This is the first comprehensive account of English Renaissance literature in the context of the culture which shaped it: the courts of Henry VIII, Edward VI, Mary, and Elizabeth I, the tumult of Catholic and Protestant alliances during and following the Reformation, the development of humanism, the age of printing and of New World discovery.

In this century courtly literature under Henry VIII moves toward a new, more personal poetry of sentiment: lyrical poetry, narrative romance, and the sonnet reached new heights, with writers such as Sidney, Spenser, Shakespeare, and the early Donne. The development of English prose is seen in the writing of More, Foxe, and Hooker, in the evolution of satire, popular culture, and in more intimate accounts of private life. Drama moved from the churches to the commercial playhouses with the plays of Kyd, Marlowe, and the early careers of Shakespeare and Jonson.

The *Companion* tackles all these subjects in fourteen newly commissioned essays, written by experts for student readers. A detailed chronology lists the major literary achievements against the political and religious background of the age and concludes with a list of authors and their dates.

THE CAMBRIDGE
COMPANION TO
ENGLISH
LITERATURE
1500–1600

CAMBRIDGE COMPANIONS TO LITERATURE

CAMBRIDGE COMPANIONS TO CULTURE

THE CAMBRIDGE
COMPANION TO
ENGLISH
LITERATURE
1500–1600

EDITED BY
ARTHUR F. KINNEY

CAMBRIDGE
UNIVERSITY PRESS

PUBLISHED BY THE PRESS SYNDICATE OF THE UNIVERSITY OF CAMBRIDGE
The Pitt Building, Trumpington Street, Cambridge CB2 1RP, United Kingdom

CAMBRIDGE UNIVERSITY PRESS
The Edinburgh Building, Cambridge CB2 2RU, United Kingdom
40 West 20th Street, New York, NY 10011–4211, USA
10 Stamford Road, Oakleigh, Melbourne 3166, Australia

First published 2000

Printed in the United Kingdom at the University Press, Cambridge

Typeset in Sabon 10/13 pt. [CE]

A catalogue record for this book is available from the British Library

Library of Congress cataloging in publication data
The Cambridge companion to English literature, 1500–1600 / edited by Arthur E. Kinney.
p. cm. – (Cambridge companions to culture)
Includes index.
ISBN 0 521 58294 6 (hardback). – ISBN 0 521 58758 1 (paperback)
1. English literature – Early modern, 1500–1700 – History and criticism.
2. Literature and history – Great Britain – History – 16th century.
I. Kinney, Arthur F., 1933– .
II. Title: Companion to English literature, 1500–1600. III. Series.
PR413.C29 2000
820.9'002 – dc21 99–21654 CIP

ISBN 0 521 58294 6 hardback
ISBN 0 521 58758 1 paperback

CONTENTS

ILLUSTRATIONS

CONTRIBUTORS

Catherine Bates, University of Warwick
Colin Burrow, University of Cambridge
Donald Cheney, University of Massachusetts, Amherst
Heather Dubrow, University of Wisconsin, Madison
Suzanne Gossett, Loyola University of Chicago
Richard Helgerson, University of California, Santa Barbara
Clark Hulse, University of Illinois, Chicago
John N. King, The Ohio State University
Arthur F. Kinney, University of Massachusetts, Amherst
Leah S. Marcus, Vanderbitt University
Lena Cowen Orlin, University of Maryland, Baltimore County
Anne Lake Prescott, Barnard College, Columbia University
Charlotte Spivack, University of Massachusetts, Amherst
Garrett Sullivan, The Pennsylvania State University
Raymond Waddington, University of California, Davis
Wendy Wall, Northwestern University
Linda Woodbridge, The Pennsylvania State University

CHARLOTTE SPIVACK

Chronologies

Events and texts

1522 Charles V, Holy Roman Emperor, visits England
1523 Barclay, *Mirror of Good Manners*; Skelton, *Garland of Laurel*
1524 Cox, *Art or Craft of Rhetoric*
1526 Tyndale, *The New Testament* in English
1527 Anon., *Godly Queen Hester*; Rastell, *Calisto and Melebea, Gentleness and Nobility*
1528 Castiglione, *The Courtier*; Heywood, *Play of the Weather*
1529 Fall of Wolsey; More becomes Chancellor
   More, *Supplication of Souls*; Rastell, *The Pastime of People*
1530 English clergy name Henry VIII Supreme Head of the Church
   Copland, *Highway to the Spital House*
1531 Act Against Vagabonds
   Elyot, *Book of the Governor*; Tyndale, *Answer to More*
1532 Henry VIII divorces Catherine of Aragon; More resigns
   More, *Confutation of Tyndale's Answer*
1533 Henry VIII excommunicated, marries Anne Boleyn; Cranmer becomes Archbishop of Canterbury; arrest of Elizabeth Barton, "Maid of Kent"
1534 Acts of Succession and Supremacy
   Elyot, *Castle of Health*; More, *Dialogue of Comfort*
1535 More and Fisher executed
   Coverdale, *Bible*
1536 Anne Boleyn executed; Tyndale strangled and burned in Antwerp; Henry VIII marries Jane Seymour; New Act of Succession; Act Against Vagabonds; smaller abbeys supressed
1537 Sumptuary legislation; death of Jane Seymour; birth of Prince Edward
1538 Breaking of images in churches
   Bale, *God's Promises, King Johan, Three Laws*; Elyot, *Latin–English Dictionary*; Lindsay, *Complaint of the Papyngo*
1539 Dissolution of the monasteries
   Coverdale, *The "Great" Bible*; Redford, *Wit and Science*
1540 Fall and execution of Cromwell; Henry VIII marries Anne of Cleves, marriage annulled; Henry marries Catherine Howard
   Lindsay, *Satire of Three Estates*
1541 Henry VIII assumes title of King of Ireland and Head of Church in Ireland
1542 Death of James V of Scotland; birth of daughter Mary, who succeeds to the throne; execution of Catherine Howard; Act Against Vagabonds
1543 Mary, Queen of Scots, betrothed to the Dauphin; Henry VIII marries Katherine Parr; Act "for the Advancement of True Religion" restricts Bible reading
1544 War with France; capture of Boulogne
   Bale, *Brief Chronicle Concerning Sir John Oldcastle*
1545 Council of Trent begins; confiscation of chantries
   Ascham, *Toxophilus*; Churchyard, *Mirror of Man*; Elyot, *Defence of Good Women*; Rhodes, *Book of Nurture*
1546 Murder of Cardinal Beaton; peace with France

Bale, *Acts of English Votaries, First Examination of Anne Askew*;
Heywood, *Dialogue of Proverbs*

1547 Death of Henry VIII; Edward VI succeeds to throne; Somerset becomes
Protector; execution of Surrey; many laws against heresy abrogated; penal
slavery for some types of vagabonds
Anon., *Impatient Poverty*; Bale, *The Latter Examination of Anne Askew*;
Baldwin, *Treatise of Philosophy*; Cranmer, *Certain Sermons, or Homilies*

1548 Arrest of Gardiner; Somerset's Commission on Enclosures
Hall, *Union of the Families of Lancaster and York*; Latimer, *Sermon of the
Plough*

1549 War with France; Kett's Rebellion; Act of Uniformity
Book of Common Prayer; Erasmus, *Praise of Folly*, translated by Chaloner

1550 Burning of books at Oxford
Anon., *Nice Wanton, Somebody and Others*; Sherry, *Treatise of Schemes
and Tropes*

1551 Council of Trent, session II
More, *Utopia*, translated from the Latin by Robynson; Crowley, *Philargyrie
of Greate Britayne*

1552 Execution of Somerset; Act of Uniformity
Book of Common Prayer II; Udall, *Ralph Roister Doister*

1553 Death of Edward VI; Mary succeeds to the throne; Sir Hugh Willoughby's
voyage begins
Anon., *Respublica*; publication of More, *Dialogue of Comfort*; Stevenson,
Gammer Gurton's Needle; Wilson, *Art of Rhetoric*

1554 Rebellion of Sir Thomas Wyatt; execution of Lady Jane Grey; Queen Mary
marries Philip of Spain
Anon., *Wealth and Health*; Lindsay, *Dialogue betwixt Experience and a
Courtier*

1555 Latimer and Ridley burned; Muscovy Company founded
Anon., *Jack Juggler*; Berners, *Arthur of Little Britain*; Heywood, *Two
Hundred Epigrams*

1556 Cranmer burned; Philip II excommunicated
Harpsfield, *Life of More*; Heywood, *The Spider and the Fly*

1557 War with France; Stationers' Company incorporated
Anon., *Court of Venus, Sackful of News*; Cavendish, *Life of Wolsey*;
publication of More, *English Works*; Tottel, *Songs and Sonnets*; Tusser,
Hundred Good Points

1558 Death of Queen Mary; death of Cardinal Pole; Elizabeth succeeds to throne;
loss of Calais
Knox, *First Blast of the Trumpet Against the Monstrous Regiment of
Women*; Wager, *Life and Repentance of Mary Magdalene*

1559 Mary Queen of Scots marries the Dauphin; Parker becomes Archbishop of
Canterbury; Acts of Uniformity, including fine for not attending church;
iconoclasm and looting of churches

Mirror for Magistrates II; *Book of Common Prayer* III; Bullein, *Government of Health*; Philip, *Play of Patient Grissell*; Wager, *The Longer Thou Livest*

1560 Statute against destruction of church monuments
Copland, *Jill of Brentford*; Heywood, *Fourth Hundred of Epigrams*; Ingeland, *The Disobedient Child*; Wager, *Enough Is As Good As A Feast*

1561 English occupation of Le Havre
Anon., *The Pedlar's Prophecy*; Awdeley, *Fraternity of Vagabonds*; Castiglione, *The Courtier* translated by Hoby; Stow, edition of Chaucer; Preston, *Cambises*

1562 Council of Trent, session III; Hawkins' voyage begins
Brooke, *Romeus and Juliet*; Bullein, *Bulwark Against All Sickness*; Heywood, *Works*; Latimer, *Twenty-seven Sermons*; Norton and Sackville, *Gorboduc*

1563 Plague in London; Elizabeth's first Poor Law
Foxe, *Acts and Monuments* (*Book of Martyrs*); Googe, *Eclogs*; Rainold, *Foundation of Rhetoric*; *Mirror for Magistrates* (enlarged, including Thomas Sackville)

1564 Influx of Flemish Protestant refugees
Bullein, *Dialogue Against the Fever Pestilence*; R.B., *Appius and Virginia*

1565 Attempts to check English and French piracy in the Channel
Anon., *Jests of Skoggan*, *King Darius*; Edwards, *Damon and Pithias*; Ovid's *Metamorphosis*, translated by Golding; Stow, *Summary of English Chronicles*; Wager, *The Cruel Debtor*

1566 Birth of King James VI of Scotland, later King James I of England
Edwards, *Palamon and Arcite I and II*; Gascoigne, *Jocasta, Supposes*; Painter, *Palace of Pleasure*

1567 Revolt of the Netherlands
Anon., *Merry Tales by Skelton*; Painter, *Second Tome of Palace of Pleasure*; Pickering, *Interlude of Vice* (*Horestes*); Turberville, *Epitaphs, Epigrams, Songs and Sonnets*; Wager, *Trial of Treasure*

1568 Mary Queen of Scots flees to England; Queen Elizabeth seizes treasure of Spanish fleet driven into Plymouth by pirates; English College of Douai founded
Anon., *Marriage of Wit and Science*; *Like Will to Like*; Howell, *The Arbor of Amity, New Sonnets and Pretty Pamphlets*; North, *Dial of Princes*; Skelton, *Pithy Works*

1569 Unsuccessful rebellion of Norfolk and the Northern Earls
Garter, *The Most Virtuous and Godly Susanna*; Hawkins, *True Declaration of the Troublesome voyage*

1570 Pope excommunicates Elizabeth I
Ascham, *The Schoolmaster*; Anon., *Clyomon and Clamydes*; Foxe, *Eccelesiastical History*; Tusser, *Hundred Good Points Married Unto a Hundred Good Points of Huswifery*

1571 Battle of Lepanto; diplomatic relations with Spain broken off
Anon., *New Custom*; Latimer, *Fruitful Sermons*

1572 Massacre of St. Bartholomew; unpatronized troops of actors declared rogues and vagabonds
Woodes, *Conflict of Conscience*

1573 Relations with Spain resumed
Gascoigne, *A Hundred Sundrie Flowres*, incorporating *Adventures of Master F.J.*; Tusser, *Five Hundred Points*

1574 Anglo-Spanish Treaty of Bristol; persecution of Papists in England
Scott, *Platform of a Hop-Garden*

1575 New Poor Law; Anabaptists burned in England
Breton, *Small Handful of Fragrant Flowers*; Gascoigne, *Glass of Government*, *Posies*; Painter, *Palace of Pleasure* (2 vols.); Turberville, *Noble Art of Venery*, *Book of Falconry*

1576 Sack of Antwerp; Grindal named Archbishop of Canterbury; Frobisher's voyage begins; priests from Douai arrive in England; the Theatre opens in Shoreditch

1577 Drake's voyage around the world begins; Curtain Theatre opens, Blackfriars Theatre opens
Northbrook, *Treatise Wherein Dicing, etc. Are Reproved*; Holinshed, *Chronicles*, Lupton, *All for Money*

1578 Anon., *Gorgeous Gallery of Gallant Inventions*; Lyly, *Euphues*; Rolland, *The Seven Sages*; Rich, *Alarm to England*, Whetstone, *Promos and Cassandra*

1579 Gosson, *School of Abuse*; Merbury, *A Marriage Between Wit and Wisdom*; Munday, *Mirror of Mutability*; *Plutarch's Lives*, translated by North; Spenser, *Shepheardes Calender*

1580 Gifford, *Poesy of Gillyflowers*; Lyly, *Euphues and His England*; Munday, *Zelauto*; Saker, *Narbonus*; Stow, *Chronicle*

1581 Execution of Edmund Campion
Mulcaster, *Positions*; *Seneca his Ten Tragedies*, translated by Newton; Peele, *The Arraignment of Paris*; Rich, *Farewell to the Military Profession*, *Strange and Wonderful Adventures of Don Simonides*; Wilson, *The Three Ladies of London*

1582 University of Edinburgh founded; plague in London
Breton, *Toys of an Idle Heart*; Gosson, *Plays Confuted*; Hakluyt, *Voyages*; Munday (?), *Rare Triumphs of Love and Fortune*

1583 Irish rebellion defeated; Whitgift named Archbishop of Canterbury; Queen's Players company formed
Greene, *Mamillia*; Stubbes, *Anatomy of Abuses*

1584 Assassination of William of Orange; failure of Ralegh in Virginia
Greene, *Mirror of Modesty*, *Card of Fancy*; Lodge, *Alarm Against Usurers*; Lyly, *Campaspe, Sappho and Phao*; Munday, *Watchword in England*; Rich,

Second Tome of Don Simonides; Scot, *Discovery of Witchcraft*; Warner, *Pan His Syrinx*

1585 Greene, *Planetomachia*; Lyly, *Gallathea*; Peele, *Pageant for Dixi*; Whetstone, *Enemy to Unthriftiness*

1586 Battle of Zutphen; death of Sidney from battle wounds; Babington plot; trial of Mary Queen of Scots
Knox, *History of the Reformation in Scotland*; Warner, *Albion's England*, Books I–IV; Webbe, *Discourse of English Poetrie*; Whetstone, *English Mirror*

1587 Execution of Mary Queen of Scots; Pope proclaims crusade against England
Gifford, *Discourse of Practices of Devils*; Greene, *Alphonsus, Euphues His Censure, Morando, Penelope's Web*; Kyd, *The Spanish Tragedy*; Marlowe, Parts 1 and 2 of *Tamburlaine* first performed; Marlowe and Nashe, *Dido*; Peele, *David and Bathsheba*; Turberville, *Tragical Tales*

1588 Defeat of the Spanish Armada
Byrd, *Psalms, Sonnets, and Songs*; Greene, *Pandosto, Perimedes the Blacksmith*; Harriot, *Brief and True Report of Virginia*; Lodge, *Wounds of Civil War*; Lyly, *Endymion*; Porter, *Two Angry Women of Abingdon*; Wilson, *Three Lords and Ladies of London*

1589 Byrd, *Songs of Sundry Natures*; Greene, *Friar Bacon and Friar Bungay*; Hakluyt, *Principal Navigations*; Lodge, *Scylla's Metamorphosis*; Lyly, *Pap with a Hatchet, Midas, Mother Bombie*; Marlowe, *Jew of Malta*; Nashe, *Anatomy of Absurdity*; Peele, *Battle of Alcazar*; Puttenham, *Arte of English Poesie*

1590 Death of Waslsingham
Anon.; *Life and Pranks of Long Meg, Edward III, Fair Em, King Leir, Mucedorus, Soliman and Perseda*; Greene, *Never Too Late, Francesco's Fortunes, George a Greene, James IV*; Holland, *Treatise Against Witchcraft*; Lodge, *A Looking Glass for London and England, Rosalynd*; Lyly, *Love's Metamorphosis*; Nashe, *Almond for a Parrot*; Peele, *The Old Wives Tale, Polyhymnia*; Sidney, *Arcadia*; Spenser, *Faerie Queene*, Books I–III; Wilson, *The Cobbler's Prophecy*

1591 Increased severity against recusants
Anon., *Arden of Feversham, Jack Straw, Locrine, True Tragedy of Richard III*; Breton, *Breton's Bower of Delights*; Drayton, *Harmony of the Church*; Fraunce, *The Countess of Pembroke's Emanuel*; Greene, *Orlando Furioso, A Notable Discovery of Cosenage*; James VI, *Poetical Exercises*; Lodge, *Robert, Duke of Normandy*; Peele, *Edward I*; Shakespeare, Parts 2 and 3 of *Henry VI*; Sidney, *Astrophil and Stella*; Southwell, *Mary Magdalene's Tears*; Spenser, *Complaints, Daphnaida*

1592 Rose Theatre opened; plague in London
Breton, *Pilgrimage to Paradise*; Churchyard, *Handful of Gladsome Verses*; Constable, *Diana*; Daniel, *Complaint of Rosamond, Delia*; Delony, *Garland of Good Will*; Greene, *Selimus, John of Bordeaux*; Marlowe, *Edward II*,

Doctor Faustus; Nashe, *Summer's Last Will and Testament*; Shakespeare, *The Comedy of Errors*, Part I of *Henry VI*; Anon., *A Knack to Know A Knave*, *Thomas of Woodstock*

1593   Theatres in London closed for plague

Anon., *Guy Earl of Warwick*; Barnes, *Parthenophil*; Chettle, *Kind Heart's Dream*; Daniel, *Cleopatra*; Drayton, *Idea*; Gifford, *Dialogue Concerning Witches*; Harvey, *Pierce's Supererogation*; Hooker, *Laws of Ecclesiastical Polity*, Books I–III; Lodge, *Phyllis and Elstred*; Lyly, *Woman In the Moon*; Morley, *Canzonets*; Nashe, *Christ's Tears Over Jerusalem*; Peele, *The Honor of the Garter*; Shakespeare, *Venus and Adonis*; *Richard III*, *Two Gentlemen of Verona*; Stubbes, *A Motive to Good Workes*; Watson, *Tears of Fancy*; Whetstone, *Aurelia*; Marlowe, *Massacre at Paris*

1594   Swan Theatre built

Anon., *Alphonsus, Emperor of Germany*, *A Knack to Know An Honest Man*; Barnfield, *Affectionate Shepherd*; Constable, *Diana* (augmented); Davies, *Orchestra*; Dickenson, *The Shepherd's Complaint*; Drayton, *Ideas Mirrour*, *Matilda*; Hume, *Treatise of Conscience*, *Of the Felicity*; Kyd, *Cornelia*; Morley, *Madrigals to Four Voices*; Nashe, *Terrors of Night*, *The Unfortunate Traveller*; Percy, *Sonnets to Caelia*; Shakespeare,*The Rape of Lucrece*, *Taming of the Shrew*, *Titus Andronicus*; Sylvester, *Monodia*; Willoby, *Willoby, His Avisa*; Yarington, *Two Lamentable Tragedies*

1595   Execution of Southwell; deaths of Drake and Hawkins on their voyage to the West Indies

Anon., *Caesar and Pompey*, *Edmund Ironside*; Barnfield, *Certain Sonnets*; Breton, *Mary Magdalene's Love*; Chapman, *Ovid's Banquet of Sense*; Chettle, *Piers Plainness*; Churchyard, *Praise of Poetry*, *Consort of Heavenly Harmony*; Copley, *Love's Owl*, *Wits, Fits, and Fancies*; Daniel, *Civil Wars* I–IV; Drayton, *Endimion and Phoebe*; Edwards, *Narcissus, Cephalus and Procris*; Lodge, *A Fig for Momus*; Morley, *First Book of Ballads*; Shakespeare, *Love's Labors Lost*, *Midsummer Night's Dream*, *Richard II*, *Romeo and Juliet*; Sidney, *Defence of Poetrie* published; Spenser, *Amoretti*, *Colin Clout's Come Home Again*, *Epithalamion*

1596   Essex storms Cadiz

Anon., *Capt. Thomas Stukeley*; Chapman, *Blind Beggar of Alexandria*; Churchyard, *Pleasant Discourse of Court and Wars*; Deloney, *Jack of Newbury*; Lodge, *Robert Duke of Normandy*; Greville, *Mustapha*; Jonson, *A Tale of a Tub*; Keymis, *Second Voyage to Guiana*; Lodge, *A Margarite of America*, *Wit's Misery*; Nashe, *Have With You To Saffron-Walden*; Ralegh, *Discovery of Guiana*; Shakespeare, *Merchant of Venice*, *King John*: Spenser, *Faerie Queene* Books IV–VI, *Prothalamion*, *Four Hymns*

1597   Bacon, *Essays*; Breton, *Arbor of Amorous Devices*; Chapman, *A Humorous Day's Mirth*; Deloney, *The Gentle Craft*; Dowland, *First Book of Songs*; Drayton, *England's Heroical Epistles*; Hall, *Virgidemiarum* Books I–III;

Hooker, *Laws of Ecclesiastical Polity* Book v; James VI (of Scotland),
Demonology; Jonson, *The Case is Altered*

1598 Edict of Nantes
Bacon, *Essays* 2nd edn.; Barnfield, *Complaint of Poetry, Lady Pecunia*;
Homer, *Iliad*, translated by Chapman; Marlowe, *Hero and Leander*,
completed by Chapman; Chettle, *The Downfall and Death of Robert Earl of
Huntington*; Deloney, *Thomas of Raiding*; Guilpin, *Skialethia*; Hakluyt,
Principal Navigations, 2nd edn.; Hall, *Virgidemiarum* Books IV–VI;
Haughton, *Englishmen for My Money*; Jonson, *Every Man In His Humour*;
Marston, *Pygmalion, Scourge of Villainy*; Meres, *Palladis Tamia*; Rankins,
Seven Satires; Shakespeare, *Much Ado About Nothing*; Speght, edition of
Chaucer; Stow, *Survey of London*

1599 Essex imprisoned, Globe Theatre opened
Anon., *Pilgrimage To Parnassus, Thracian Wonder, A Warning for Fair
Women, Wisdom of Dr. Dodypoll, Look About You, A Larum for London*;
Chapman, *All Fools*; Daniel, *Musophilus, Poetical Essays*; Dekker, *Old
Fortunatus, The Shoemaker's Holiday*; Drayton, *Heroical Epistles*;
Hayward, *Life of Henry IV*; James VI (of Scotland), *Basilikon Doron*;
Marston, *Scourge of Villainy, Antonio and Mellida, Histriomastix*; Porter,
Two Merry Women of Abingdon; Shakespeare, *As You Like It, Henry V,
Julius Caesar*; T.M., *Micro-Cynicon*; Weever, *Epigrams in the Oldest Cut*

1600 Bruno burned at Rome; East India Company founded; Fortune Theatre built
Anon., *Return from Parnassus, Thomas Lord Cromwell, Maid's
Metamorphosis, Weakest Goeth to the Wall*; Cornwallis, *Essays*; Chettle,
Blind Beggar, Patient Grissill; Dowland, *Second Book of Songs, England's
Helicon, England's Parnassus*; Heywood, *Four Prentices of London*; Kemp,
Nine Days Wonder; Marston, *Antonio's Revenge, Jack Drum's
Entertainment*; Shakespeare, *Merry Wives of Windsor, Twelfth Night*;
Tourneur, *Transformed Metamorphosis*; Vaughan, *Golden Grove*

Contemporary Lives

George Cavendish, 1500–1561
Thomas Wyatt, 1503–1542
Nicholas Udall, (?)1505–1556
George Buchanan, 1506–1582
John Calvin, 1509–1564
Thomas Smith, 1513–1577
John Knox, (?)1514–1572
Roger Ascham, 1515–1568
John Foxe, 1516–1587
Henry Howard, Earl of Surrey,
    1517–1547
Robert Crowley, 1518–1588
Thomas Churchyard, (?)1520–1564
Richard Eden, (?)1521–1576
Thomas Tusser, (?)1524–1580
George Gascoigne, (?)1525–1577
John Stowe, (?)1525–1565
Thomas Wilson, (?)1525–1581
John Lesley, 1527–1596
Richard Mulcaster, (?)1530–1611
William Allen, 1532–1594
John Hawkins, 1532–1595
Alexander Scott, (?)1532–(?)1584
Thomas Cartwright, 1535–1603
Thomas North, (?)1535–1601
Arthur Golding, (?)1536–(?)1605
Thomas Sackville, 1536–1608
Reginald Scot, (?)1538–1599
Humphrey Gilbert, (?)1539–1583
Thomas Campion, 1540–1581
Barnabe Googe, 1540–1594
William Painter, (?)1540–1594
Barnabe Rich, (?)1540–1617
George Turberville, (?)1540–(?)1610
Thomas Deloney, (?)1543–(?)1600
George Whetstone, (?)1544–(?)1587
Thomas Bodley, 1545–1613
Nicholas Breton, (?)1545–1626
Gabriel Harvey, (?)1545–1630
Richard Stanyhurst, 1547–1618
George Pettie, 1548–1589
Giles Fletcher, (?)1549–1611

Henry Smith, (?)1559–1591
William Camden, 1551–1623
Richard Hakluyt, (?)1552–1616
Philemon Holland, 1552–1637
Edmund Spenser, 1552–1599
Anthony Munday, 1553–1633
Stephen Gosson, 1554–1624
Fulke Greville, 1554–1628
Richard Hooker, 1554–1600
John Lyly, 1554–1606
Walter Ralegh, (?)1554–1618
Philip Sidney, 1554–1586
Lancelot Andrewes, 1555–1626
Thomas Watson, (?)1557–1592
Robert Greene, 1558–1592
Thomas Lodge, (?)1558–1625
George Peele, (?)1558–1596
William Perkins, 1558–1602
William Warren, (?)1558–1609
George Chapman, (?)1559–1634
Henry Chettle, (?)1560–(?)1607
Alexander Hume, (?)1560–1609
Francis Bacon, 1561–1626
John Harington, 1561–1612
Robert Southwell, 1561–1595
Henry Constable, 1562–1613
Samuel Daniel, 1562–1619
Michael Drayton, 1563–1631
Joshua Sylvester, 1563–1618
Christopher Marlowe, 1564–1593
William Shakespeare, 1564–1616
Francis Meres, 1565–1647
John Davies, (?)1565–1618
John Hoskyns, 1566–1638
Anthony Copley, 1567–1607
Gervase Markham, 1568–1637
Henry Wotton, 1568–1639
Barnabe Barnes, (?)1569–1609
Thomas Middleton, (?)1570–1627
Samuel Rowlands, (?)1570–(?)1630
John Donne, 1572–1631
Ben Jonson, 1572–1637

William Laud, 1573–1645
Richard Barnfield, 1574–1627
Joseph Hall, 1574–1656
Thomas Heywood, 1574–1641
William Percy, 1575–1648
Samuel Purchas, (?)1575–1626
Cyril Tourneur, (?)1575–1616
George Sandys, 1578–1644
John Fletcher, 1579–1625
John Webster, 1580–1625
Thomas Overbury, 1581–1613
Phineas Fletcher, 1582–1650
Philip Massinger, 1583–1640
Francis Beaumont, 1584–1616

William Drummond, 1585–1649
John Ford, 1586–c.1640
Thomas Hobbes, 1588–1679
George Wither, 1588–1667
Richard Brome c.1590–c.1652
William Browne, 1591–1643
Robert Herrick, 1591–1674
Francis Quarles, 1592–1644
George Herbert, 1593–1633
Izaak Walton, 1593–1683
Thomas Carew c.1598–c.1639
Oliver Cromwell, 1599–1658
William Prynne, 1600–1669

I

ARTHUR F. KINNEY

Introduction

A currently recognized representation of the Tudor aesthetic in the sixteenth century is Hans Holbein's double portrait of "The Ambassadors" painted in the spring of 1533 in London (Figure 1), yet its significance and its actual meaning have been debated. For Stephen Greenblatt, the painting represents a cultural poetic that is essentially humanistic. The work is seen from the perspective of the courtly and social and it emphasizes the vast and varied knowledge humanism had come to represent at the Henrician court:

> Jean de Dinteville, seigneur de Polisy and Francis I's ambassador to the English court, and his friend Georges de Selve, shortly to be bishop of Lavaur, stand at either side of a two-shelved table. They are young, successful men, whose impressively wide-ranging interests and accomplishments are elegantly recorded by the objects scattered with careful casualness on the table: celestial and terrestrial globes, sundials, quadrants and other instruments of astronomy and geometry, a lute, a case of flutes, a German book of arithmetic, kept open by a square, and an open German hymn book, on whose pages may be seen part of Luther's translation of the "Veni Creator Spiritus" and his "Shortened Version of the Ten Commandments" ... The terrestrial and celestial spheres, the sword and the book, the state and the church, Protestantism and Catholicism, the mind as measurer of all things and the mind as unifying force, the arts and sciences, the power of images and the power of words – all are conjoined then in Holbein's painting and integrated in a design as intricate as the pavement ...[1]

on which the two men stand. Greenblatt's verbal portrait is meant to match Holbein's painterly one, persuading us to accept a humanist poetics of cultural accomplishment that leads to optimism and even complacency. It is a poetics that joins Platonic epistemology of Idea to Aristotelian mimesis of authentic representation, just as the literary works of Erasmus and Thomas More were doing at the time. Greenblatt continues, "And yet slashing across the pavement, intruding upon these complex harmonies and disrupting

1 *The Ambassadors*, by Hans Holbein.

them, is the extraordinary anamorphic representation of the death's-head. Viewed frontally, the skull is an unreadable blur in the center foreground of the painting; only from the proper position at the side of the painting is it suddenly revealed" (*Renaissance Self-Fashioning*, p. 18).

Practicing a twentieth-century formalism to read a work of art, Greenblatt looks, much as the sixteenth-century grammar school student would, at the work's harmony, integration, and meaning. Noting what is out of place, the grim reminder of death, Greenblatt moves on to the kind of dialectic that advanced humanist training fostered, implying that truth lies finally either in paradox of the kind that lies behind the *Utopia*, Petrarchan lyric, and much public drama, or an ongoing interrogation, in which meaning is finally indeterminate, as in George Gascoigne's *Adventures of Master F. J.*, Christopher Marlowe's *Hero and Leander*, or Shakespeare's *Twelfth Night*. Either way, as proposition or dialectic, statement or argument, Holbein's double portrait is essentially a work of humanist poetics coincident with the teaching of Tudor grammar schools and fundamental to courtly aesthetic.

Lisa Jardine, however, observing that the painting was executed by a foreign artist with strong mercantile interests, and that it did not remain in England long, sees a work far more troubling.

> Holbein's "The Ambassadors" was painted (for Jean de Dinteville) in London in the spring of 1533 (the painting left England when François I's ambassador returned to France late in 1553, and was hung in de Dinteville's chateau at Polisy). The artist, Hans Holbein, was a German from Basle, most of whose commissions in London had been portraits of German merchants resident in the city. The setting for this painting (identified by the pavement on which the two men stand) is the chapel in Westminster Cathedral in which Henry VIII's new queen, Anne Boleyn (whom he had secretly married at the end of January, 1533), was crowned with great pomp and ceremony at the end of May. This was an acutely fraught period of English diplomatic activity (Anne was pregnant and Henry VIII would not risk the "boy's" being born a bastard by delaying her recognition as his legitimate wife; François I was meanwhile trying to persuade him not to go public until he had smoothed the path of divorce and remarriage with the Medici Pope, Clement VII). Jean de Dinteville's brother, Francois, Bishop of Auxerre, was François I's ambassador to Rome. A week before the coronation Jean de Dinteville wrote to his brother (in a letter whose evasive phrasing clearly shows he expected it to be vetted) with a veiled warning that it might be necessary for him to intervene with the Pope since things in London were coming to a head.[2]

For Jardine, then, the painting is not an emblem of the humanist movement and its wide cultural aesthetic constrained by mortality, but the consequence of particular historic forces joining at a particular historic moment: not only the painter and subject are important but the precise time the work was executed and a particular use to which it might be put. Armed with historic specificity, she is alerted to other features in what is perhaps history's first double portrait:

> Some of the issues foremost in the French envoy's mind at the time are elegantly and precisely figured in the conjunctions of objects painted on the lower (mundane) shelf on which he leans. The foreshortened uncased lute (its discarded case lies under the table on de Dinteville's side) with its prominently broken string is still recognizably an emblem of current discord. Beneath its neck lies an open hymn-book, in which we can still read the opening verse in German of Luther's "Kom Heiliger Geyst" ["Come Holy Ghost"] on the left, and "Mensch wiltu leben seliglich" ["Man wilt thou live blessedly"] (with the music of tenor voice); the discord here specified, then, is that within the Christian Church, a discord within which Henry's impending marriage to a known sympathizer with the Reformation movement played a significant part. The collection of harmonizing flutes under the hymn-book remain out of use, in their case. ("Strains of Renaissance Reading," p. 298)

Moreover, the polyhedral sundial and quadrant are misdirected and reversed, so that they cannot perform their measurements accurately; the skull at the center of the base of the portrait forms a direct diagonal line with another emblem of death (and life) in the crucifix of Christ showing behind the drapery at the top left of the painting. The book of mathematics is open at the start of a section on Division. Such a sense of the cultural moment does not permit integration for Jardine, but quite the opposite: "Holbein's meticulously rendered globe [set at Polisy] represents discord as violent and as destructive of international peace as doctrinal difference within the Christian Church" (p. 299). The imperialistic need and the failure of a negotiated empire is the explicit message encoded in the work: "for Holbein and his sitters Empire is indeed a key issue, but that it already figures in the painting as the *problem* around whose absent presence the entire composition is structured. In other words, far from being itself imperialistic, it struggles with imperialism elsewhere" (p. 302).

For all their apparent difference, however – in their approaches, their concerns, their observations, and their conclusions – Greenblatt and Jardine are more alike than not in their diverse interpretations of Holbein's work. Both attempt to narratize a picture, to transfer paint into words and to make sense of the painting by showing how it tells a story. For Greenblatt, it is a story of human accomplishment; for Jardine, it is a story of breakdown and anxiety. In their desire to account for each element in this crowded painting of details, Greenblatt and Jardine attempt to order their reactions controlled by their own aesthetic, one that makes sense of the details. They are both practicing what readers of the Tudor period practiced – receiving texts by intervening in them to establish meaning. It is this understanding, as the various authors of the following chapters demonstrate in various ways, that governed both the conception and reception of public and private writing. This Tudor aesthetic, at first enunciated by Renaissance painters in Italy, rested centrally on two principles. First, works were seen as pluralistic (not simply anamorphic), quite unlike the monolithic mathematical perspective that characterizes much modern thought. In other words, the painters and writers of the Renaissance with whom we are concerned placed a premium on the potential multiplicity of perspective. Painters did not expect viewers to remain fixed in looking at a work of art, but to move around to various positions to view it, just as the writers at Henry's court expected to be read: More's *Utopia*, for instance, is about a land and a people seen, simultaneously, by Hythlodaeus, Peter Giles, the More-persona, More the author, and the reader (who might attempt to consolidate some or all of these views). Shifting stances allow various readings; Edmund Spenser's *Faerie Queene*, to take another example, can be read as an epic, an allegory, a romance, an heroic narrative, or an elaborate plea for patronage. Not all perspectives can be held simultaneously: to see the death's head in "The Ambassadors" prevents the viewer from seeing the two human figures; concentrating on the objects on the table and their meanings takes the viewer away from the ambassadors, while they in turn may be viewed individually or in conjunction with one other (one is more formal and yet more modest than the other). As James Elkins remarks, "Instead of simple, rational, symmetrical pictures of perspective 'hollow-space,' we find a number of complicated practices."[3] Thus conditioned, readers of a work of dialectic such as Erasmus' *Praise of Folly* would not be frustrated as the subject of folly shifts in matter and attitude, but instead derive pleasure from such a work. They would also be prepared for the segmentation of acts and scenes in a play like *The Spanish Tragedy* when in the theatre as well as for the cross-cutting of scenes in the *Arcadia* when at home.

A second aesthetic principle of Tudor culture (and Tudor writing) is what Elkins calls "the object-oriented purpose of much Renaissance picture making: the idea that the artists' attentions, and their perspective methods, were focused on the delineation of particular objects rather than the erection of a scaffolding of fictive space" (*The Poetics of Perspective*, p. 56). The interest Tudors had in their material existence is illustrated throughout their writing, as in the material object of gold chamber pots in

Utopia or the material practice of hawking in Skelton's poetic attack on his curate at Diss, the tournaments in Sidney and Nashe, the Wood of Error in Spenser. But like the painters this emphasis on the concrete rather than the abstract provided means more often than ends. "Drawings of objects set against indeterminate or empty backgrounds, as was the practice, appear ready to be inserted in paintings whenever a painter might want," Elkins writes (*The Poetics of Perspective*, p. 59). Rather than appreciate what we have termed singular or essential paradigms of unchanging truth, the Tudors, especially after the Reformation, relished and recorded the plenitude of life, combining their reason and passion to make provisional approximations of the world teeming with change all about them. Similar to the royal palace of Whitehall that came to dominate London in this period – seen variously as "the largest and ugliest palace in Europe" and "a heap of houses"[4] – Tudor aesthetics always admitted both a single central palace of the King that was itself once the house of archbishops, and the separate entities that surrounded it, including the Queen's chambers, the old state rooms occupied by Wolsey, gardens, parks, and gates. A palace built from necessity and desire as well as pleasure, it argued more for plenitude than integration.

The literary and cultural texts examined in this volume, then, reflecting this Tudor aesthetic, were neither passive receptacles of the culture nor outside the cultural history in which they played out their ideas. Rather, they were productions of a Renaissance culture whose works were conditioned by the social, political, and religious forces with which they participated, which they reflected, and to which they in turn contributed. A written text was not a work suddenly and wholly inspired by a muse of poesy but rather was a work constructed from various if discordant perceptions of various cultural forces and practices. Indeed, the forces which distinguished a text were often but not always congruent with the various practices of a poetics inherited from classical works. Thus even the most literary of works was created through a process of "discovering," imitating and diverging from a classical model and so mapping something new. Contending multiple narratives could therefore address the same issue – such as the perfect courtier, heroic action, or the prerequisites to salvation – and could appear in various forms – such as folios, quartos, or manuscripts – intended for different and sometimes discrete audiences. While the common property of all such texts was language, various lexicons – such as the vocabulary of the court, the talk of the street, and the specialized cant of the underworld – and various linguistic formations – such as the variety of short lyrics lumped together as "sonnets" or "songs" – promoted the cultural principles of pluralism and plentitude. Richard Helgerson has shown how this happened in connection with the murder in 1551 of Thomas Arden, a gentleman of Faversham, Kent, by his wife, her lover, and a number of accomplices. Here different perspectives also took different forms. "For more than half a century – from its first brief mention in the *Breviat Chronicle* of 1551 through the long and detailed account in Holinshed to the retellings in Stow and Heywood – Arden's murder was very much part of England's history," he tells us. "But then ... it left history (or was forcibly ejected from it) to reappear in a succession of genres well off the main line of English historical writing – stage play, ballad, collection of wonders, calendars of crime, antiquarian treatise, puppet show, ballet, novel, and opera."[5] Different genres, themselves often elastic, admitted or even encouraged different concerns and attitudes different readers might have on different occasions. Together they inscribe a cultural moment and separately help to constitute the literature of Tudor England.

Plenitude which invited multiple perspective characterized the age from its start. In *De ratione studii*, written with John Colet as a plan of study for St. Paul's School, London, and published in 1511, Eramus insisted a teacher should not be "content with the standard ten or twelve authors, but would require a veritable universe of learning (*sed orbem illum doctrinae requiram*)." His *De Copia* was written at about the same time to show endless ways of varying words to make a single statement or promote a single idea. The consequence was, as Lauro Martines notes, that "humanism in itself had no strict or narrow political ideology ... it spoke up for princely rule or for republican government; and it could plump for absolute power under kingship, or instead, favor republican states based upon an educated urban nobility and *haute bourgeoisie*."[6] At once classical and contemporary, international and national, humanist pedagogy, says James Tracy, functioned as "an optical glass for seeing the world, whose uses were as diverse as the intentions of those who thought and wrote within its framework."[7] Indeed, by 1586 William Webbe was complaining of "innumerable sorts of English Bookes, and infinite fardles of printed pamphlets, wherewith this Country is pestered, all shopps stuffed, and every study furnished."[8] Yet James Cleland delights in such variety and number. Cleland comments in *The Institution of a Young Noble Man* (1607) that "learning is circular, and the Muses stand round about Apollo, having no beginning nor ending more than a geometrical circle, so that he who would enjoy one of the disciplines must labour to be acquainted with them all." For Roger Ascham in *The Scholemaster* (1570), books could even replace experience. He posited his famous judgment that, to escape the dangerous state of Italy, it was better for students of the world to read about that country than to take the fashionable Grand Tour. (Philip Sidney apparently believed in both, writing letters to his brother Robert about his European travels so that Robert would not have to go himself, but if he did, telling him what to watch out for.)

Just so: written works not only reflected a dispersed culture but could intervene and help to direct it. Such a conjunction is seen with special clarity during the brief reign of Edward VI when political and social order were often connected to orderly speech and measured by it. At such an interstice, the word *quiet*, for instance, was more than descriptive; it was also prescriptive. The proclamation of Edward's government issued in 1551 against political and religious rumors that were seen as subversive asks each man to "apply himself to live obediently, quietly, without murmur, grudging, sowing of sedition, spreading of tales or rumors, and without doing or saying of any manner of thing (as near God will give them grace) that may touch the dignity of his majesty, his council, his magistrates or ministers." Conversely, irresponsible speech could cause social unrest. A number of governmental documents argue a close connection between disorderly language, unlawful gatherings, and rebellion. The state-authored "Homilie agaynst Contencion and Braulynge" (1547), paraphrasing Paul's epistles to Timothy, claims that "foolish and unlearned questions, knowing that they breed strife" endanger the church and, employing the literary form of sermon and the literary practice of biblical exegesis, points to contemporary instances in "gospeler," "papist," and "heretic."

Such writing examines the ideas of the state or the church following the literary techniques introduced into Tudor classrooms by Tudor rhetorics. Through these books and repeated lessons and drills, Henrician humanists promoted a rhetorical culture whereby counselors to the prince were those most educated and eloquent. Similar training was given both lawyers and preachers. Their advice and methods would direct, but not integrate, the works of state and church as well as writings for leisure and reflection. Later Elizabethan writers continued such practices. John Lyly's *Euphues* was designed to give the court a new, elevated, and delightfully varied if schematic language; *The Faerie Queene* was written, according to Spenser, to fashion a gentleman by modeling multiple forms of behavior embodying thoughts and acts of virtue; and even Sidney's *Arcadia*, circulated privately in manuscript, attempted to define the ideal citizen through the conflicting formulations of his characters. Such works were constructed through anthologies of incidents that made them pluralistic in narrative viewpoint and plentiful in character and incident.

Furthermore, the horizons of expectations for cultural texts steadily expanded throughout the sixteenth century. In 1540 Thomas Cranmer notes in his preface to the second edition of the Great Bible that it is intended for "all manner of persons, men, women, young, old, learned, unlearned, rich, poor, priests, laymen, Lords, Ladies, officers, tenants, and mean men, virgins, wifes, widows, lawyers, merchants, artificers, husbandmen, and all manner of persons of what estate or condition soever they be" concluding that it is "sufficiently determined and approved, that it is convenient and good, the scripture to be read of all sorts & kinds of people, and in the vulgar tongue." In the event, he was ahead of his time; both Henry (in a proclamation of 1541) and Mary resisted such circulation. But the "golden age" of Elizabeth I may have been most golden in its profusion of bibles and other works – the works that Webbe abhorred; in the aggregate, such works preserve a thick description of the Elizabethan culture. Reading thus demanded even more active and deeper engagement. But Richard Hooker found readers had the capacity needed: "the mind, while we are in this present life whether it contemplate, meditate, deliberate, or howsoever exercise itself, worketh nothing without continual recourse unto imagination the only storehouse of wit end peculiar chair of memory." In a world of swift cultural change, disparate audiences, and indeterminate meanings, each reader had for Hooker, writing in his *Laws of Ecclesiastical Polity* (1593), the ability to reflect on what he or she reads, finding there exemplary and pleasurable mirrors of the self. Hooker's interests were chiefly religion and philosophy, but Sidney's poetics for the artist is not altogether dissimilar. Sidney's poet is "lifted up with the vigour of his own inventions, [and] doth grow in effect another nature, in making things either better than nature bringeth forth, or, quite anew, forms such as never were in nature." He mixes Platonic ideals with an Aristotelian mimesis in order to convey, through metaphor and even unities of action, time, and place, how the poetic world is analogous to an intricate natural one by means of varying perspectives. The golden world of the poet – if it is to reach the multitude of the poet's readers – must abstract like the philosopher but cannot do so without "pleasaunt riuers, fruitfull trees, sweete-smelling flowers":[9] the quotidian world of nature, the messiness of history. But then, through such a process, Sidney's poet also produces works for the Tudor century distinctive in the pluralism and plenitude they harbor. Such writing opens things up rather than closes them down, forever inviting readers to join in the production of meaning. Perhaps this is the key to why such a body of English writing has been called "the Renaissance" – and why it is so alive, so varied, and so popular, then as now illuminating a world that often seems very much like our own.

NOTES

1 Stephen Greenblatt, *Renaissance Self-Fashioning: From More to Shakespeare* (Chicago: University of Chicago Press, 1980), pp. 17–18.
2 Lisa Jardine, "Strains of Renaissance Reading," *English Literary Renaissance* 25:3 (Autumn 1995): 296–97.
3 James Elkins, *The Poetics of Perspective* (Ithaca, NY and London: Cornell University Press, 1994), p. 117.
4 Simon Thurley, "The Lost Palace of Whitehall," *History Today* 48:1 (January 1998): 51.
5 Richard Helgerson, "Murder in Faversham: Holinshed's Impertinent History," in *The Historical Imagination in Early Modern Britain: History, Rhetoric, and Fiction, 1500–1800*, ed. Donald R. Kelley and David Harris Sacks (Cambridge: Cambridge University Press and Woodrow Wilson Center Press, 1997), p. 145.
6 Lauro Martines, "The Protean Face of Renaissance Humanism," *Modern Language Quarterly* 51 (1990): 107.
7 James Tracy, "From Humanism to the Humanities: A Critique of Grafton and Jardine," *Modern Language Quarterly* 51 (1990): 139.
8 William Webbe, *A Discourse of English Poetrie* (1586), from *Elizabethan Critical Essays*, ed. G. Gregory Smith, 2 vols. (Oxford: Oxford University Press, 1904), vol. I, p. 226.
9 Sir Philip Sidney, *The Defence of Poetrie* (1595), sig. Cl; also in Smith, ed., *Elizabethan Critical Essays*, vol. I, p. 156, as *An Apologie for Poetrie*.

2

COLIN BURROW

The sixteenth century

What makes a century? It is clearly something more than the simple passage of a hundred years, but equally clearly is something less than a perfectly connected sequence of events with an interconnected beginning, middle, and end. History rarely shapes itself to the motions of the planets or to the arbitrary divisions of the calendar: as Hayden White has shown us, it is more usually shaped by the demands imposed on it by different kinds of narrative structure.[1] Monarchs do not obligingly succumb to *fin de siècle* gloom in order to die with the century, nor do social or literary movements terminate with a bang the moment a century draws to an end.

The sixteenth century is particularly unobliging in its relation to the calendar. Nothing of great note happened in 1500, and nothing of great note happened in 1600 either, as the timeline appended to this volume shows. As a unit of political history the century effectively begins in 1485, when Henry Tudor defeated Richard III at the Battle of Bosworth field. Henry VII, as he became, was keen to present this event as a beginning: he employed historians such as Polydore Vergil and Bernard André to construct a Tudor version of history in which Richard III was portrayed as a murderous tyrant, and in which the marriage of Henry himself to Elizabeth of York was presented as the final resolution of fifteenth-century battles between the rival houses of York and Lancaster over the succession.

To many English subjects the era which began in 1485 would appear to have ended in 1603 with the death of Henry VIII's childless daughter Elizabeth. Fears of the Queen's decline and anxiety as to who would succeed her ran through the last thirty years of her reign. In the event the death of Elizabeth was followed by the peaceful accession of James VI of Scotland to the English throne. Although panegyrists of James hurried into print with poems which promised the beginning of a new age in 1603, many Londoners (and by 1603 Londoners comprised roughly 10 percent of the population of England) would have felt that year to be one of endings rather than of beginnings: it was marked by a severe plague, in which more than 30,000 people died.[2] Thomas Dekker in his *Wonderful Year* (1603) describes how after the death of Elizabeth plague transformed the geography of London into a map of death: "Imagine then that all this while, Death (like a Spanish leaguer, or rather like stalking Tamberlaine) hath pitched his tents (being nothing but a heap of winding sheets tacked together) in the sinfully-polluted suburbs: the plague is muster-master and Marshall of the field: burning fevers, boils, blains, and carbuncles, the leaders, Lieutenants, Sergeants, and Corporals."[3] 1603 was, for Dekker, the wonderful year that promised the marriage of Scotland and England through the accession of James VI and I; and yet it was not the future King James, but Death who made his triumphal entry into the city. The year 1603 felt terminal.

So a beginning and an end can be found for the century. But what about a middle? Grand unified narratives about the sixteenth century should be treated with suspicion. There are many residual versions of such fables lurking around: that the Tudors united the nation at the cost of imposing on it absolute rule; that the literature of the period consistently sings the praises of its monarchs; that the Reformation brought with it the rise of a forward-looking Puritan spirit which finally rose against Stuart absolutism in the 1640s. All of these stories have been dismantled by historians over the past twenty years, and with good reason: many of their outlines first take shape in the mythologies constructed about the sixteenth century by Tudor and Protestant propagandists. From 1485 to 1603 English monarchs sought consciously to fashion an image and a posthumous reputation for themselves, and to construct a version of history for popular consumption. The arts of history, poetry, drama, painting, engraving, woodcutting, religious prose-writing, and even architecture were deployed to shape their subjects' perceptions of the dynasty. The title page of Edward Hall's *Union of the Two Noble ... Families of Lancaster and York* (1550) (or Hall's *Chronicle*, as it is usually known) depicts interwoven rose trees which represent the houses of York and Lancaster, and which eventually merge at the top of the page in the substantial figure of Henry VIII. In Bernard André's history of Henry VII (c. 1502) the climactic battle of Bosworth is an event so great that the blind historian professes he is unable to represent it, and so leaves a dramatically blank page in his narrative.[4] Even the death of Elizabeth was not simply a biological accident, but an act of self-shaping, mediated to the population of England through a careful propaganda campaign. According to John Clapham,

> She sat up six days together without any sleep and yet was she not bereaved of any understanding, but had the use thereof, even after her speech failed, as

appeared by divers motions of her eyes and hands lifted up, when she was required by the Bishops to give testimony of the hope and comfort she had had in God. It is reported that when she was demanded whom she would have to sit in her seat after her death, she made answer "No base person, but a king."[5]

With a dumb sign with her hand she is then said to have indicated that the King she meant was James VI of Scotland. It is impossible to tell if this gestural affirmation of the continuity of Tudor and Stuart rule actually occurred, or whether it is what Elizabeth's subjects needed to be told had occurred. But it does show that careful manipulation of images, even in death, was a means by which this family sought to ensure national stability and dynastic continuity. This program was reinforced in one of the major new beginnings within this period, the state entry of Elizabeth I into London in 1558. At one of the mini-pageants that punctuated her progress through the capital ("the whole pageant garnished with red roses and white," as one observer recorded)[6] the Queen was presented with a book called *Verbum Veritatis* (the word of Truth) by an allegorical figure representing Truth, the daughter of Time. Elizabeth is reported to have kissed the volume and to have held it up so all could see, signaling to the London aldermen and livery companies who had paid for the pageant that she would return to the Protestantism of her brother Edward, after the efforts of her sister Mary to draw the nation back to Roman Catholicism. This was a century in which representations were a crucial tool of government.

This is one reason why its literature is so strong: as an art of representation it knows it matters. But it is also why we should be uneasy with mythically unified tales about the period. Tudor rule was not all (heraldic) roses. Revisionist historians over the past few years have noted the ways in which the success of the dynasty depended upon perilous improvization, the careful distribution of patronage, the delicate balancing of faction against faction, and the dispersal of power to the localities. From the 1530s humanist writers such as Thomas Elyot and Thomas Starkey emphasized an ideal of counsel, with its roots in Cicero's *De officiis*, which urged the duty of an educated and eloquent nobility to advise the monarch. Conceptions of government throughout the period were divided between the ideal of a sacred, imperial monarchy on the one hand, and the potentially conflicting ideal of regal government limited by counsel on the other. England was frequently presented as a mixed polity, which counterpoised the power of the Crown with the moral force of parliament and counsel.[7] The literature of the period frequently explores the potential lines of stress within this delicate balance of monarch and advisors. It also frequently reflects some of the less than fully desired by-products of the often less than perfectly conceived policies of the government. It certainly does not present a static "Elizabethan world picture," as E. M. W. Tillyard called it, of harmonious equipoise between monarch and commons.

In order to flesh out these bald propositions we might take a closer look at some of the attempts made in this period to fashion a Tudor mythology through art. This strategy intrinsically involves risk: those who seek to employ the power of art to their own dynastic ends necessarily acknowledge its potential power over themselves. The example given above of Elizabeth's gracious acceptance of the book given to her by Truth during her state entry illustrates this very clearly. The Queen played a role which was scripted for her by those who wished to advise her: the hotly Protestant Richard Grafton was the chief coordinator of her state entry, and the Latin verses for the occasion were probably composed by another zealous Protestant, Richard Mulcaster, who was to be the schoolmaster of Edmund Spenser.[8] They knew, and Elizabeth probably knew, that half a dozen years before Mary had witnessed a similar pageant at her state entry, and that Stephen Gardiner, Bishop of Winchester, had ordered that the same book called *Verbum Dei* be painted out in a symbolic erasure of the legacy of reform. Elizabeth's role in her state entry was made for her by factional interests, and that role may well have sat awkwardly with her own religious opinions (her insistence in 1559 that her private chapel contain a crucifix gave rise to some tension with her leading churchmen). As her reign progressed Elizabeth was repeatedly positioned within courtly entertainments and fictions which attempted to shape her actions under pretexts of praising her. The Earl of Leicester's literary comperes, including Sir Philip Sidney, mounted a concerted aesthetic campaign against the Queen's entertaining the courtship of the Catholic duc d'Alençon in the later 1570s.[9] Spenser's *Faerie Queene*, which may have origins in the factional interests of the Earl of Leicester in the 1570s, is often claimed to have presented an idealized image of Tudor polity. It may do so, but its imaginary polity displays the distinct points of stress in Tudor rule. The poem enacts an unresolved battle of a characteristically Tudor kind between the wish to praise an idealized monarch and the urge to refashion the Queen's image and redirect her policies. Spenser's noblemen heroes fight their battles independently of their Queen Gloriana, who appears in the poem only in a dream; and frequently the allegory of the poem privily counsels the Queen to favour policies to which she was resistant, such as expensive anti-Spanish policies in the Low Countries.[10] Art does not passively shape itself to the demands of power in this period; it beguilingly demands that the relationship between monarch and artist be reciprocal, that power is exchanged between the two.

There are many respects in which Tudor policy did have a significant impact on the writing of the period, but it rarely did so in ways which the architects of policy would have wished for or designed. In the period up to the death of Henry VIII in 1547 the majority of writing which has come down to us was composed by people (Skelton, Hawes, More, Wyatt, Surrey) who had direct experience of the Tudor court. The court, which was originally no more than the household of the monarch, became by the end of Henry VII's reign an administrative center which was located for an increasing proportion of the year in London. In the 1490s the inner or Privy Chamber emerged as a separate department of the royal household in which the King performed the majority of his private business, and courtiers who could charm the King in this realm within the court were likely to enjoy economic and political favor. By the 1520s Henry VIII's penchant for giving influential positions in the Privy Chamber to men whom he liked (his "minions" as they were disparagingly called) made the ability to win access to the inner sanctum of the court through persistence, gentle bribery, or artful self-display the central requirement of success in early Tudor England.[11] It also increased the likelihood that the court would become a center of faction and a source of resentful exclusion by those who felt shut out from the process of counsel. The centrality of the court, and the secrecy of the Privy Chamber at the center of that center, meant that unless one gained near access to the monarch – and that often meant getting a piece of paper into his or her hand by fair means or foul – a request for a suit of land or for patronage would fail.

These changes in the court, the primary imaginative locale of writing, had an immediate and continuing impact: from Skelton's *Bowge of Court* (*c.* 1500), through the allegorical narratives of Stephen Hawes in the first decades of the sixteenth century, and the satires of Sir Thomas Wyatt, right up to Spenser's satirical attack on the court in *Colin Clout's Come Home Againe* (1595) and Sir Walter Ralegh's complaint to his Queen in "The Ocean to Cynthia" (probably composed during his imprisonment in 1592), poets meditate on what it is to be excluded from court, indulge the agonies of yearning which result from their exclusion, and contemplate the compensatory freedoms which they might create for themselves in the absence of direct access to authority. The supremely "literary" posture of the Petrarchan lover, yearning for an ever-elusive mistress, and creating from the void of desire a voice of personal lament, grows in its English form from the Tudor court: the first English imitations of Petrarch were composed by the Henrician courtiers Wyatt and Surrey, and the most influential sonnet sequence of the later part of the century, Sidney's *Astrophil and Stella* (printed in 1591), draws on Sidney's frustratedly edgy relations with a courtly milieu.[12] The closed circle of the court, which by the end of Elizabeth's reign was open only to a tiny group of noblemen, was the gravitational center of Tudor literature, and like all gravitational centers it was so powerful that few could survive for long at its heart – but writing grew from its excluded margins.

The most complex process of the sixteenth century, the Reformation, also has a major influence on literary activity. But here too the whole long process of breaking from the authority of Rome and constructing a viable alternative church had effects on literature and the nation which were not exactly what its initiators would have desired. In the 1960s and 1970s the dominant view of the Reformation was that it marked a concerted effort to revolutionize the government of the nation, and that the move to Protestantism reflected popular hostility to the excesses of the late medieval church.[13] It did indeed begin – at least in its political aspect – with a string of Acts of Parliament in the 1530s which sought to center authority on the substantial figure of Henry VIII, as the preamble to the Act in Restraint of Appeals illustrates: "Where by divers sundry old authentic histories and chronicles it is manifestly declared and expressed that this realm of England is an empire, and so hath been accepted in the world, governed by one supreme head and king having the dignity and royal estate of the imperial crown of the same, unto whom a body politic, compact of all sorts and degrees of people divided in terms and by names of spiritualty and temporalty, be bounden and owe to bear next to God a natural and humble obedience ..."[14] There is revolution hidden in that lumbering legalese, and it lies in the claim that the English monarch enjoyed "imperial" dominion within his realm over matters both temporal and spiritual. That meant the authority of the Pope in England was in theory at an end. A string of further acts was energetically put forward by Henry's chief minister Thomas Cromwell through the 1530s in order to enforce this rejection of papal authority within the realm of England. The Act of Supremacy of 1534 declared that the King "shall be taken, accepted and reputed the only Supreme Head in earth of the Church of England" (Elton, ed., *The Tudor Constitution*, p. 364). A new treason act, which extended treason to include words, followed closely in 1534, and was the legal instrument which gave a thin justification to the executions of Bishop John Fisher and Thomas More, the two most influential figures to refuse to take the oath appended to the Act of Succession (which required subjects to abjure "any foreign potentate," including the Pope). By 1535 Henry VIII was established, in English law at least, as at once the supreme secular authority in the nation and the Supreme Head of the Church of England.

The desired constitutional effect of the Reformation is best illustrated by the engraved title page of the Great Bible of 1539. It shows the massy form of Henry VIII handing a book called "Verbum Dei" to his chief ministers of church and state, who pass the book down to the commons beneath. The commons cry, as though in gratitude, "God Save the King." But things are always less simple than Tudor iconography makes them appear: the political reformation proceeded at different rates and in different ways depending on which faction enjoyed favor at court, and it interacted in unpredictable ways with popular responses to it. Reformed religion was received with very different levels of understanding and enthusiasm in different areas of the country: Lancashire and Suffolk, for example, were particularly resistant to change. It was not initially a popular movement (although historians argue hotly about this). In the early years of the sixteenth century small groups of "Lollards" (followers of the fourteenth-century reformer John Wycliffe) kept up pressure for reform of the church in London, and their radical voices were given some authority by influential humanist reformers such as John Colet. Zealous Lutherans such as William Tyndale also advanced the cause of religious reform by active campaigns of translation in the 1520s.[15] But in the years which preceded the break with Rome there was no evident diminution in the popularity of the Catholic church in the majority of English parishes – and John Skelton was the most vocal poetic opponent of reform. There were few signs of any major change in popular attitudes to worship for at least the next twenty years. In 1548, when Henry's son Edward VI began a concerted policy of confiscating or destroying the ornaments of Catholic piety – church plate, crucifixes, rood screens – many churchmen did not believe that a permanent change in modes of worship would result. Chalices and clerical vestments, roodscreens and crucifixes, were hidden away in many parishes in the hope of a restoration of traditional practices of worship. As late as 1570 parishioners were leaving gold candlesticks to their churches "should mass ever be said there again" (Haigh, *English Reformations*, pp. 252–53). Martin Bucer regarded the transformation of the church as a reformation from above "by means of ordinances which the majority obey very grudgingly, and by the removal of the instruments of the ancient super-stition."[16] The commons, who were squeezed into the very lowest section of the title page of the Great Bible, had their own experiences of reformed religion, which frequently liberated itself from the weighty presence of royal authority. Throughout the sixteenth century, and well on into the next, the English church battled within itself over the best modes of church government, over clerical dress, over the articles of faith, and over the extent to which the constitutional break with Rome should be matched by a break with its theology of grace, intercession, and atonement.

The return to Catholicism attempted by Edward VI's sister Mary from 1553 to 1558 offers further examples of how unpredictable the long-term consequences of Tudor legislation could be. Mary's restoration of the traditional modes of worship was greeted warmly by many lay people (Haigh, *Reformations*, ch. 12), but the persecution and burning of Protestants which followed her accession led about 450 Protestant men and their families to leave England for the European centers of Protestant piety – Emden, Zurich, Strasbourg, Frankfurt, and Geneva. This group of exiles cannot be said to have a unified position on church government, beyond their opposition to Mary and papal supremacy,[17] but after Mary's death in 1558 their writings came to have a defining influence on English Protestantism. During Mary's reign more than eighty separate printed works had arrived in England from the pens of the exiles, including the first unequivocal expressions in English of Protestant resistance theory (the view that a legitimate hereditary monarch who transgresses God's law to become a murderer or a tyrant should be opposed by force) from Christopher Goodman and John Ponet.[18] During these years too the most popular translation of the bible in the period, the so called "Geneva Bible," was produced by William Whittingham and his collaborators. It contained several marginal notes which reflected Protestant resistance theory. Meanwhile in Frankfurt, and later in Basle, John Foxe was gathering material for what was to become the most powerful work of Protestant propaganda of the period and the most popular book of the century apart from the bible itself, the *Acts and Monuments*, or "Foxe's Book of Martyrs," as it became known. The title page of the 1563 edition shows two churches, the reformed and the unreformed (there is no need to say which side is peopled by devils and monks), and that image permeated the religious thought of the Elizabethan period: the twinning of the saintly Una with the duplicitous Duessa in Book 1 of Spenser's *Faerie Queene* is founded on Foxe's vision. The years of Marian exile gave to English Protestants a missionary zeal which Mary's renovated Catholic church under Cardinal Pole had lacked.

The Marian period also gave English Protestants a stimulus to catalogue and canonize their literary saints. John Bale's *Scriptorum illustrium maioris Brytanniae*, printed in Basle in 1557, was by no means the first catalogue of canonical English writers – Skelton and Hawes at the start of the century had created their own pantheons including Chaucer, Gower, and Lydgate – but it is by far the fullest in range and detail, and the first to present British literary achievements in Latin to a wider European audience. With the urgency of a Protestant exile Bale insists on the anticlerical and antipapist credentials of the writers whose lives and works he records (Pettegrew, *Marian Protestantism*, pp. 122–24 and 159–61). It is extremely difficult to say whether or not the majority of communicants in the Anglican church by 1580 could meaningfully be termed "Protestant," since most lay people at that date probably believed in the effectiveness of prayers and works as means to salvation; but the number of members of the gentry and of the priesthood who were united in their hostility to the Pope, to idolatry, and to the notion that men could merit salvation by their own actions, was considerably greater by 1580 than it had been in 1557. The mythology of the Reformation created by the Marian exiles played as great a part in this transformation as any act of government.

A general picture is emerging from this discussion of Tudor government, one in which many strands of authority coexist and occasionally struggle against each other, and in which efforts to assert or centralize regal authority often have unpredictable literary consequences. In a period in which there was no standing army or a regular police force this is not surprising: the chief ways of winning influence were through grants of offices, land, or licenses to sell particular commodities. Artfully distributed patronage could win allegiances and loyalty from networks of individuals, but it was not a method of rule which could effectively enforce spiritual or intellectual orthodoxy. The medium which could affect the minds of many people, however, was print. By the end of this period the printed word was the dominant mode of literary publication, but print was never in any full sense under the control of monarchs or their ministers. The rapid development of printing from Caxton's single press in the 1470s to a significant industry by 1590 has given rise to two equally misleading myths. According to the first, print, allied to the Reformation, liberated the minds of Englishmen from the dark clouds of Catholic oppression and made everyone start to think for him- or herself (after a millennium and a half in which the population had presumably gone around staring at their boots and muttering Hail Marys). According to the second myth the Tudor regime exerted a stranglehold of censorship over the press, recognizing both its potential as a medium of propaganda and the dangers posed by popular literacy. The first is really a scaled down version of Protestant propaganda: John Foxe claimed that the Pope "must abolish knowledge and printing, or he must seek a new world to reign over; for else, as this world standeth, printing doubtless will abolish him."[19] The second is substantially false. Control over the presses was in fact exercised, in a characteristically Tudor fashion, by occasional grand (and usually ineffective) gestures of assertiveness, combined with a more or less systematic use of patronage and financial incentives. After Caxton had printed the first book to issue from an English press in 1476 sporadic efforts were made to ally the new medium to the Crown through the establishment of royal printers, by a number of acts which sought to protect the business interests of the press, and, in 1557, by the granting of a monopoly over printing to members of the Stationers' Company. The mechanism of control was chiefly that of patronage rather than suppression. The authorities did respond *ad hoc* to particular localized threats, but when they did so the absence of means of enforcement tended to result in proclamations which issued big threats but which had in practice only limited effects. After the printing of Tyndale's New Testament in Cologne in 1526, Bishop Tunstall warned booksellers against importing such inflammatory material, but with little effect. Possession of heretical books was made a capital crime by Mary in June 1558, but this did little to stem the flow of Protestant books into English ports (Pettegrew, *Marian Protestantism*, pp. 164–65).[20] From 1586 the Star Chamber required that licenses be obtained for printing individual books, but the sheer number of volumes printed each year at the end of the century made it increasingly difficult to exercise any practical control over the presses: even after 1586 probably no more than half of the books printed each year were ever "allowed" – that is cleared for printing – by those in authority. And the process of having a work "allowed" may often have involved little more than an act of paraphrasing its contents to a member of the Commission.[21] In 1588–89 the illicit printing of anticlerical works by a group of writers who called themselves "Martin Marprelate" did initiate a spate of crack-downs by the authorities on particular genres: the Archbishop of Canterbury John Whitgift and Richard Bancroft, Bishop of London, ordained in 1599 that "no *Satyres* or *Epigrams* be printed hereafter" and that "noe Englishe historyes be printed excepte they be allowed by some of her maiesties privie Counsell."[22] Satires by Marston, Hall, and Nashe were burned by the public hangman, but nonetheless histories and satires continued to be allowed after that date by the Commission responsible for pre-publication censorship.

From 1581 plays were scrutinized by the Master of the Revels before they were performed, notionally to see if they might be acceptable for performance at court. But here again the Master of the Revels had a financial interest in the theatre (if theatres were closed and he had no plays to license, then he would lose the fee he was paid for scrutinizing each one) and so seems often to have acted in defense of the stage against the city authorities of London.[23] Plays which contained scenes in which monarchs were deposed, or historical plays with uncomfortable analogies with the present, were on several occasions printed without the offending scenes. When Shakespeare's *Richard II* was first printed in 1597 it lacked the scene which dramatizes the deposition of the King. In the best documented instance of theatrical censorship in the period, the Master of the Revels

Edmund Tilney directed the authors of the *Book of Sir Thomas More*, which contained an account of More's role in putting down the "Ill May Day" riot against foreign merchants in 1517, to "leave out the insurrection wholly with the cause thereof." This is not likely to have been the result of Tilney's wish to act as the instrument of civic order: it was probably the result of specific fears about the timing of the performance of the play in the aftermath of the anti-alien riots of 1593.[24] Such blunt measures were deployed only fitfully, and the evidence suggests that the authorities' focus of attention was on religious opinion and on works which might impair the dignity of rulers or noblemen. Ideas, experimental forms, provocatively innovative thinking of the kind which runs through the work of Christopher Marlowe, seem persistently to have hit a blind-spot in the censor's vision. The creaky mechanisms by which the authorities sought to regulate the press left plenty of room for the sharper wits of creative writers to fashion invisible or semi-visible means of reconfiguring the political orthodoxies of the period.[25] For simple reasons of scale the medium of print surged away from the mechanisms of control: according to the *Short-Title Catalogue of English Books* thirty-five works were printed in 1500 (of which the majority were practical manuals of piety); in 1600 no fewer than 268 books are known to have been printed. And this was not just an explosion in volume: the works printed in 1600 included *The Merchant of Venice, Much Ado About Nothing*, as well as Ben Jonson's *Every Man out of his Humour*. Something had happened to English writing between those dates.

What? Well, that innocent question is murderously difficult to answer. The chapters which follow each describe some of the huge number of complex changes which ran through the period. But the most extraordinary literary phenomenon of the century was the sudden burst of literary activity in the 1580s and 1590s, when Shakespeare, Marlowe, Jonson and Donne were all at work within a few miles of each other. There is inevitably a shortfall between any quasi-causal "explanation" of this kind of miracle and the phenomenon itself. But those writers were the beneficiaries of many things: an expansion of grammar schools had produced an increasingly eloquent, classically learned body of men from relatively humble backgrounds for whom public offices (as secretaries to noblemen or as minor civil servants) were in critically short supply. For men who could not get any other job which would enable them to make use of their training in eloquence, writing provided an opportunity to use their eloquence in a public forum. After about 1560, as chapter 4 shows, there also began a complex set of realignments in the ways in which poets, dramatists, and prose writers regarded their activity, and in the ways in which they were regarded by their readers. In 1562 Barnabe Googe's *Eclogues* were prefaced by a note from their author protesting that they had been smuggled into print without his knowledge. In 1573 George Gascoigne's *Hundred Sundrie Flowres* was preceded by an elaborate set of epistles which purport to describe how the printer had obtained the manuscript without the author's consent. These, however, were almost certainly composed by Gascoigne himself to give his printed work the *cachet* of a privately circulated manuscript. By 1590 attitudes toward print had changed significantly: poets who were not primarily courtiers frequently printed their works with signed epistles which revealed both their identity and their involvement in the process of printing (although courtiers such as Sir Walter Ralegh appear to have gone to great lengths to keep their work anonymous if it did sneak into print). Sir Philip Sidney, who died in 1586, did not print any of his literary works in his lifetime, but by 1595 all of his works had posthumously seen the light of print. The *Defence of Poetrie* printed in 1595, presented poetry as occupying a distinctive logical category: it was not the bare summary of events offered by history, nor the indigestible abstractions of philosophy, but a hypothetical realm of events as they might be. But the simple fact that Sidney's works were printed, first illicitly and then with the collaboration of his sister Mary, did even more than his theoretical arguments to raise the social status of printed works. This is not to say that circulation of poems in manuscript to a small coterie of friends ceased in the 1590s: manuscript – often in multiple copies – continued to be a major method of publication until the latter part of the seventeenth century and beyond. The majority of the poems of John Donne circulated in manuscript alone until after his death, and readers would regularly transcribe works into their own manuscript compilations for the enjoyment of themselves and their friends.[26] But by 1590, when Spenser printed *The Faerie Queene* with his name on the title page, an environment had emerged in which it was both possible and respectable to present oneself to the world as a professional author.[27] And by 1598 the name of Shakespeare, rather than simply the name of the company which had performed his plays, was frequently appearing on the title pages of the printed versions of his plays. This foregrounding of the author, which is explored more fully in chapter 4, was heightened by a tendency of much literary criticism in the later sixteenth century to create canons of named writers who had contributed to the growth of English language and literature, and to oppose these named figures – usually Chaucer, Wyatt, Surrey, Golding, Gascoigne, Sidney, Spenser – to unnamed poetasters and ballad-mongers. Sometimes, as in Francis Meres' catalogue of English writers in *Palladis Tamia* (1598), these lists are underwritten by ennobling parallels between the literature of London and that of Augustan Rome: as Meres put it "the sweet witty soul of Ovid lives in mellifluous and hony-tongued Shakespeare."[28] By the 1590s poetry could claim for its producers something of the *cachet* of laureateship.

These processes occurred above all in one place: London. And it is no exaggeration to say that without London the literary revolution of the 1580s and 1590s would not have occurred. The city's presses fed the center of the English book trade in the precincts of St. Paul's Cathedral, the hub of the social and religious activity of the capital. London also boasted the only purpose-made theatres in the country. The consumers of these media were drawn from a population which showed the highest levels of literacy in the nation, and which included the smart young men who attended the Inns of Court (the centers of legal training which were often called the country's third university). The city dominated more than 90 percent of the wool trade, which was the chief export industry in the period, and contained a massive body of wealthy and would-be wealthy hangers-on to the court and its attendant bureaucracies. But more than this, London, with its sprawling suburbs, its shady inns, and wandering back streets, was by the 1590s an imaginary locale of extraordinary energy. It was a place in which one could get caught by a debt-collector, lost without trace, robbed, raped, plague-struck, or very rich.

London was governed by a tight and reciprocal collaboration between the Crown and the guilds, livery companies, merchants, and aldermen who had created most of the wealth of the city (Rappaport, *Worlds Within Worlds*). Through the 1590s even these very effective forms of government were creaking under the weight of a population which had expanded from about 35,000 in 1500 to about 200,000 in 1600. In June 1602 there was the first vain attempt to curb the growth of the city by proclamation, since "such multitudes could hardly be governed by ordinary justice to serve God and obey her Majesty."[29] The growth continued unchecked, however, as men and a large number of women from the provinces thronged toward the center of work and wealth, the city which uniquely among European capitals was the center of both power and of mercantile activity. The rate of urban growth was matched in the 1590s by a phenomenal increase in the frequency with which new words entered the language, from about 50 new words per year in 1500 to about 350 in 1600.[30] Among anxious debates as to whether a "homespun" native English vocabulary was preferable to exotic words imported from Rome and Europe, the cosmopolitan London idiom became virtually institutionalized as that of literary English. As George Puttenham put it in his *Arte of English Poesie* (1589): "Ye shall therefore take the usual speech of the Court, and that of London and the shires lying about London within 60 miles, and not much above" (Smith, *Elizabethan Critical Essays*, vol. II, p. 150).

Writing in London grew and mutated in the 1580s and 1590s as rapidly as the city itself. Ballads, chapbooks, accounts of robberies and hangings, all circulated in the same space (and often among the same readers) as writing which laid claim to august literary status. London writers read each others' works, imitated each others' styles, and tried eagerly to overgo each other, with the result that sonnet sequences, plays, epigrams, satires, and prose pamphlets had each year to differ from last year's model. Genres developed and died with an almost unhealthy rapidity. A single genre, the erotic narrative poem (the "epyllion," or brief epic as it is sometimes called) illustrates the almost unhealthy vigor of generic development and transformation in the period.[31] The genre effectively began with Thomas Lodge's *Scylla's Metamorphosis* (1589), but probably took off as a fashionable form with Marlowe's *Hero and Leander*. Marlowe's poem was not printed until 1598, but was almost certainly read in manuscript in the early 1590s by a young poet-playwright called William Shakespeare. Marlowe glancingly describes Hero's sleeves "bordered with a grove, / Where Venus in her naked glory strove / To please the careless and disdainful eyes / Of proud Adonis, that before her lies" in one of the densely inlaid pictorial images in which his poem and the genre abounds. Shakespeare may well have sought to expand and ornament this tiny detail into the first printed work to which his name was attached, *Venus and Adonis*, in 1593. By 1601 the sheer smartness of those who had attempted the genre had all but worked it out: Francis Beaumont's *Salmacis and Hermaphroditus* takes the key features of the earlier exemplars of the genre, their gender-bending delight in polymorphous sexuality, their unstoppably digressive narrative form, to a point of excess which it is all but impossible to overgo, and, exhausted, the form dropped from the fashionable repertoire. London in the 1580s and 1590s generated a giddily accelerated literary history, fueled by competition, by the desire to earn and to win patronage, and by the desire to pass into the magic circle of named, canonical writers.

This overheated atmosphere generated many of the anxieties that make authors present their writings as "literary," as a special form of discourse over which they have rights of ownership and control. Some key elements in the vocabulary with which to assert literary ownership emerge in this period: the word "plagiary" first enters the language in Joseph Hall's satires (he has the ghost of Petrarch claiming his own from "a plagiary sonnet-wright" in *Virgidemiarum* 4. 2); John Donne's satire 2 vents its spleen against those "who (beggarly) doth chaw [chew] / Others' wits' fruits." Anxieties about the theft and misinterpretation of poems run through Ben Jonson's *Poetaster* (1601), and surface in many of his earlier works. Jonson responds to these anxieties by shaping a physically and dramatically substantial character of "the Author" for himself in several of his plays, a character who argues about the interpretation of his texts and the critical principles on which they rest. The fear that printed words could disperse among a multitude of readers, be misinterpreted, stolen, or simply used as wrapping or lavatory paper has a profound effect on the way in which writers in the 1590s present their own personae: their efforts to be lords and owners of their work are partly the consequences of recognizing the actual vulnerability and ephemerality of their words.[32] Donne, Jonson, and Shakespeare are all writers whose literary careers and literary personae developed in the overheated atmosphere of late Elizabethan London, in which they fought for survival; and without London, that sprawling monster on the threshold of the court, the majority of the writing for which the sixteenth century is remembered would never have been produced.

This chapter began with some reflections on periodization. I suggested that a story of a kind began in or around 1485. In the light of the latter part of this chapter we might wish to allow the starting date of the literary century to drift back to 1476, the introduction of printing into England, or perhaps forward to the 1518 edition of More's *Utopia*, which was one of the earliest works to use the arts of printing to advance its author's career, and which was also one of the first works to attempt to remove the court and the noble household from its picture of a predominantly urban society.[33] The shifts toward print and from a literature of the court toward a literature which has a dominantly urban focus and feel are the central changes in the nature of literary activity in the sixteenth century. Beginnings for these processes can be found toward the end of the fifteenth century and at the start of the sixteenth. These beginnings do not of course mark absolute breaks with the past, since the styles, and the styles of self-presentation, of Wyatt and Skelton and Hawes are deeply indebted to Chaucer, Lydgate, and Gower; but they do anticipate the high-point of English writing in the 1590s. It is not clear that the story which follows these beginnings is entirely continuous: certainly the repeated changes in official religion through the century would have seemed bewildering to many Englishmen, since each reign marked a new beginning. By 1603 it would have been apparent that the accession of James I and the consequent union with Scotland would lead to major changes in how England itself was perceived as a geographical and political entity.

It is also not clear that the story can be said to have ended in 1603. The 1616 first Folio of Ben Jonson's *Workes* – and he was much mocked for using that grandiose word of mere poems and plays – with its monumental title page; the 1623 Folio of Shakespeare's *Tragedies, Comedies and Histories*, with its engraving of the playwright which presides over a prestigious and costly volume; even perhaps the 1645 volume of *Poems of Mr. John Milton both English and Latin*, all testify to the emergence of a

COLIN BURROW

dignified profession of literary authorship which worked in collaboration with the medium of print. The start of this chapter gave some examples of royal self-fashioning, and explored some of the ways in which Tudor monarchs were not entirely in control of their images. The same goes, *mutatis mutandis*, for authors, whose written words were subjected to the unpredictable effects of the early modern presses, and then read by a public which prided itself on its autonomy and taste for innovation. No one, monarch or author, enjoyed absolute rule in the commonwealth of Tudor England. The following chapters explore the bewildering riches of the sixteenth century, which extend through its literary criticism, drama, chronicles of private life, the writing of reformation, popular chapbooks and ballads, to (in the final chapter) an emerging literature of the localities. The development of a form of authorship which was located in London life and articulated through the medium of print was by no means the sole source of riches in the sixteenth century; but after the death of Elizabeth in 1603 it was perhaps the chief legacy left by the dying century.

NOTES

1 Hayden White, *Tropics of Discourse: Essays in Cultural Criticism* (Baltimore and London: Johns Hopkins University Press, 1978).
2 Steve Rappaport, *Worlds Within Worlds: Structures of Life in Sixteenth-Century London* (Cambridge: Cambridge University Press, 1989), p. 72.
3 Thomas Dekker, *The Wonderful Yeare. 1603* (London, 1603), p. 24.
4 Bernard André, *De Vita atque Gestis Henrici Septimi*, ed. James Gairdner, *Rerum Britannicorum Medii Aevi Scriptores* (London: Longman, 1858), p. 32.
5 John Clapham, *Elizabeth of England*, ed. Evelyn Plummer Read and Conyers Read (Philadelphia and London: University of Pennsylvania Press, 1951), pp. 98–99.
6 J. Nichols, ed., *The Progresses and Public Processions of Elizabeth I*, 3 vols. (London: Society of Antiquaries, 1823), vol. I, p. 41.
7 See John Guy, "Tudor Monarchy and its Critiques" and Patrick Collinson, "The Monarchical Republic of Elizabeth I," in *The Tudor Monarchy*, ed. John Guy, (London: Arnold, 1997), chs. 3 and 4.
8 For Grafton and Mulcaster's involvement, see Roy Strong, *The Tudor and Stuart Monarchy: Pageantry, Painting, Iconography: II Elizabethan* (Woodbridge: the Boydell Press, 1995), pp. 38–40.
9 See further Blair Worden, *The Sound of Virtue: Philip Sidney's* Arcadia *and Elizabethan Politics* (New Haven and London: Yale University Press, 1996).
10 See Colin Burrow, *Edmund Spenser* (Plymouth: Northcote House, 1996); David Norbrook, *Poetry and Politics in the English Renaissance* (London: Routledge and Kegan Paul, 1984), ch. 5.
11 See Steven Gunn, "The Courtiers of Henry VII," in *The Tudor Monarchy*, ed. John Guy (London: Arnold, 1997), ch. 9; David Starkey et al., eds., *The English Court: from the Wars of the Roses to the Civil War* (London: Longman, 1987); David Loades, *The Tudor Court*, rev. edn. (London: Headstart History, 1992);

and G. R. Elton, "Tudor Government: the Points of Contact: III the Court," in *Studies in Tudor and Stuart Politics and Government III* (Cambridge: Cambridge University Press, 1983), pp. 38–57.

12 See Arthur F. Marotti, "Love is not Love: Elizabethan Sonnet Sequences and the Social Order," *ELH* 49 (1982): 396–428.

13 Notably by G. R. Elton, *The Tudor Revolution in Government* (repr. Cambridge: Cambridge University Press, 1969). The triumphalist account of the rise of Protestantism by A.G. Dickens, *The English Reformation*, 2nd edn. (London: Batsford, 1989) is still valuable, but has been questioned by a number of revisionist studies, notably J. J. Scarisbrick, *The Reformation and the English People* (Oxford: Blackwell, 1984); Christopher Haigh, *English Reformations: Religion, Politics, and Society under the Tudors* (Oxford: Clarendon Press, 1993); and Eamon Duffy, *The Stripping of the Altars: Traditional Religion in England c.1400–c.1580* (New Haven and London: Yale University Press, 1992). These works have won the battle on the ground, since they convey the impact of the Reformation on individual parishioners as Dickens does not; but they have not won the war. Dickens takes much fuller account than they of the mythologies of Reformation, and these mythologies, rather than parochial dissent, are more often reflected in the literature of the period.

14 G. R. Elton, ed., *The Tudor Constitution*, 2nd edn. (Cambridge: Cambridge University Press, 1982), p. 353.

15 On London reformers see Susan Bridgen, *London and the Reformation* (Oxford: Clarendon Press, 1989), ch. 2.

16 Quoted in Christopher Haigh, *Reformation and Resistance in Tudor Lancashire* (Cambridge: Cambridge University Press, 1975), p. 145.

17 C. H. Garrett, *The Marian Exiles* (Cambridge: Cambridge University Press, 1966); also A. G. Dickens, *The English Reformation*, pp. 339–49 and Andrew Pettegrew, *Marian Protestantism: Six Studies* (Aldershot: Scolar Press, 1996).

18 See Quentin Skinner, *The Foundations of Modern Political Thought: volume II, the Reformation* (Cambridge: Cambridge University Press, 1978), pp. 221–24.

19 J. Foxe, *Acts and Monuments*, ed. S. R. Cattley and J. Pratt, 4th edn. (London: Religious Tract Society, 1877), vol. III, p. 720.

20 For the use of printed works by the Marian regime to influence opinion abroad, see Jennifer Loach, "The Marian Establishment and the Printing Press," *English Historical Review* 101 (1986): 135–48.

21 Cyndia Susan Clegg, *Press Censorship in Elizabethan England* (Cambridge: Cambridge University Press, 1997), p. 61.

22 Edward Arber, ed., *A Transcript of the Stationers' Register*, 5 vols. (London and Birmingham, 1875–94), vol. III, pp. 677–78.

23 See Richard Dutton, *Mastering the Revels* (London: Macmillan, 1991).

24 See *Sir Thomas More: a Play by Anthony Munday and others*, ed. Vittorio Gabrieli and Giorgio Melchiori (Manchester and New York: Manchester University Press, 1990), p. 17, and Dutton, *Mastering the Revels*, pp. 84–86.

25 See Annabel Patterson, *Censorship and Interpretation: the Conditions of Writing and Reading in Early Modern England* (Madison: University of Wisconsin Press, 1984). On theatrical censorship, see Gerald Eades Bentley, *The Professions of Dramatist and Player in Shakespeare's Time, 1590–1642* (Princeton: Princeton University Press, 1986), pp. 145–96.

26 See Arthur F. Marotti, *Manuscript, Print, and the English Renaissance Lyric* (Ithaca, NY and London: Cornell University Press, 1995) and Harold Love, *Scribal Publication in Seventeenth-Century England* (Oxford: Clarendon Press, 1993).

27 Richard Helgerson, *Self-Crowned Laureates: Spenser, Jonson, Milton, and the Literary System* (Berkeley and London: University of California Press, 1983); Patrick Cheney, *Spenser's Famous Flight: a Renaissance Idea of a Literary Career* (Toronto and London: University of Toronto Press, 1993).

28 G. Gregory Smith, ed., *Elizabethan Critical Essays*, 2 vols. (Oxford: Oxford University Press, 1904), vol. II, p. 317.

29 Paul L. Hughes and James F. Larkin, eds., *Tudor Royal Proclamations, Volume III: The Later Tudors, 1588–1603* (New Haven: Yale University Press, 1969), p. 245. On the relative stability of London, see Rappaport, *Worlds within Worlds*.

30 See Geoffrey Hughes, *Words in Time: A Social History of the English Vocabulary* (Oxford: Basil Blackwell, 1988), pp. 101–03. These figures are likely to be exaggerated, since documentation in the OED, on which they are based, is relatively poor for the period 1500–50.

31 For a fuller account, see Clark Hulse, *Metamorphic Verse: The Elizabethan Minor Epic* (Princeton: Princeton University Press, 1981).

32 See Ian Donaldson, *Jonson's Magic Houses* (Oxford: Clarendon Press, 1997), chs. 3 and 12.

33 On the artful shaping of the epigrams printed with the 1518 *Utopia*, see David R. Carlson, *English Humanist Books: Writers and Patrons, Manuscript and Print, 1475–1525* (Toronto, Buffalo, and London, 1993), ch. 7; on the urban structures of *Utopia*, see Lawrence Manley, *Literature and Culture in Early Modern London* (Cambridge: Cambridge University Press, 1995), ch. 1.

FURTHER READING

Collinson, P., *The Birthpangs of Protestant England* (Basingstoke: Macmillan, 1988).

Dickens, A. G., *The English Reformation*, 2nd edn. (London: Batsford, 1989).

Duffy, Eamon, *The Stripping of the Altars: Traditional Religion in England c. 1400–c.1580* (New Haven and London: Yale University Press, 1992).

Elton, G. R., *Reform and Reformation* (London: Edward Arnold, 1977).

Guy, John, *Tudor England* (Oxford: Oxford University Press, 1988).

Guy, John, ed., *The Tudor Monarchy* (London: Arnold, 1997).

Haigh, Christopher, ed., *The Reign of Elizabeth I* (Basingstoke: Macmillan, 1984).

Haigh, Christopher, *Elizabeth I* (London: Longman, 1988).

  English Reformations: Religion, Politics, and Society under the Tudors (Oxford: Clarendon Press, 1993).

James, Mervyn, *Society, Politics, and Culture: Studies in Early Modern England* (Cambridge: Cambridge University Press, 1986).

Manley, Lawrence, *Literature and Culture in Early Modern London* (Cambridge: Cambridge University Press, 1995).

Williams, Penry, *The Later Tudors: England 1547–1603* (Oxford: Clarendon Press, 1995).

3

CLARK HULSE

Tudor aesthetics

TWO FABLES

What is "literature"? Who writes it, and who reads it? What good or harm does it do? How is it related to other cultural forms? And what is the appropriate language and kind of writing within which these issues can be framed and argued? These simple questions, which provide the fodder for the complex aesthetic debates of the Enlightenment and the Romantic eras and for the theory wars of the late twentieth century, were likewise disputed in the sixteenth century. It is possible, indeed, to think of the sixteenth century as the first great age of literary criticism,[1] in which a distinctive category of literature was established, and a distinctive way of talking about it and the other arts was developed.

For Tudor writers and readers, the answers to these questions depend primarily on their understanding of literature as a kind of *imitation*. The word *imitation* is a complex one, though, for it allows two important meanings. The first of these is imitation as the copying or echoing of other speech or writing, an understanding of the term that places literature, as imitative writing, in a close relationship to rhetoric, and emphasizes its power to speak to human desires and hence to act as a force either of order or disorder in society. The second important meaning is imitation as the representation of nature, or what Aristotle in his *Poetics* calls *mimesis*. Modern accounts of Renaissance aesthetics, especially accounts that draw primarily on the experience of Renaissance Italy, often describe the transition from medieval to Renaissance poetics as a shift from a rhetorically based imitation to an Aristotelian understanding of *mimesis*. While Aristotle's *Poetics* has an undeniably greater importance at the end of the sixteenth century than it had at the beginning, it is better to understand the two meanings of imitation as always present in Tudor aesthetic discourse and always in dialogue with each another. The exact relationship between them is a primary subject of debate in the period, one from which Tudor writers then generate answers to the whole set of questions that make up their aesthetic understanding. As we shall see, the debate about the nature of imitation is itself represented by Tudor writers through metaphors of the human body, so that Tudor aesthetics can with justice be called an aesthetics of the body.

An initial sense of these debates can be found in the contrast between a passage at the end of Geoffrey Chaucer's "Nun's Priest's Tale," from *The Canterbury Tales*, written around 1390, and a passage from Sir Philip Sidney's *Defence of Poetrie*, written around 1580. In Chaucer's tale, a fox named Don Russel has flattered Chauntecleer the rooster by praising his song-like crowing. When the rooster closes his eyes to crow all the better, the fox grabs him by the neck and dashes away. As he flees, the captured Chauntecleer persuades him to shout defiance at the pursuing farmhands, but when Don Russel opens his mouth for his boast, Chauntecleer breaks free and flies to safety high in a tree. When Don Russel tries to persuade him to come down, pleading that he meant no harm, Chauntecleer replies this way (Chaucer's Middle English is here lightly modernized):

> "Thou shalt no more through thy flattery
> Do me to sing and winken with mine eye.
> For he that winketh when he should see,
> All willfully, God let him never thrive."
>   "Nay," quoth the fox, "but God give him mischance
> That is so indiscrete of governance
> That jangleth when he should hold his peace."[2]

This curious conversation between animals is simultaneously a reflection on the nature and function of language. Chauntecleer acknowledges that he has been misled through language not only by the fox's duplicity, but by the self-deception of his own desire for flattery. At the same time, he recognizes that language is an instrument – and a divinely ordained one at that – for understanding truth through self-examination. Don Russel for his part understands that God has also ordained a social purpose for language, which is an instrument by which the individual can avoid "indiscrete governance" within the group.

If this seems like an over-reading of a simple barnyard story, one must take heed of the commentary that the Nun's Priest himself adds by way of conclusion:

> But ye that holden this tale a folly
> As of a fox, or of a cock and hen,
> Taketh the morality, good men,
> For Saint Paul sayeth that all that written is

To our doctrine it written is, ywis:
Taketh the fruit, and let the chaff be still.
("The Nun's Priest's Tale," lines 3438–43)

The Nun's Priest not only ratifies the theory of language developed by his creatures, but extends it to the poetic tale itself. While the tale is in some sense a "folly," all writing has the capacity to teach. Whether this story leads to folly or doctrine may depend less on the story itself, since it has the capacity for both, than on whether or not we are "good men," people of "discrete governance," who know how to take the "fruit" of its morality and dispense with the "chaff," which is nothing less than the story itself, in all its literary elements of character, plot, discursive style, and poetic form.

Chaucer's tale thus exhibits a curious self-division, in which the nature of literature is understood only through its close relation to other forms of language, specifically rhetoric and theology. The value of literature likewise lies outside itself, in its capacity to produce or obstruct individual enlightenment and civil order, and the internal qualities of literature that might mark it as different from other language are subjected to an almost deconstructive process, in which they are the means for the construction of the poem's meaning, but then themselves dissolve into non-meaning once that activity of understanding is complete.

In contrast, Sidney describes a conversation not between a fox and a rooster, but between himself and an Italian horseman, Gian Pietro Pugliano, who is esquire to the Holy Roman Emperor Maximilian II. Pugliano, like Chauntecleer, is infatuated with his own art, though in this case it is horsemanship he is crowing about:

> He said soldiers were the noblest estate of mankind, and horsemen the noblest of soldiers. He said they were the masters of war and ornaments of peace, speedy goers and strong abiders, triumphers both in camps and courts. Nay, to so unbelieved a point he proceeded as that no earthly thing bred such wonder to a prince as to be a good horseman – skill in government was but a *pedanteria* [pedantry] in comparison. Then would he add certain praises, by telling what a peerless beast the horse was, the only serviceable courtier without flattery, the beast of most beauty, faithfulness, courage, and such more, that if I had not been a piece of a logician before I came to him, I think he would have persuaded me to have wished myself a horse.[3]

Like Chaucer's Chauntecleer, Sidney sees in Pugliano's discourse the capacity of language to mislead its hearers, though he sees the danger of self-delusion to be far greater. Like Don Russel, he replies with a boast of his own, that he will speak in defense of his own vocation of poetry, although it is, under the circumstances, a strange one. Sidney justifies his mimicry of Pugliano's "strong affection and weak arguments" in the praise of horses on the grounds that poetry is all the more in need of praise because even the most eminent philosophers have joined in attacking it, "with great danger of civil war among the Muses" (*Defence*, p. 212).

Sidney's comic fable here has its points of resemblance to that of the Nun's Priest, suggesting that even the most foolish tale may bear the fruit of some moral doctrine. Still, there are important differences between the two. Whereas Chauntecleer and Don Russel saw that poetry and rhetoric must lead ultimately to self-knowledge and good governance, Sidney instead embraces, however ironically, the capacity of language to produce self-delusion and "civil war." And where the fox, the rooster, and the priest understood that the imitative "chaff" of poetic fable must in the end be cast aside in favor of philosophy and theology, Sidney argues, in a very subtle way, that poetry is superior to philosophy precisely in the power of its mimetic chaff to capture our attention. For the philosopher who has most vehemently attacked poetry is of course Plato, who argues incessantly in the *Republic* that if you want to gain true knowledge about horses, you will not ask the painter or the poet who gives you a copy of a horse in pigments or in words, but will go to the horseman, who has direct knowledge of the thing itself. In his own love for horses, Philip Sidney (Philip = phil-hippos = lover of horses!) has gone to the most expert horseman, only to discover not the thing itself promised by philosophy, but the most elaborate self-delusions of language. From this verbal chaff he wrests a curious self-knowledge, that through his greater love for poetry he may come to understand these paradoxical powers of language, and by embracing them rather than discarding them, may produce self-knowledge and good governance after all. And how better to produce these results than through a fable about fables – through, that is, this very story, which starts out sounding like an autobiographical anecdote and ends in doctrine. In short, the "chaff," the fable, the formal characteristics of mimetic language, are not something to be discarded as Sidney makes his point, but are themselves the point.

This shift in the status of poetic language, from a nervous marginality to a nervous centrality, is enacted not only in the content of these two passages but in their form as well. For Chaucer's reflections on the nature of his poetic art come as an epilogue to a tale purportedly told not by Chaucer but by another, and are conveyed in a vocabulary derived ultimately not from poetry itself but from rhetoric and theology. Sidney in contrast places his anecdote at the beginning of a work devoted entirely to reflections on poetic art. (Its precise generic identity as "defense," "treatise," or some other form is an intricate question that we will take up later.) The space between the two ways of talking about literature is the space in which aesthetic discourse emerges as a separate way of talking or writing, separate, that is, from rhetoric, philosophy, or theology. Hence the changes from Chaucer to Sidney, the changes that underpin this chapter on "Tudor aesthetics," are changes not only in the content of aesthetic discourse, but also are changes in the place of that discourse itself within the world of learning.

At the same time that they embody important changes, the two passages have equally important features in common. Each places at the center of discussion the relationship of literature to rhetoric, which is the discourse about the nature of language, and of literature to philosophy or theology, which are the discourses about the nature of truth. But each proceeds through an imitative mode that is characterized both by the representation of multiple voices and by the representation of nature, whether in the form of "fictive" animals or "real" humans. In each case, none of the voices within the fable – neither Chauntecleer nor Don Russel nor the Nun's Priest nor Pugliano nor Sidney himself – is a voice of unquestioned and absolute authority. Rather, it is only by an appeal to discursive authority that lies outside the fable itself – outside both the linguistic and natural "imitation" of the text – that any doctrinal authority can be established (as in the case of Chaucer's text), or even imagined (as in the case of Sidney's). It is precisely this rhetorical and dialogized characteristic of Tudor aesthetic discourse that marks it as different from the more abstracted discourse of modern and postmodern literary theory. It is an aesthetic discourse that both debates the nature of imitation and enacts it, as a dialogue on dialogue, and as a mimesis of mimesis.

AESTHETICS, POETICS, RHETORIC

Before proceeding to a detailed examination of the central texts that make up the body of Tudor aesthetics, it is important that we look at the history of the terms that we have used already in talking about Chaucer and Sidney, especially the terms "rhetoric," "poetics," and "aesthetics" itself. Of these, the most important is the word "aesthetics," since the very idea of a "Tudor aesthetics" is an anachronism, though it is a useful one. The term "aesthetics" is an eighteenth-century invention, introduced by A. G. Baumgarten in 1750, and given currency by Immanuel Kant in his *Critique of Judgment* (1790). Baumgarten defined the aesthetic as "the theory of the liberal arts, a lower grade of knowledge [than logic], the art of thinking beautifully, the art of the analogy of reason," or "the science of sensuous knowing."[4] This formulation aligns literature with music and the visual arts, in opposition to science, philosophy, and (later) the social sciences.[5] It establishes literature, along with the other fine arts, as a way of knowing through what is represented to the senses. Hence literature is mimetic – that is, it follows nature, but only by distancing nature from itself through representation. And, ironically, Baumgarten's formulation divides aesthetic theory from the aesthetic itself, since the theory of the aesthetic, as conducted by Baumgarten or Kant, uses the logical language of philosophy rather than the metaphoric language of literature.

Our own aesthetic thinking usually shares these Enlightenment assumptions, especially the assumptions that "theory" is a separate category from literature itself, that literature is secondary to science as a logical form of knowledge, and that any critique of literature, including a social critique, must also be a critique of beauty. In contrast, sixteenth-century debates over literature take for granted only the last of these assumptions. Formulations of the nature of literature and of the writer were deeply encoded with gendered assumptions about the beauty of the human body, and in many ways literature became an arena for working out tensions within the gender system. The status of literature as a form of knowledge, and hence its relationship to other forms of knowledge, including the fine arts, philosophy, and science, was in continual crisis throughout the century, and was an important term in wider debates about the proper form of education and even of religion. And finally, the forms and languages of debate were themselves multiple, ranging from poems about poetry to polemical defenses of literature to philosophical treatises.

Indeed, the term that would have been most familiar to sixteenth-century writers and readers was not "aesthetics" but "poetics." "Poetics" is established by Aristotle as the philosophical inquiry into language that is characterized by *mimesis* or the imitation of nature; hence it potentially encompasses everything we call "literature," and not just poetry. Aristotle treated poetics in a separate treatise from "rhetoric" or language that is characterized by its force of persuasion. Each of these forms of language is accompanied by an art – that is, a set of methods or techniques by which imitation or persuasion can best be achieved. There are large areas of overlap in Aristotle's understanding of the two arts of language, especially in their common use of metaphor. In the important formulations of the Middle Ages, especially that of the twelfth-century theologian Hugh of St. Victor, poetic is considered a subcategory of rhetoric, since the quality of imitation is to give vividness to language, which is central to persuasion. Rhetoric in this inclusive sense is one of the seven liberal arts, which are subdivided into the *trivium* of grammar, logic, and rhetoric, and the *quadrivium* of arithmetic, geometry, astronomy, and music. The arts of the *trivium* are qualitative, useful in describing the properties of nature and humanity, while the arts of the *quadrivium* are quantitative, useful in describing their proportions. Overarching all of the arts were the supreme forms of study, philosophy and theology.

After the publication of a newly recovered Greek text of Aristotle's *Poetics* in 1509, the subject of poetics was increasingly treated as distinct from rhetoric, because of its focus on *mimesis*, but never in the sixteenth century is it treated as wholly separate from rhetoric. Rather, the two lines of inquiry describe two different aspects of literature. Like all language, literature is rhetorical, and like other imitative arts such as painting, literature is mimetic. But the effect of literature having a quality different from other language – a quality, that is, more important than the jangle of rhyme – was to give writers and critics a ground for removing literature from its subordinate status in the *trivium*. And the more literature was characterized first and foremost as an art of "making" by which the poet created a "second world" or "golden world" (about which more later) the more poetry could be linked to the arts of the *quadrivium*, by which the forms and proportions of that world might be measured. Hence "poetics" or the "art of poetry" is an important term throughout the sixteenth century, used repeatedly by leading writers to define the characteristics that belong specifically to literature.

Nonetheless, "poetics" never exists in isolation, and is always overlapping, contesting, combining, and separating from the other arts, especially the arts of rhetoric, music, philosophy, theology, and even geometry. It is precisely in those zones of interaction that theorists are best able to work out the important issues of poetics, concerning the nature, function, and forms of literature. For that reason, the broader term "aesthetics" remains useful as an umbrella beneath which we can place poetics and its connected arts, as together they seek to answer the central questions of the nature, function, and form not only of literature, but also of all language and other forms of art as well as questions about the proper shaping of the human body, human society, and human soul.

Because "poetry" and "poetics" were such unstable categories, the forms of aesthetic writing were likewise unstable, prior to their consolidation by the likes of Baumgarten and Kant as a branch of philosophy. Hence almost a century ago, G. Gregory Smith, the first important anthologizer of Tudor poetics, noted the common perception that "the critical writings are a mere miscellany of stray pamphlets, a 'gallimaufry' of treatises in the old rhetorical vein, tracts on prosody, or prefaces of abuse: and that the writers who disclose something of the critical temper were indifferent to the things which interest modern criticism."[6] This bewildering disorder of forms and preoccupations has led modern scholars to impose a variety of evolutionary schemes on the century. J. E. Spingarn in 1899 and O. B. Hardison in 1963 wrote approvingly of a growing classicism that developed under the influence of Italian literary theorists.[7] Smith in turn perceived two strands at work, a dominant classical one, and a submerged Romantic one, which he considered "are always found co-existing in the greatest periods and the greatest writers" (*Elizabethan Critical Essays*, p. lx). In each of these cases we can see the modern scholar actively imposing elements from late nineteenth- and early twentieth-century aesthetic theory on the sixteenth century to construct a shapely narrative for their material. But while there is clearly a difference between Sidney's conception of poetry and Chaucer's two centuries earlier, any such shapely narrative of development is impossible to sustain as an account of the year-by-year production of aesthetic writings from the accession of Henry VII to the death of Elizabeth I. A similar air of unreality hangs over these accounts insofar as they attempt to describe not only an evolution of content, but also suppose that the form of Tudor aesthetic discourse aspired somehow to leave behind that "gallimaufry" of epistles, prefaces, rhetorical handbooks, and prosodic tracts in order to achieve that mature form of aesthetic discourse which was embodied in the classical past by Aristotle's *Poetics*, in the Renaissance present by the treatises of Minturno or Castelvetro, and in the Enlightenment future by Kant's *Critique of Judgment*.

Writing in the wake of England's close call in World War II, J. W. H. Atkins offered an alternative hypothesis. He found the same disorder of forms and preoccupations to be the signs not of an unsuccessful imitation of classical or Italian Renaissance aesthetic treatises, but of a "continuous but unregulated effort to lay anew the foundations of the native literature in the light that had dawned at the Renascence." The progressive direction of criticism over the sixteenth century and into the seventeenth was the result of "free minds bent on investigating matters both old and new, working meanwhile from first principles."[8] Atkins' account still has a bit of the linear and teleological quality that dogs Spingarn, Smith, and Hardison, and clearly it involves some imposition of his own aesthetic and political values on earlier material – a defect that Sidney has warned us to beware of in all discourses on the arts, including the one you are now reading. But Atkins nonetheless makes a crucial swerve from the work of the others in rejecting the automatic priority of either classical or Italian material over the English. Rather, he perceives that the apparent disorder of the material is precisely the measure that it does not follow the progressive developmental scheme laid down by sixteenth-century Italian criticism, a scheme derived in no small part from Giorgio Vasari's description of the development of Italian painting, and a scheme that still controls with an astonishing tenacity most writing about the development of "Renaissance" culture in general. Rather, Atkins sees that the adoption of Italian or classical materials is of secondary importance compared to the underlying questions – questions that are as often political and social as aesthetic – that the material is being deployed to answer within and for its own culture.

In Atkin's swerve, then, we can see the seeds of an account of Tudor aesthetics comparable to that outlined for African–American aesthetics by Henry Louis Gates, Jr., in *The Signifying Monkey*. The project is to describe how a culture theorizes itself to itself[9] – that is, to uncover the specific forms and contents by which Tudor culture represents to itself its theories of language, literature, and culture. Such a culturally reflexive account of Tudor aesthetics proceeds not as a linear progression toward classical or Italianate perfection but as a series of dialogues and interplays of discourses, whether they be dialogues between roosters and foxes or between English diplomats and Italian horsemen. The gallimaufry of forms, then, reflects the specific settings of these dialogues and discourses within the cultural institutions of Tudor England, especially the schools, the court, and the law societies or Inns of Court, all of which shaped in powerful ways not only who was writing and who was reading, but the specific disputes and struggles with which the writings were concerned. The following sections will examine the major texts of Tudor aesthetic discourse as the variety of forms in which Tudor culture thinks itself to itself, within the terms of its indigenous languages and institutions.

POETICS OF THE SCHOOLMASTER

We must turn therefore to the debate over the proper positions of rhetoric and poetic in education. A crucial cultural development of the early Tudor period was the impact of humanist learning on elementary schooling, and the emergence of a reformed school curriculum that emphasized training in rhetoric. John Colet's plan for St. Paul's School in London, developed with the aid of Erasmus, Europe's leading scholar, in 1512, is justly regarded as the setting-on point for this movement. John Milton was educated there a century later. Edmund Spenser was taught the books in the 1560s at the Merchant Taylors' School just east of St. Paul's, and even the rustic Stratford Grammar School, where Shakespeare is presumed to have learned his lessons, is in many ways an outgrowth. Nor was the movement limited to primary schools. It affected the nature of the private tutoring provided for aristocratic males and exceptional women (only boys went to organized schools; if a girl was to receive education, she received it at home from a tutor). And it found a ready home at the universities and at the law societies, or Inns of Court.

Arthur F. Kinney rightly points out how astonishingly intense the primary school focus was on language skills, a focus that now appears narrow to the modern mind, which expects a broader range of study in science and social sciences as well as the humanities. Under what the Tudor schoolmaster might consider ideal conditions, a schoolboy would be "restricted to language study, even using Latin while at play and in recess. So thorough was his training and so frequent and repetitive the drills that, at the end of three years, the Tudor student knew well his *syntaxis, figura,* and *prosodia* [syntax, rhetorical figures, and versification]: a child of eleven or twelve could construe simple, compound, and complex Latin sentences, recognize a large number of figures of speech and so constantly rearrange his own writing, and scan Latin verse in a variety of meters."[10] Kinney observes that this training prepared the pupil to use imitative language in both senses: not only was he drilled to write in the manner of ancient Latin writers, but he was trained to use specific forms that required the invention of fictive situations such as: letters to imaginary persons, fables, descriptions of historic events, and orations in imaginary settings.

The fullest account of Tudor humanist teaching is contained in Roger Ascham's *The Scholemaster*. Although the book was first printed in 1570, it is shaped by Ascham's experiences with Sir John Cheke, who was Ascham's teacher at Cambridge, tutor to King Edward VI, and private secretary to Lady Jane Grey. Ascham in turn was tutor to the Princess Elizabeth before she became Queen, and to Lady Jane Grey, as well as Latin Secretary to Queen Mary. The two men embody learning in the service of the state in the Tudor mid-century. When Elizabeth came to the throne in 1558, Ascham became Greek preceptor at her court, and set about gathering his educational principles into a treatise.

The second half of Ascham's *Scholemaster* focuses on methods for teaching eloquence in Latin, which was the primary language of learning. Ascham isolates six learning activities for teaching eloquence: translation, paraphrase, metaphrase (loose paraphrase), epitome (summary), declamation, and imitation. Of these, the one most closely connected with poetic issues is obviously imitation, although Ascham does not explicitly use the term in the Aristotelian sense of a copying of nature. Rather, by "imitation" he primarily means the copying of other language, or "a faculty to express lively and perfectly that example which ye go about to follow."[11] Hence he finds imitation in this sense to be fundamental to all use of language, and indeed to be the means by which language is acquired. "All languages, both learned [i.e. Latin and Greek] and mother tongues, be gotten, and gotten only, by imitation. For as ye use [are accustomed] to hear, so ye learn to speak" (*The Scolemaster*, p. 114). If you never heard anyone speak you would never learn to speak yourself, and you learn to speak only from those you hear speak.

Language for Ascham does not refer directly to things; it is always mediated by other language: by the conversations of those around us and by the texts we read. His idea of imitation, then, is perhaps closer to Mikhail Bakhtin's idea of dialogic language than it is to Aristotle's idea of *mimesis*. Writing is filled with predecessory texts, learned and vernacular, wise and foolish, and the process of rhetorical education is largely a process of training the mind to control the interplay of those predecessory texts through linguistic imitation. Indeed, the trained mind is constructed in and through this interplay of texts, and to some extent can be identified with it. For good writing, asserts Ascham, is always found to accompany good doctrine, at least in the Latin and Greek authors used in the schools, while "whosoever be found fond [foolish] in judgment of matter, be commonly found as rude in uttering their mind" (*The Scholemaster*, p. 115). The process of imitating good writing is identical to the process of forming wisdom. Hence, however dialogic Ascham's theory of language may be, he has none of Bakhtin's love of the carnival. The play of voices that shape the mind must remain controlled and hierarchical, with the pattern of ancient wisdom always dominant. The congenial but authoritarian relation of teacher to student must in effect be internalized as the foundational structure of character through the arduous exercise of the classroom.

If imitation is a process of the internalizing of the speech of another in order to form the self, then it is not surprising that Ascham compares the universe of language to a human body, so that the various forms of eloquence make up a whole body of eloquence. He divides this body of eloquence into four "members" or "genres": Poetic, Historic, Philosophic, and Oratorical, and then subdivides each genus into parts, so that the Poetic is composed of comic, tragic, epic, and melic (or lyric). "Poetic" remains a subset of rhetoric or eloquence generally, and Aristotelian *mimesis*, or language imitating nature, is a subset of that broader imitation of language by language. Hence the imitation of nature is never direct: a poet imitates nature by imitating other poets imitating nature. Indeed, of all the forms of imitation, the poetic is the least stable and most playful. Whereas the imitation of the historians and orators is compared to walking and speaking, that of the poets is dancing and singing (*The Scholemaster*, pp. 152–53). This is perhaps Ascham's moment of closest approach to a notion of linguistic carnival, but this dancing and singing is a carefully measured revelry, not to be confused with the licentious dance of the bacchanal.

The form of Ascham's discourse on imitation enacts in a sophisticated way the very principles that it explains. Ascham divides eloquent language between the present and the Greco-Latin past, and examines each through a different mode of imitation. The past – the eloquence of Cicero or Vergil or Varro – is examined by examples and precepts, as an unfolding of a linguistic authority that is hierarchically superior but somewhat removed and distant. The present, in contrast, is examined dialogically, through anecdotes about conversations that Ascham has had with learned friends, especially the English humanist Sir John Cheke, and the German Sturmius, or Johann Sturm. In this way, Ascham enacts the interplay of language with the language of others that characterizes his theory of imitation, and at the same time enacts the subjection of the speaking self to those other voices, those discourses belonging to his own teachers and to the past.

Indeed, so strong is this imitative displacement of the self into the measured play of language that Ascham even disavows his authority over his own discourse on imitation. He sees the possibility that "a very profitable book might be made *De imitatione* [about imitation] ... unto the which should be gathered and applied plenty of examples, out of the choicest authors of both the tongues" [i.e. Latin and Greek] (*the Schole-master*, p. 127), but his own treatise can only function to "give some good student occasion to take some piece in hand of this work of imitation." Or perhaps, if he lives long enough, Ascham himself "will turn the best part of my study and time to toil in one or other piece of this work of imitation" (p. 130). So his own treatise is self-marginalizing in form as well as in content, as it positions itself as a prospectus for this future work, and proclaims itself as the imitation not only of past and present eloquence, but of future eloquence as well.

In his promulgation of imitation as a fundamental rhetorical trait of all language, Ascham provides a general theory for a series of Tudor treatises on rhetoric that draw their figures from poetry as well as from nonliterary writing. Such treatises include Leonard Cox's *The Art or Craft of Rhetoric* (1524), Richard Sherry's *Treatise of the Figures of Grammar and Rhetoric* (1555), Richard Rainolde's *Foundation of Rhetoric* (1583), and Henry Peacham's *The Garden of Eloquence* (1577). Abraham Fraunce's *Arcadian Rhetoric* of 1588 is notable for using illustrations fromh Philip Sidney's *Arcadia* and from Edmund Spenser's *Faerie Queene*, both of which were circulating only in manuscript at that point.

The most important rhetorical treatise of the century, however, is Thomas Wilson's *Art of Rhetoric*, first published in 1553, expanded in 1560, and reprinted continuously thereafter. Addressed primarily to lawyers, Wilson's work was standard reading in the universities as well as at the royal court, where Wilson himself became secretary to the Privy Council. The *Art of Rhetoric* provides for adults what Ascham provided for children: an argument for the disciplining of the individual mind and of human society through the power of figurative language. Before the advent of language, Wilson argues in the famous preface to the 1560 edition, "all things waxed savage: the earth untilled, society neglected, God's will not known, man against man, one against another, all against order."[12] This Hobbesian state of nature was put to an end not by force of arms but by force of language:

> And therefore the Poets do feign that Hercules, being a man of great wisdom, had all men linked together by the ears in a chain to draw them and lead them even as he lusted. For his wit was so great, his tongue so eloquent, and his experience such, that no one man was able to withstand his reason ...
>
> Neither can I see that men could have been brought by any other means to live together in fellowship of life, to maintain cities, to deal truly, and willingly to obey one another, if men at the first had not by art and eloquence persuaded that which they full oft found by reason. For what man, I pray you ... would not rather look to rule like a lord, than to live like an underling, if by reason he were not persuaded that it behooveth every man to live in his own vocation, and not to seek any higher room than whereunto he was at the first appointed? Who would dig and delve from morn til evening? Who would travail and toil with the sweat of his brows? Yea, who would for his king's pleasure adventure and hazard his life, if wit had not so won men, that they thought nothing more needful in this world, nor anything whereunto they were more bounden, than here to live in their duty and to train their whole life according to their calling?   (Wilson, *The Art of Rhetoric*, p. 42)

This passage rings oddly in modern ears, with its long paean to the role of rhetoric and poetry in upholding not only peace and civil order but also a hierarchical class system, the exploitation of labor, and the sacrifice of unwitting men in battle for the "king's pleasure." It is an argument in praise of eloquence as an instrument of power, which describes its place in an ideal order dreamed of by the schoolmaster, the lawyer, and the official of the Privy Council. But the praise of eloquence must also be recognized as a tactical boast offered on behalf of rhetoricians and poets as a class, a boast that through their logocentric fantasy they can better wield the power of the state that would otherwise have to be written on the ears, the tongues, and the bodies of its subjects with the branding iron and the sword.

THE AESTHETICS OF PROPORTION

The fantasy of order in figurative language and through figurative language described so vividly by Ascham and Wilson is carried in another direction by the authors of treatises on poetic form. For while Ascham focused on the twists and turns of metaphor and the infinite linguistic dances of such figures as *paranomasia* and *anadiplosis*, others focused on the raw sound of the words themselves, as embodied in the prosodic forms of meter and rhyme. Ascham himself was among the many Tudor writers who was critical of what he called the "rude, beggarly rhyming" of English and the other modern vernaculars (*The Scholemaster*, p. 145). This fault, found in Chaucer himself as well as in Surrey, Wyatt and others, is in Ascham's mind the result of a yielding to "time and custom" (p. 146), that is, to the medieval Gothic influence that should be supplanted by a return to the examples of Latin and Greek versification, which generally avoids rhyme. Surrey has made such a return in his translation of Vergil's *Aeneid*, which to Ascham's mind shows England taking the lead over Italy in reestablishing a cultural dialogue with the ancients.

But the question of rhyme was not simply a small technical question about the following of ancient models. It was a fundamental element in the definition of poetry itself and the description of its relationship to the other half of the liberal arts, the *quadrivium*, those arts concerned with measure and proportion. The opponents of rhyme – among whom we may principally number William Webbe and Thomas Campion, along with Ascham himself – all acknowledge the close relationship of poetry to rhetoric, or eloquence in general, and thereby agree that poetry has been a principal source of civil order. Poetry is to be distinguished from rhetoric, however, not by any particular subject matter or way of using of figural language, but by a particular sort of internal relationship of words to words and words to meanings. Thus Webbe, in his *Discourse of English Poetrie* (1586), defines poetry itself as "any work [which] is learnedly complied in measurable speech, and framed in words containing number or proportion of just syllables, delighting the readers or hearers as well by the apt and decent framing of words in equal resemblance of quantity, commonly called verse, as by the skillful handling of the matter whereof it is entreated."[13]

Webbe's elusively simple definition maintains the rhetorical definition of eloquence as persuasion by reason and delight, while weaving into it a second set of criteria contained in the words "measurable," "proportion," "just," "apt," "decent," and "quantity." Each word is cryptic in itself. Taken together, they suggest a system for the framing of verse analogous to other systems of order. For Campion, a skillful lyricist and composer, the most important analogy is to music. The measures, proportions, and quantities of music, however, were not considered by the Tudors to be just an abstract matter of 8s and 12s and so forth. They were an imitation of cosmic order, first defined by Pythagoras and best expressed by Lorenzo in Shakespeare's *Merchant of Venice*:

> Here will we sit, and let the sounds of music
> Creep in our ears. Soft stillness and the night
> Become the touches of sweet harmony.
> Sit, Jessica. Look how the floor of heaven
> Is thick inlaid with patens of bright gold.
> There's not the smallest orb which thou behold'st
> But in his motion like an angel sings,
> Still choiring to the young-eyed cherubins.
> Such harmony is in immortal souls,
> But whilst this muddy vesture of decay
> Doth grossly close it in, we cannot hear it.[14]

The measure or proportion of language to itself is analogous, therefore, to the measure of sound in music, the measure of the heavenly orbs of the planets, and the measure of the well-ordered mind that has emerged from Ascham's schoolhouse. Robert Fludd depicted Lorenzo's proportionate orbs in his *Utriusque cosmi historia* (1617) (figure 2) as a series of concentric spheres with the "young eyed cherubin" in the outermost orb, and at the center, Adam and Eve in Eden at the last instant of perfection before the Fall. But even in the postlapsarian world one could pursue the arts of proportion, as William Cuningham demonstrated in his 1559 treatise *The Cosmographical Glasse, containing the Pleasant Principles of Cosmography, Geography, Hydrography, or Navigation* (figure 3). Cuningham lays out mathematical methods for mapping not only the heavens, but also the earth, cities, and natural features.

As a "doctor of physicke" (MD), Cuningham is interested in the measure not only of the inanimate universe but of the animate world as well. The reach of his project is perhaps best summarized by the frontispiece to the volume (figure 4). Cuningham's hand rests on a globe circled by the band of the zodiac and behind him is a hilly landscape pierced by a river. Together these elements suggest the arts of measure identified on the title page: cosmography, geography, and hydrography. The open volume before him is an herbal, or guidebook to plants, in which he studies the forms of nature. Finally, the half-length figure of Cuningham himself, in a standard pose of Renaissance portraiture, suggests that the final study is the measure of the human mind and the human body.

The arts of human proportion suggested by Cuningham's frontispiece were pursued on the Continent by such monumental figures as Leon Battista Alberti, Leonardo da Vinci, and Albrecht Dürer, and in Tudor England by the significantly less-renowned Richard Haydocke. In 1598 Haydocke published a translation of Paolo Lomazzo's *Treatise on Painting*, illustrated by figures of human and animal proportions modeled on those

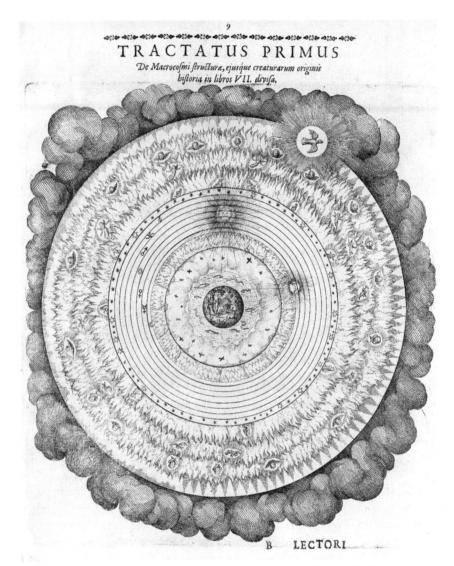

2 Robert Fludd, *Utriusque cosmi historia* (1617) p. 36, diagram of spheres.

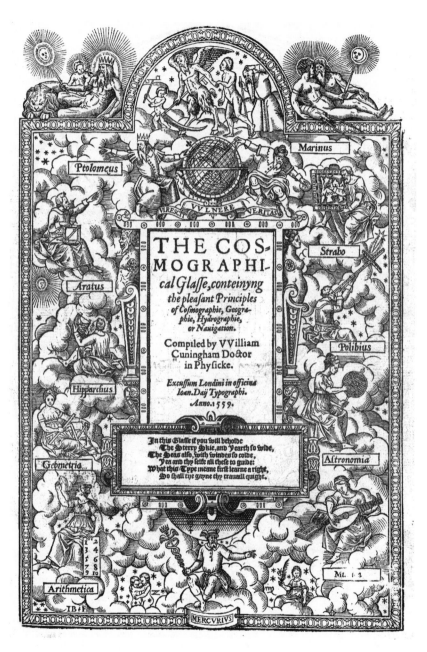

3 William Cuningham, *The Cosmographical Glasse* (London, 1559), title page.

4 William Cuningham, *The Cosmographical Glasse* (London, 1559), frontispiece.

of Dürer (figure 5). Here the body – whether of man or of the horses beloved of Socrates, Sidney, and Pugliano – is laid out as a set of ratios of one part to another, a set of ratios that can then be used as a canon or measuring rod for determining the relative perfection of individual specimens.[15] The arts of measure and proportion, then, claim to set out a system of what Robert Williams calls "absolute art"[16] – an art that is based on a closed system of self-referential proportions, and simultaneously has a place in a system of analogous proportional relationships in a cosmic order. It is a system that thereby purports to banish from within its boundaries any dependence on the messy relativities of "time and custom," as Ascham termed the conditions of history that produced such barbaric forms as rhyme.

Yet at the core of the arguments for absolute art lay a contradiction, in that such systems depended on the very principles of "time and custom" that they hoped to banish. First of all, the examples of Greek and Latin poetry or sculpture that gave Campion or Haydocke their systems of canonical proportions for language or for the body were themselves generated out of a specific "time and custom," one that was as subject to the messy relativity of culture as were the works of the sixteenth century. Indeed, Webbe, in a gesture of compromise, offers provisional approval of rhyme if only "it were by men of learning and ability bettered, and made more artificial, according to the worthiness of our speech" (A Discourse of English Poetrie, p. 267). In this gesture, he acknowledges that rhyme would have to be made proportional not just to Latin or Greek, but to "our speech," English, and so has acknowledged that the canons of proportion are themselves subject to "time and custom."

Insofar as systems of proportion in human language or the human body are self-reflexive, they are systems of the proportion of the human to the human, not just of the human to the divine. And in that turn back toward the human, Tudor proportional systems remain caught in the complex of human desire that underlies that most unabsolute source of aesthetic form, which is rhetoric. Indeed, the very metaphor in which Ascham imagined a perfected body of eloquence – a body composed of well-proportioned members assembled harmoniously – is derived from Cicero's Rhetoric. The same metaphor underlies the perfected visual body delineated by Alberti in his treatise On Painting.[17] The arguments for an absolute art of poetic language, which were advanced in the cause of the banishment of rhyme, are ultimately if covertly dependent on the same grounds as the arguments for the socially reflexive nature of rhetorical eloquence. And it is those socially reflexive arguments that would ultimately produce the counter-arguments that maintained the position of rhyme in Tudor literature.

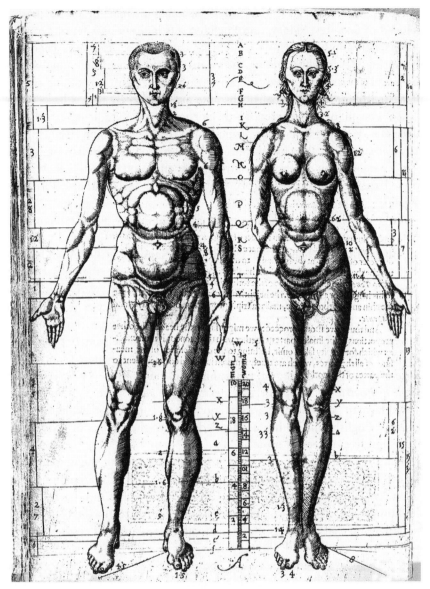

5 Richard Haydocke after Albrecht Dürer. Proportional figures of man and woman. *A Tract Containing the Arts of Curious Painting, Carving and Building* (Oxford, 1598), 1, 36.

The ultimate convergence of absolute and socially reflexive aesthetics may be demonstrated by an ironic detail in the famous diagram depicting Queen Elizabeth in Richard Case's *Sphaera Civitatis*, published in 1588, in which Elizabeth's body is equated with the well-ordered state (figure 6). Like his Oxford friend Haydocke (or, for that matter, like Cuningham), Case is a physician interested in the proper ordering of the human body and in anything analogous to the human body, such as the body politic or the heavenly bodies. Here the familiar concentric circles of the heavenly spheres are made analogous to the qualities of a ruler: majesty, prudence, fortitude, religion, mercy, eloquence, productivity or fecundity. Elizabeth stands over and behind the state, measuring it as the artist of proportion might judge the canonical measures of the heavens, of the human body, or of the body politic.[18] At the fixed center of the scheme, which is the position of the earth in a Ptolomaic diagram of the cosmos, Case places "unmovable Justice." The unintended irony of his scheme, though, is that he has placed his centric quality immediately under the embrace of eloquence and fecundity, and in a position analogous to Elizabeth's genital organs. The aesthetic order of proportion has been graphically located in the seat of desire, and the principle of a fixed and unchanging aesthetic remains implicated with the forces that give motion to the human and social body.

The reply to the attacks on rhyme are mounted by two practicing poets, George Gascoigne and Samuel Daniel. Gascoigne's *Certayne Notes of Instruction Concerning the Making of Verse or Rhyme in English* (1575) is at heart a practical handbook of metrical and rhyme schemes, but it acknowledges the argument against rhyme by continually insisting that rhyme must never be "without reasons" nor should distract from the pursuit of the underlying invention, and so should remain continuously apt to the "just measure" of the verse.[19] Gascoigne's treatise is in effect a feeble attempt to justify rhyme by the very principles that were being deployed much more powerfully by its opponents. Daniel, on the other hand, mounts a sophisticated counterattack in his *Defence of Rhyme* (1602), which is a direct response to Campion's treatise. Rather than limiting himself to the immediate question of versification, he goes straight to the underlying question of whether literature, or indeed any art, is based on a single principle found to be perfected in the canons of ancient art, or whether art is produced and evaluated in a culturally reflexive process.

Along the way, Daniel demolishes once and for all every argument advanced by Ascham, Webbe, and Campion. He rejects their denial of history and celebrates custom and nature as the true grounds of culture, or "Custom that is before all Law, Nature that is above all Art."[20] He rejects

Philosophorum ΣΟΦΩΤΑΤΩ Æscvlapio Svo.

V Iuere cui vires & robora sana dedisti
    Scribere ni vellem, næ robore durior essem.
Ergo mihi (quæ priuato pertingere nulli
CASE datur)tecum satis & satis Astra tueri est.

6 Richard Case, *Sphaera Civitatis* (Oxford, 1588), frontispiece.

the very notion that rhyme must lack proportion, if it is handled with any skill. He rejects the notion that the revival of classical learning goes back no further than the early sixteenth century – that is, to the time of More and Erasmus. Most importantly, he rejects the denigration of the Middle Ages themselves as a time of Gothic "barbarity." Rather, he asserts that they had their own measure, their own proportion, and it is one far more relevant to the nation and language of England than are the measures and proportions of Greece or Italy.[21] Thus "every language hath her proper number or measure fitted to use and delight, which Custom, entertaining by the allowance of the Ear, doth indenize [make a denizen] and make natural" (*Defence of Rhyme*, p. 131).

Daniel then proposes to reform Ascham's fundamental notion of a "body of eloquence" around the principles of Nature and Custom. For if "the body of our imagination" begins as an "unformed Chaos without fashion," it can through poetic inspiration "be wrought into an Orb of order and form" (p. 138). But since in this postlapsarian world we do not readily understand that which is infinite, it is far better for language "to have those closes [of rhyme] rather than not to know where to end, or how far to go, especially seeing our passions are often without measure" (p. 138). Moving from the spherical proportions of the heavenly orbs, he turns to the human body for final metaphor, declaring that "the best measure of man is to be taken by his own foot, bearing ever the nearest proportion to himself" (p. 143). In his punning on the human foot, the measuring unit of the foot, and the poetic foot, he aptly turns the entire debate over English meter back on itself, as the source and endpoint of its own principles of art. If the self-reflection of proportional measure has in Daniel's hands been transformed into the self-reflection of the cultural moment, then he can reasonably conclude that "we have but one body of justice, one body of Wisdom, throughout the whole world; which is but apparelled according to the fashion of every nation" (p. 145). If the unchanging and essential subject matter of imitation is Justice and Wisdom, then it is all the variable materials of rhetorical figures, meters, and rhyme that make up the forms of literature that are specific to its culture.

DEFENDING THE INDEFENSIBLE

In their different ways, the treatises that we have just examined all imagine that the arts of imitation can produce a perfected and healthy body of eloquence, if only they are artful enough. They all make some such claim, regardless of whether they are speaking of verbal imitation or of *mimesis*, whether they oppose the use of rhyme or support it, and whether they base their principles of aesthetic order on a canon of proportions or on a reflexive relation to culture. All of these Tudor writers are caught up in "shaping fantasies" (to adopt Louis Montrose's suggestive phrase), fantasies of authorship in which the act of writing aligns the writer psychically, physically, and socially with the sources of authority in nature, in the state, in human history, and in the cosmos.

Yet we have seen running through these writings another possibility, a possibility against which their assertions of aesthetic authority are a collective defense. It is the possibility that all imitation – and especially the kinds of persuasive verbal imitation that appeal to human desires – leads ultimately to chaos or to tyranny. The dialogue of ancient and contemporary voices imagined by Ascham may reduce itself to a carnivalesque Babel. The Herculean chaining of men by their ears imagined by Wilson might become the enslavement of free people through propaganda. The perfect music sought by Campion or Webbe might be "like sweet bells jangled, out of time" (*Hamlet* III.i.157). Only Daniel, in his deep embrace of cultural relativity, seems to imagine that the annihilating forces of human imperfection and cultural change provide a certain positive measure of freedom from the oppressive weight of ancient cultural standards. He finds an abject solace at the end of the *Defence of Rhyme*, where he concludes that "the perpetual revolution which we see to be in all things that can never remain the same, and we must herein be content to submit ourselves to the law of time, which in few years will make all that for which we now contend, *Nothing*" (p. 158).

A fear of annihilation, disorder, disharmony, and disease is thus always implicit in the Tudor praise of imitation and eloquence as sources of order, harmony, and psychic and social health. A full confrontation with these fears, however, is rarely acted out within the institutional confines of the *trivium* or the *quadrivium* – within, that is, the discussions of the trivial arts of rhetoric and poetic or the quadrivial arts of music and astronomy, as they were pursued in the schools, universities, court, and Inns of Court. Among canonical literary forms, only love poetry, with its focus on personal sexual desire, and satire, with its focus on social rancor, were likely targets for criticism. Rather, it was a different institution and practice of eloquence and imitation – the theatre – that acted as the primary site for this confrontation. Tudor theatre drew on many of the same intellectual skills as the literary forms of writing, but the "place of the stage" (to use Steven Mullaney's phrase) was always marginal. The body of the actor therefore served as the culturally appropriate site for saying what one might be loath to say about the body of eloquence.

The 1570s and 1580s were marked by a series of official and unofficial attacks on the theatres, including a 1573 Act of Parliament, sermons at prominent sites in London, and pamphlets such as John Northbrook's *Treatise Wherein Dicing, Dancing, Vain Plays or Interludes ... are Reproved* (1577), Stephen Gosson's *School of Abuse* (1579) and *Plays Confuted in Five Actions* (1582), Henry Denham's *Second and Third Blast of Retreat from Plays and Theaters* (1580), and John Stubbes' *Anatomy of Abuses* (1583). These works are sometimes characterized as the product of a middle-class puritanical and mercantile consciousness which just didn't understand literature, with the implication that the minds of such persons would have been improved by joining the leisure class, going to the university, and majoring in English. While the class basis of the attack on the theatres is important, it is just as important to beware of the residual class bias in such characterizations, and instead treat the attacks as expressions of something that is endemic within Tudor culture, and indeed is shared, however nervously, by the defenders of literature themselves.

Of the attacks, the most significant is Gosson's *School of Abuse*. Gosson takes aim not only at the drama, but at classical poetry itself, using Plato as his ally in claiming that poetry is mostly a waste of time, and not all that entertaining either. But his particular venom is reserved for the recently established professional theatres of London:

> In our assemblies at plays in London, you shall see such heaving and shoving, such itching and shouldering to sit by women, such care for their garments that they be not trod on, such eyes to their laps that no chips light in them, such pillows to their backs that they take no hurt, such masking in their ears I know not what, such giving them pippins to pass the time, such playing at foot saunt without cards [playing footsie?], such ticking, such toying, such smiling, such winking, and such manning them [women] home when the sports are ended, that it is a right comedy to mark their behavior, to watch their conceits, as the cat for the mouse.[22]

For his first line of attack, Gosson adapts a passage from Ovid's *Art of Love* that testifies to the power of theatre to incite lust and to give opportunity for its enactment. But where Ovid saw a spectacle of desire, Gosson sees the pageantry of disgust, a disgust that centers in every way on the body: the obsession of the audience with bodily comfort, the unregulated movement of the body, the contact of body with body, the satisfying of the appetites of touching, tasting, smelling, seeing, and hearing. From the unregulated indulgence of the body he moves to the bodies of the prostitutes who, he says, congregate at the theatres, for they emblematize the disease and disorder both of the natural body and the social body:

> If it were as well noted as ill seen, or as openly punished as secretly practiced,

I have no doubt but that … these pretty rabbits [prostitutes] [would be] cunningly ferreted from their burrows. For they that lack customers all the week, either because their haunt is unknown, or the constables and officers of their parish watch them so narrowly that they dare not queatche [stir], to celebrate the Sabbath flock to theatres, and there keep a general market of bawdry. Not that any filthiness, indeed, is committed within the compass of that ground, as was once done in Rome, but that every wanton and paramour, every man and his mistress, every John and his Joan, every knave and his queane [whore] are there first acquainted, and cheapen the merchandise [set the price] in that place, which they pay for elsewhere, as they can agree. These worms, when they dare not nestle in the peascod at home, find refuge abroad and are hid in the ears of other men's corn.   (Gosson, *Abuse*, p. 95).

To some extent, Gosson is upset at the mere fact of licentiousness, at this "general market of bawdry." At some level, though, he seems to accept the existence of whores and whoremongers so long as the rabbits keep to their burrows. It is particularly the breakdown of regulation that distresses him, a breakdown that is promoted by the openness of the theatre, and which is epitomized by the violation of the Sabbath and the failure of police supervision. His distress reaches its height when he moves from the female bodies of prostitutes to the unregulated male bodies of the actors themselves, especially the boys:

How often hath her Majesty, with the grave advice of her whole Council, set down the limits of apparel to every degree, and how soon again hath the pride of our hearts overflown the channel? How many times hath access to theatres been restrained, and how boldly again have we re-entered? Over-lashing in apparel is so common a fault, that the very hirelings of some of our players, which stand at reversion [receive wages] of 6 shillings a week, jet under gentlemen's noses in suits of silk, exercising themselves in prating on the stage, and common scoffing when they come abroad, where they look askance over the shoulder at every man of whom the Sunday before they begged an alms.   (Gosson, *Abuse*, pp. 95–96)

The body of the actor as it represents a character in the play is in itself a rhetorical figure, a kind of living *mimesis*. At the same time, the actor's costume clothes his figural body as the garment of eloquence clothes rhetorical speech. Gosson focuses on this mimetic garment as the focus for all of his fears that her Majesty's order (by which he seems to mean both her proclamations and the order of society itself), will be undermined by the cancer of imitation. The silky overdressing of the journeymen and the boys, as they prate and scoff and look askance at their olders and betters, constitutes for Gosson an undermining of age hierarchy and class hierarchy, a disruption in manners and gestures, a disruption of the posturing of the body as they "exercise," a disruption of the posturing of speech as they scoff and prate. There is a hint too at Gosson's recurring fear of sexual arousal, as the actors flirtatiously "look askance over the shoulder," though the disruption is now doubled by the shift in gender from the loosely regulated female whores to the wholly uncontrolled male actors. The garment of eloquence which Daniel imagined as the expression of cultural difference becomes in Gosson's phobic reaction the mark of cultural degradation.

A telling aspect of Gosson's attack is his recognition that the social abuse he denounces is harbored not only by whores and actors but also by the very people who claim to be most upset about it. While the gentlemen in the theatrical audience may be offended by the prancing of the actors in silks, they have themselves been the first to be driven by "the pride of our hearts" to violate the sumptuary laws by which the Queen establishes a proportion within costume that corresponds to the proportions of class hierarchy. Gosson's prescription, in effect, is to balance the loathing of the diseased body of the social other with a self-loathing of one's own psychic disease. In Gosson's mis-shaping fantasy, the structures of the Tudor fantasy of aesthetic order have been doubly perverted, so that the proportioning of the mimetic body to the order of society and to the order of the self is in either case an act of mis-proportion.

The greatest and most enduring piece of aesthetic writing of the Tudor period, Sir Philip Sidney's *Defence of Poetrie*, is constructed around this dialectic structure of the self as other and the other as the self. Written around 1580, the work was simultaneously printed in 1595, under the title of *Defence of Poetrie* as well as under an alternative title of the *Apology for Poetry*. Margaret Ferguson points out that each title has its appropriateness, since the title of *Defence* better indicates Sidney's rejection of the external attacks on literature, while the title of *Apology* (with the Latin meaning of "self-justification") better indicates Sidney's response to the internal critique. Ferguson identifies the *Defence* as a response to three threats: the threat to imitation posed by the factual truth of external reality, the threat from morality as expressed by Stephen Gosson and others who see literature as disruptive to the state, and the threat posed to literature by itself through its power to inflame the passions.[23] It was, indeed, that last threat that we saw weighing on Sidney's mind in his opening passage, examined at the beginning of this chapter, as he contemplated the power of language to act in the service of self-love and self-deception.

Sidney's defense against the threat to poetry and the threat from poetry centers on his definition of imitation. Noting that the Greek word for poet means "maker," he argues that poetry alone among the arts does not just copy or improve nature, but makes something independent of nature that supplants and surpasses nature. In Sidney's formulation, the traditional arts of geometry, arithmetic, grammar, and so forth, are themselves imitative in that they consist of and depend on nature. Poetry is of a different sort:

> Only the poet, disdaining to be tied to any such subjection, lifted up with the vigor of his own invention, doth grow in effect another nature, in making things either better than nature bringeth forth, or, quite anew, forms such as never were in nature, as the Heroes, Demigods, Cylops, Chimeras, Furies, and such like: so as he goeth hand in hand with nature, not enclosed within the narrow warrant of her gifts, but freely ranging only within the zodiac of his own wit. Nature never set forth the earth in so rich tapestry as divers poets have done: neither with so pleasant rivers, fruitful trees, sweet-smelling flowers, nor whatsoever else may make the too much loved earth more lovely. Her world is brazen, the poets only deliver a golden. (*Defence*, p. 216).

Sidney's description of the nature of poetic imitation has several important consequences. Most importantly, poetry is now positioned as superior to the other arts, rather than the stepchild of rhetoric. At the same time, it shares the persuasive purpose traditionally ascribed to rhetoric. Invoking Aristotle's term of *mimesis*, Sidney defines poetic imitation as "a representing, counterfeiting, or figuring forth – to speak metaphorically, a speaking picture – with this end, to teach and delight" (*Defence*, p. 217). While poetry uses the same linguistic material as rhetoric and pursues the same ends, it does so in a more intensely metaphoric way, through its creation of the "golden world," or what Sidney alternatively calls a "second nature,"[24] over which humanity rules as God rules over the world of reality. At the same time, by calling poetry's world "golden" and nature's "brazen," Sidney invokes the classical myth in which human history devolves from an original golden age through an age of bronze to the iron age of the present. Analogously, the myth of the golden age recalls the Judeo-Christian doctrine of a fall from Eden. Indeed, Sidney argues that the power of the poetic imagination to imagine a better world is a kind of recollection of Eden itself.

Sidney develops his argument about poetic imitation by contrasting it with two other forms of imitative discourse, that of the historians and that of the philosophers. Sidney turns each into a character, imagining the philosophers tracking him down with a "sullen gravity," badly dressed, their arms full of books, their mouths spewing definitions and distinctions. The historian is scarcely less ridiculous, "laden with old mouse-eaten records," boring children and adults alike with his endless monologues on obscure events. The philosopher has wise precepts, if only anyone could understand them. The historian has the facts, if only they added up to something. It is the poet who "coupleth the general notion with the particular example," creating vivid pictures in our minds. This alone is a form of language capable of making things happen in the world, creating imitations with such force that the audience determines to imitate those imitations. Poetry's effect derives from the internal mimetic nature of the language, not from external incidentals such as whether or not it rhymes. Hence Sidney singles out a prose work, Xenophon's *Cyropedia*, as an example of an excellent heroic poem, since in the accomplishments of the Persian commander and emperor one may see what an ideal ruler and a well-run kingdom would be. The goal of the poet, then, is "not only to make a Cyrus, which had been but a particular excellency as nature might have done, but to bestow a Cyrus upon the world to make many Cyruses, if they will learn aright why and how that [poetic] maker made him" (*Defence*, pp. 216–17).

Sidney's idea of the poetic second world in a sense redefines *mimesis* as an act of *prosthesis*: a repairing of a defect of nature, a defect that exists both in the material world and in language.[25] The idea of the defect is itself nothing less common than a restatement of the doctrine of the fall. The idea of a prosthetic second nature achieved through poetic language, however, contains within it a demand for a perfection that is not quite human since it is not quite to be achieved through primary nature itself. The *prosthesis* is a repairing of a body that adds something that is not natural to the body. Alan Sinfield identifies in Sidney's demand for the perfecting of nature a strain of authoritarianism, and the promulgation of a cultural program that asserts an absolute notion of humanity.[26]

Sidney's focus on the figure of Cyrus is an index of the extent to which Sidney is not describing a restoration of the human body, of the body politic, or of the body of eloquence to an originary perfection, but instead is describing and fashioning a new ideal: an armored male body, a warrior body, capable of defending itself against the forces of imperfection at home and abroad. The extant portraits of Sidney have often been considered unsatisfactory because they depict a youthful courtier and warrior, not a thoughtful writer (figure 7). But they reflect accurately enough the figure that Sidney says poetry should create, a figure who is simultaneously graceful and invulnerable, with the throat carapaced in masculine steel and left hand on the sword, while the remainder of the body is softened and made courtly with the slashed doublet and loose skirt of material about the waist, that in turn opens to reveal the erect codpiece. In his project of transforming himself into a Cyrus and becoming a begetter of Cyruses, Sidney imagines the garments of rhetoric as both steel and silk. He in effect returns in the body of his *Defence* to the project that had failed at the

7 Anonymous. *Sir Philip Sidney* (*c.* 1580).

outset in his conversation with Pugliano: to control rhetorical self-love in the name of rhetorical action, and thereby to discover the true nature of the horse, of the horseman, and of the kingdom he ruled.

The prosthetic armoring of the body of eloquence that Sidney advances in the *Defence* is necessitated not only by the threats to poetry from material reality and from morality, but by the threat that it poses to itself. For precisely to the extent that poetry can so possess the mind and direct the will, it is equally capable of misleading the mind and the will. Hence Sidney can defend poetry only by excluding parts of poetry from his defense, specifically those parts that threaten to violate the ordering of the human, social, and linguistic bodies. Erotic love poetry is especially suspect, though it is a form in which Sidney himself excelled. However, the form that is particularly singled out for criticism is the English theatre. Sidney abhors everything about it: its mangy plots, its indecorous mixing of social classes, and above all, its inability to represent a battle properly. It is often assumed that the problem is simply that Sidney died too soon; if only he had lived long enough to see Marlowe and Shakespeare, surely he would have changed his mind. But in Sidney's rejection of the theatre, we may see at work the accusation from within: the inner puritan and the inner schoolmaster alike demand a sacrifice. In order to preserve his ideal of the heroic, Sidney offers as his scapegoat the marginal, excluded, malproportioned element of Tudor literature, the popular stage.

POESY, PROPORTION, ORNAMENT

If Sidney's *Defence* is the most brilliant piece of aesthetic writing of the Tudor age, the most representative is probably George Puttenham's *Arte of English Poesie* (1589). As such, it provides an ideal summary of Tudor aesthetics. Puttenham arranges his treatise in three books: "Of Poets and Poesy," "Of Proportion," and "Of Ornament." The plan of the work thus promises what the likes of Spingarn and Hardison always dreamed of finding: a well-ordered treatise on the model of Italian treatises that gave full and appropriate measure to each topic and brought Tudor aesthetic thought into classical frame. Delightfully, Puttenham's treatise is nothing of the sort. While it recites appropriate anecdotes of the ancient glory of poetry, cites Aristotle and Horace, reviews poetic genres, and examines an array of proportional forms in cadence, verse form, and rhyme scheme, it intermixes these orderly disquisitions with a bewildering gallimaufry of anecdotes, recollections, and digressions upon digressions. It is less an orderly work on aesthetic order than a babble of aesthetic discourses, or an internalized but eloquent debate over the nature of eloquence.

Something of the texture of Puttenham's argument can be found in his definition of ornament, which opens the third book. After an abstract but familiarly rhetorical definition of ornament as a fashioning of poetic language and style to delight and allure the mind and the ear, he illustrates his point by comparing ornament to the costly garments of the ladies at the court of Elizabeth:

> And as we see in these great Madams of Honor, be they for personage or otherwise never so comely or beautiful, yet if they want [lack] their courtly habiliments [clothing] or at leastwise such other apparel as custom and civility have ordained to cover their naked bodies, would be half ashamed or greatly out of countenance to be seen in that sort, and perchance do then think themselves more amiable in every man's eye, when they be in their richest attire, suppose of silks or tissues and costly embroideries, than when they go in cloth or in any other plain and simple apparel. Even so cannot our vulgar Poesie shew itself either gallant or gorgeous, if any limb be left naked and bare and not clad in his kindly clothes and colors, such as may convey them somewhat out of sight, that is from the common course of ordinary speech and capacity of the vulgar judgment, and yet being artificially handled must needs yield it much more beauty and commendation. This ornament we speak of is given to it by figures and figurative speeches, which be the flowers, as it were, and colors that a Poet setteth upon his language of art, as the embroiderer doth his stone and pearl, or passements of gold upon the stuff of a Princely garment, or as the excellent painter bestoweth the rich Orient colors upon his table of portrait.[27]

As the painter fashions an artificial body in a painting, or a costumer forms a second body out of fabric, the artful body of rhetoric hides and substitutes for the natural body. In doing so, it preserves that natural body from shame, either from the moral shame of indecent exposure or from the social shame of underdressing, while simultaneously preserving or even enhancing the sexual and social allure of the natural body.

Puttenham here confronts the contradictory fears and desires of the Tudor age about the body of eloquence, and offers a synthetic conciliation, not so much through the force of argument as through the force of self-reflection upon the customs and practices of his own society. In the passage above, it is the court ladies who serve as his metaphor for metaphor. In the following pages, he defends eloquence by contrasting the fine parliamentary declamations of Sir Nicholas Bacon (Elizabeth's Speaker of the House and father to Sir Francis Bacon), with the fumbling, unintelligible ramble of Mary Tudor's first speaker, who had unfortunately lost his teeth. Like Daniel's *Defence*, Puttenham's *Arte* is a study of the cultural appropriateness of native forms, which serve within Tudor society in ways analogous to the function of classical forms within their society. And so it is at heart utterly rhetorical, and nowhere more so than in its conception of ornament as both an external appeal to the senses and an inward conveying of meaning to the mind within the context of a specific social situation.

In his comic anecdotes about perfecting the body of eloquence, Puttenham also straddles the gender politics that pervade Tudor aesthetic discourse. Running underneath his praise of the court ladies is a masculine desire for and suspicion of the feminized body of eloquence. But by setting eloquence at the court, Puttenham makes that feminized body one that is politically powerful, in contrast to the marginal female rhetorical bodies that Gosson described, cowering in their burrows under police surveillance. Puttenham's own rhetorical discourse is a continual appeal to the power of those court ladies and to the Queen herself for favor. Indeed, he concludes that "I write to the pleasure of a Lady and a most gracious Queen, and neither to priests nor to prophets or philosophers" (*The Arte of English Poesie*, p. 314). Whereas Chaucer had ultimately dismissed the material substance of eloquence as "chaff," Sidney had given that chaff a nervous centrality by imagining a half-armored masculine body of eloquence, ready to wield power in defense of social order and human perfection. Puttenham has removed the armor, and imagined the body of eloquence as the body of the Queen.

NOTES

1 Baxter Hathaway, *The Age of Criticism: The Late Renaissance in Italy* (Ithaca, NY: Cornell University Press, 1962).
2 Geoffrey Chaucer, "The Nun's Priest's Tale," from *The Canterbury Tales*, *The Works of Geoffrey Chaucer*, ed. F. N. Robinson, 2nd edn. (Boston: Houghton Mifflin, 1957), lines 3429–35.
3 "The Defence of Poesy," in *Sir Philip Sidney*, ed. Katherine Duncan-Jones (Oxford: Oxford University Press, 1989), p. 212.
4 Quoted by Donald G. Marshall, "The History of Eighteenth-Century Criticism and Modern Hermeneutical Philosophy: The Example of Richard Hurd," *The Eighteenth Century* 21 (1980): 200.
5 Paul Oskar Kristeller, "The Modern System of the Arts," in *Renaissance Thought II* (New York: Harper, 1965), pp. 163–227.
6 G. Gregory Smith, ed., *Elizabethan Critical Essays* 2 vols. (Oxford: Oxford University Press, 1904), vol. I, p. xi.
7 J. E. Spingarn, *A History of Literary Criticism in the Renaissance* (New York: Macmillan, 1899); O. B. Hardison, Jr., ed., *English Literary Criticism: The Renaissance* (New York: Appleton-Century-Crofts, 1963).
8 J. W. H. Atkins, *English Literary Criticism: The Renascence* (London: Methuen, 1947), pp. 343–44.

9 Henry Louis Gates, Jr., *The Signifying Monkey: A Theory of African–American Literary Criticism* (Oxford: Oxford University Press, 1988), pp. xix–xxv.

10 Arthur F. Kinney, *Humanist Poetics: Thought, Rhetoric, and Fiction in Sixteenth-Century England* (Amherst: University of Massachusetts Press, 1986), p. 8.

11 Roger Ascham, *The Scholemaster*, ed. Lawrence V. Ryan (Ithaca, NY: Cornell University Press, 1967), p. 114.

12 Thomas Wilson, *The Art of Rhetoric* (1560), ed. Peter E. Medine (University Park: Pennsylvania State University Press, 1994), p. 41.

13 William Webbe, *A Discourse of English Poetrie*, in Smith, ed., *Elizabethan Critical Essays*, vol. I, p. 248.

14 William Shakespeare, *The Merchant of Venice* v.i.54–64, from *The Norton Shakespeare*, ed. Stephen Greenblatt et al. (New York: Norton, 1997).

15 Clark Hulse, *The Rule of Art: Literature and Painting in the Renaissance* (Chicago: University of Chicago Press, 1990), pp. 137–41.

16 Robert Williams, *Art, Theory, and Culture in Sixteenth-Century Italy : From Techne to Metatechne* (New York: Cambridge University Press, 1997).

17 Michael Baxandall, *Giotto and the Orators: Humanist Observers of Painting in Italy and the Discovery of Pictorial Composition 1312–1450* (Oxford: Clarendon Press, 1971), pp. 130–32.

18 The best and fullest reading of the diagram, especially in relation to diagrams of God as creator or measurer of the universe, is that of Andrew and Catherine Belsey, "Icons of Divinity: Portraits of Elizabeth I," in *Renaissance Bodies: The Human Figure in English Culture c. 1540– 1660*, ed. Lucy Gent and Nigel Llewellyn (London: Reaktion Books, 1990), pp. 11–35. My analysis extends parts of their reading of George Gower's "Armada" portrait to the Case diagram.

19 George Gascoigne, *Certayne Notes of Instruction Concerning the Making of Verse or Rhyme in English*, in *The Complete Works of George Gascoigne*, ed. John W. Cunliffe (Cambridge: Cambridge University Press, 1907), 2 vols., vol I, pp. 466, 469.

20 Samuel Daniel, *Poems and a Defence of Rhyme*, ed. Arthur Colby Sprague (Chicago: University of Chicago Press, 1965), p. 131.

21 Clark Hulse, "Samuel Daniel: The Poet as Literary Historian," *SEL* 19 (1979): 62–64.

22 Gosson, *Abuse*, in Hardison, *English Literary Criticism*, pp. 94–96.

23 Margaret Ferguson, *Trials of Desire: Renaissance Defenses of Poetry* (New Haven: Yale University Press, 1983), pp. 137–39.

24 Harry Berger, Jr., *Second World and Green World: Studies in Renaissance Fiction-Making* (Berkeley: University of California Press, 1988), pp. 3–40.

25 I take this use of the the the term *prosthesis* from Harry Berger's reconsideration of his earlier discussions of "second nature" in "Mannerly Dissections: Supplying Deficiencies of Nature in the Renaissance," forthcoming in *The Visual Culture of Early Modern England*, ed. Peter Erickson and Clark Hulse.

26 Alan Sinfield, "Sidney's Defence and the Collective-Farm Chairman: Puritan Humanism and the Cultural Apparatus," in *Faultlines: Cultural Materialism and the Politics of Dissident Reading* (Oxford: Clarendon Press, 1992).

27 George Puttenham, *The Arte of English Poesie*, ed. Baxter Hathaway (Kent, OH: Kent State University Press, 1970), pp. 149–50.

FURTHER READING

Atkins, J. W. H., *English Literary Criticism: The Renascence* (London: Methuen, 1947).
Berger, Harry, Jr., *Second World and Green World: Studies in Renaissance Fiction-Making* (Berkeley: University of California Press, 1988).
Ferguson, Margaret, *Trials of Desire: Renaissance Defenses of Poetry* (New Haven: Yale University Press, 1983).
Heninger, S. K., Jr., *Sidney and Spenser: The Poet as Maker* (University Park: Pennsylvania State University Press, 1989).
Levao, Ronald, *Renaissance Minds and their Fictions: Cusanus, Sidney, Shakespeare* (Berkeley: University of California Press, 1985).
Smith, G. Gregory, ed., *Elizabethan Critical Essays*, 2 vols. (Oxford: Oxford University Press, 1904).

4

WENDY WALL

Authorship and the material
conditions of writing

> We should note the force, effect, and consequences of inventions which are
> nowhere more conspicuous than in those three which were unknown to the
> ancients, namely, printing, gunpowder, and the compass. For these three have
> changed the appearance and state of the whole world.
>
> Francis Bacon, Novum Organum[1]

To grasp the conditions of writing in the early English Renaissance, we
need to imagine a world poised between manuscript and print cultures.
Although William Caxton set up the first press in England in 1476 and set
into motion a slowly unfolding debate about the meaning and significance
of print technology, a lively manuscript culture continued to thrive alongside the print marketplace for the next hundred years or more. The result is
a fascinating cross-fertilization between two kinds of textual production,
each with its own practices and forms. In turn, these new forms of
production gave rise to new conceptions of authorship and meaning. It is
impossible "to divorce the substance of a text on the one hand," observes
D. F. McKenzie, "from the physical form of its presentation on the other."[2]
McKenzie reminds us that a literary text's material embodiment, as a loose
page or bound book, is a critical part of its meaning. The physical form of
sixteenth-century texts is thus intimately connected with the social conditions which produced them, and the social scene into which they emerged.
How did factors such as class, gender, and religious affiliation determine
whether a person produced a manuscript or a printed text? How did the
Gutenberg invention authorize specific institutions and groups? How did
the book object become important to cultural, social, and political issues?
And how did authorship emerge from within larger cultural debates?

Scholars have long recognized the sixteenth century as a time when
definitions of authorship were being transformed, but had not yet crystal-
lized into the modern meaning that would arise in the late eighteenth
century: the author as the ultimate origin and governing force for a text.

Having inherited medieval notions of the sacred *auctor* and classical models that did not apply to rapidly changing social conditions, people in the Tudor and Elizabethan periods eagerly tested out different roles for the author. Yet the most monumental volumes of poetry in the period – the 1557 lyric anthology, *Tottel's Miscellany*; Philip Sidney's 1591 sonnet sequence *Astrophil and Stella*; and John Donne's 1633 *Songs and Sonets* – were published after their authors died. Edmund Spenser's inaugural 1579 *Shepheardes Calender*, a landmark of poetry, was published anonymously; and Renaissance plays were produced collaboratively under the auspices of theatre companies rather than individual writers.[3] In order to understand writing in this period, we thus have to dispense with our modern notion of the author who publishes a signed and finished text for the public and posterity. Instead we find that the author had a limited role in the dominant modes of writing – the early print industry and manuscript exchange. Although writing has always been enmeshed in historical circumstance, the material forces governing texts were certainly more visible at a time when authorship was just one of many conventions controlling the reception of written works.

Bacon may have overstated the case when he claimed that print "changed the appearance and state of the whole world," but he was right to see that print had profound implications for religion, politics, and literature. The social struggles surrounding the press in its English infancy reveal an intense negotiation over the authority that this new technology made possible. By the end of the century, when writers and publishers had shifted the debate to the more specific issue of literary authorship, something like the seeds of our modern conception of the author began to emerge. Using the characteristics of the book form to claim the text's monumental "literariness," writers such as Spenser and Jonson attempted to create what Richard Helgerson terms the "laureate" status of the poet. As we shall see, however, authorship had not yet attained any consistent or unified meaning, and instead remained one of the many "authorizing forces" that gave meaning to early modern English writing.

SOCIAL STRUGGLES SURROUNDING THE PRESS

Between the fourth and twelfth centuries, illuminators and scribes crafted books in the scriptoria of medieval monasteries. In the twelfth century, universities also began producing elaborately ornate manuscripts. With Gutenberg's 1450 invention of the movable type press, Europe acquired the technology to reproduce books efficiently and cheaply. But the author did not become the preeminent figure in the story of the early English press. In fact, there was little distinction between the activities of writing, printing, and bookselling in the early sixteenth century. William Caxton learned the craft of printing in order to publish one of his own translations for a patroness. Richard Tottel juggled the tasks of editing verse, competing for royal patents, and setting type for his mid-century anthology of poetry. The few contemporary English authors published in the early years of printing had only the most tenuous link to the process of publication.[4] The author was willing to resign works to a publisher, or to allow others to do so, for the simple fact that writing was not perceived as a vocation and publishing was not the most obvious way to circulate literary works.

Rather than establishing an entitlement for the author or addressing the potentially new characteristics of a mass produced book, the earliest issues surrounding the press concerned the economic protection of printers and the mechanisms for censorship.[5] Although Henry VIII tested out a preliminary licensing system in the 1530s and issued a list of prohibited books, it was not until the incorporation of the Stationers' Company in 1557 that the book trade became centralized. Enjoined to license publication, this organization served as the main organ through which the book trade was managed. With the right to levy fines, deny promotions to the rank of journeyman and master printer, and seize illegal equipment, the company became a powerful player in London economic structures.

The first printing regulations attempted to address the fact that foreigners dominated the book trade; in 1535, four-fifths of all printers and booksellers were aliens. By limiting the number of non-native apprentices and regulating the importation of foreign books, these regulations gradually "Englished" the industry.[6] But as late as 1578, the Stationers' Company, believing that foreign printers profited by evading laws governing apprenticeship, petitioned "that no work be put to foreigners or strangers."[7] Helgerson has noted that the Englishing of letters in the latter half of the sixteenth century expressed part of a broader nationalist project taken up by writers of history books, legal theory, cartography, and literature.[8] The very existence of books in English created "print communities" organized around national boundaries rather than Latin Christendom.[9] When poets used print to redeem the "barbarous" English tongue, they consolidated a project that had its own stakes within the print industry.

Printing also introduced a second set of economic struggles concerning royal patents and monopolies, the exclusive rights granted to a printer for a particular book or *type* of book (e.g., law books, devotional guides). Fredrick Siebert argues that monopolies were instrumental in allowing the monarch to control the content of texts as well, for the court could penalize and reward printers for conforming to various orthodoxies (*Freedom of the*

Press). The unexpected result of this system was that some printers, out of economic necessity, printed prohibited books. Before long, a network of secret presses was operating in London. Between 1575 and 1586, a group of insurgent printers, led by John Wolfe, protested the system of monopolies. Announcing that he would reform the printing trade just as Luther had reformed religion, Wolfe proceeded to print the Latin grammars and religious books held under patent by other printers. Instead of imprisoning the renegade Wolfe, state authorities co-opted him by giving him a lucrative patent. The rights of printers remained a crucial issue throughout the century.

But economic conflicts within the printing business were perhaps overshadowed by struggles over who had the right to censor writing. Designed to erode "seditious opinions," Henry VIII's 1538 proclamation granted the power of censorship to the Privy Council (the monarch's cabinet) rather than ecclesiastical authorities. Beginning in 1542, the Privy Council attempted to crack down on printed ballads and broadsides (inexpensively printed sheets) which debated current events. In her Star Chamber decree of 1586, Elizabeth reinstalled church authorities in the licensing system by making the Archbishop of Canterbury and the Bishop of London the final arbiters for censorship. But an order issued by these prelates at the end of the century indicates that the regulatory system was not successful. This 1599 decree isolated particular genres as subversive (e.g., satires, epigrams), reiterated the need for pre-approval of texts, and ordered particular books to be burned.

These debates about the English press were centrally ignited and shaped by the Reformation, for Protestantism shifted authority away from the visible church to the power of the book. In opposing a culture organized around iconography and ceremony, reformers emphasized literacy and endowed the book with an almost mystical power; access to scripture became central to a person's salvation.[10] The individual was urged to judge tenets of faith by appealing directly to God's word, newly printed in the English tongue. Inadvertently splintering doctrine into the more flexible form of public opinion, Henry VIII's break with the Church of Rome also unwittingly opened up new venues for debate and for the dissemination of knowledge, for it licensed people to question the foundations of church and state authority. Early print regulations were devoted almost entirely to monitoring the circulation of theological texts, given that religion was the foundation on which politics was predicated. Following a wave of deliberations about the printing of English Bibles in the 1530s was a series of tracts in the 1560s attacking the church for not completing the Reformation project. And because a conjoined humanist and religious inquiry became the prerogative of all Christians, new sectors of the population felt free to take up intellectual and spiritual issues. One result was an outpouring of inexpensive popular "godly" ballads, which made matters of faith into popular tunes. Another consequence was that female aristocrats entered intellectual life and educated lower gentry moved into court positions. In inspiring questions about the control of knowledge and speech, the press served as a technological counterpart to the Reformation.

As Elaine Beilin argues, the Reformation was crucial for the early emergence of women writers in print: its emphasis on individual salvation shaped the roles that English writers could assume.[11] Tracts urging women to be silent often pointed to the frailty of Eve, whose disobedience proved that the pursuit of knowledge and theological matters were best left to men. Discussing translated religious devotions, Beilin suggests that women writers resolved this dilemma by establishing the persona of the virtuous woman. Female piety became a strong justification for women's writing, since religious texts could preempt a charge of moral jeopardy and cement the female author's claim to speak. Margaret Roper, daughter to Sir Thomas More, helped to start this trend by translating a 1523 meditation by Erasmus. Bearing the simple attribution that it was written by a nineteen-year-old girl, Roper's work was "authored" not by an individual but a type of person. Her translation was thus evidence of humanism's success in inspiring intellectual achievement even by unlikely subjects. Katherine Parr, Henry VIII's sixth Queen, became the first Englishwoman to publish an original work bearing her name. Initiating the first humanist education of noblewomen and serving as the first influential female Reformist figure, Parr fused piety with patronage to encourage more extensive reform than Henry allowed. Publishing *Prayers Stirring the Mind unto Heavenly Meditations* (1545) and *The Lamentation of a Sinner* (1547), Parr influenced theologians and scholars such as John Bale, John Foxe, Hugh Latimer, Roger Ascham, and Thomas Becon. The four daughters of Anthony Cooke – Mildred, Anne, Elizabeth, and Katherine – also published significant religious translations that furthered the consolidation of the Church of England, clarified doctrine, and discussed the nature of the holy sacraments.[12]

The Reformation set off a wave of debates, however, that extended beyond the confines of aristocratic circles. During the reign of the Catholic Queen Mary (1554–58), a group of people, mainly ministers, left England to take refuge in the Protestant low countries. These exiles, possibly including the printers John Day, Richard Jugge, and Hugh Singleton, returned to England upon Elizabeth's succession filled with a zeal for Genevan doctrines and a taste for ardent reform.[13] Dissatisfied with transformations of church vestments and rituals, they became the first group to use the press to engage in organized opposition to the Crown. The first weapon in their battle for reform was an anonymous 1572 pamphlet entitled *An Admonition to Parliament*, which pointed to errors in doctrine. John Field and Thomas Wilcocks, who were imprisoned for transcribing the pamphlet, argued their case on the basis of the Englishman's ancient right to petition Parliament. This sparked a contest in which writers appealed to public opinion to defend and criticize the Crown's position on religious reform. Rather than silencing dissenting voices, the bishops published replies which further stimulated the debate.

When the church sought to contain the force unleashed by the *Admonition*, it set off an anonymous guerrilla pamphlet war that not only posed a challenge to church and state authority, but also made literary style critical to the power amassing in the printed book. Published between 1588–89, a group of tracts called the Martin Marprelate pamphlets argued against an episcopal, or more hierarchical, form of church government. Using the pseudonym of Martin, various writers attacked church structures by blending theological argument with satire, ridicule, humorous quips and the idiom of holiday festivity.[14] Hesitant to respond with equal wit and colloquialism, church authorities commissioned secular writers such as Thomas Nashe, John Lyly, Anthony Munday, and Robert Greene to offer witty counterattacks. The history of censorship and church reform thus began to intersect explicitly with the emergence of authorship; for these Elizabethan writers were compelled to create stylized personae as part of the debate. Drawing on a humanist training that encouraged imitation, rhetorical wordplay, wit, and the creation of a self-conscious "I," writers generated a wildly energetic pamphlet war filled with uproarious caricatures and high irony. In the late 1580s, the "Martinets" were finally silenced when the church suspended their hired writers, seized an illegal press, and tortured some of the perpetrators. But this controversy indicates that the press had become an important tool for the dissemination of opinion; and the introduction of satire and performance into the debate showed the importance of "literary" training to social struggles of the day.

The writer gradually joined the printer as a player in the story of sixteenth-century censorship. After the printing of a 1579 tract protesting the Queen's marriage negotiations with a Catholic prince, the author (John Stubbes), printer (Hugh Singleton), and publisher were all three tried and sentenced to having their rights hands cut off. In other notable cases, authors suffered a range of punishments – from mutilation, to imprisonment, to simple demotion or loss of court favor. Among writers for the theatre, Ben Jonson and George Chapman were just two of many playwrights imprisoned for their authorship of "slanderous" scripts. While a 1599 ordinance conventionally identified individual texts and genres as scurrilous, it specifically singled out and banned several authors, including Thomas Nashe, from publishing. Yet, even in such cases, the author clearly was perceived as just one component within a broader system that created and distributed writing.[15] The crises incited by the expansion of the print industry did not intially focus on literary authorship but on the force and limits of religious, economic, and state authorities.

MANUSCRIPT CULTURE AND LITERARY AUTHORITY

The author occupied a similarly restricted place in the thriving literary manuscript culture of the sixteenth century. Because writing was not cordoned off from social life, it functioned as a communal and collective endeavor. Poetry and other kinds of texts commonly circulated in the enclosed environments of the Inns of Court (schools in which lawyers were trained), aristocratic and middle-class households, universities, and the royal court. Performed in court and civic pageantry, used to celebrate noteworthy occasions, offered as compliments to recipients, exchanged as gifts, and imparted as love tokens, poetry was the currency by which writers displayed the humanist education that equipped them for governmental service. Trivialized as a mere "toy," poetry had little formally acknowledged cultural esteem but a great deal of utility. Because writing was not categorized as "literary," lyrics appeared in odd places: scribbled on walls and furniture, inscribed in banqueting dishes such as marzipan cakes, etched on rings and jewelry. While an interest in occasional writing is hardly specific to the early modern period, it is clear that writers generally felt little compunction to preserve texts in any durable form that might transcend the occasion. We only have proof that Queen Elizabeth composed a poem about her cousin Mary because it was collected in a private manuscript by members of the Harington family, the Arundel Harington Manuscript. Modern readers also only know about the poetic complaint that Elizabeth scrawled on a wall because Continental visitors copied and printed it.[16] Lest we think that more accomplished authors' works were clearly distinguished from such ephemeral writing, we need only point to the fact that poems by Sidney and Donne were intermixed in private notebooks called commonplace books with the works of now unknown writers and with other "nonliterary" items such as recipes, letters, business transactions, and household accounts. And lower down on the social scale, between 600,000 and three million ballads were published anonymously as single-sheet penny broadsides in the second half of the sixteenth century;

decorated with woodcuts and designed to be sung aloud or pasted on walls, these texts blended oral and literate cultures. An entire range of "author-less" literatures surfaced within the practices of everyday life.[17]

The social dimension of Renaissance writing fostered what Walter Ong has called the "participatory poetics" of manuscript culture.[18] While writers occasionally produced complete handwritten books, they more often circulated writing on loose sheets. Unlike the ornate "finished" works produced in monasteries, sixteenth-century manuscript writing resembled theatre scripts. Traveling through households and schools, texts were open to inscription by readers, who felt free to amend rhymes, alter lines, and integrate "answer poems" into the poem proper. Christopher Marlowe's famous love poem, "Come Live with Me and Be My Love," spawned numerous imitations and revisions as well as several verse replies, the most famous of which was Walter Ralegh's "Nymph's Reply." Written as part of the active social life of educated men, the literary text had unusually unfixed parameters. An author might write several copies of a poem at the request of friends, each slightly different. As these copies circulated, readers might transcribe them with varying degrees of accuracy and place them in new settings that altered the poem's theme or focus. A poem might become recontextualized, and even reattributed, as it found its way into common-place books and miscellanies. Arthur Marotti has shown that poems by Ralegh, for instance, which editors previously labeled as "corrupt," now can be recognized as the perfectly proper emendations made by readers: what looks like sloppiness, plagiarism, or a disregard for authorial inten-tion, if viewed through a modern lens, simply demonstrates the energetic life of a popular manuscript poem in its sixteenth-century setting. The period's participatory poetics clearly do not square with the scholarly assumptions about authorial autonomy and control that we have inherited from the nineteenth century.

Sir John Harington, a writer and courtier in Elizabeth's court, poetically describes the collaborative nature of writing poetry:

> When Lynus thinkes that he and I are friends,
> Then all his Poems unto me he sends:
> His Disticks, Satyrs, Sonnets, and Exameters,
> His Epigrams, his Lyncks, his Pentameters.
> Then I must censure them, I must correct them,
> Then only I must order, and direct them.[19]

According to Harington, writing is the product of exchanges between "frends"; and the "director" of the work is properly its reader. But, of course, one had to be included in a particular social environment in order to be part of this network of "frends." Harington's allusion to Sidney's sonnets seven years before they appeared in print testifies to the lively private circulation of verse within a select readership. Literary reputation did not depend on a writer's appearance in print as much as his or her access to the right circles of readership.

Because gentlemanly amateurism was the most acceptable form of writing, the author who wanted to appear in print faced the dilemma of fashioning a persona that could overcome the stigma of print. While writers from earlier periods grappled with similar problems when presenting themselves in manuscript texts, the growth of the print industry and its perceived link to the lower class put English sixteenth-century writers in the fairly new position of establishing authority for the living publishing author.[20] On the Continent, lyrics had a more secure place in the print marketplace, mainly because of the prestige of Petrarch. But in England, the absence of a powerful vernacular tradition and the stronger emphasis on class decorum inhibited authorship.

Because it bridged readers from different classes and eroded the boundaries that distinguished an "in-the-know" social clique, print was seen as potentially disruptive. Writers were nervous that printing would make it possible for anyone with ready cash to become privy to the writings that previously proved social status. Harington declared proudly of his Muse:

> Mine never sought to set to sale her writing;
> In part her friends, in all her self delighting,
> She cannot beg applause of vulgar sort,
> Free born and bred, more free for noble sport.
>
> (*Letters*, no. 424, 320)

Fending off the encroaching marketplace, Harington opted to protect the "noble sport" of writing from the "vulgar" commodification of print. The courtier John Davies similarly complained that people of all social standings mixed in the marketplace: "great Hearts doe scorne, / To have their Measures with such Nombers throng'd, / as are so basely got, conceiv'd, and borne."[21] To publish was to become part of the common "throng," or crowd, where illegitimate and legitimate verse mingled indiscriminately.

Given low literacy rates and the select readership of literary works, the press had little chance of wreaking the social havoc that these writers feared; nevertheless it did foster new ways of identifying texts since it required that poems travel far from the social site in which they were written into new communities of readers. Although the average print run consisted only of 300 to 400 copies, publishing held out the possibility of creating circuits of readership independent of existing social circles. With its increased volume and new affordability, the press altered the way in which people conceptualized texts while also making the author a subject of debate.

REDEFINING THE AUTHOR

Print had a stronger impact on literary development in the second half of the century, when the fashion for gentlemanly amateurism began to erode. In 1557, Tottel changed the literary landscape and established the English lyric by publishing the now famed *Songs and Sonets*, also known as *Tottel's Miscellany*. In presenting a collection of poems that had previously circulated in manuscript, Tottel sought to provide a rationale for his book that might ward off the stigma of print and successfully merge occasional verse with the form of the book commodity. In doing so, he chose to emphasize both the nationalist project of creating a vernacular tradition and the aristocratic credentials of the verse he released to the public. Accusing elite readers of "hoarding" national treasures, Tottel claimed that his poems would enhance the moral fiber of a broad reading populace. "It resteth now (gentle reader)" he announces, "that thou think it not evil done, to publish, to the honor of the English tongue, and for profit of the studious of English eloquence, those works which the ungentle hoarders up of such treasure have heretofore envied thee."[22] With these words, Tottel dethroned manuscript readers as "ungentle" and nominated print readers as the truly aristocratic textual consumers.

What role does the author play in this anthology? The entire *Miscellany* appears to be neatly divided into four sections classified by author – Henry Howard, Thomas Wyatt, Nicholas Grimald, and "uncertain authors." But the book's organizational framework everywhere collapses, as poems by various writers seep into all sections. The fact that Tottel felt free to revise the poems by regularizing meter and rhyme clearly reveals his sense of the author's limited standing in the text. While editing the poems, Tottel also imposed titles that de-emphasized the occasional nature of the verse and emphasized instead its more "literary" aspects. One poem, for instance, is entitled "The means to attain happy life." Yet Tottel also provided titles that displayed the poems' close proximity to social circumstances: "Wyatt being in prison, to Brian"; "A song written by the Earl of Surrey to a lady that refused to dance with him." The result is a text that identifies poetry as occasional and contingent, on the one hand, and as the exemplar of timeless human feeling, on the other. While Tottel made writers into authors posthumously, he did not arrogate to them a sovereign role in the text; instead the poems were authorized as much by their place in a moment of social exchange as their status as personal utterance. These multiple identifications document the text's intermediary place between manuscript and print environments.

According to H. S. Bennett the output of printed titles doubled between 1558 and the 1580s.[23] Humanism's emphasis on education strengthened the Tudor system of grammar schools, with the result that literacy increased dramatically in the period.[24] Printers, eager to expand their reach, sought to devise books intelligible to these new markets. Gentlemen and would-be elites began to see the advantages of publishing, mainly because they sought a broader means for attracting patrons and advertising the grandeur of the English tongue to the Continent.

The first individual to publish a collection of his own poems was a gentleman named Barnabe Googe, whose *Eclogues, Epitaphes and Sonnets* (1563) appeared six years after *Tottel's Miscellany*. As Arthur Marotti observes, the publisher echoes Tottel's claim that manuscript exchange permits people to "hoard" the literary treasures that more rightfully belong to a national public (*Manuscript*, p. 297). But Googe himself does not put forth this defense; instead it is craftily presented by the printer, who admits to taking advantage of Googe's travels abroad by publishing poems that he left with a friend.[25] As Marotti notes, however, the collection "has the marks of a deliberate authorial strategy" (p. 297), for the book includes a commendatory letter from a family member and Googe's own dedicatory epistle to a friend from the Inns of Court. Writing of his embarrassment on returning to London to find his poems about to be issued from the press, Googe seeks to safeguard them by declaring them a private "gift" for a friend. The *Eclogues* thus reveals the elaborate ruses necessary for the publishing author to make a claim to gentility but also take advantage of the possibilities of print.

The first Englishwoman to publish a secular text, Isabella Whitney was a member of the minor gentry who did not have access to elite manuscript circulation. While placing her works in the public eye could not jeopardize her social position, it did require that she combat widespread cultural attitudes against women's public writing as she attempted to define the book commodity. Numerous writers warned women of the dangers of publicity. Humanist court educator Juan Luis Vives wrote, for instance, that it was unseemly for a woman to "speak abroad, and shake off her demureness and honesty ... it were better to be at home within and unknown to other folks, and in company to hold her tongue demurely."[26] While male scholarly study was expected to materialize as public service, female education was designed to promote private virtue. Whitney broke decorum by publishing a 1567 complaint against male inconstancy and a

1573 book of moral adages, called *A Sweet Nosegay*. In this second book, Whitney styled herself as an author by placing her "primary material," 110 moral poetic sayings, alongside two other sections: a poetic epistolary exchange in which Whitney laments her loss of position to family and friends, and a concluding verse written as if the speaker were making a will and testament. Whitney's verse letters conjure up the comforting idea of a circle of friends as the text's ideal readership even though she clearly seeks an audience beyond that scope. Her readers thus became part of an intimate social circuit of exchange elasticized to incorporate the book commodity.

Like other publishing writers, Whitney also attempted to create a metaphor for the text that located authorship within manuscript conventions. Yet the strategies used by her male counterparts were simply not available to her: she could not allege, as did Googe, to have had her coterie texts stolen while traveling abroad, nor could she claim, as did George Turberville in a 1567 book of poems, to be a reformed prodigal. Presenting her work instead as a medicinal recipe, Whitney identifies herself as a good housewife who protects readers by warding off the spiritual, economic, and physical disease of the culture. Founding her poetic authority on a Renaissance housewife's prescribed task of attending to bodily ailments, Whitney classifies her book as a curative "nosegay" fashioned out of a male writer's intellectual "garden." Yet her concluding "Will and testament" extends her authority in this intimate setting to a broader urban community, as her metaphor shifts from domestic worker to dying citizen. In leaving items to London that she could not possibly own – shops, gallows, streets – Whitney emphasizes the one "possession" that she can bequeath to readers: her book. Like Googe, who appealed to "private" writing in the Inns of Court, Whitney presents an authorial role founded on an "extra-literary" basis; both writers show us how gender and class shaped the authorial roles available to Tudor writers.[27]

In the history of authorship, George Gascoigne proves to be a pivotal figure between early Tudor writers and the later Elizabethans, for Gascoigne manipulated the form of the book more studiedly to announce a role for the public "literary" author. When published in 1573, *A Hundred Sundrie Flowres* appeared to offer a miscellaneous collection of works by ancient, Continental and contemporary English writers, one of whom was Gascoigne. The opening letters narrate the sensational origins of the text: the printer confesses to intercepting a manuscript sent from a man identified as G.T. to someone named H. W. Bookbuyers are thus invited to feel privileged at being able to peek at the private materials exchanged between friends. When the editor later claims to know the story of adulterous seduction behind the poems for one of the included works, "The Adventures of Master F.J.," however, he redefines the meaning of "privacy" for the reader. Signaling the text's place in a socially exclusive but also sexually scandalous world, the publisher represents the print marketplace as promising access to an enticing world of letters.

As the title to the work suggests, the *Flowres* appears to be an assortment of "sundry" texts. Identifying the poems as gathered from existing poetic gardens, the printer urges the reader to sample the work piecemeal: "you shall not be constrained to smell of the flowers therein contained all at once," he advises, "but you may take any one flower by itself."[28] The text's diversity indicates the poems' "true" affiliation with circuits of gentlemanly amateurism. Elsewhere, however, when G.T. compares these works to Chaucer's accomplishments and evaluates the merits of the poems, he invites readers to imagine the texts as part of a literary canon. Alternately trivializing the poems as "games" and heralding them as significant cultural achievements, the edition reveals the collision between two modes of writing.

The entire frame for the work, however, was later revealed to be a staged fabrication; for two years later, Gascoigne republished a slightly revised version of the same text, renamed as *The Posies of George Gascoigne, Esquire, Corrected, perfected and augmented by the Author* (1575). Rather than a collection of poems by different writers, the book is attributed to a single author, whose status rests on his ability to control and correct the text. The new title also hints at a more cohesive organizational frame: instead of "sundry" works, the "posies" are carefully subdivided into "flowers," "herbs," and "weeds." Branding the *Flowres* as the juvenilia of his wayward youth, Gascoigne claims to make amends by publishing a corrected and purified text. Apparently the *Flowres* had been censored by the Privy Council because the book was understood to refer to contemporary political events. But Gascoigne capitalizes on the notoriety of the text in order to justify the need for clear authorial intervention and revision. As Lorna Hutson notes, books could be suppressed because of their apparent uselessness, or their "purposeful" references to current events.[29] Maneuvering through this double bind, Gascoigne downplays the text's link to frivolous manuscript entertainments and instead emphasizes the book's national, moral, and literary utility. He does so by strategically substituting the earlier *Flowres'* claims to be a true story with a literary frame that highlights the text's fictional status (it is now a tale written by "Bartello"). The book's status as "literature" and as the product of a single author, then, emerges from within a social controversy. Assuming the roles previously attributed to the editor, writer, real life characters, and "sundry" authors, Gascoigne redefines a gentlemanly anthology as the more established literary effort of an ambitious author.

It was Edmund Spenser, however, who succeeded in generating a more exalted role for the author by using the materiality of the printed book to merge humanist intellectual value with civic duty. Endowing the role of poet with the ancient dignity of classical authors, Spenser rescripts the basic idea of the poetic profession to make the author instrumental in producing a national and moral vernacular literature. Four years after the printing of Gascoigne's *Posies*, Spenser made his carefully orchestrated debut with the publication of the 1579 *Shepheardes Calender*. Dedicating the work to Sir Philip Sidney, Spenser strategically presents a group of twelve eclogues anonymously. But the text appeared to its readers as if already a "classic": it included a scholarly gloss by an unknown writer named E.K., who carefully places the poem in a literary history including Chaucer, Skelton, Marot, and Vergil. According to E.K., the unidentified writer follows in the footsteps of Vergil by writing a lowly pastoral that seeks to define a new role for poetry in the realm. The text's meaning was partially dependent upon its "printed" state, for in boasting woodcut illustrations, glosses, carefully designed borders, emblems, and addresses to the reader, the *Calender* made its status as a tangible object important to its self-definition (figure 8). Discussing the poems' literary allusions and praising particular motifs, E.K. announces "*the* new poet" as a figure who has already cultivated a readership fully appreciative of the literary merits of the text. The *Calender*'s printed form heightened its literary claims rather than jeopardized its cultural prestige.[30]

In an opening poem, Spenser whets the reader's desire to know who has written this seemingly monumental anonymous text:

> Goe little booke; thy selfe present,
> As whose parent is unkent . . .
> And asked, who thee forth did bring,
> A shepheardes swaine saye did thee sing . . .
> But if that any aske thy name,
> Say thou wert begot with blame.[31]

By producing an "unkent" (unknown) and bastard work ("begot with blame"), Spenser makes the text's origin a matter of speculation; the effect is that the author appears to be the crucial absent center. Refusing to identify himself, Spenser cedes possession of the text to its dedicatee, Sidney, and the pastoral-poet figures who function as author-figures within the text (the "shepheardes swaine"). Although one of the poet-shepherds, Colin Clout, is heralded as embodying the noble potential of poetic letters,

Aprill.

Aegloga Quarta.

Argument.

THis *Aeglogue is purposely intended to the honour and prayse of our most gracious soueraigne,* Queene Elizabeth. *The speakers herein be* Hobbinoll *and* Thenot, *two shepheardes: the which* Hobbinoll *being before mentioned, greatly to haue loued* Colin, *is here sette forth more largely, complaining him of that boyes great misaduenture in Loue, whereby his minde was alienate and with drawne not onely from him, who most loued him, but also from all former delights and studies as well in pleasaunt piping, as cunning ryming and singing, and other hys laudable exercises. Whereby he taketh occasion for proofe his more excellencie and skill in poetrie, to recorde a song, which they sayd* Colin *sometime made in honor of her* Maiestie, *whom abruptly he termeth* Elisa.

8 The woodcut to Edmund Spenser's "April" eclogue of *The Shepheardes Calender* (London, 1579).

he finally can offer only a failed model of authorship; for while Colin's poetic song to "Eliza" (Queen Elizabeth) in the "April" eclogue successfully fuses political praise, religious ardor, and poetic vision, he is finally unable to transform his erotic passions into a moral and nationally useful vocation. Incapable of creating a durable literary monument out of the trials of human experience, Colin throws into relief the greater achievements of the mysterious *Calender* writer, who does offer a model for integrating poetry into a Protestant and nationalist project. As the shepherds in the text debate poetry's moral and social mission, E.K. provides a running gloss which assesses the poems sung by the characters. E.K.'s argument, that the poems fuse imperial Vergilian aims with sacred gospel and classical tradition, gives the lie to Spenser's professed "modesty." In declaring that the book is "begot with blame," Spenser hints that this seemingly illegitimate form (the anonymous poet in print) will birth a newly legitimated vocation for the author. "Loe I have made a Calendar for every yeare," the author declares grandly at the closing of the poem. With this presumptuous parting gesture, Spenser proclaims a change in the Elizabethan profession of letters. He goes beyond the playful endeavors of the courtly gentleman and the love-struck shepherd to create a transcendent vocation for the imperial Protestant poet.

Spenser creates a book that also claims affinities to the world of contemporary gentility. Emerging from the text's manuscript-like authorizations – the voices of the fictional poet Colin, the annotator E.K., the poet Immerito – the author steps forward with a promise to write more poetry. Indeed, Spenser abandons the disguise of anonymity and identifies himself as the author of the *Calender* in his next grand work, the epic *Faerie Queene*, which opens:

> Lo I the man, Whose Muse whilome did maske,
> As time her taught in lowly Shepheardes weeds,
> Am now enforst a far unfitter taske,
> For trumpets sterne to chaunge mine Oaten reeds[32]

The multiple voices of the *Calender* are subsumed into the confident voice of the single author, whose boldness in undertaking the project of epic-writing is justified by the success of his previous, more modest, work. Throwing off the "maske" of "lowly" pastoral to undertake the more arduous role of Vergilian epic poet, Spenser also sheds the anonymity of amateurism to enter without disguise into the print marketplace. He thus offers a new conception of authorship that rises out of the trappings of manuscript exchange, one steeped in the authority of classical writing.

While Spenser addressed his *Calender* to the living Sidney as a "precedent" for a new Protestant humanism, later writers authorized their writing by referring specifically to Sidney's posthumous publication. Sidney, who had been indifferent to the press, ironically became the model for writers eager to enter the print marketplace without jeopardizing their social status. Thomas Newman's 1591 publication of *Astrophil and Stella*, followed by the 1590 and 1593 folio releases of Sidney's *Countess of Pembroke's Arcadia*, became watershed publishing events; for these texts nominated the printed book as the proper haven for aristocratic authorship. If Sidney – cultural hero, Protestant martyr, and member of the inner sanctum – could appear in print, then who could worry about the press's perceived baseness? Numerous writers at the turn of the century, including Michael Drayton, Samuel Daniel, and Giles Fletcher, attempted to capitalize on Sidney's "published" status by citing him in their prefaces. Daniel explained that he was forced to print his sonnet sequence *Delia* because his poems had been included in Newman's edition of Sidney's *Astrophil*. Thomas Moffett and Fulke Greville published biographies of Sidney. And a significant anthology, *The Phoenix Nest* (1593), unusual because it presented the verse of prominent gentlemen, opened with an elegy to Sidney.

While the legend of Sidney provided aristocratic credentials for the socially ambitious author, other writers and printers combated the stigma of print by creating models for authorship that were highly gendered and sexualized. As we have seen, Gascoigne was willing to brand himself a profligate in his authorial self-fashioning and Spenser temporarily inhabited the role of lovestruck shepherd in the *Calender*. In prefaces to numerous sonnet sequences, publishers pun on their titles – *Delia*, *Phillis*, *Chloris*, *Fidessa* – so as to personify their books as the idealized women of Petrarchan love, "Delia" the anagram of "ideal." In using this analogy, publishers and authors invite readers to imagine book purchase as the act of entertaining and owning a "female" object; "May it please you to looke and like of homlie Phillys," Thomas Lodge bids his reader.[33] The publisher of Thomas Sackville and Thomas Norton's influential play *Gorboduc* (1570) describes the text as a "fair maid" who had been raped and cast out to the reading public before being rehabilitated by the responsible printer who redresses her "shame." And Daniel protests that his "private passions" (sonnets) were "betrayed" to print readers when his Muse was "thrust" "rawly" (or nakedly) into the world.[34] Texts strangely became figured as wanton maidens or secrets unwillingly displayed to voyeuristic readers.[35] The goal of such rhetoric was to transfer the stigma of print into a titillating game and thus create a recognizable role for author and commodity; one effect was to gender both the emergent author and reader as male.

Given the popularity of these gendered models, how did women establish themselves as authors? Books published by women earlier in the century, mainly humanist and religious translations, inserted female voices into the marketplace but failed to mold an enduring model for female authorship. Yet some women associated with the court at the turn of the century created literary texts that claimed the identity of the writer. Mary Sidney's collaborative *Psalmes* explicitly addressed the issue of a woman's public writing. An accomplished lyricist and one of the primary patrons of the period, Sidney translated and published three works, wrote poetry, and collaborated with her brother Philip on a translation of the Psalms. Her literary reputation was attested to by numerous writers, including John Donne, George Herbert, Thomas Moffet, Nicholas Breton, Edmund Spenser, and Aemilia Lanyer. Sidney chose to present her Psalms in manuscript form in order to display her access to a readership of the highest rank. In designing her text for public presentation to Queen Elizabeth, Sidney included prefatory poems that defined her authorial role in relation to two authoritative men – the biblical King David and Philip Sidney – and two traditions – a militant Protestantism and aristocratic collaborative writing. By presenting her "coupled work" at court, she emphasized the social command of her Protestant-identified family and Philip's standing in political-religious circles. By foregrounding Philip's "bleeding veins," Sidney casts the text as a public elegy linking her family's sacrifice to a Protestant mission fueled by scripture.[36] The case of the Sidneian Psalms proves that scholars' commonsense assumptions about manuscript writing need qualification: her decision to produce a manuscript was not based on the notion that this ostensibly "private" form was suitable for female modesty, but rather on her particular social position.[37]

In 1610, Aemilia Lanyer published a different religious work, *Salve Deus Rex Judaeorum*, in which the writer's gender was central to both her self-presentation as author and her poetic interpretation of scripure.[38] Unusual because it was addressed solely to female readers, this text couched a defense of women within the narrative of Christian redemption. The *Salve Deus* consists of nine dedicatory poems, a lengthy poem on Christ's passion, a spirited defense of Eve, and the first country house poem published in England. Like other writers, Lanyer generated a fictional community of readers through multiple dedications, but she wrote to the most notable women in the realm, including Queen Anne, Princess Elizabeth, Arbella Stuart, and Anne Clifford. She thus touted court society as the appropriate site of reception for the printed book, while attempting to make a more defined place for the author within that society.

Married to a court musician, formerly mistress to a prominent courtier, and descendant of a Jewish family, Lanyer sought to consolidate her tenuous link to aristocratic culture by publishing. In the *Salve*, she locates herself within an elite community of virtuous women stretching from biblical tradition to contemporary aristocrats. Arguing for women's privileged relationship to Christian piety, Lanyer implies that her gender can overshadow the status lines that divide her from her dedicatees, and her religious subject matter can authorize her foray into print. Combining gestures of humility before Christ and aristocratic women, the poem invites readers to prove Christian charity by accepting the Christ-like book and its humble but spiritually apt author. Writing from the social margins, Lanyer transforms book-buying into a gendered act of devotion and a sign of gentility.

The history of sixteenth-century authorship must conclude with the figure of Ben Jonson, the writer most influential in extending the author's power over the text. Jonson's publication of *The Workes of Benjamin Jonson* in folio form in 1616 illustrates what one critic calls his "bibliographic ego," the personality he developed through the features of the book.[39] Prior to the printing of his *Workes*, Jonson, like other actors, trafficked writing by selling plays to acting companies, but he also made direct appeals to patrons by designing court masques and circuating manuscript verses. Jonson was unusual in his quest to control the meaning of his works, particularly in his success in reclaiming his scripts back from the acting company, who rightfully controlled these texts. Arranging for a printer named William Stansby to secure the rights to his plays from other printers, Jonson became the first dramatist to oversee the publication of his work; he corrected, revised, and annotated his plays as they were set into type. Cleansing the text from the residue of the stage, Jonson sought to restore ideas that had been altered in performance. While title pages for published plays conventionally foregrounded the theatrical success of the work, the title page to Jonson's 1600 *Every Man out of His Humour*, advertised the text "as it was first composed by the author B.I. Containing more than hath been Publicly spoke or Acted." Distinguishing between the authorial and acted version of a play, this text claimed to supplement the deficient performance with the author's more significant guidance. In explicating sources for particular passages, Jonson redefined the script as literary. In addition to highlighting the erudition of the playtext, Jonson regularized punctuation, spelling, and capitalization, with the result that the text became more uniform and carefully crafted. He thus emphasized the text's proximity to the library rather than to the stage.[40]

But Jonson's 1616 *Workes* carried the goals of his carefully printed quartos further; for this text set a precedent that reshaped the definition of theatrical and poetic writing. Preparing the way for the later folio works of Shakespeare (1623) and Beaumont and Fletcher (1647) this text signaled its affiliation with grand collections of poetry, such as Samuel Daniel's 1603 *Works*. The huge, durable, and expensive folio form impressed the reader with the text's lasting importance, for folios were usually reserved for classical editions and had only recently been used to publish English authors such as Chaucer. Jonson's *Workes* tellingly bore an elaborate title page with a pictorial frontispiece that identified the book's monumental status specifically with its author (figure 9). In this image, mythological icons representing the classical genres of the book frame Jonson's ornately presented name. Through careful manipulation of the print apparatus, Jonson offered to contemporary authors a role previously reserved for classical writers. Jonson thus attempted to consolidate and extend the laureate status that Spenser generated by including plays in the ongoing process of monumentalizing literature. Critics have long recognized Jonson's contribution to the legitimation of drama, but, given the widespread biases against published poetry, Jonson's success in binding authorial control to both the fixed properties of print and the literary characteristics of the text made him instrumental in producing a new concept of authorship. Jonson's career thus marks an important moment in literature's institutionalization.

THE EARLY MODERN AUTHOR

In now famous essays, Michel Foucault and Roland Barthes argue that the author is an historical construct rather than a universal idea. Foucault sees the author as "a certain functional principle by which, in our culture, one limits, excludes, and chooses; in short, by which one impedes the free circulation, the free manipulation, the free composition, decomposition, and recomposition of fiction."[41] According to Foucault, the "restrictive" force called the author comes into visibility in certain historical moments for particular social reasons. In one sense, authors in the Renaissance were much like those from other periods: they spent energy shaping personae through language, revising established conventions, and complaining about the trials of writing. But, in our modern understanding of the term, there were no Renaissance authors at all. For legal definitions require an author's proprietorial control over a work, and authors in an age before copyright did not govern the way that texts were read or classified. Instead readers saw texts as part of a social network which was authorized variously by multiple groups and institutions. The degree to which the author became significant to a particular

9 Title page to the monumental folio edition of Ben Jonson's collected works (London, 1616).

work depended on factors that were often not "literary." Tottel named Surrey as the primary author for his *Songs and Sonets* although Surrey wrote only 40 of the 213 poems in the book, half as many as were written by Wyatt; Surrey's impeccable aristocratic credentials nominated him to be an author.

Tottel's promotion of Surrey to the rank of authorship only points to the fact that sixteenth-century authorship was shaped by scribes, publishers, and stationers as well as ambitious writers.[42] Gascoigne's printer accentuated the authorial name on the title page simply by manipulating typeface; and the publishers of Daniel's and Drayton's collected works "authorized" these collections by presenting elaborate portraits of their laureate authors on the title pages. Providing an authorial figure to preside over the work, such frontispieces organized the readers' interpretation of the text and constituted the author as a more powerful cultural sign. Marotti points out that typeface itself could signal a work's status: old-fashioned black-letter texts were associated with a native tradition while roman style books indicated a classicizing mode (*Manuscript*, pp. 282–83). There was also a hierarchy in the size of books: the durable and expensive folios carried more prestige than quartos, which were cheaper and readily available to a wider populace. The extremely tiny duodecimo book might solicit readers to imagine the text as an intimate personal possession, easily slipped in a pocket. Although these manipulations may seem to have their analogies in the market-driven formatting of modern printed books, they had a cultural force that was historically distinctive; for these conventions conjured an authority for the literary writer and book that simply had not existed. And when a printer changed the format of a text from octavo to quarto, altered a play's list of characters or organized its speeches into acts and scenes, contributed prefatory poems, or changed the book's title, he transformed the reader's understanding of both the literary object and its author to a degree unimaginable in a modern literary world. When we recognize the fact that publishers', typesetters', and booksellers' interventions dovetailed with the elaborate authorial strategies for self-presentation that I have described, we make clear that people other than writers shaped the "idea of the author," and authorship emerged from the reader's experience with the book's form and not only its content. While the sixteenth-century humanist emphasis on a person's heightened potential generated a spirit of rhetorical self-fashioning that perhaps prompted bold authorial assertions, the individual's role in defining authorship went hand in hand with other forces that shaped the material conditions of writing.

As the examples of Donne, Sidney, Spenser, and Jonson make clear, the advent of print technology did not insure, or even produce, a single definition of authorship. Sidney and Donne were widely known as "authors" based largely on the circulation of manuscript poems, although their "authority" did not fit the definition that Foucault articulates for the author: the figure who patrols the text's boundaries and provides limits for the reading experience. When Spenser and Jonson used the book format to generate the author's laureate status, however, they produced more modern and familiar images of literary authority – classically authorized writers who serve as the origin and arbiter of a literary monument that exceeds its place in everyday cultural transactions. In the overlap of manuscript and print cultures, an array of different and sometimes competing conceptions of authorship emerged.

One of the pleasures afforded by reading Renaissance literature is a heightened appreciation of its remoteness, for that difference can remind us of the flexibility of our own most precious ideas and models. What would it mean to read differently? Because authorship is now such a seemingly "natural" category of reading that we use to make sense of a text, we can easily forget that this concept has changed over time. Learning that Renaissance citizens had distinctly un-modern ideas about such basic ideas as "authorship" and "literature" not only allows us to see the interaction between individuals, social forces, and technology, but also unleashes some of the extraordinary characteristics of a moment when manuscript and print cultures coexisted in the literary landscape.

NOTES

1 Francis Bacon, *A Selection of his Works*, ed. W. Warhaft (Toronto: University of Toronto Press, 1965), Aphorism 129, p. 455.
2 D. F. McKenzie, "Typography and Meaning: The Case of William Congreve," in *The Book and The Book Trade in Eighteenth-Century Europe*, ed. Giles Barber and Bernhard Fabian (Hamburg: Ernst Hauswedell, 1981), p. 82.
3 Gerald Eades Bentley, *The Profession of Dramatist in Shakespeare's Time: 1590–1642* (Princeton: Princeton University Press, 1971).
4 H. S. Bennett, *English Books and Readers, 1475–1557* (Cambridge: Cambridge University Press, 1952).
5 Fredrick Seaton Siebert, *Freedom of the Press in England, 1476–1776: The Rise and Decline of Government Controls* (Urbana: University of Illinois Press, 1952), esp. pp. 21–40.
6 Marjorie Plant, *The English Book Trade: An Economic History of the Making and Sale of Books* (London: George Allen and Unwin, 1939), esp. p. 28.
7 *A Transcript of the Registers of the Company of Stationers of London 1554–1640*, ed. Edward Arber, 5 vols. (London, 1857–77; rpt. London: W. Aldis Wright, 1978), vol. II, pp. 881–82.
8 Richard Helgerson, *Forms of Nationhood: The Elizabethan Writing of England* (Chicago: University of Chicago Press, 1992).

9 On print's impact on nationalism, see Elizabeth L. Eisenstein, *The Printing Press as an Agent of Change* (Cambridge: Cambridge University Press, 1979), esp. pp. 117–18 and 358–64; and Benedict Anderson, *Imagined Communities: Reflections on the Origin and Spread of Nationalism* (London and New York: Verso, 1983; rvd. 1991).

10 See Stephen Greenblatt, *Renaissance Self-Fashioning: From More to Shakespeare* (Chicago: University of Chicago Press, 1980), pp. 74–114.

11 Elaine V. Beilin, *Redeeming Eve: Women Writers of the English Renaissance* (Princeton: Princeton University Press, 1987).

12 Mary Ellen Lamb, "The Cooke Sisters: Attitudes toward Learned Women in the Renaissance," in *Silent But For the Word: Tudor Women as Patrons, Translators, and Writers of Religious Works*, ed. Margaret P. Hannay (Kent, OH: Kent State University Press, 1985), pp. 107–25.

13 Christina Hollwell Garret, *The Marian Exiles: A Study of the Origins of Elizabethan Puritanism* (Cambridge: Cambridge University Press, 1966).

14 Jonathan V. Crewe, *Unredeemed Rhetoric: Thomas Nashe and the Scandal of Authorship* (Baltimore: Johns Hopkins University Press, 1982), pp. 31–37.

15 Margreta de Grazia, *Shakespeare Verbatim: The Reproduction of Authenticity and the 1790 Apparatus* (Oxford: Clarendon Press, 1991), p. 190.

16 These poems are recorded and discussed in *The Poems of Queen Elizabeth*, ed. Leicester Bradner (Providence, RI: Brown University Press, 1964).

17 On manuscript exchange, see Arthur F. Marotti, *Manuscript, Print, and the English Renaissance Lyric* (Ithaca, NY: Cornell University Press, 1995); and J. W. Saunders, "From Manuscript to Print: Notes on the Circulation of Poetic MSS. in the Sixteenth Century," *Proceedings of the Leeds Philosophical and Literary Society* 6 (1951): 507–28. On broadsides, see Tessa Watt, *Cheap Print and Popular Piety, 1550–1640* (Cambridge: Cambridge University Press, 1991).

18 Walter Ong, *Interfaces of the Word* (Ithaca, NY: Cornell University Press, 1977), pp. 274–79.

19 John Harington, *The Letters and Epigrams of Sir John Harington*, ed. Norman Egbert McClure (Philadelphia: University of Pennsylvania Press, 1930), no. 67, p. 173.

20 J. W. Saunders, "The Stigma of Print: A Note on the Social Bases of Tudor Poetry, " *Essays in Criticism* (1951): 139–64.

21 John Davies, *The Muse's Sacrifice*, in *The Works of John Davies*, ed. Alexander B. Grosart. (Edinburgh: Cherlsey Worthies Library, 1878) vol. II, p. 5.

22 *Tottel's Miscellany*, ed. Hyder Edward Rollins, 2 vols. (Cambridge: Harvard University Press, 1965), vol I, p. 2.

23 H. S. Bennett, *English Books and their Readers, 1558–1603* (Cambridge: Cambridge University Press, 1965), pp. 269–71.

24 Arthur F. Kinney, *Humanist Poetics: Thought, Rhetoric, and Fiction in Sixteenth-Century England* (Amherst: University of Massachusetts Press, 1986); Margaret Spufford, *Small Books and Pleasant Histories: Popular Fiction and its Readership in Seventeenth-Century England* (Athens: University of Georgia Press, 1981).

25 Barnabe Googe, *Eclogues, Epitaphs, and Sonnets*, ed. Judith M. Kennedy (Toronto: University of Toronto Press, 1989), p. 39.

26 Juan Luis Vives, *The Instruction of a Christian Woman*, trans. Richard Hyrde (London, 1540), sig. C6.

27 Isabella Whitney, *A Sweet Nosegay*. Rpt. Fac. in *The Floures of Philosophie (1572) by Hugh Plat and A Sweet Nosgay (1573) and The Copy of a Letter (1567) by Isabella Whitney*, ed. Richard J. Panofsky (Delmar: NY: Scholars' Facsimiles & Reprints, 1982).

28 *The Complete Works of George Gascoigne*, ed. John W. Cunliffe, 2 vols. (Cambridge: Cambridge University Press, 1907), vol. I, p. 476.

29 Lorna Hutson, *Thomas Nashe in Context* (Oxford: Clarendon Press, 1989).

30 Louis Montrose, "The Elizabethan Subject and the Spenserian Text," in *Literary Theory/Renaissance Texts*, ed. Patricia Parker and David Quint (Baltimore: Johns Hopkins University Press, 1986), pp. 319–20; David Lee Miller, "Authorship, Anonymity, and *The Shepheardes Calender*," *Modern Language Quarterly* 40 (1979): 219–36; Richard Helgerson, *Self-Crowned Laureates: Spenser, Jonson, Milton and the Literary System* (Berkeley and London: University of California Press, 1983).

31 Edmund Spenser, *The Shepheardes Calender*, in *The Yale Edition of the Shorter Poems of Edmund Spenser*, ed. William A. Oram et al. (New Haven: Yale University Press, 1989).

32 Edmund Spenser, *The Faerie Queene*, ed. Thomas P. Roche (Harmondsworth: Penguin, 1987), p. 39.

33 Thomas Lodge, *Phillis* (London, 1593), sig. A2.

34 Samuel Daniel, *Poems and a Defence of Ryme*, ed. Arthur Colby Sprague (Chicago: University of Chicago Press, 1965), p. 9.

35 Wendy Wall, *The Imprint of Gender: Authorship and Publication in the English Renaissance* (Ithaca, NY: Cornell University Press, 1993), pp. 169–226.

36 Mary Sidney, "Even Now that Care" and "To the Angell Spirit," in *The Triumph of Death and Other Unpublished and Uncollected Poems*, ed. Gary Waller (Salzburg: Universität Salzburg, 1977).

37 See Margaret Ezell, *The Patriarch's Wife: Literary Evidence and the History of the Family* (Chapel Hill: University of North Carolina Press, 1987).

38 Aemilia Lanyer, *The Poems of Aemilia Lanyer: Salve Deus Rex Judaeorum*, ed. Susanne Woods (Oxford: Oxford University Press, 1993). See Barbara Kiefer Lewalski, *Writing Women in Jacobean England* (Cambridge: Harvard University Press, 1993); Lisa Schnell, "'So Great a Difference is There in Degree': Aemilia Lanyer and the Aims of Feminist Criticism," *Modern Language Quarterly* 57 (1996): 23–35.

39 Joseph Loewenstein, "The Script in the Marketplace," *Representations* 12 (1985): 101–14.

40 Timothy Murray, *Theatrical Legitimation: Allegories of Genius in Seventeenth-Century England and France* (Oxford: Oxford University Press, 1987).

41 Michel Foucault, "What is an Author?," in *Textual Strategies: Perspectives in Post Structuralist Criticism*, ed. Josué Harari (Ithaca, NY: Cornell University Press, 1977), p. 159; Roland Barthes, "The Death of the Author," in *Image, Music, Text*, trans. Stephen Heath (New York: Hill and Wang, 1977).

42 Margreta de Grazia and Peter Stallybrass, "The Materiality of the Shakespearean Text," *Shakespeare Quarterly* 44 (1993): 255–83.

FURTHER READING

Beilin, Elaine V., *Redeeming Eve: Women Writers of the English Renaissance* (Princeton: Princeton University Press, 1987).

Bennett, H. S., *English Books and Readers, 1475–1557* (Cambridge: Cambridge University Press, 1952).

English Books and their Readers, 1558–1603 (Cambridge: Cambridge University Press, 1965).

Bentley, Gerald Eades, *The Profession of Dramatist in Shakespeare's Time: 1590–1642* (Princeton: Princeton University Press, 1971).

De Grazia, Margreta, *Shakespeare Verbatim: The Reproduction of Authenticity and the 1790 Apparatus* (Oxford: Oxford University Press, 1991).

De Grazia, Margreta and Peter Stallybrass, "The Materiality of the Shakespearean Text" *Shakespeare Quarterly* 44 (1993): 255–83.

Eisenstein, Elizabeth L., *The Printing Press as An Agent of Change* (Cambridge: Cambridge University Press, 1979).

Ezell, Margaret, *The Patriarch's Wife: Literary Evidence and the History of the Family* (Chapel Hill: University of North Carolina Press, 1987).

Foucault, Michel, "What is an Author?" *Textual Strategies: Perspectives in Post Structuralist Criticism*, ed. Josué Harari (Ithaca, NY: Cornell University Press, 1977).

Greenblatt, Stephen, *Renaissance Self-Fashioning: From More to Shakespeare* (Chicago: University of Chicago Press, 1980).

Helgerson, Richard, *Self-Crowned Laureates: Spenser, Jonson, Milton and the Literary System* (Berkeley and London: University of California Press, 1983).

Marotti, Arthur F., *Manuscript, Print, and the English Renaissance Lyric* (Ithaca, NY: Cornell University Press, 1995).

Masten, Jeffrey, *Textual Intercourse: Collaboration, Authorship and Sexualities in Renaissance Drama* (Cambridge: Cambridge University Press, 1997).

Montrose, Louis, "The Elizabethan Subject and the Spenserian Text," *Literary Theory/Renaissance Texts*, ed. Patricia Parker and David Quint (Baltimore: Johns Hopkins University Press, 1986).

Murray, Timothy, *Theatrical Legitimation: Allegories of Genius in Seventeenth-Century England and France* (Oxford: Oxford University Press, 1987).

Saunders, J. W., "The Stigma of Print: A Note on the Social Bases of Tudor Poetry," *Essays in Criticism* (1951): 139–64.

Siebert, Fredrick Seaton, *Freedom of the Press in England, 1476–1776: The Rise and Decline of Government Controls* (Urbana: University of Illinois Press, 1952).

Wall, Wendy, *The Imprint of Gender: Authorship and Publication in the English Renaissance* (Ithaca, NY: Cornell University Press, 1993).

Watt, Tessa, *Cheap Print and Popular Piety, 1550–1640* (Cambridge: Cambridge University Press, 1991).

5

CATHERINE BATES

Poetry, patronage, and the court

In the sixteenth century poetry followed patronage like a shadow. At a time when the newly invented printing press was disseminating texts at a rate never before imagined, writers, editors, translators, and compilers did not earn a living from their labors. Receiving a single payment for their manuscripts but no royalties thereafter, writers remained as dependent on patrons for employment, retainerships, and cash rewards as they had done in the age of scribal reproduction.[1] To publish was not to profit, and the days when a writer might make a fortune from his pen and claim, as Pope did, to be "Above a Patron," were still a long way off. Literature that was written at the behest of a patron, literature that aimed to attract a patron, literature that ruminated the vagaries of the patronage system, literature that deplored its shortcomings – these account for so large a proportion of sixteenth-century writing that the literature of the period has not unreasonably been described as a "literature of patronage."[2]

Many writers looked with hopeful prospect toward the court. The Tudors used patronage as a way of regulating the flow of gifts in order to implement their overall policy of centralizing political power, and – in their canny distribution of titles, lands, livings, offices, sinecures, monopolies, and wardships – they successfully transformed what had once been an overweening nobility into what Lawrence Stone calls a "set of shameless mendicants."[3] Patronage extended, pyramid-fashion, all the way down the social hierarchy – favored nobles and gentry themselves bestowing the positions and livings that were within their gift – but the monarch remained at the apex of the triangle and was perceived as the ultimate source of bounty and munificence.

That the court was, in addition, a center of literary and cultural patronage owed much to the Tudor flair for publicity and a shrewd recognition that writers could serve the royal turn. Henry VII was the first English king to appoint an official King's Poet; and, if the lavish rewards paid out each year to Bernard André for his eulogistic *Annales* are anything to go by (an annual pension of £24 plus 100 shillings on the presentation of each new *Annal*), the first incumbent evidently more than fulfilled his brief. Henry VII was concerned that his court appear a place of culture and seat of learning and to this end he appointed a permanent Royal Librarian to look after a fast-expanding book collection. Court poets such as Pietro Carmeliano, Giovanni Gigli, Stephen Hawes, and John Skelton were expected to turn out verse to mark special events and royal occasions, and poets were appointed as tutors and chaplains to the royal princes. Henry VIII continued the tradition his father had begun and in 1512 appointed his old tutor Skelton to the post of King's Poet, while also gathering around himself scholars and lettered men of the younger, humanistic generation, such that an admiring Erasmus could compare the royal court to a university. Writing in what he perceived to be a more niggardly age, George Puttenham was to recall how Henry VIII "for a few Psalms of David turned into English meter by [Thomas] Sternhold, made him groom of his privy chamber and gave him many other good gifts," although not long after these words were published even the parsimonious Elizabeth was to reward Spenser with an annual pension of £50 in return for *The Faerie Queene*, a sum which appears to have been paid out regularly until his death.[4] The court also commissioned writers for more overtly propagandist purposes, Thomas Cromwell employing such talented polemicists as Thomas Starkey to take up the cause of the King's "great matter" in the 1530s, and the Elizabethan bishops hiring popular writers such as Lyly and Nashe to counter the seditious Marprelate tracts in the late 1580s. Indeed, since the post-Reformation church was no longer independent of secular jurisdiction but under the government of the state, church patronage – including the appointment of talented men to livings, bishoprics, and university fellow-ships – naturally became an extension of court patronage. The church fielded apologists for the state religion, and ecclesiastical patronage must include among its cultural productions such celebrated contributions to English prose-writing as John Foxe's *Acts and Monuments* – that vast history and martyrology of the church, a copy of which was ordered to lie in every parish church – and Richard Hooker's reasoned defense of balance and toleration, the *Laws of Ecclesiastical Polity*.

The court had an interest in setting forth its magnificence – a princely virtue newly reendorsed by the *Nichomachean Ethics* – and throughout the sixteenth century Europe witnessed an unprecedented princely expenditure on palace-building, portraiture, and pageantry. A successful prince, Machiavelli advised, should entertain his people with festivities and shows, and the Tudors immediately grasped the promotional power of such displays. The century began as it was to go on with the lavish entertainments designed by William Cornish, a Gentleman of the Chapel Royal, to celebrate the marriage of Prince Arthur to Katherine of Aragon in 1501 and the consolidation of the dynasty that such a union was intended to represent. An extravagant multimedia event followed, involving Burgundian allegorical pageant cars – a castle full of ladies, a fully rigged ship, a "Mount of Love" containing amorous knights – together with poetry, music, singing, and dancing. Such disguisings were to continue unabated throughout Henry VIII's reign (to be faithfully chronicled by Edward Hall), lay behind those state-sponsored displays of public devotion, the Elizabethan Accession Day Tilts, and were to culminate in that collaboration of writer and artist in the celebration of royal hegemony that, in the days of Jonson and Inigo Jones, was to be the fully fledged Stuart court masque.

Seen in terms of payments made to writers in return for panegyrics and apologias, patronage appears at its simplest and most direct. But the transaction was, of course, a two-way process, and, if the court was, in Gabriel Harvey's words, "the only mart of preferment and honor," then it was, like any marketplace, thronged with as many sellers as buyers.[5] From the top down in this overcrowded exchange, poetry served as a form of unofficial currency and was used to buy anything from royal favor to a straightforward cash reward. "Verses are grown such merchantable ware," wrote Sir John Harington, "That now for sonnets, sellers are and buyers."[6] Courtier-poets like Ralegh and Essex would rifle poetic convention in order to catch the favor of the Queen: "Then must I needs advance my self by skill, / And live to serve, in hope of your goodwill" – and would do exactly the same if they lost it.[7] At the next level were those who, like Donne, had been educated at the universities or Inns of Court and used their writing as a way of displaying their credentials with a view to gaining employment as tutors, secretaries, chaplains, or lawyers in the noble households. Such men – for whom writing was a means to an end – poetry "hath done much for," Jonson was drily to remark, "and advanced in the way of their own professions (both the Law, and the Gospel) beyond all they could have hoped, or done for themselves, without her favor."[8]

Suitors turned their hands to a variety of poetic forms and genres in order to bend their prospective patrons' ears. One of the most direct means was the drama and spectacle for which there was already a tradition and style well established by court-sponsored pageants and shows. The Earl of Leicester's lavish entertainment of Queen Elizabeth at Kenilworth in 1575 – a medley of dramatic entertainments and costumed devices interspersed with bear-baiting, hunting, and jousts – became a prototype for the entertainments laid on during later Elizabethan progresses and one of the ways in which courtiers sought to flatter, petition, or appease their sovereign. In 1578 or 1579 Philip Sidney composed his playlet, *The Lady of May* – a drama in which Elizabeth was suddenly accosted, while walking in the garden at Leicester's Wanstead House, by a troupe of actors who drew her into their fiction and invited her to arbitrate a dispute between two rival suitors for the May Lady's hand. Sidney's drama has traditionally been linked to the political issue most current at the time – the question of Elizabeth's marriage and the deep unpopularity (among Leicester's Protestant faction) of the Catholic French prince, Alençon, as a proposed suitor. By courteously leaving Elizabeth to adjudicate the quarrel, however, Sidney stresses the delicate balance of the question – debated, like any academic disputation, *in utramque partem* (on either side) – rather than its resolution, thus dramatizing the courtier's own vulnerability, not to say powerlessness, in the face of royal whim. At the same time, entertainments staged during state visits gave individuals an opportunity to make themselves noticed and were an invaluable first step on the ladder to appointment and success. On the occasion of Elizabeth's visit to Oxford in 1566 the University presented a host of orations and plays, both in Latin and in English. One of the spectacles to which Elizabeth was treated was a two-part performance of *Palemon and Arcite*, an English play based on Chaucer's *Knight's Tale* and composed by the Master of the Children of the Chapel Royal, Richard Edwards. The performance took place in Christ Church and included a simulated fox-hunt (reportedly very realistic). The liveliness and press of the crowd was such as to make a stone wall collapse, causing several in the audience to be killed or injured. But, this accident aside, the show brought to Elizabeth's attention the talents of the cast, which included the young Tobie Matthew (later Dean of Christ Church and Archbishop of York) and John Rainolds (future president of Corpus Christi College). The latter received eight angels (eighty shillings) from the Queen for his performance of Hippolyta.

Writers also dedicated works to patrons in the hope that their elevated status would enhance the book, stimulate sales, and protect it from detractors: "If your Highness will read it," wrote Harington to Elizabeth, dedicating to her his translation of the *Orlando Furioso* (1591), "who dare reject it? if allow it, who can reprove it? if protect it, what MOMUS barking or ZOILUS biting can any way hurt or annoy it?"[9] Multiple dedications allowed poets to spread their portfolio of assets more widely: Spenser appended first ten and then seventeen dedicatory sonnets to the 1590 edition of *The Faerie Queene*, Henry Lok sixty to his *Ecclesiastes* (1597), and Geoffrey Whitney over ninety to his *Choice of Emblems* (1586). It was hoped that a dedication might elicit a cash reward from the individual so favored, and it was presumably to milk this system that writers such as Robert Greene dedicated seventeen books to sixteen different patrons, or Thomas Lodge, eighteen of his works (including translations) to as many "true Mæcenases." Quite what a writer might hope to receive for his trouble could vary a good deal. Richard Robinson, a hard-pressed Freeman of the Leathersellers' Company who sought to eke out a living by translating works and dedicating them to wealthy patrons, records receiving anything from a niggardly two shillings from the Bishop of Chichester ("not so thankful as I deserved," he comments) to an ecstatic six angels (sixty shillings) from the Earl of Rutland, "my best benefactor and patron."[10] In literature, the tight-fisted patron is a regular butt of satire, giving away now a "french crown," now a paltry two groats, now a mere "cap and thanks" – "wherefore," advises Nashe's Pierce Penniless, "I would counsel my friends to be more considerate in their dedications, and not cast away so many months labor on a clown that knows not how to use a scholar: for what reason have I to bestow any of my wit upon him, that will bestow none of his wealth upon me?"[11]

Pierce – the impoverished poet who for lack of patronage is forced to sue to the Devil for favor – advises his peers to lower the value of their stock in order to bring it into line with the current rate of exchange. Nashe ironically projects a system in which value is calculated exactly: a tightly managed exchange in which there is no surplus, neither a surplus of poets to patrons nor a surplus of poetic capital (what is left over when the product of "many months labor" is bought on the cheap). What is ironic is his alignment of two quite different worlds: a stable and regulated exchange-economy as against the deregulated, inflationary economy of capitalistic venture. Throughout this period, writers hark back to the former as an idealized, feudal past in which the circulation of benefits was wholly balanced and contained – a world in which a perfect reciprocity existed between poet and patron and between what one party "bestowed" upon the other. In Alexander Barclay's fourth Eclogue, "treating of the behavior of rich men against poets," the disgruntled poet Minalcas evokes such a world when he puts it to the wealthy Codrus that

> If I feed thy ears, feed thou my mouth again,
> I loth were to spend my gifts all in vain.
> Meat unto the mouth is food and sustenance,
> And songs feed the ears with pleasance.
> I have the Muses, if thou wilt have of mine,
> Then right requireth that I have part of thine.[12]

This ancient "right" – elsewhere described as a hallowed "law" (line 192) – underpinned this sentimentalized economy in which what was given was exactly recompensed by what was received. In this system there was no trading because the trade-off was guaranteed, and the value of the product was not at issue because it was stable and assured. Spenser evokes the same world in the dedicatory sonnets which he attached to the 1590 edition of *The Faerie Queene*. Addressing Lord Grey of Wilton as "Patron of my Muses pupillage" to whom he is "bound yours by vassalage," Spenser also suggests in the poem to Northumberland that "by like right" those who are praised by poets "are tied / T'embrace the service of sweet Poetry" and therefore obliged "To patronize the author of their praise."[13] Yet this world of *noblesse oblige*, in which ties of debt and obligation regulated the flow of gifts, is (if it ever existed) always presented as part of a long-vanished past. By contrast, the needy poet now finds himself in a fallen, mercantile economy of open competition where he is forced to sell his wares and, like Pierce Penniless, to adjust the value of his commodity to the going price. The same clash between two antithetical economic systems is adumbrated in *Timon of Athens*. Although the surplus here is that of the patron rather than the poet, its effect – that of destabilizing prices – is the same. An old-world courtesy where favor is met by favor is shown to be antiquated and hopelessly marooned in the self-serving and opportunistic present. Timon's fantastic liberality does not fit in with this system but instead generates a grotesque inflation in which the objects of exchange are correspondingly devalued and the query "What dost thou think 'tis worth?" becomes the unanswerable question of the play. In a world where goods are "rated / As those which sell would give," any sense of inherent value is put in doubt, and poets and painters are at one with jewelers and merchants in their enforced submission to market trends.[14]

These texts each rehearse the conflict between an old world in which poetry was "recompensed" (inherently valued) and a new world in which poetry is bought and sold (forced to find its price within a fluctuating market). Since the old days when poetry had been simply valued and rewarded are universally regarded as long gone, writers of the period constantly find themselves confronting the question of what price their art can command. There was a relentless calculation and evaluation of what the poet had to offer or to sell. Indeed, the sixteenth-century patronage system promoted an intense preoccupation with what poetry was worth. What exactly did the poet have to "bestow" upon a patron and what precisely was the value of the cultural capital at his disposal?

Writers were, unsurprisingly, apt to present the market as a buyers' rather than as a sellers' one, and, since they were writers, it is their struggles and frustrations with the system which have tended to get left on record. From the writer's point of view, it was a rare patron who valued the poet's gift more highly than he did, or who would protest (as Lord Mountjoy did to his protégé Erasmus in 1509) that "whereas you say you owe much to me, I am on the contrary so much in your debt for giving me immortality through your writings that I believe I must declare myself insolvent."[15] Mountjoy's patrician courtesy puts the writer's art on a different scale of reward so that the flow of goods is clearly weighted in the latter's favor. Far more common are the complaints that poetry is undervalued, incommensurate with a system of crude commodification and sullied by being brought into contact with it. "All Artists," wrote Nashe, are like

> the Indians, that have store of gold and precious stones at command, yet are ignorant of their value, and therefore let the Spaniards, the Englishmen and every one load their ships with them without molestation. So they, enjoying and possessing the purity of knowledge (a treasure far richer than the Indian Mines), let every proud Thraso be partaker of their perfections, repaying them no profit; and gild himself with the titles they give him, when he will scarce return them a good word for their labor.
>
> Nashe, *Pierce Penniless*, pp. 241–42

Here the relation between poet and patron is less one of exchange than of straightforward exploitation. Presented as the innocent inhabitants of a utopian world in which knowledge is prized above gold, writers are fleeced and defrauded by unscrupulous pirates who subscribe to a quite different set of values. Indeed, poets lose out on both counts, receiving by way of reward neither the commodity which the alien system values (gold) nor that upon which they set such store themselves, namely the "good word."

This theme is reiterated countless times. Complaining that poetry is undervalued, poets resort to claiming that poetry is above valuation – that it possesses a virtue which can neither be calculated nor quantified. This is the humanistic poetics whereby the poet enriches the world – converting the brazen into the golden, but according to some purifying alchemy by which the golden cannot then be converted back again into the brute cash value of "this beneath world" (*Timon of Athens*, 1.i.44). The poet lays claim to an aesthetic and moral economy where, in the words of Thomas Lodge, "wisdom is better than wealth, and a golden sentence worth a world of treasure."[16] Yet distinguishing between different kinds of gold – the aureate and the exchangeable – smacks of expediency and constantly begs the question of the correspondence between the two. "Cuddie, the praise is better than the price," says Piers, attempting to reinvigorate the disconsolate poet of Spenser's October Eclogue, "The glory eke much greater then the gain." But, in the harsh, practical world where poets have to earn their bread, this humanistic optimism offers Cuddie little comfort:

> So praysen babes the peacocks spotted train,
> And wondren at bright Argus blazing eye:
> But who rewards him ere the more for thy?
> Or feeds him once the fuller by a grain?
> Sike praise is smoke, that sheddeth in the sky,
> Sike words bene wind, and wasten soon in vain.[17]

The golden sentence of humanist poetics is forced of necessity to exchange itself for money. The poet must sing for his supper – a situation which gives rise to the disingenuous convolutions of the New Year's gift which Jonson presented to the Countess of Rutland (Sidney's daughter) in 1600:

> Madam,
> > Whilst that for which all virtue now is sold,
> > And almost every vice, almighty gold,
> > . . .
> > I, that have none to send you, send you verse.[18]

Putting poetry above pelf, Jonson attempts to invest his word-gift with a higher worth which, on recognizing, the Countess will properly reciprocate; except that what Jonson hopes for in return are, presumably, not the windy words (which he offers her in such abundance) but the very commodity of which he has "none" and which he spends most of the poem deriding – gold.

If the system of patronage provoked intense speculation about the worth of poetry, it also led to a rigorous reassessment of the poet himself. "They who write to Lords, rewards to get," wrote Donne scornfully, "Are they not like singers at doors for meat?"[19] The poet's dependence on patronage exposed him to the obvious charge of servility or worse – of "prostituting my pen like a courtesan," as Nashe puts it[20] – and the conflict between the poet's moral integrity on the one hand and his enforced servitude on the other did much to develop thinking on the poet's standing and status and on his claims to poetic authority. "In these days," wrote George Puttenham, ". . . as well poets and poesy are despised," and he defends poets against the accusation that they are mere "cunning Princepleasers" by taking the line, usual with the humanist educator, that the ability to write poetry signified the possession of other, ultimately more useful, transferable skills: "so as the poets seemed to have skill not only in the subtleties of their art, but also to be meet for all maner of functions civil and martial" (*Arte of English Poesie*, pp. 18, 17, 18). Throughout the period, writers would present themselves as "amateurs" or gentlemen-poets whose verses – modestly deprecated as "trifles" – were intended to display the poet's intellectual abilities and to indicate his commitment to the higher responsibilities of state service as churchman, statesman, or civil servant.

Patronage necessarily put the poet's autonomy into question. Over the last twenty years literary historians have looked more inquiringly into the dependent relation of poet to patron and have alerted us to the subtle negotiations, reciprocities, and circulations of power that existed between the two. In a recent essay, Louis Montrose compares the title pages of the 1590 and the 1596 *Faerie Queene* and suggests that, in the typographical advancement from a lowly "*Ed. Spenser*" in the first to a grandiose "EDMVND SPENSER" in the second – the poet's name here centered and presented in the same sized capitals as that of Elizabeth – this humble subject of the Queen is flexing his poetic muscle and asserting his own sovereign authority over the subject of his verse.[21] As the sociologist Pierre Bourdieu has noted, the exchange of gifts creates ties of debt and obligation between giver and receiver that amount to a form of "symbolic violence."[22] Although poets in this period were materially obliged to patrons for benefits and maintenance and universally presented themselves as their patrons' bounden servants to command, they were also able to turn the tables in their writings and, by placing the patron under obligation, to exert a symbolic violence of their own. The ways in which they might do this varied in subtlety. Nashe crudely literalizes this violence when he threatens that if no "Maecenas bind me to him by his bounty," he will, by way of revenge, "rail on him soundly ... in some elaborate, polished poem" with terms steeped in "aquafortis and gunpowder, that shall rattle through the skies, and make an earthquake in a peasant's ears" (*Pierce Penniless*, p. 195). Alexander Barclay is more cunning in his bid for patronage from the second Duke of Norfolk when he includes a doleful elegy on the latter's son within an eclogue that deplores the niggardliness of patrons – a device which amounts, in the words of one critic, to a kind of "fictional blackmail by proxy."[23] Craftier still is Spenser's gracious suggestion in the Proem to Book VI of *The Faerie Queene* that he has drawn his model of courtesy from Elizabeth herself:

> Then pardon me, most dreaded Sovereign,
> That from your self I do this virtue bring,
> And to your self do it return again:
> So from the Ocean all rivers spring,
> And tribute back repay as to their King.

This idealized model of gift-exchange – by which the poet returns only what he has received – carries with it the distinct implication that the poet's courteous tribute, flowing outwards like the tributary on which it puns, will keep the cycle turning and will bring him back some kind of reward.

The fact that, according to the metaphor, royal favor would involve the unnatural perversion of rivers flowing uphill, however, hints ruefully that even such gentle pressure can be guaranteed to yield no results, and Donne gives a more cynical version of the same motif in one of his satires when he describes suitors as "Springs; now full, now shallow, now dry; which, to / That which drowns them, run."[24]

In the undignified scramble by too many poets for too few favors, "It cannot be," wrote Daniel, "but they must throng the more, / And kick, and thrust, and shoulder with debate."[25] But if the patronage system did not ease the poet's situation, it did have one important literary payoff. For in this tense and tricky environment – fraught with frustration and compromise, in which autonomy and necessity constantly struggled with one another – poets developed a particular sensitivity to performance and role-play, and the result is some of the most densely multilayered literature of the period. Writers increasingly resorted to allegorical forms under whose "dark terms" and "dark conceit" they might, like Chapman, "labor to be shadowed," and behind whose smooth and discreet forms they might – like their poetry itself – contrive successfully to masquerade.[26] As Puttenham put it, "beau semblant" was "the chief profession as well of courting as of poesy" (*Arte of English Poesie*, p. 158). Moreover, this kind of playacting also allowed poets to protest, complain, and criticize the system while still belonging to it and hoping to benefit by it. One standard motif in the repertory of roles is that of the plain man or "silly shepherd" who, like Spenser's Colin Clout, refuses to playact and rejects the inveigling duplicities of "courting vain."[27] In the best satirical tradition, this plain soul asserts his autonomy by retiring in despair from the court to the earthy simplicity of "Kent and Christendom" (as Wyatt) and to the moral integrity of the centered self, "At home in wholesome solitariness" (as Donne).[28] Rustic retirement freed the poet from the compromising exigencies of patronage, and, as Sidney wrote, since shepherds "know not how to feign, / Nor with love to cloak disdain," their words bear the imprint of their sincerity.[29] The point, however, is that this role is entirely conventional and that, as a rhetorical device, it allowed poets to rehearse their discontents while at the same time displaying their qualities of seriousness (all the stronger for being differentiated from mere empty flattery) as part of a bid to get back into the system and to sell themselves to the highest bidder.

Finally, it was through the system of patronage – more, perhaps, than anything else – that women were to have an important impact on the history of sixteenth-century letters. From Lady Margaret Beaufort, who sponsored the printer Wynkyn de Worde, and Katherine Parr, who patronized such humanist projects as a translation of Erasmus' *Paraphrases* on the

New Testament, to those great Elizabethan patronesses, the Countesses of Bedford and Pembroke, women did much to provide writers with both practical support and more general literary encouragement. Lucy Russell, wife of the third Earl of Bedford, received dedications from a host of writers, including Florio, Chapman and Davies, and was friends with Daniel, Drayton, Jonson, and Donne. Mary Herbert, Countess of Pembroke – the sister of that cultural legend and "general Mæcenas of learning," Sir Philip Sidney – was hailed by Nashe as "a second Minerva ... [whom] our poets extol as the patroness of their invention."[30] Samuel Daniel, who was tutor to her children, gratefully recalls how the family seat at Wilton was his own "best school," and John Aubrey was to perpetuate her reputation as "the greatest patroness of wit and learning" again by describing Wilton as "like a College."[31]

In addressing themselves specifically to female patrons, moreover, male poets had recourse to a literary role that was as conventional but, if anything, even more adaptable than that of the disillusioned shepherd – namely, that of the lover. Throwing himself at the feet of a lady, protesting his own insufficiency and dependence on her grace, the male poet was able to play on the positional pun of being a suitor and to raid the tradition of courtly love for every trope of self-abasement and courteous request that lent itself to his petition. Dismissed on the accession of Henry VIII from the court position he had held under Henry VII, Stephen Hawes sued to the King's sister to be restored to royal favor by presenting himself, in *The Comfort of Lovers*, as the worthy if secret admirer of a lady who is far above his station. After some coy dissimulation, he eventually confesses to the "Pucell" that "It is your grace, that hath the interest / In my true heart, with love so fervently," and, although she does not yield to his passion, this gracious lady evidently appreciates his worthiness and expresses a fervent admiration for his poetry: "Of late I saw a book of your making / Called the pastime of pleasure, which is wond[rous]."[32] The role of lover and rapt admirer put at the poet's disposal a whole vocabulary of service and devotion and provided a context in which the most excessive expressions of ardor might be used to flatter a patroness into action. When the monarch herself happened to be a queen, of course, this model of the courtly suitor developed a particular resonance, and under Elizabeth poets from the most elevated to the most humble ransacked the tropes of Petrarchan convention in order to present themselves as worthy lovers of that object of universal devotion, England's Eliza.

One of the reasons why this motif enjoyed the vogue that it did in the period is that it allowed poets to examine and meditate on so many of the conditions and compromises of the patronage system. In the courtly lover's timeworn obsequies, for instance, the poet was able to rehearse his dependency and give voice to his disempowerment. At the same time, "by gesturing toward the controlling power of the writing subject over the representation he has made," he was also – as Montrose here suggests of Spenser – in a position to assert, or at least to explore the question of, his own poetic autonomy ("The Elizabethan Subject and the Spenserian Text," p. 320). If the suitor was not in control of his destiny, he was at least in command of his text, and, in his mastery both of rhetoric and of the mistress of his own inventing, he was able to exercise (even if only in fantasy) a "symbolic violence" all his own. In the lover's many roles, the poet might play out the period's fascination with masks and self-display, and, equally, cultivate a rhetoric of "cloudy figures" and "doubtful show."[33] And finally – in the intense and conceitful poetry that was the distillation of all these projections and desires – he might contemplate the intrinsic value of a literature which was, *faute de mieux*, a product of that busy mart of bargain and exchange that constituted the sixteenth-century patronage system.

NOTES

1 The standard price for a pamphlet or small volume of poetry in the Elizabethan period was forty shillings. The only writers in the period who were in a position to profit from their pens were the dramatists, but it was specifically the performance and not the publication of their plays that netted an income.
2 Patricia Thomson, "The Literature of Patronage 1580–1630," *Essays in Criticism* 2 (1952): 267–84.
3 Lawrence Stone, *The Crisis of the Aristocracy 1558–1641* (Oxford: Clarendon Press, 1965), p. 477.
4 George Puttenham, *The Arte of English Poesie* (1589), ed. G. D. Willcock and Alice Walker (Cambridge: Cambridge University Press, 1936), pp. 16–17.
5 Gabriel Harvey, *Marginalia*, ed. G. C. Moore Smith (Stratford on Avon: Shakespeare Head Press, 1913), p. 142.
6 Sir John Harington, *The Letters and Epigrams of Sir John Harington*, ed. Norman Egbert McClure (Philadelphia: University of Pennsylvania Press, 1930), p. 164.
7 From "Sweet are the thoughts," lines 11–12, in *The Poems of Sir Walter Ralegh*, ed. Agnes M. C. Latham (London: Routlege and Kegan Paul, 1951), p. 4.
8 Ben Jonson, *Discoveries*, in *Ben Jonson*, ed. C. H. Herford, Percy and Evelyn Simpson, 11 vols. (Oxford: Clarendon Press, 1925–52), vol. VIII, p. 583.
9 Sir John Harington, trans., *Ludovico Ariosto's Orlando Furioso*, ed. Robert McNulty (Oxford: Clarendon Press, 1972), p. 18.
10 Robinson's text, preserved in BM MS Royal 18 A.lxvi, is printed in George McGill Vogt, "Richard Robinson's *Eupolemia* (1603)," *Studies in Philology* 21 (1924): 629–48, these citations pp. 631, 633.
11 *Pierce Penniless his Supplication to the Devil* (1592), in *The Works of Thomas*

Nashe, ed. Ronald B. McKerrow, 5 vols. (Oxford: Blackwell, 1904–10, repr.1966), vol. I, p. 241.

12 Fourth Eclogue, lines 299–304, in *The Eclogues of Alexander Barclay*, ed. Beatrice White (London: Early English Text Society, 1928), pp. 150–51.

13 Edmund Spenser, *The Faerie Queene*, ed. A. C. Hamilton (London: Longman, 1977), pp. 742, 741.

14 *Timon of Athens*, I.i.213, 168–69, in *The Riverside Shakespeare*, ed. G. Blakemore Evans et al., 2nd edn. (Boston: Houghton Mifflin, 1997).

15 Letter from William Blount, Lord Mountjoy, to Erasmus, 27 May 1509, in *Collected Works of Erasmus*, 86 vols. (Toronto: University of Toronto Press, 1974), vol. II, p. 148 (letter no. 215).

16 Thomas Lodge, *Rosalynde* (1590), sig.B3.

17 *The Shepheardes Calender* (1579), October Eclogue, lines 19–20, 31–36, in *The Yale Edition of the Shorter Poems of Edmund Spenser*, ed. William A. Oram et al. (New Haven: Yale University Press, 1989), pp. 171, 172.

18 Jonson, *Epistle to Elizabeth, Countess of Rutland*, lines 1–2, 19, in *Jonson*, ed. Herford and Simpson, vol. VIII, p. 113.

19 Donne, *Satyre* II, lines 21–22, in *The Complete English Poems of John Donne*, ed. C. A. Patrides (London: Dent, 1985), p. 219.

20 Nashe, *Have With You to Saffron-Walden* (1596), in *Works*, ed. McKerrow, vol. III, p. 30.

21 Louis A. Montrose, "Spenser's Domestic Domain: Poetry, Property, and the Early Modern Subject," in *Subject and Object in Renaissance Culture*, ed. Margreta de Grazia, Maureen Quilligan, and Peter Stallybrass (Cambridge: Cambridge University Press, 1996), pp. 83–130, esp. pp. 87–91; Montrose here expands on the discussion on Spenser's authority which he first broached in "The Elizabethan Subject and the Spenserian Text," in *Literary Theory/Renaissance Texts*, ed. Patricia Parker and David Quint (Baltimore: Johns Hopkins University Press, 1986), pp. 303–40.

22 Pierre Bourdieu, *Outline of a Theory of Practice*, trans. Richard Nice (Cambridge: Cambridge University Press, 1977), pp. 190–97.

23 Alistair Fox, *Politics and Literature in the Reigns of Henry VII and Henry VIII* (Oxford: Blackwell, 1989), p. 54.

24 Donne, *Satyre* V, lines 15–16, in *Poems*, ed. Patrides, p. 241.

25 Samuel Daniel, *Musophilus* (1599), lines 456–57, in *Poems and A Defence of Ryme*, ed. Arthur Colby Sprague (Chicago: University of Chicago Press, 1930), p. 82.

26 "Dark terms," from Puttenham, *The Arte of English Poesie*, p. 186; "dark conceit" from Spenser's Letter to Ralegh, prefatory to *The Faerie Queene*; the reference to Chapman comes from *Ovids Banquet of Sense* (1595): "Obscurity in affection of words and indigested conceits, is pedantical and childish; but where it shroudeth itself in the heart of his subject, uttered with fitness of figure and expressive epithets, with that darkness will I still labor to be shadowed."

27 Spenser, *Colin Clout's Come Home Againe* (1595), line 790, in *The Yale Edition of the Shorter Poems*, ed. Oram, p. 555.

28 Wyatt, "Mine own John Poins," line 100, in *Collected Poems of Sir Thomas Wyatt*, ed. Kenneth Muir and Patricia Thomson (Liverpool: University of Liverpool Press, 1969), p. 91; Donne, *Satyre* IV, line 155, in *Poems*, ed. Patrides, p. 236.

29 Sidney, "Disprayse of a Courtly life," lines 39–40, in *The Poems of Sir Philip Sidney*, ed. W. A. Ringler (Oxford: Clarendon Press, 1962), p. 263.
30 Fulke Greville, "A Dedication to Sir Philip Sidney," in *The Prose Works of Fulke Greville, Lord Brooke*, ed. John Gouws (Oxford: Clarendon Press, 1986), p. 21; Nashe, Preface to *Astrophil and Stella* (1591), in *Works*, ed. McKerrow, vol. III, p. 331.
31 Daniel, *A Defence of Ryme* (1603), in *Poems*, ed. Sprague, p. 129; John Aubrey, *Brief Lives*, ed. Oliver Lawson Dick (Harmondsworth: Penguin, 1972), p. 297.
32 Stephen Hawes, *The Comfort of Lovers* (?1510–11), lines 808–09, 785–86, in *The Minor Poems*, ed. Florence Gluck and Alice Morgan (London: Early English Text Society, 1974), p. 117.
33 "Cloudy figures," from Hawes, *The Comfort of Lovers*, line 1, in *Minor Poems*, ed. Gluck and Morgan, p. 93; "doubtful show" from George Gascoigne, "The Adventures of Master F. J.," in *A Hundred Sundrie Flowres* (1573), ed. C. T. Prouty (Columbia: University of Missouri Press, 1942), p. 53.

FURTHER READING

Anglo, Sydney, *Spectacle, Pageantry, and Early Tudor Policy* (Oxford: Clarendon Press, 1969).
Bennett, H. S., *English Books and Readers 1475–1557*, and *English Books and Readers 1558–1603* (Cambridge: Cambridge University Press, 1952, 1965).
Brennan, Michael, *Literary Patronage in the English Renaissance: The Pembroke Family* (London: Routledge, 1988).
Dorsten, Jan van, *Poets, Patrons, and Professors: Sir Philip Sidney, Daniel Rogers, and the Leiden Humanists* (Leiden: Leiden University Press, 1962).
Eisenstein, Elizabeth L., *The Printing Press as an Agent of Change* (Cambridge: Cambridge University Press, 1979).
Fogle, French R. and Louis A. Knafla, *Patronage in Late Renaissance England* (Los Angeles: William Andrews Clark Memorial Library, 1983).
Hannay, Margaret P., ed., *Silent But For The Word: Tudor Women as Patrons, Translators, and Writers of Religious Works* (Kent, OH: Kent State University Press, 1985).
Helgerson, Richard, *Self-Crowned Laureates: Spenser, Jonson, Milton and the Literary System* (Berkeley and London: University of California Press, 1983).
Hutson, Lorna, *The Usurer's Daughter: Male Friendship and Fictions of Women in Sixteenth-Century England* (London: Routledge, 1994).
Kipling, Gordon, *The Triumph of Honour: Burgundian Origins of the Elizabethan Renaissance* (Leiden: Leiden University Press, 1977).
Lytle, Guy Fitch and Stephen Orgel, eds., *Patronage in the Renaissance* (Princeton: Princeton University Press, 1981).
Rosenberg, Eleanor, *Leicester, Patron of Letters* (New York: Columbia University Press, 1955).
Sheavyn, Phoebe, *The Literary Profession in the Elizabethan Age*, 2nd edn. (Manchester: Manchester University Press, 1967).
Wall, Wendy, *The Imprint of Gender: Authorship and Publication in the English Renaissance* (Ithaca, NY: Cornell University Press, 1993).

6

JOHN N. KING

Religious writing

Elizabeth I (1558–1603) may never have uttered the famous words attributed to her in a letter by Sir Francis Bacon: "I would not open windows into men's souls."[1] Her division between conformity in public worship and private religious sensibility reverses the authoritarian view that governmental fiat determines religious conviction. Elizabeth's acknowledgment of liberty of conscience free from surveillance sounds apocryphal, but the remark does correspond to the Queen's secretiveness about her personal beliefs.

Liberty of conscience was not the case when Sir Thomas More, despite his legalistic strategy of maintaining silence concerning his refusal to acquiesce to the Royal Supremacy over the church, was convicted of treason at the outset of the political Reformation under Henry VIII (1509–47). Perjured testimony that the humanist scholar, lawyer, and former Lord Chancellor of England had denied the King's supremacy in the Church of England led to his condemnation. Before his death sentence was handed down, More discharged his conscience by defending ecclesiastical unity and objecting to royal control of the church.

Cunning silence protected Elizabeth, however, during the regime of her elder Catholic sister, who enjoys a lurid reputation as "Bloody Mary" (1553–58) because of the persecution of hundreds of Protestant martyrs during her reign. John Foxe records the shrewd Princess Elizabeth's masterstroke of self-fashioning when she departed from Woodstock Manor, where she had been held under house arrest. Wittily employing a diamond to inscribe the following epigram upon a pane of glass, she closed a window into her soul:

> Much suspected by me,
> Nothing proved can be;
> Quoth Elizabeth prisoner.[2]

The narrative account of Elizabeth's imprisonment that concludes Foxe's *Book of Martyrs* idealizes the princess as a Protestant heroine who eluded a close brush with martyrdom, despite conformity to Roman-rite worship and attendance at Mass during her sister's reign. Keeping her own counsel throughout her life, Elizabeth's inward beliefs concerning religion and other matters remained enigmatic. Needless to say, Foxe and other Protestants gave little note to the execution of 180 Jesuit missionary priests by the Elizabethan regime.

Both Thomas More and Queen Elizabeth fully understood that politics and religion were inseparable in Tudor England. The Vatican canonized Thomas More in 1935 as a saint and martyr for resisting Henry VIII's schism from the Church of Rome, but his stance was treasonous in the eyes of the King, who seized control of the Church of England as an "English Pope" under the Act of Supremacy (1534). Modern readers have misunderstood More's *Utopia* (1516) as a forerunner of arguments of religion because of the Utopians' apparent insistence upon religious tolerance, but the citizens of Utopia are forbidden to profess mortality of the soul and atheism. In line with Michel Foucault's views on the pervasive surveillance of the early modern state ("panopticism"), Utopian law permits governors to brainwash dissenters until they agree.

We need to remember that *Utopia* was published in elegantly stylized Latin, without an English translation, for an audience of Continental humanists. It appeared only one year before Martin Luther triggered the Protestant Reformation when he attached his Ninety-five Theses detailing the alleged failures of the Roman church to the door of Castle Church in Wittenberg. Before and after More became Lord Chancellor upon the fall of Cardinal Thomas Wolsey in 1529, he emulated the verbal violence of Luther's invective style to attack the emergent Reformation. His *Dialogue Concerning Heresies* (1529) elicited William Tyndale's *Answer unto Sir Thomas More's Dialogue* (1531), in response to which More wrote *The Confutation of Tyndale's Answer* (1532).

Heretics' pyres may be absent in mythical Utopia, but Lord Chancellor More had heretics tortured at his Chelsea household, burning them alive. Protestants attacked his savagery before Henry VIII initiated the political Reformation that resulted in More's decapitation. Ascending the scaffold in 1535, he jested with the Lieutenant of the Tower of London: "See me safe up and, for my coming down, let me shift for myself." In a speech delivered before his execution, he affirmed "that he should now there suffer death in and for the faith of the Holy Catholc Church."[3] His execution, like that of Bishop John Fisher, aroused an international furor. Little more than a year later, Imperial agents in the Low Countries burned alive More's Protestant antagonist, William Tyndale, for translating the Bible into the English language. Meeting the same end as More, his last words were "Lord, open the King of England's eyes."[4]

In investigating windows into the soul opened by the rich variety of Tudor religious writing, this chapter considers the interplay among literary and nonliterary texts within their historical, political, and cultural contexts. This was an age dominated by the Henrician Reformation, which transformed the Church of England while leaving Catholic theology and ritual intact (1529–38); King Henry's rejection of evangelical Protestantism (1538–47); the radically Protestant Reformation under Edward VI, a sickly and short-lived boy (1547–53); Mary I's restoration of Catholicism (1553–58); and the Elizabethan reinstatement of the Edwardian Reformation in the guise of a compromise between Protestant theology and Catholic ritual (1558–63), which remained in place until long after Elizabeth's death in 1603. Only recently have revisionist historians like Christopher Haigh and Eamon Duffy initiated a controversial attempt to dismantle the long-standing understanding of sixteenth-century English history as a triumph of Protestantism.[5] Instead, they call attention to the vagaries of dynastic politics and the survival of Catholic resistance to changes in religion under Henry VIII and his Protestant offspring, Edward and Elizabeth.

BIBLE TRANSLATION

No printed version of the English Bible existed until Tyndale undertook its translation. Forced to emigrate by hostile authorities, Tyndale secured publication of his New Testament at Worms in 1526. He acted upon the Lutheran principle of "scripture alone" which insisted upon the primacy of the Bible and heeded the humanist call to return to the Hebrew and Greek texts of the Bible. Tyndale's colloquial diction owes much to Erasmus' appeal in *Paraclesis* ("Exhortation"), the preface to his Greek New Testament, that humble plowmen and "even the lowliest women" be allowed to read the Bible.[6] Tyndale defined his audience thus: "If God spare my life, ere many years I will cause a boy that driveth the plow shall know more of the Scripture than thou dost."[7] Tyndale's publication was an affordable text that appealed to a popular lay readership. By contrast with the periodic sentence structure of Thomas More's Latinate prose style, Tyndale's scripturalism is marked by binary constructions, syntactic parallelism, and radical antitheses as, for example, in this memorable passage from the Sermon on the Mount: "No man can serve two masters. For either he shall hate the one and love the other: or else he shall lean to the one and despise the other: ye cannot serve God and Mammon" (Matt. 6:24).[8]

Tyndale antagonized Henry VIII and English prelates by publishing an unauthorized biblical translation and incorporating Lutheran ideology in his prefaces, notes, and translations. The evangelical Protestant bias denoted by his use of "congregation" instead of "church" and "elder" instead of "priest" is well known. Recognizing the dissident potential of Tyndale's version, Thomas More defended readings like "church" and "priest" in his *Dialogue Concerning Heresies*.[9] In addition to the New Testament, Tyndale finished the Pentateuch, Jonah, and other portions of the Old Testament by the time of his execution. Filled with what are now proverbial expressions like "Seek, and ye shall find" (Matt. 7:7) and "Neither cast ye your pearls before swine" (Matt. 7:6), Tyndale's Bible has exerted a greater influence upon English language and literature than Shakespeare's plays.

Published in 1535, the first complete English Bible contains translations by Tyndale and its compiler, Miles Coverdale. Unlike Tyndale, who worked from the original Hebrew and Greek, Coverdale used Luther's German New Testament, the Vulgate, and other Latin versions. Although the Coverdale Bible was not authorized, the title page border by Hans Holbein the Younger, court portraitist to Henry VIII, implies the existence of official approval. It portrays the King handing the translation to the bishops kneeling before him (figure 10). In 1537 John Rogers anonymously compiled the officially licensed "Matthew" Bible out of translations by Tyndale and Coverdale.

These works led the way for the landmark appearance of the Great Bible (1539) under Henry VIII, whose Second Royal Injunctions ordered the purchase of "one book of the whole Bible of the largest volume, in English"[10] by every parish church, where chained copies were freely accessible to parishioners. Revising the "Matthew" Bible, Coverdale combined Tyndale's suspect work and his own translations. The Great Bible in England had gone in the direction of evangelical reform despite the retention of traditional theology and the Mass. The absence of doctrinal notes and prefaces provides an index of the volume's theological conservatism, because the King understood that uncontrolled interpretation would lead to divisiveness in religion.

John Bale recognized the subversive potential of the English Bible in *The Image of Both Churches* (1545?), the first commentary upon the Book of Revelation printed in the English language. It interprets Christian history as a conflict between the "true" Christian church and the "false" church of the papal Antichrist. Bale's interpretation of the golden cup carried by the Whore of Babylon (Rev. 17:4) typifies his turgid propagandistic style: "This cup is the false religion that she daily ministereth, besides the chalice whom

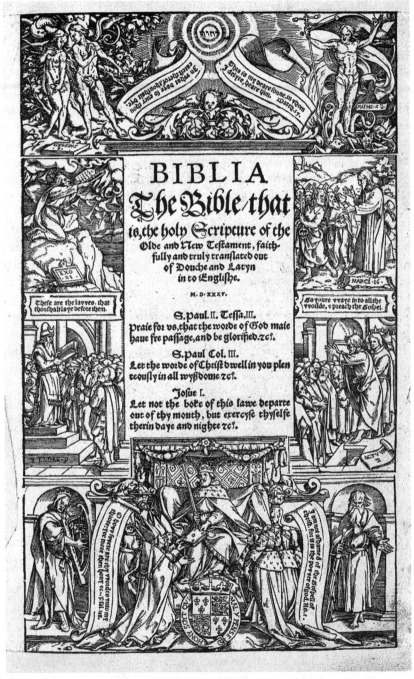

10 Hans Holbein the Younger, *The Coverdale Bible* (Antwerp, 1535), title page.

her merchants most damnably abuse."[11] Of course, Roman Catholic opponents reversed the equation by opposing the "true" church of Rome, identified with the Woman Clothed with the Sun (Rev. 12), to Protestantism as the Babylonian Whore.

Protestant exiles who fled to the Continent from persecution under Mary I created a radically different translation: the Geneva Bible (1560). It improves upon the philological scholarship in Tyndale's text and other earlier versions. Intended for popular readership, this version introduces the division of the text into verses to facilitate quick reference and includes a didactic concordance, illustrations, maps, and tables. Modern English Bibles retain the layout of this edition. The Geneva Bible's strident annotations held out a special appeal to the Puritans. Its readers included poets such as William Shakespeare and Edmund Spenser and even Matthew Parker, Archbishop of Canterbury, who opposed its public use. Parker organized production of the noncontroversial Bishops' Bible (1568), a modification of the Great Bible, for use in church services and to counter the popular appeal of the Geneva Bible.

The Rheims-Douai Bible provided a Roman Catholic alternative to English Protestant Bibles. A group of exiles at the seminary at Rheims produced the New Testament in 1582; publication of the Old Testament followed at Douai in 1609–10. This literal translation of the Vulgate version employs Latinate diction and technical vocabulary dissimilar from the more popular, vernacular style of the Protestant Bibles.

The continuing opposition of Puritans to the Bishops' Bible led to the production of the King James Bible, also known as the Authorized Version (1611). Like the Great Bible and the Bishops' Bible, it incorporates conservative ecclesiastical vocabulary and lacks annotations. The translation is justly famous for its stylistic virtuosity, but it should be remembered that Tyndale's diction provides the foundation for all later Renaissance Bibles. Despite its archaic resonance to the modern ear, the King James Bible and the Tyndale diction that it preserves are still in use today.

BIOGRAPHY, AUTOBIOGRAPHY, AND MARTYROLOGY

The heretical interpretation of the Bible by Anne Askew provides a classic example of the divisiveness so feared by Henry VIII. She violated the prohibition against the participation of women in theological debate and denied the Catholic doctrine of transubstantiation and the ritual of the Mass. Her interrogation by ecclesiastical and secular authorities ended in the unprecedented torture and racking of a woman. She was burned alive in 1546, near the end of Henry VIII's reign.

Askew wrote an eloquent autobiographical account of her interrogations, trial, and conviction. The two parts of her *Examinations* (1546–47) were edited by John Bale during his first Continental exile and smuggled into England. The texts accord with Bale's transformation of traditional saint's life into Protestant martyrology by means of the commentaries that he added to those editions. Rejecting the medieval formula that presented miracle-working saints as intermediaries between believers and Christ, Bale follows New Testament precedent in styling the genre of a Protestant saint's life as an account of a humble believer who is faithful to Christ to the point of death.

The clearly drawn gender conflict in Askew's *Examinations* highlights important questions concerning the Protestant attack on transubstantiation and the Mass, transmission of texts, martyrology, the education of women, and narrative art. Even though Bale presents Askew in the stereotypical role of a weak woman who can resist injustice only through divine grace, the victim fashioned her own identity as a strong woman motivated by intense religious conviction, but one who avoids hyperbolic polemical rhetoric. Laced with scriptural references and ironic applications of biblical typology, her plain colloquial language violates the patriarchal expectation that a virtuous woman remain silent and obedient. Thus she lodges the startling claim that despite torture on the rack, which left her unable to stand, she "sat two long hours reasoning with my Lord Chancellor upon the bare floor, where as he with many flattering words persuaded [i.e., attempted to persuade] me to leave my opinion. But my Lord God (I thank his everlasting goodness) gave me grace to persevere." Bale alters the tenor of Askew's plain language, however, by adding a highly fraught commentary filled with outbursts against the tyrannous "practice of devilishness," "forsaken reprobates," and "wicked desperates [that] have the voluptuous pleasures of this vain world so dear."[12] On different occasions Askew quietly employed sarcastic devices including rhetorical questions, ironic smiles, and gestures to mock transubstantiation, the Mass, and other Roman Catholic beliefs and worship practices. Nevertheless, she remained capable of exploiting the feminine obligation of silent obedience when she refused to confess and implicate aristocratic women who sent money to her in prison.

Just before the Anne Askew affair broke open, the eleven-year-old Princess Elizabeth translated "The Glass of the Sinful Soul" (1544), a loosely structured penitential meditation by Margaret of Navarre, *Le Miroir de l'âme pécheresse* (1531). Elizabeth embroidered the covers for the manuscript, fashioning it as a 1544 New Year gift to Katherine Parr, Henry VIII's sixth and final wife. The test demonstrates the princess' learning to the stepmother who commissioned humanist tutors like John Cheke and Roger Ascham to educate her along with Lady Jane Grey and others at the royal school that Parr organized for the education of young Prince Edward. A few mistranslations, notably Elizabeth's rendering of "Père" as "Mother,"[13] open a window into the soul of a daughter deeply troubled by her father's judicial murder of her mother, Anne Boleyn, from whom she may have inherited the French original. Even though the pious meditations in Elizabeth's "Glass" do not contain Protestant doctrine as such, the "Epistle Dedicatory" and "Conclusion" of the printed text, *A Godly Meditation of the Christian Soul* (1548), demonstrate how John Bale edited it alongside Askew's *Examinations* as a document compatible with the radical Protestant climate of Edward VI's reign.

Queen Katherine occupied a precarious position within a royal court dominated by a cruel spouse notorious for executing two wives, Anne Boleyn and Katherine Howard. In keeping with the prohibition upon dissemination of Protestant ideas in the Act of Six Articles (1539), Parr's *Prayers Stirring the Mind unto Heavenly Meditations* (1545) contains noncontroversial, evangelical devotions akin to those in Elizabeth's "Glass," a text symbolic of a mirror for, not a window into, the soul. It consists of rewritten excerpts from an English translation of Book 3 of Thomas à Kempis' later medieval devotional masterpiece, *The Imitation of Christ*, to which Parr adds a set of five original prayers including one "for the King" and another concerning warfare, which may reflect her own position as Regent during Henry's absence from England during his invasion of France in 1544.

The devout meditations in Parr's *Lamentation of a Sinner* open a window into a queenly soul that is utterly lacking in precedent. William Cecil, secretary to Protector Somerset, who controlled England at the onset of Edward VI's reign, edited the text for publication at the behest of Catherine, Duchess of Suffolk. Its publication is compatible with the radical temper of Edwardian England, when advanced Protestant theology held sway. Written under the influence of Tyndale's New Testament, writings by Cranmer, and Hugh Latimer's sermons, this conversion narrative is filled with Protestant assertions concerning justification by faith alone, saving grace, divine election, and predestination. It takes the form of highly personalized, free-flowing, vernacular meditations like the following: "But we worse than frantic or blind will not follow Christ's doctrine, but trust to men's doctrines, judgments, and sayings, which dimmeth our eyes: and so the blind leadeth them, and both fall into the ditch."[14]

Autobiographical narrative was the preserve of men as well as women.

The Vocation of John Bale (1553) records the author's experience from the time of his appointment by Edward VI as Bishop of Ossory, a diocese in southern Ireland, until his flight into a second Continental exile upon the accession of Mary I one year later. With its focus upon individual salvation, the *Vocation* looks like a precursor of the spiritual autobiographies that became fashionable within seventeenth-century Puritan circles. The text documents continual conflict between an uncompromising missionary bishop and the Irish clergy, upon whom he vents fury for the breaking of religious vows, and the people whom he attempted to convert. Styling himself as a martyr (Greek "witness"), Bale fashions an identity as one who testifies to Christian faith, to the point of death if necessary.

Bale's brisk narrative recounts the poisoning of his superior, Archbishop Goodacre; the murder of Bale's own servants for obeying his orders to mow hay on a Catholic feast day; his flight from priests who attempted to kill him; his captivity by a sea rover and ensuing voyage to a safe haven on the Continent. He retells ludicrous anticlerical anecdotes about a supercilious cleric who boasts about being sired by an abbot; about a priest who uses Eucharistic bread as fish bait; and about another who "pissed" in the mouth of a parishioner, he "being gaping asleep in the church after evensong."[15]

The history of the church and collection of martyrologies in John Foxe's *Acts and Monuments of the English Martyrs* is the most renowned Elizabethan prose text after the English Bible (figure 11). Foxe followed the model of Bale's printed accounts of Anne Askew and "saints" like Sir John Oldcastle in attempting to supplant medieval hagiographies, which featured the alleged ability of the saints to work miracles, cures, and magical feats. It affords a sharp contrast to the hagiographical lives of Thomas More by William Roper, Nicholas Harpsfield, Thomas Stapleton, and the unknown Ro. Ba., for example, by celebrating Protestant testimonials by humble lay people. By "monuments" Foxe means not relics, but religious writings left behind by or concerning martyrs.

Known from the beginning as the *Book of Martyrs*, the text contains scores of highly charged, polemical accounts of the suffering of Christians whom Foxe alleges, on the model of Bale's *Image of Both Churches*, to have maintained faith with the "true" church of Christ as opposed to the "false" church of Rome. The collection functions as an encyclopedia of popular literature, in verse and prose, that contains a diverse array of literary genres including anecdotes, autobiographical memoirs, legal documents, sermons, ballads, beast fables, letters, tales, and romanticized adventure narratives. Foxe constructed four increasingly massive editions (1563–83) during his lifetime, before the work took on a life of its own

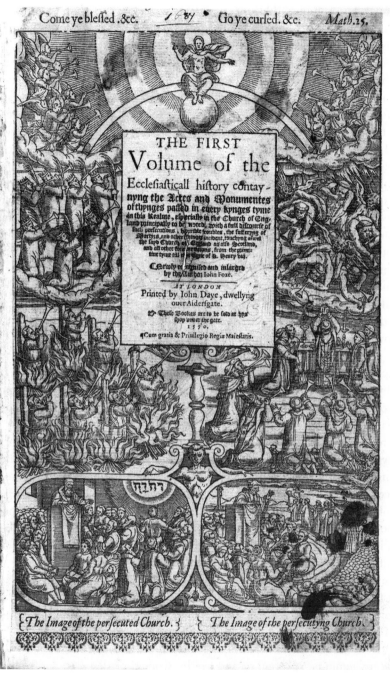

11 John Foxe, *Acts and Monuments of these Latter and Perilous Days* (London, 1563), title page.

through posthumous additions over the centuries. It is perhaps second only to the English Bible in the enduring influence it has exerted upon the consciousness of English-speaking Protestants.

Foxe collaborated with John Day, arguably the most successful Elizabethan master-printer, in producing a collection that is not only the most complicated publishing venture, but also the best illustrated English book of its age. In the popular imagination, the *Book of Martyrs* is remembered for the lurid woodcuts of the "roasting" of Sir John Oldcastle, the hangings of Lollards, and the seemingly countless burnings of Protestant martyrs. Foxe claims that the historicity of his martyrologies contradicts the alleged "superstition" of medieval legends of saints. In place of alleged examples of saintly intercession, healing, and prophecy, Foxe provides instances of providential intervention to deliver the faithful or work vengeance against their opponents. The suffering experience of saints is a common element in Protestant and Catholic accounts, but Foxe and his coreligionists insist that sainthood inheres in risking even life itself to testify to faith in Christ, rather than in the marvelous elements emphasized in legends of the saints. Sainthood of that kind is accessible to any elect Christian. In place of the fabulous miracle workers of medieval tradition, Foxe celebrates the little-known artisans and lowly workers who died for their faith under Mary I.

Some of the best-known narratives in the collection are those that describe the death of John Rogers, assistant of Tyndale and editor of the "Matthew" Bible, who was the Marian proto-martyr; the burning of the renowned preacher, John Bradford; the suffering of John Hooper, noted preacher and Bishop of Gloucester; and the recantation, reaffirmation of faith, and burning of Thomas Cranmer at Oxford. Perhaps the most poignant narrative is the description of the double execution of the Protestant heroes, Nicholas Ridley and aged Hugh Latimer, also at Oxford. According to the stirring account in the 1570 edition, Latimer made the symbolic gesture of wearing a funeral shroud to the stake, where he is reported to have uttered words modeled on those of Polycarp, an early Christian martyr, which are justifiably famous as a rallying cry of the English Reformation: "Be of good comfort, Master Ridley, and play the man. We shall this day light such a candle by God's grace in England, as I trust shall never be put out."[16] That story and its cartoonlike woodcut left an indelible imprint on the consciousness of Protestant England.

Many readers have viewed Foxe's book as both a product of and contributor to Protestant patriarchal discourse, but many of its narratives concern feminine spirituality and are by women or designed for a female audience. The *Book of Martyrs* contains stories about lowborn women in addition to a number of setpiece narratives concerning royal or aristocratic women such as Katherine Parr, Lady Jane Grey, and the Duchess of Suffolk. The feminine coloration of the text therefore pertains not only to Queen Elizabeth, the heroine of a climactic narrative concerning her allegedly miraculous preservation during her sister's reign, but also to women of all social ranks.

PROTESTANT RELIGIOUS PROSE

Foxean martyrs like William Tyndale, Hugh Latimer, and Thomas Cranmer are remembered for some of the finest English religious prose. Published by John Day as a companion to the *Book of Martyrs*, Foxe's edition of *The Whole Works of William Tyndale, John Frith, and Doctor Barnes* (1573) may be the most important collection of Tudor religious prose. Containing all of Tyndale's works aside from bible translation, the collection also contains writings by Robert Barnes, the antipapal campaigner, and John Frith, assistant to Tyndale and author of polemics against Thomas More and John Fisher. Tyndale, Barnes, and Frith were burned alive under Henry VIII. Foxe's edition is memorable primarily for the clarity and expressiveness of Tyndale's extraordinarily influential prose treatises, which afford bedrock for the English Protestant tradition. Chief in importance are *A Parable of the Wicked Mammon* and *The Obedience of a Christian Man* (both 1528). The first expounds justification by faith alone, whereas the second counters More's accusation that the reformers were traitors with the argument that the New Testament teaches subjects to obey governmental authority at the same time that it revolutionizes inward spirituality. According to tradition, Henry VIII exclaimed, "This is a book for me and all kings to read,"[17] when Anne Boleyn gave him a copy of the *Obedience*. The enumeration of clerical misdeeds in *The Practice of Prelates* (1530) anticipates scores of Protestant pamphlets, notably John Bale's *Acts of English Votaries* (1546–51). In addition to a variety of bible introductions and commentaries, notably *A Pathway into the Holy Scripture* (1536?), Tyndale also wrote *A Dialogue concerning Heresies* and *An Answer unto Sir Thomas More's Dialogue*, a point-by-point rebuttal of his opponent's attacks.

Hugh Latimer was the most renowned preacher during an age of great preachers, who included John Hooper and Thomas Cranmer. Latimer advocated social justice as strongly as he attacked allegedly corrupt worship practices. Rising to prominence under Henry VIII, his sermons in favor of bible translation and against the cult of the saints, pilgrimages, and adoration of relics made him famous. He attacked ecclesiastical abuses before the Convocation of Clergy and delivered the funeral sermon for Jane

Seymour, mother of Edward, Prince of Wales. Appointed Bishop of Winchester, he resigned that office when the conservative swing of King Henry's later years brought the Act of Six Articles (1539), notorious for its harsh punishment of Protestant heresy.

Latimer's reputation as a prose stylist rests largely upon sermons from the reign of Edward VI, notably the famous "Sermon on the Plowers" that he delivered to a throng of Londoners at St. Paul's Cathedral. In his plain and familiar sermonic style, filled with anecdotes and compelling allegories, he expounded Jesus' Parable of the Sower in order to define the reformed ministry:

> And now I shall tell you who be the plowers, for God's word is a seed to be sown in God's field, that is, the faithful congregation, and the preacher is the sower. And it is in the Gospel ... 'He that soweth, the husbandman, the plowman, went forth to sow his seed' [Luke 8:5]. So that a preacher is resembled [i.e., compared] to a plowman.[18]

As the chief preacher at the court of Edward VI, he coupled advocacy of a program of radical reform in the Church of England with attack on the misappropriation of ecclesiastical wealth by Henry VIII and Protestant lords who came to power when his son was crowned as a minor. Overflow attendance at his Lenten sermons resulted in the erection of a wooden pulpit in the gardens of Whitehall Palace. Going into edition after edition, during Latimer's lifetime and beyond, his sermons were among the best-selling texts printed by John Day, the publisher of the *Book of Martyrs*, who shrewdly catered to the Protestant market.

Even though Latimer's pulpit manner afforded a precedent for plain-style preachers during the reign of Queen Elizabeth, the copious sermonic style of Henry Smith, the most popular preacher of his era, is notable not only for humble eloquence and homely analogy, but also for innovative use of verbal repetition and irony, including self-mockery. Booksellers sold dozens and dozens of editions of the sermons of "silver-tongued Smith." Although he opposed separation from the Church of England, his opposition to the retention of Roman Catholic practices led to a short-lived suspension of his license to preach by the Bishop of London, John Aylmer, at a time when John Whitgift, the last Archbishop of Canterbury to serve under Elizabeth I, led an anti-Puritan campaign.

Thomas Cranmer's enduring reputation as a prose stylist rests upon liturgical texts that he oversaw during the reign of Edward VI. Supplanting an ancient Latin ritual that had become incomprehensible to ordinary people, Cranmer's self-contained set of books shifted the center of worship from the altar, where priests had celebrated the Mass, to the pulpit and lectern, where Protestant clerics preached and read from the vernacular Bible. He presided over an ecclesiastical revolution by instituting a worship service in the language of the people, one based upon readings from the Great Bible (for which he provided a preface), the *Book of Homilies*, and the *Book of Common Prayer*. After a return to the Latin rite under Mary I, the restoration of Cranmer's liturgy under Elizabeth I established an order of worship for the Church of England that has endured to the twentieth century. Cranmer's highly eclectic achievement bears the imprint of the Bible, notably the epistles of St. Paul, but also the theology of Fathers of the Church like St. Augustine and St. Jerome, in addition to Erasmus, Luther, Tyndale and many other theologians, both Catholic and Protestant.

The provision of official sermons in *Certain Sermons, or Homilies, Appointed to be Read* (1547) compensated for the scarcity of university-educated ministers at the same time that it allowed the government to control pulpit discourse. The collection of twelve sermons contains con-tributions by different hands including Hugh Latimer, who wrote against strife and contention, and Edmund Bonner, the conservative Bishop of London who provided the sermon on charity. In all likelihood, Cranmer himself composed the doctrinal homilies "Of the True and Lively Faith" and "Of Good Works," which follow Luther by expounding the doctrine of justification by faith while leaving room for good works not as a means of justification, but as posterior "fruits" of a "true and lively faith."[19] Those sermons reply to the conservative criticism that justification by faith alone exempts believers from doing good works. "Of Good Works" veers into an impassioned iconoclastic attack on Roman Catholic practices like pil-grimages, purchase of indulgences, and veneration of images and relics. Even though evangelical critics opposed the reading of formulaic sermons, congregations heard preachers read the complete *Book of Homilies* repeat-edly during the course of the church year.

Replacing the profusion of texts in the old Latin rite, Cranmer designed the first *Book of Common Prayer* (1549) in order to open a set of windows, both subjective and collective, into the human soul. Because Cranmer's studied ambiguity placed the widest possible limits on individual interpreta-tion, militants like John Hooper and John Knox forced him to issue a revised text in 1552, which veered in a more Protestant direction by eliminating the Mass, elaborate vestments, prayers for the dead, private confession, and extreme unction. By directing the minister to turn toward the people and stand in the part of the church where they could hear him most clearly, the 1552 prayer book invites active lay participation in public worship, by contrast with the medieval rite that insisted upon the inter-cessory role of priests.

In line with Cranmer's goal of employing language "easy and plain for the understanding of both of the readers and hearers," the collects (i.e., short prayers) in his prayer book synthesize Latinate elements distinctive in the prose style of humanists like Thomas More with native English sentence structures and colloquial diction typical of Tyndale's prose. The collect for Matins on Easter Sunday, for example, typifies what Janel Mueller has identified as Cranmer's distinctive ecclesiastical style, which combines ornate and suspensive Latinate sentence structure with the successiveness of conjunctive clauses characteristic of native English: "We humbly beseech thee, that as by thy special grace preventing us, thou dost put in our minds good desires, so by thy continual help, we may bring the same to good effect; through Jesus Christ our Lord, who liveth and reigneth ..."[20]

The accession of Elizabeth I allowed for a great outpouring of religious tracts and treatises by those who favored or opposed her settlement of religion, which attempted to compromise between Protestant theology and more conservative traditions based upon Catholic religious practices. Bishop John Jewel's *An Apology [for] the Church of England* (1562) defended the Elizabethan Compromise against accusations of Roman Catholic heresy by denying papal supremacy and defending reformation of religion as an affair of state. A consensus existed among Elizabethan churchmen that affirmed a predestinarian theology of grace, which, although compatible with almost any aspect of Genevan Calvinism except ministry and discipline, essentially reaffirmed the Zwinglian settlement in religion imposed under Edward VI.

Puritan authors began to speak out during the 1560s controversy concerning clerical vestments and the *Admonition* controversy of the 1560s and 1570s. John Field and Thomas Wilcox triggered the latter dispute with their *Admonition to Parliament* and *Second Admonition* (1572), which denounced the bishops and appealed for completion of a half-finished process of religious reform. Continental presses and secret presses in England turned out consolatory pamphlets for oppressed Roman Catholics. Presbyterian proponents of church government by the elders of individual congregations rather than an episcopal hierarchy threatened the structure of the Church of England that Queen Elizabeth, whose motto was *semper eadem* ("always the same"), regarded as unchangeable. The raffishly satirical Marprelate Tracts challenged the Queen's settlement in religion by attacking episcopacy from a Presbyterian vantage point in the late 1580s.

Among competing Protestant voices that diverged from the Elizabethan religious settlement, William Perkins, a theologian who swayed a generation of students at Cambridge University, was the most powerful spokesman for Puritans who saw themselves as a "godly" minority believing in strict observance of official Protestant theology as opposed to a Pelagian majority that denied original sin, believed in free will, and accepted ritualistic practices with a perceived Catholic tinge. Although few Elizabethan Puritans separated from the established church, they believed that collective worship ordained by the *Book of Common Prayer* and *Book of Homilies* was insufficient without heartfelt, individualistic scriptural exegesis or "prophesying." Perkins' *Act of Prophesying*, a translation of his *Prophetica* (1592), defines bible-based preaching as "prophesying in the name and room of Christ whereby men are called to the state of grace, and conserved in it."[21] *A Golden Chain, or the Description of Theology, Containing the Order of the Causes of Salvation and Damnation, According to God's Word* (1591) is a translation of Perkins' *Armilla Aurea*, a Latin treatise concerning predestination. Edition after edition appeared in print until William Laud disestablished official predestinarian theology. Laud, the controversial Archbishop of Canterbury, was beheaded in 1645 by parliamentary order for wielding arbitrary ecclesiastical authority under Charles I (1625–49).

Richard Hooker wrote *Of the Laws of Ecclesiastical Polity* near the end of the Elizabethan era as the last great defense of the religious settlement of 1559. Unlike his patron, John Jewel, whose *Apology of the Church of England* responded to Roman Catholic opposition, Hooker wrote his *Laws* primarily in response to the presbyterian appeal for congregational church governance, even though he followed Jewel in enumerating "papist" errors. The text modifies the predestinarian consensus subscribed to by both Jewel and Perkins when it defines Elizabethan religion as a *via media* between Geneva and Rome. It defends the *Book of Common Prayer* against Puritan attack. Hooker differs from Puritans in acknowledging that the Church of Rome possesses some merit as a "catholic" church and in questioning Protestant beliefs concerning justification by faith, grace, predestination, and the sufficiency of the Bible as a guide concerning church governance.

Only the first five books of *Laws* (1593–97) were published during Hooker's lifetime. Controversy has existed concerning the authenticity of the manuscripts which provided the basis for posthumous publication of the remaining three books (1648–62). The unorthodox arguments lodged by those books for episcopal authority and royal supremacy on the basis of public acceptance rather than divine right were compatible with political thought during an era when republican theorists opposed divine-right arguments favored by Elizabeth I and later embellished by James I and Charles I.

Hooker's prose is notable for its grandiloquent, Latinate style, which differs sharply both from the nativist plain style of Tyndale and Latimer and from Cranmer's synthesis of English and Latin syntax. The following periodic sentence from *The Laws of Ecclesiastical Polity* exemplifies Hooker's elegant vocabulary, inversion of word order, construction of balanced clauses, and Ciceronian suspension of meaning:

> Though for no other cause, yet for this; that posterity may know we have not loosely through silence permitted things to pass away as in a dream, there shall be for men's information extant thus much concerning the present state of the Church of God established amongst us, and their careful endeavor which would have upheld the same.[22]

RELIGIOUS SATIRE

Tudor England spawned a host of religious satires. Among the best-known examples are poems by John Skelton. Grounded upon the Catholic liturgy, his attacks on religious abuses reflect his priestly vocation. Although the apparent subject of *Philip Sparrow* is a lament upon the death of the pet of Jane Scrope, a novice nun, the poem delicately mocks her construction of a Requiem Mass for her bird out of elements from the Office for the Dead. *Ware the Hawk* defends the sanctity of both clerical vocation and liturgy by attacking a hedonistic priest whose fondness for hunting results in the desecration of a church altar when his hawk sheds blood on it in a parody of transubstantiation and the Mass.

Skelton attacks Cardinal Wolsey in three satires that date from the early 1520s. Employing the persona of a bird, *Speak, Parrot* employs obscure metaphor, allegory, and dazzling rhyme leashes typical of the poet's idiosyncratic verse form, Skeltonics, to attack a prelate whose princely magnificence subverts clerical humility. Continuing the attack on Wolsey's abuse of his offices as Archbishop of York and Lord Chancellor of England through the voice of a humble truth-teller, *Colin Clout* afforded a flimsy basis for Protestant reformers to appropriate Skelton as a proto-Protestant satirist, despite his religious orthodoxy. *Why Come Ye Not to Court?* is Skelton's most violent attack on Wolsey's subversion of the Bible, the liturgy, and other bases for worship and devotion.

John Heywood is the other important Henrician satirist in the Catholic tradition. A notable dramatist, musician, and versifier of proverbs, Heywood engaged in a defense of dogmatic Catholicism and practices such as pilgrimages and the sale of pardons in farces written under King Henry: *Pardoner and Friar, Four PP,* and *Johan Johan.* Heywood dropped his guise of impartiality in *The Spider and the Fly* (1556), an obscure allegory in which protracted conflict between a Protestant spider and a Catholic fly culminates in the predator's death and the cleansing of England's house by

Queen Mary, whom he had tutored, as a divine handmaid. Heywood went into exile in opposition to the Protestant settlement of religion under Elizabeth I.

The host of contentious satires that poured from the printing press during the militantly Protestant reign of Edward VI have received little attention despite their importance as a seedbed for satire by Spenser and others. The prominence of parody and lampoon contradicts the stereotyped view of early Protestants as somber and humorless opponents of fiction and drama. Writers modeled satirical verse and drama upon late medieval allegorical interludes, satires tinged with Lollardry including the pseudo-Chaucerian *The Plowman's Tale*, and Skelton's *Colin Clout*. They include dialogues in which skeptical lay people bluntly mock the mystifying ignorance of pompous clerics, and morality plays in which bawdy allegorical Vices symbolic of the old religion trick unwary youths into "spiritual fornication," despite the counsel of ministerial Protestant Virtues.

John Bale's interpretation of Revelation in terms of apocalyptic conflict between "true" and "false" churches was highly influential. The risqué humor of his satires has led conservative opponents to stigmatize him as "Bilious Bale." *King Johan* stands out among the many allegorical interludes and biblical mysteries that Bale composed in the late 1530s for performance by itinerant dramatic troupes. It praises Henry VIII in order to advance Protestant ideas. *Three Laws* relies upon allegorical costuming to satirize Roman Catholic "error." Covetousness appears in disguise as a bishop while False Doctrine plays a "popish" doctor. The costume of an old witch identifies Idolatry with the Whore of Babylon, a type for papal Rome, the city where Sodomy resides as a monk. Clad as a Franciscan friar, Infidelity employs the blasphemy and vulgar comic diction of the medieval Vice character.[23]

Deeply imbued with the densely scriptural style favored by the Edwardian "gospelers," Robert Crowley modeled his prophetic poems on *The Visions of Piers Plowman* (1550). His edition of that important medieval poem misrepresents it as a powerful attack against monasticism and the Roman Catholic hierarchy. The most interesting of his own works is *Philargyry of Great Britain* (1551), an appeal for completion of religious reforms blocked by Henry VIII's failure to redistribute the wealth of the monasteries that he suppressed to poor commoners. The title-page woodcut accordingly portrays Philargyry ("lover of silver") as an avaricious giant who employs a Bible to rake gold coins into a sack (figure 12).[24]

Like Crowley, Luke Shepherd emerges from the native tradition of late medieval verse satire. He shares Skelton's idiosyncratic fondness, for run-

12 Robert Crowley, *Philargyry of Great Britain* (London, 1551), title page.

on rhyme leashes, short lines of irregular length and measure, vigorous colloquial vocabulary, alliteration, puns, macaronic diction, copious verse catalogues, and scatological and sexual innuendo. Shepherd structures *John Bon and Master Parson* as a dialogue between a rural malcontent descended from Piers Plowman and an ignorant cleric. It hinges upon the commonsense rationality of John Bon, who denies transubstantiation because he cannot taste or see it. *Doctor Double Ale* ridicules an actual London priest who neglected his pastoral calling for the sake of haunting alehouses. A cobbler's son descended from Tyndale's plowboy risks execution as a heretic by using subversive bible interpretation to oppose a drunken priest who mistakes an ale pot for his Mass-book.[25]

Like Bale and Crowley, William Baldwin was involved with the London book trade as an author, editor, proofreader, and publisher. His often reprinted edition of *The Mirror for Magistrates*, a set of *de casibus* tragedies by various hands, influenced the stagecraft of Shakespeare and Marlowe. Baldwin's little-known novella, *Beware the Cat*, is a truly memorable religious satire that focuses on a fictive world of talking cats who witness the survival of forbidden Catholic ceremonies. As a witness to secret rituals, a cat named Mouse-slayer peers through the shuttered windows of recalcitrant souls during her picaresque progress among hypocritical priests, bawds, cheats, and cuckolds. In one ludicrous instance, the lover of an adulterous wife guilty of "spiritual fornication" learns to beware the cat. Mouse-slayer recounts how she revealed that "bare-arst gentleman," hidden behind a tapestry, when she "leaped up and caught him by the genitals with my teeth, and bote [bit] so hard that, when he had restrained more than I thought any man could, at last he cried out, and caught me by the neck thinking to strangle me."[26]

UNDERGROUND RESISTANCE AND EXILE

Old-fashioned critics have claimed that the Edwardian "Homily on Obedience" reflects a social order in which citizens unquestioningly bowed to monarchical authority, but the fates of hundreds of Protestant and Catholic martyrs exposes that view as fallacious. Roman Catholic resistance to changes in official religion stretched across the sixteenth century. Because most Protestant apologists suppressed their distaste for Henry VIII, on the ground that he and his heir, Prince Edward, afforded the only reasonable prospect for Protestant reform, the religio-political critique in Crowley's *Philargyyry of Great Britain* is exceptional. Indeed, the government of Edward VI suppressed domestic Catholic printing. Forced to recant for his defense of traditional doctrine, *A Brief Treatise Setting Forth Divers Truths*

(1547), Richard Smith fled to France, where he published a tract against Cranmer's new English liturgy.

The accession of Mary I reversed the equation, when Smith and Robert Caly, a Catholic printer, returned from French exile. Preaching prior to the burning of Latimer and Ridley, Smith cited scriptural authority for declaring "they were heretics and died out of the Church." James Cancellar's *Path of Obedience* (1556?) lodged a counterattack upon the *Vocation* of the newly exiled John Bale as the work of "a notable heretic apostate and runagate [i.e., exile] ... compelled of necessity to run with the thief or murderer... from country to country for the assurance of [his] life."[27]

Despite the widespread view that the Marian government misunderstood the importance of printing, it did attempt to control publication, ban Protestant propaganda, and foster lay education through sermons, primers, and catechisms. Caly printed tracts by Miles Hogarde, the artisan poet who provides the single example of a Catholic propagandist who exploited the resources of late medieval complaint and satire. Composed surreptitiously when the Edwardian government banned his books, Hogarde's *The Assault of the Sacrament of the Altar* (1554), an allegorical dream vision, defends the Mass against attacks from Wyclif, Luther, Cranmer, and others. His other Marian polemics include *The Displaying of Protestants* and *Pathway to the Tower of Perfections*.

Queen Elizabeth's reputed disinclination "to open windows into men's souls" recalls her precarious position as a princess, when she inspired Protestant dissidents under Mary I. The massive flight of Protestant intellectuals to the Continent represented an unprecedented shift from passive obedience to active dissent; indeed, the Marian exile gave birth to radical resistance theory. At a safe haven in Strasbourg, John Ponet wrote *A Short Treatise of Politic Power* (1556), which declares that scriptural warrant entitles subjects to choose and depose governors, and even resort to tyrannicide. Christopher Goodman published *How Superior Powers Ought to Be Obeyed of Their Subjects: And Wherein They May Lawfully Be Disobeyed* (1558) in Calvin's Geneva, where John Knox published *The First Blast of the Trumpet against the Monstrous Regiment of Women* in the same year. They committed the unwitting blunder of vilifying feminine government not long before the death of Mary I. Giving grave offense to Elizabeth I, they contributed to her hostility to Calvin and distaste for more extreme forms of evangelical piety.

Recusancy (i.e., refusal to attend established church services) gathered strength during the 1570s, when Elizabeth, newly excommunicated by the Pope, imprisoned Mary Queen of Scots as a Catholic claimant to the throne. Edmund Campion and Robert Parsons endangered the Elizabethan religious settlement when they initiated the Jesuit Mission to England in 1580. *Campion's Challenge* (1580), an open letter to the Privy Council in the form of a quickly suppressed pamphlet, fashions the identity of the Jesuit missionary-martyr in terms of paradoxical interplay between self-concealment and conspicuous self-representation. Parsons directed the English Mission from abroad after Campion's arrest in July 1581 before moving on to Spain, where he established seminaries for English priests at Valladolid, Seville, and Madrid. Jesuit presses at locations such as Antwerp and St. Omer, Normandy, produced most of the tracts and devotional works that Parsons composed for surreptitious export to England. *A Christian Directory, Guiding Men to Their Salvation* (1585) achieved considerable popularity among both Catholics and Protestants. He wrote *A Jesuit's Memorial for the Intended Reformation of England* (comp. 1596) in anticipation of a restoration of Roman Catholicism. The third part of his *Treatise of Three Conversions of England* (1603), "An Examin[ation] of the Calendar or Catalogue of Protestant Saints ... Devised by Foxe," initiated an attack on the historical accuracy of the *Book of Martyrs* that has endured into modern times.

The Queen's chief minister, William Cecil, responded to the Jesuit "peril" with *The Execution of Justice in England* (1583), a legalistic argument that Jesuits like Campion were executed not as martyrs, but as traitors loyal to a foreign sovereign, the Pope. William Allen (later made cardinal), founder of English colleges for missionary priests at Douai and Rome, eloquently rejected Cecil's argument regarding treason in *A True, Sincere and Modest Defense of English Catholics* (1584).

Chidiock Tichborne and Robert Southwell, SJ, were notable Elizabethan recusant poets. Tichborne's three extant poems reflect circumstances at the end of his life, when, after delivering a moving final speech, he was hanged, drawn, and quartered at Tyburn because of his role in the 1586 conspiracy of Anthony Babington to assassinate Queen Elizabeth. The poignancy and antithetical style of "Tichborne's Lament," his best lyric, anticipates verse by Southwell, the Jesuit martyr.[28] A participant in the English Mission spearheaded by Campion and Parsons, Southwell composed *An Epistle of Comfort* (1587?) to console recusants subject to persecution. A press concealed at the London house of the Duchess of Arundel published that eloquent devotional work. Hiding at Arundel House, Southwell opened windows into the recusant soul in poems including "Of the Blessed Sacrament of the Altar" and "The Burning Babe," an often anthologized masterpiece that rivals sacred lyrics by Donne and Herbert. Torture preceded Southwell's martyrdom at Tyburn, a pilgrimage site to the present day, after the infamous priest-catcher, Richard Topcliffe, hunted him down.

"St. Peter's Complaint," part of a collection of poems published posthumously by a Jesuit press in Normandy, is a lengthy penitential lament in the voice of St. Peter, the disciple of Christ and martyr honored by Catholics as the first pope.

PSALM VERSIFICATION

Tudor poets habitually employed "Englished" Psalms as vehicles for opening meditative windows into their own souls. In his "Paraphrase of the Penitential Psalms," for example, Sir Thomas Wyatt follows the long-standing tradition of expressing remorse by versifying seven Psalms thought to articulate King David's repentance for adultery with Bathsheba and the consequent murder of her husband, Uriah the Hittite. The Henrician courtier attaches Protestant values to a set of Psalms controversial in the late 1530s because readers could apply them with reference to a latter-day David, Henry VIII, and his ill-fated Bathsheba, Anne Boleyn. Attack on the King is almost explicit in the sonnet in praise of "Wyatt's Psalms" by Henry Howard, Earl of Surrey, who notes that "Rulers may see in a mirror clear / The bitter fruit of false concupiscence."[29] As Henry lay dying, Surrey was beheaded for contesting the succession of Edward VI.

Psalms were in vogue under Edward VI, to whom Thomas Sternhold dedicated a version in fourteeners (a variant of ballad measure) because the pietistic boy preferred secular carols and love lyrics. The courtier originally received royal favor for singing his Psalms in the presence of Henry VIII. Published in more than five hundred editions during the next century, *The Whole Book of Psalms* completed by Sternhold, John Hopkins, and others was the most popular collection of English Renaissance verse. Despite its metrical crudity, it gained renown as a collection of hymns used by Puritans to examine their souls.

In accordance with the declaration in Sir Philip Sidney's *Defence of Poetrie* that "divine" poetry is the most excellent and highest kind of verse, he and his sister, Mary, Countess of Pembroke, collaborated on versifying translations of the complete Psalter (he contributed the first forty-three). Their manuscript collection circulated within a tiny aristocratic circle, by contrast with the vast audience Sternhold and Hopkins' published version reached. The acknowledgment in the *Defence* that "learned Hebricians" have yet to determine the metrical "rules" of "holy David's Psalms"[30] liberated the siblings to experiment with a virtuoso array of sophisticated stanzaic and metrical forms, often borrowed from Continental poets. Most scholars agree that Sidney's Psalms incorporate Protestant theology and advice to the Queen concerning religious faith, but the precise nature of Philip Sidney's theological position is uncertain.

SPENSER, SIDNEY, MARLOWE, AND SHAKESPEARE

The Reformation tradition left its imprint upon Spenser and other Elizabethan authors. The May, July, and September Eclogues in *The Shepheardes Calender* (1579) incorporate ecclesiastical satire compatible with the views of "Algrind," an allegorization of Edmund Grindal, the Archbishop of Canterbury ruined by Queen Elizabeth for refusing to suppress Puritan "prophesyings" (i.e., extempore sermons) of the kind advocated by William Perkins. Piers, the reformist speaker in "May," is a descendant of Piers Plowman, Tyndale's plowboy, John Bon, and the cobbler's boy who antagonizes Doctor Double Ale.

Book One of *The Faerie Queene* (1590–96), or "The Legend of Holiness," affords a theological foundation for the heroic romance in which Spenser defends the Protestant nation refounded by Elizabeth I. The inseparability of politics and religion necessitated a Protestant structure in an Elizabethan national epic. The historical allegory in Book One recounts the return of England to "true" religion after centuries of domination by the Church of Rome. It embodies an apocalyptic worldview aligned with Bale's *Image of Both Churches* and Foxe's *Book of Martyrs*. For example, the conflict between Una and Duessa recalls Bale's interpretation of the Woman Clothed by the Sun and Whore of Babylon as types of the "true" and "false" churches. The Red Cross Knight functions as a Protestant Everyman, St. George (patron of England), and a type of Jesus Christ. The swarming offspring of monstrous Error bring Jesuit missionaries to mind, and personification of Hypocrisy in monklike Archimago recalls dramatization of the same Vice in Bale's *Three Laws*. At the core of the theological allegory in the House of Holiness, Fidelia and Charissa recall Cranmer's crucial definition of good works as the "fruit" of a "true and lively faith" in the *Book of Homilies*.

Spenser dedicated *The Shepheardes Calender* to Philip Sidney, nephew of Robert Dudley, Earl of Leicester, and son-in-law of Sir Francis Walsingham, Elizabeth's zealously anti-Catholic Secretary of State. Against the Queen's pacifistic wishes, they favored English intervention in the Low Countries in defense of Protestants beleaguered by the forces of Catholic Spain. More so than Sidney's metrical Psalms, the different versions of his sprawling pastoral romance bear the imprint of Protestant politics. Written *c.* 1577–85, during the era when Queen Elizabeth raised the specter of foreign Catholic domination with her proposal to marry the duc d'Anjou, heir apparent to the throne of France, Sidney's *Old Arcadia* and *New Arcadia* employ pastoral disguise to veil a critique of royal failure deeply imbued with apocalyptic fears of foreign Catholic tyranny. At the same time, we need to remember that Sidney's notional Protestantism left room for an apparent flirtation with some Catholic ideas.

Parodic inversions in plays by Christopher Marlowe transferred Reformation ideology to the Elizabethan stage. Even though scholars debate the degree to which the different texts of *Doctor Faustus* incorporate the predestinarian theology of unmerited grace versus the Arminian view that free will plays a role in damnation or salvation, the play's Vatican scene invokes the iconoclastic attack on the papal Antichrist familiar from woodcuts in Foxe's *Book of Martyrs*. In the final scene, Faustus plays a role in the Protestant drama of salvation when he speaks, without intercession by Catholic saints or the Virgin Mary, of the enormous gulf between his sinful self and an angry God.

Despite Shakespeare's avoidance of overt politicization, plays like *Hamlet* are engaged with Protestant ideology. In *King Lear*, the resistance to tyranny of the serving man and Gloucester dramatizes theories of political resistance and tyrannicide propounded by Ponet, Goodman, and others. Comical parodies of monastic characters in *Measure for Measure* recall satirical allegories by Bale and others. Indeed, Shakespeare tends toward comic portrayals: Sir Oliver Martext in *As You Like It* and Nathaniel in *Love's Labor's Lost*. The 1613 staging of *Henry VIII* reverts to the apocalyptic fervor familiar from Foxe's *Book of Martyrs* when a speech delivered by Archbishop Cranmer at the christening of Princess Elizabeth prophesies the completion of the Protestant Reformation during her reign. It is worthy of note that William Sankey, SJ, expurgated the whole of *Measure for Measure* from the second edition of Shakespeare's plays (1632) in the library of the English Jesuit College at Valladolid in Spain. (The Folger Shakespeare Library now preserves that copy.) Father Sankey also excised Cranmer's futuristic praise of Elizabeth in *Henry VIII* as a Protestant heroine nurtured by Truth and counseled by "Holy and heavenly thoughts" (V.iv.29). One may only speculate whether those cuts in the Valladolid Folio identify windows into Shakespeare's soul.

NOTES

1 Angela Partington, ed., *The Oxford Dictionary of Quotations*, 4th edn., rev. (Oxford: Oxford University Press, 1996), p. 274. Reliable editions of certain texts mentioned in this essay are as yet unavailable, but collections of writings by Elizabeth I, Miles Hogarde, Katherine Parr, and Luke Shepherd, and my own edition of *English Reformation Texts: From Tyndale to Spenser*, are currently in

progress. Editorial teams are at work on critical editions of the polemical prose of William Tyndale and Foxe's *Acts and Monuments*. Quotations are modernized.

2 John Foxe, *Acts and Monuments of the English Martyrs*, 1st edn. (1563), sig. 4N7v. Known from the beginning as the *Book of Martyrs*.

3 William Roper, *Life of Sir Thomas More*, in *Two Early Tudor Lives*, ed. Richard S. Sylvester and Davis P. Harding (New Haven: Yale University Press, 1962), p. 254.

4 Foxe, *Acts and Monuments* (1570), sig. 3D4.

5 Eamon Duffy, *The Stripping of the Altars: Traditional Religion in England 1400-1580* (New Haven: Yale University Press, 1992); Christopher Haigh, *The English Reformations: Religion, Politics, and Society under the Tudors* (Oxford: Clarendon Press, 1993).

6 Desiderius Erasmus, *Christian Humanism and the Reformation: Selected Writings*, ed. J. C. Olin (New York: Harper, 1965), p. 97.

7 Foxe, *Acts and Monuments* (1563), sig. 2A5v.

8 David Daniell, ed., *Tyndale's New Testament: Translated from the Greek by William Tyndale in 1534* (New Haven and London: Yale University Press, 1989).

9 *The Yale Edition of the Complete Works of St Thomas More*, ed. Richard Sylvester et al., 10 vols. in 15 parts (New Haven: Yale University Press, 1963–1998), vol. VI, p. 286.

10 A. G. Dickens and Dorothy Carr, eds., *The Reformation in England to the Accession of Elizabeth I*, Documents of Modern History (London: Edward Arnold, 1967), p. 82.

11 John Bale, *The Select Works of Bishop Bale*, Parker Society, vol. 36 (Cambridge, 1849), p. 497.

12 Elaine V. Beilin, ed., *The Examinations of Anne Askew*, Women Writers in English 1350-1850 (Oxford: Oxford University Press, 1996), pp. 130-31.

13 Anne Lake Prescott, "The Pearl of the Valois and Elizabeth I: Marguerite de Navarre's *Miroir* and Tudor England," in *Silent But for the Word: Tudor Women as Patrons, Translators, and Writers of Religious Works*, ed. Margaret P. Hannay (Kent, OH: Kent State University Press, 1985), p. 69. See Marc Shell, *Elizabeth's Glass with "The Glass of the Sinfull Soul" (1544) by Elizabeth I and "Epistle Dedicatory" and "Conclusion" (1548) by John Bale* (Lincoln: University of Nebraska Press, 1993).

14 Janel Mueller, ed., *The Works of Katherine Parr*, in progress.

15 Peter Happé and John N. King, eds., *The Vocacyon of Johan Bale*, ed. Renaissance English Text Society, vol. 14 (1989), (Binghamton, NY: Medieval and Renaissance Texts and Studies, 1990), pp. 51-52, 72-73.

16 Foxe, *Acts and Monuments* (1570), sig. 4Q6r.

17 From a manuscript once in the possession of Foxe, cited in J. F. Mozley, *William Tyndale* (London: SPCK, 1937), p. 143.

18 Hugh Latimer, *Selected Sermons of Hugh Latimer*, ed. Allan Griffith Chester, Folger Documents of Tudor and Stuart Civilization (Charlottesville: University Press of Virginia; Folger Shakespeare Library, 1968), p. 29.

19 Ronald B. Bond, ed., *Certain Sermons, or Homilies, Appointed to be Read* (Toronto: University Of Toronto Press, 1987), "Of the True and Lively Faith" and "Of Good Works."

20 John E. Booty, ed., *The Book of Common Prayer 1559: The Elizabethan Prayer Book* (Charlottesville: University Press of Virginia, 1976), pp. 152-53; Janel M. Mueller, *The Native Tongue and the Word: Developments in English Prose Style, 1380-1580* (Chicago and London: University of Chicago Press, 1984), p. 231.

21 Perkins, *The Art of Prophesying: Or A Treatise Concerning the Sacred and Only True Manner and Method of Preaching* (1607), sig. A4r.

22 Richard Hooker, *Of the Laws of Ecclesiastical Polity: An Abridged Edition*, ed. A. S. McGrade and Brian Vickers (London: Sidgwick & Jackson, 1975), p. 63.

23 *The Complete Plays of John Bale*, ed Peter Happé, 2 vols. (Cambridge: D.S. Brewer, 1985-86), vol. II, p. 121.

24 John N. King, ed., "*Philargyrie of Greate Britayne* by Robert Crowley," *English Literary Renaissance* 10 (1980): 46-75.

25 Janice Devereux's edition of the collected works of Luke Shepherd is forthcoming from the Renaissance English Text Society.

26 William A. Ringler, Jr. and Michael Flachmann, ed., *Beware the Cat by William Baldwin: The First English Novel* (San Marino, CA: The Huntington Library, 1988), pp. 50-51.

27 Transcribed in Bale, *Vocacyon*, ed. Happé and King, p. 130. Intending it for the press of John Day, Bale never published his response, "A Return of James Cancellar's Railing Book Upon his Own Head" (London, Lambeth Palace MS 2001).

28 Richard S. M. Hirsch, "The Works of Chidiock Tichborne (text)," *ELR* 16 (1986): 303-18.

29 Richard Sylvester, ed., *English Sixteenth-century Verse: An Anthology* (New York: Norton, 1984), p. 187.

30 Katherine Duncan-Jones, ed., *Sir Philip Sidney: Selections* (Oxford: Oxford University Press, 1989), p. 215.

FURTHER READING

Collinson, Patrick, *The Birthpangs of Protestant England: Religion and Cultural Change in the Sixteenth and Seventeenth Centuries* (London: Macmillan, 1988).

Gless, Darryl, *Interpretation and Theology in Spenser* (Cambridge: Cambridge University Press, 1994).

Hadfield, Andrew, *Literature, Politics, and National Identity: Reformation to Renaissance* (Cambridge: Cambridge University Press, 1994).

King, John N., *English Reformation Literature: The Tudor Origins of the Protestant Tradition* (Princeton: Princeton University Press, 1982).

  Tudor Royal Iconography: Literature and Art in an Age of Religious Crisis (Princeton: Princeton University Press, 1989).

  Spenser's Poetry and the Reformation Tradition (Princeton: Princeton University Press, 1990).

Kinney, Arthur F., *John Skelton, Priest as Poet: Seasons of Discovery* (Chapel Hill: University of North Carolina Press, 1987).

Mueller, Janel, "A Tudor Queen Finds Voice: Katherine Parr's *Lamentation*," *The Historical Renaissance: New Essays on Tudor and Stuart Literature and*

Culture, ed. Heather Dubrow and Richard Strier (Chicago and London: Chicago University Press, 1988), pp. 15–47.

The Native Tongue and the Word: Developments in English Prose Style, 1380–1580) (Chicago and London: Chicago University Press, 1984).

Norbrook, David, *Poetry and Politics in the English Renaissance* (London: Routledge, Kegan Paul, 1984).

Weiner, Andrew, *Sir Philip Sidney and the Poetics of Protestantism* (Minneapolis: Routledge, Kegan Paul, 1978).

White, Paul, *Theatre and Reformation: Protestantism, Patronage, and Playing in Tudor England* (Cambridge: Cambridge University Press, 1993).

Worden, Blair, *The Sound of Virtue: Philip Sidney's* Arcadia *and Elizabethan Politics* (New Haven: Yale University Press, 1996).

7

LEAH S. MARCUS

Dramatic experiments: Tudor drama, 1490–1567

In the prologue to John Dryden's revised version of Shakespeare's *Troilus and Cressida* (1678), Dryden had "Mr. Betterton, representing the ghost of Shakespeare" rise up and intone to the audience,

> Untaught, unpractic'd, in a barbarous age,
> I found not, but created first the stage.

Before Shakespeare was the void – an uncouth, dark time with nothing to offer England's first master dramatic poet. There are traces of Dryden's perspective in the titles of this chapter and the one that follows it. While the age of Shakespeare proudly sets forth "Dramatic Achievements," the pre-Shakespearean era can offer only "Experiments." To be sure, we have abandoned Dryden's formulation in some ways. No scholar would now contend that Shakespeare took nothing from the drama that preceded him; indeed, a flourishing twentieth-century scholarly industry has devoted itself precisely to demonstrating how Shakespeare's achievement needs to be understood as the culmination of earlier developments in the Tudor theatre. Shakespeare was neither "untaught" nor "unpractic'd" in an earlier English drama, but found much to emulate and adopt.

Although the more recent developmental paradigm escapes Dryden's error of effacing a pre-Shakespearean theatre altogether, it nevertheless devalues earlier dramatic activity except insofar as that can be seen as contributing to the brilliant final decades of the sixteenth century, when, we have long been told, the English stage achieved a poetic intensity, realism, and autonomy unprecedented in the theatrical history of any nation. Typically, earlier Tudor drama has interested scholars only as a transition to something else; the dominant critical mode has been genealogical, attending to origins and influence, but somehow embarrassed by the rudeness of the plays considered in themselves. The present chapter will make every effort to avoid the developmental paradigm that enables such judgments, for the plays we will be discussing deserve to be valued in their own right, not only as "specimens" or "precursors" of what would come later. For that reason, we will avoid the unconsciously derogatory nomenclature that has pigeonholed the early Tudor entertainments as mere "interludes" or "moralities" (even though both terms date from the period) rather than plays. But we will also consider some of the playing conditions that made it possible for Dryden to overlook the existence of a vibrant, healthy English theatre before Shakespeare.

In the Restoration, the London theatrical scene could boast several competing commercial theatres whose offerings rivaled and commented upon one another, enriching the experience of playgoers. London had an established theatrical culture of actors and playwrights who were lionized in the same way that later cultures have venerated opera stars, sports heroes, and race horses. London also had a committed public of literate theatregoers who not only attended plays and commented upon them, but also bought them in printed versions, and in numerous ways made them part of the emerging "public sphere." Small wonder that Dryden saw none of this in England before Shakespeare, for the "stage" as he understood it did not yet exist. In considering the earlier Tudor theatre, we have to work our way out of the long process of cultural conditioning that causes us to regard fixed theatres and a quasi-autonomous theatrical culture as normative and other forms of theatre as inferior and subordinate, provisional, and striving to become what they were not. The present chapter will not attempt to be all-inclusive; rather, we will consider several of the most important plays in roughly chronological order as a way of illustrating defining features of this theatre without a stage.

This chapter adopts as its terminus the year 1567, for in that year London acquired its first independent structure built expressly for the purpose of showing plays to the public, the scaffold stage at the Red Lion in Whitechapel, erected by John Brayne, a grocer.[1] There may have been earlier attempts; indeed, the evidence suggests that there may have been a specially built London theatre operating briefly during the 1520s. With the construction of the Red Lion, however, even though it appears not to have been successful, we can identify the instauration of a tradition: the Theatre in Shoreditch (1576) was built by the same John Brayne in partnership with James Burbage; then followed the Curtain, the Rose, the Swan, the Globe (built in 1598 out of transported timbers from the dismantled Theatre), and the Fortune, all of which had been constructed by 1600. As we have begun to recognize, these permanent or at least quasi-permanent structures, and the public taste for playgoing they catered to, helped to transform Tudor drama and the expectations audiences brought to it. One of our tasks here will be to recover some of the alternative expectations audiences brought to the earlier Tudor theatre, before it had achieved the autonomy implied by the building of fixed London stages expressly designed for the performance of plays.

As the recent REED project has begun to demonstrate, it was not only Dryden who was unaware of the extent of pre-Shakespearean theatrical life. The *Records of Early English Drama*'s researchers are methodically canvassing early modern manuscript records of all kinds for signs of theatrical activity, and finding it to be unexpectedly widespread in early Tudor England. In the absence of fixed public theatres, dramatic activity was often attached to some larger occasion or institution. In towns and villages, the church served as an important locus for plays and kindred productions: many towns kept their traditional mystery plays until the late sixteenth and even the seventeenth century, albeit often in an altered form that omitted material offensive to Protestant doctrine. Religious plays were often performed in churches, which in many communities would be the largest available space, but so were secular plays, particularly if the weather was too foul to permit performance in the churchyard.[2] Towns also sponsored plays and pageants as part of their communal civic activities, and as guild-sponsored mystery and miracle plays fell into disuse these secular productions became more prominent: Lord Mayors' shows, guildhall productions, entertainments for visiting royalty and aristocrats, and performances by traveling players belonging to the households of territorial magnates. The most famous of these civic entertainments from the early Tudor period was London's ceremonial welcome of Elizabeth in January 1559, the day before her coronation, when the Queen proceeded through the City to Westminster, encountering allegorical tableaux and interacting with the speakers who explicated them for her as she passed. According to Richard Mulcaster's highly charged description of the event in *The Passage of Our Most Dread Sovereign Lady* (London, 1559), "if a man should say well, he could not better term the City of London that time than a stage wherein was showed the wonderful spectacle of a noble-hearted princess toward her most loving people and the people's exceeding comfort in beholding as worthy a sovereign and hearing so princelike a voice" (Sig. A2 v). Indeed, it would not be an exaggeration to state that the collective, public "stages" of English streets and marketplaces in times of political and religious festivity were the primary sites for dramatic activity during the early Tudor period.

The schools and universities were another fertile locus of dramatic performance: indeed, we need to remind ourselves that were it not for its preservation much earlier as a school text, Sophocles' *Oedipus Rex* would have been lost to the Renaissance and to us. The universities valued the drama for offering language and oratorical training and put on extravagant theatrical productions for the edification (and stultification) of visiting monarchs. The new humanist grammar schools were similarly devoted to oral language training of a decidedly dramatic type, as witnessed by the many school dialogues that have survived, some of which were no doubt performed as dramatic skits by the students. The Inns of Court were also rich in dramatic activity that complemented the usual emphasis on oral debate that characterized legal training, and the Inns were particularly noted for their Christmas revels and "misrule." At the royal court and in noble houses throughout the realm, holidays were especially favored times for maskings, disguisings, and plays, or all of these intermingled into a single vast season of managed revelry. Folk plays of Robin Hood, St. George and the Dragon, and other time-honored subjects were perhaps the most ubiquitous form of drama, performed in humble households, village squares, churchyards, and the royal court alike, often as part of a larger program of holiday revels.

Unfortunately, however, for most of these recorded events, nothing but titles, intriguingly brief lists of props or payments, and perhaps brief descriptions of the plot, have survived. Indeed, many such plays – particularly the folk plays – were probably not transcribed at all, but handed down through oral tradition and partially improvised every time they were performed. Only the most highly literate cultural groups made a regular practice of recording and publishing the texts of dramatic entertainments, and then, it would appear, only if the event carried special political significance or if repeat performances were planned for the future or for other locations. Entertainment first performed at festival banquets in a nobleman's household could, through the medium of print, become available for use by unrelated troupes of players. Some of the plays to be discussed here, such as *Gammer Gurton's Needle*, had a performance life decades beyond the occasion of their original production because of the medium of print. The early Tudor drama no doubt appeared quite solid and reliably present to audiences at the time of its performance, but for us all of that lively, prolific activity has receded into fleeting glimpses since so little of it has typically survived on paper.

Even the dramatic productions that have survived in manuscript or printed transcriptions often appear disappointingly thin to modern readers because we lack the shared community knowledge necessary to interpret them adequately. Usually such transcriptions are aimed less at reproducing the event for readers remote from the original performance, and more at creating a written "memory" of it for those who were involved. For that reason, written accounts are often quite sparse, recording only words, with little sense of accompanying dances, music, and revels, or of the specific milieu and purpose of a performance. Early Tudor dramatic performances, since they typically occurred as part of some larger collective activity on the part of a household, parish, town, or other institution, could count on a high degree of common knowledge and group cohesion on the part of most members of their audiences. That shared knowledge has to be recovered by way of painstaking historical investigation before we can fully appreciate the vitality and daring of the plays. Not coincidentally, some of the very features that make early Tudor plays fundamentally different from the plays that gradually came into fashion after 1567, during the era of permanent playhouses, are the same features that made them lively and successful theatre for their original audiences.

In the fixed playhouses, the relationship between audience and actors quickly became conventionalized because it was dictated by the structure of the theatres themselves, which offered clearly differentiated spaces for the stage and for the audience. The separation was, of course, not always observed; particularly in the private playhouses, young swells in the audience liked to sit on stage, and in numerous plays of late century, the actors on stage would still address the audience as though it constituted a collective personage within the world of the play rather than observers outside it. But in the early Tudor drama, each play of necessity had to carve its own performance area out of space that was also used for other purposes; hence the traditional mummers' cry of "Room, room!" by which the players requested that an area be cleared for the duration of their performance. The relationship between actors and audience was also less conventionalized than it became later, in part because most actors were amateurs rather than professionals, and even if they did accept money or goods as a reward for performance they probably held down other jobs as well. In community productions actors and audiences were likely to know each other well, and there was little or no professional divide between them.

The differentiation and identification of actors from audience is accomplished with particular wit in Henry Medwall's very early *Fulgens and Lucrece*, a two-part drama offered at the household of Cardinal John Morton during the 1490s, perhaps in the great hall of Lambeth Palace during the Christmas festivities of 1497, when Morton entertained the ambassadors of Spain and Flanders. As Suzanne Westfall has recently concluded, this play was probably put on by members of Morton's own household. Medwall, the author, was Morton's chaplain. As the play begins, A. and B. come up out of the audience and at first masquerade as simple onlookers like the rest of those at the feast. Each denies that he is one of the players: A. suspects B., who retorts, insulted, "Nay, I am none; /

I trow thou speakest in derision / To liken me thereto" (lines 45–47), whereupon A. goes into a brief disquisition about how little can be assumed by "nice array" among such a company of gallants. But both, of course, belong to the play: each manages later on to attach himself to one of the two youths who are wooing the young Roman maiden Lucrece, whose father Fulgens, a noble Roman senator, has given his daughter free rein to choose between them. By mediating between the audience and the play proper, A. and B. help to define the playing space and orient the audience to the action that follows: B. has at least been made privy to the plot of the play, which he proceeds to offer in precis form for the information of A. and also for the benefit of the audience. Through the rest of the action, as the two suitors, the patrician Publius Cornelius, and the recently ennobled Gaius Flaminius, vie for the hand of Lucrece, the "low" characters A. and B. comically vie for the hand of her maid, a fair "flower of the frying pan" (line 1174). Typically for early Tudor household revels, the play includes music, combat (a mock joust between A. and B.), and a holiday mumming brought in by B. to help win Lucrece for his master, Publius Cornelius.

In the form in which it has come down to us *Fulgens and Lucrece* could not be performed on a stage: it requires the atmosphere of a banquet and the intimacy of a household to succeed (and modern college revivals that can exploit the same conditions of performance have indeed been successful). Somewhat against the characters' own expectations, Lucrece chooses the lowly born but virtuous Gaius Flaminius over the patrician but dissolute Publius Cornelius: a particularly appropriate message for a cardinal who was a "new man" serving a monarch, Henry VII, who was also a relative newcomer to a throne which he had seized from the ancient but (at least from a Tudor perspective) decaying house of Plantagenet. *Fulgens and Lucrece* brilliantly exploits the format of the household revel not only to bring good holiday cheer, but also to communicate a political message supporting Henry Tudor's new order based on merit and virtue as opposed to the traditional aristocracy. Indeed, the choice made by Lucrece mirrors the choice made by Henry's consort Elizabeth, daughter of King Edward IV, when she married Henry VII although rumored to be the chosen bride of his rival and victim Richard III.

Early Tudor drama almost invariably increases in interest the more we are able to immerse ourselves in its immediate political contexts. John Skelton's *Magnificence* provides a good illustration. We do not know precisely when this brittle, daring play was composed – the traditional date assigned to it is 1516, but Greg Walker has recently suggested 1519 for reasons that will become clear later on. Nor do we have the wealth of information provided about performance that is imbedded in *Fulgens and Lucrece*. It may be that when Skelton wrote it, he was not yet sure for what occasion it would be performed. Suzanne Westfall has plausibly suggested that it may have been performed at some holiday feast of the household of the Earl of Northumberland, but the poet also had connections with the Duke of Norfolk, and there is at least the possibility that he hoped the play would be performed at court. Alternatively, as the play's most recent editor, Paula Neuss, has suggested, it may have been performed in the London hall of one of the liveried companies, perhaps the Merchant Taylors. *Magnificence* has usually been read as an attack on Cardinal Wolsey, whose high-handed, opulent lifestyle had already made him many enemies in and around the court of the young King Henry VIII. Indeed, it would appear that Wolsey himself took *Magnificence* personally – after familiarizing himself sufficiently with it, he is reported to have became Skelton's lifelong enemy. But Skelton's barbed wit may have been aimed more directly at Henry VIII himself. The play applies a traditional redemption pattern rather like that of the fifteenth-century play *Mankind* to the conditions of rule.

At the beginning of the play, Magnificence rules wisely, with Moderation tempering and guiding Liberty; but soon he falls into bad company. Sinister characters like Counterfeit Countenance, Crafty Conveyance, and Cloaked Collusion, unrecognized in their true nature by Magnificence, introduce him to Vices like Fancy and Folly who are eventually replaced by the far more sinister Adversity, Poverty, and Despair. Indeed, in this bitterly satirical play the traditional mummers' demand for "room" becomes a conniving plea for advancement at court. At the play's lowest ebb, Magnificence's government lies in ruins and he is on the verge of stabbing himself, but is rescued by Goodhope, Redress, and other Virtues, whereupon he and his court are quickly reformed.

Thus summarized, Skelton's play could offer useful advice to any person in power, not only to Cardinal Wolsey. But the play becomes particularly interesting if it is imagined as relating to Henry VIII and his court "reformation" of 1519. As Greg Walker explains, in 1518 Henry VIII had made several of his young, madcap companions Gentlemen of the Privy Chamber. They abused their new power, quickly antagonized everyone, and embarrassed the English government through their irresponsible behavior during an embassade to Paris and their gallicized affectation after their return. Recognizing his error, Henry hastened, in a sensational and widely publicized move, to dismiss several of these minions in May 1519, replacing them with what Edward Hall's contemporary *Chronicle* described as "sad and ancient knights" who helped him to reform his demoralized court. The play's term "Magnificence" was, in fact, used in earlier court records to refer to the Presence Chamber and the King's private apartments. Moreover, the many French affectations used by the Vices in the play link them closely with the King's gallicized companions. Taken with reference to Henry VIII, Skelton's play becomes a daring, trenchant accolade to the monarch for his 1519 household reforms, with an implied warning that a repeat lapse into bad companionship could produce the same disorders again. Thus understood, Skelton's *Magnificence* has a moral strenuousness and precision quite akin to that of the Stuart court masque of a century later, which both praised the monarch and held up his vices for royal acknowledgment and reform. In *Magnificence*, by contrast with *Fulgens and Lucrece*, a tried and true older nobility – like Skelton's allies Norfolk and Northumberland – are preferred over erratic upstarts. *Magnificence* brilliantly parodies the maneuvering and posturing by which would-be favorites gained and lost access to the monarch in the court of Henry VIII.

As we have noted, the late-medieval cycle plays that had been performed in various English towns during pre-Reformation times did not uniformly die out with the onset of the Protestant Reformation in England, though many of them were revised to suit the times. Rather, during the early Tudor period, Protestant dramatists attempted to create an alternative form of drama that existed for a while alongside the medieval plays, using some of the traditional plot structures but delivering an updated message. John Bale is one of the most interesting of the early Protestant dramatic polemicists. Having commenced his career as a Carmelite monk, he later joined the secular clergy and began promulgating strongly iconoclastic Protestant views. By the end of the 1530s we find him leading a troupe of actors apparently under the patronage of Thomas Cromwell, Henry VIII's principal secretary, and writing religious plays, many of them with scriptural subjects, designed to wean their audiences away from Catholicism or cement their allegiance to the new religion. As Walker has convincingly demonstrated, Bale's *King Johan*, or at least an early version of it that was considerably shorter than the composite text we have now, was performed during the Christmas holidays in 1539 at the house of reforming Archbishop Thomas Cranmer. *King Johan* is drawn from English history, and attempts to portray the thirteenth-century King John, who had been vilified by monastic chroniclers, as a righteous proto-Protestant who was hounded into destruction by the Roman Catholic hierarchy, local and international. In the play, poor widow England complains to King Johan about clerical abuses that have brought her low. But Sedition prevails upon Clergy, Civil Order, and Nobility to conspire against King Johan's attempted reforms, which bear a strong resemblance to the religious reforms advocated by Cromwell and Cranmer. Widow England is besieged by the "wild boar of

Rome" and his followers: "Like pigs they follow in fantasies, dreams, and lies, / And ever are fed with his vile ceremonies" (lines 72–73). Under Catholicism, as we have seen, mummings and other holiday shows would normally have been part of a household Christmas feast such as that at which *King Johan* was performed. But Bale cleverly assimilates such gambols to the activities of the corrupt Catholic clergy, a "rabble of Latin mummers" who disorient the people with mumbo-jumbo and hypocrisy. Throughout the play, Bale mockingly exploits the theatricality of Catholic religious practices – processions, auricular confession, the singing of Latin litanies, the assertion of spiritual vocation through monastic rules and habits, and the like – as empty devices employed to bring down the just King by setting his subjects against him.

The parallels between King Johan in the play and Henry VIII in the late 1530s are clear, although Henry was considerably less zealous than Cromwell and Cranmer in his desire to cleanse the church of any remaining trappings of popery. Like Henry, King Johan faces excommunication by the Pope for his attempted control over the English church, and threatened invasion by Continental powers opposed to his reforms. Contemporaries saw the resemblances all too well: one sympathetic auditor at the 1539 performance sponsored by Cranmer baited his more conservative neighbor by saying, "It is a pity that the bishop of Rome should reign any longer, for if he should, the said bishop would do with our king as he did with King John" (cited in Walker, *Plays*, p. 172). Bale and his players evidently took this show (and many others with similar messages), on the road and performed it in numerous locales. Although *King Johan* began its career at a household feast, it went through many revisions over the years, and was performed as Protestant polemic during the reigns of Edward VI and Elizabeth I, just as, during the intervening reign of the Catholic Mary Tudor, a polemical anti-Protestant drama flourished. At two points during the period, in proclamations from the reign of Edward VI (1549) and Mary 1553), the environment had become so heated that "interludes and plays" were banned altogether; in 1559 Elizabeth forbade all such plays to be performed without permission beforehand.[3] In its published Elizabethan form, *King Johan* ends happily, with Imperial Majesty redeeming Civil Order, the Clergy, the Nobility, and England, blessed with a "queen – thanks to the Lord above! – / Which may be a light to other princes all / For the godly ways whom she doth daily move, / To her liege people, through God's word special" (lines 2671–75). But even Elizabeth had her limits when it came to antipopery. She walked out offended from one polemical play that burlesqued the Catholic Mass.

One of the features of early Tudor drama that has led to its marginalization by Dryden's age and our own is its frequent reliance on allegorical personages, as illustrated in *Magnificence* and *King Johan*. For us, allegory is offensive or at least uncomfortable because it seems to flatten the juicy fullness of human personality into the sterility of abstraction. For the early decades of the sixteenth century, I would suggest, it had just the opposite effect. In the absence of fixed playhouses, creating a world of interrelated allegorical characters was one of the primary ways in which the early Tudor drama defined its own conceptual space, both closely related to and of necessity distinguishable from the everyday space inhabited by the audience. We need to reimagine the ways in which allegory may have functioned for such audiences: like poetic metaphor, allegory needs to be seen as expanding and complicating the human situations of the play rather than diminishing them.[4] On this reading, allegorical personages are not people reduced to abstractions, but abstractions attached to people – a compound entity that uses ideas to deepen our view of human transactions, sometimes with troubling ambiguity, by placing them within a dynamic matrix of ideas and moral insights.

In the plays we have discussed thus far, allegorical personages rarely operate simply; the actor performing one idea will frequently also perform its negation and sometimes take positions in between. By reading the plays in modern editions that identify the allegorical persons by name before they speak, we receive a false sense of certainty about the relationship of concept to person that was probably far less readily available to early audiences. Magnificence first takes Courtly Abusion for Pleasure: does the audience as well? *King Johan*'s Civil Order doubles as Sedition, but does the costume change happen on stage or off? Early printed texts of such plays often suggest possible doublings for performance by the traditional four men and a boy; part of the theatrical pleasure of such doubling came from the weighing of ambiguities it created. But familiarity with the practice would not necessarily make it less intriguing for viewers because it would be mobilized differently from one play to the next. The abstract language of allegory enlivens these plays by giving them a mercurial conceptual dimension and tying them to specific ethical situations of concern in the community at large.

With the development of fixed stages in the final decades of the sixteenth century, the physical and psychological distance between actors and audiences gradually increased and the line dividing them became more clearly defined. As Anne Higgins has wittily put the matter in her essay in *New History*, "It took a long time for spectators to learn passively to watch someone else's play, silent in someone else's theatre, ignored by the play itself, but eventually we did" (Cox and Kastan, eds., p. 92). Early Tudor drama usually assumes a more highly charged immediacy between players and onlookers; a modern American analogue might be the strong interactivity between preacher and congregation in a gospel church, by contrast with the customary sedateness and muteness of Presbyterians and Episcopalians. In the latter setting, the preacher performs before a seemingly passive audience who may dutifully intone their liturgical responses, but are not expected to show outward signs of active engagement with the ritual; in the former, much of the electricity of the performance is generated by the spontaneous vocal interplay between preacher and congregation.

A favorite early Tudor device is for the allegorical personage to insult or otherwise stir up the audience, as in John Rastell's *The Nature of the Four Elements* (c. 1517), where Ignorance claims "all they that be now in this hall, / They be the most part my servants all" (lines 1301–02). John Heywood's *The Four PP*, probably performed in a noble household sometime during the 1520s, is more cleverly devious. The play features a debate among a Palmer (pilgrim), a Pardoner, a Pothecary (apothecary), and a Pedlar. First the four Ps debate their rival accomplishments, but, in the normal manner of such plays, they soon descend into a lying contest. The Pardoner shows off his relics and the Pothecary his various medicines; both tell tall tales of the miraculous cures they have effected. The Pardoner's tale includes a heavy dose of antifeminism: he visits his friends, the devils in hell, to extricate the lost soul of Margery Coorson, evidently an actual historical person. The devils are glad to see her go for "all we devils within this den / Have more to do with two women / Than with all the charge we have beside" (Boas, ed., *Five Pre-Shakespearean Comedies*, lines 937–39). The Palmer responds, surveying an audience whose female part is no doubt by now bristling with indignation:

> Much marvel to me ensu'th,
> That women in hell such shrews can be,
> And here so gentle, as far as I see.   (lines 990–92)

Does the Palmer tell the truth or lie? When he asserts that in all his travels he has never met a woman out of patience, the Pedlar scoffingly retorts that the women in the audience should be canvassed as proof to the contrary, and awards the Palmer the prize for the "most excellent" lie of all. On most matters, however, the Palmer appears more reliable than the other Ps, and amid the conceptual tangles of their debate, a lie becomes hard to identify. The debate is projected out into the audience; its elaborate maze of lies within truths within lies is left unsettled; and how it is settled will depend on the individual beliefs of the onlookers.

The audience is enlisted in a more positive way in the later humanist school play *Wit and Science*, written by John Redford, master of the choir school of St. Paul's Cathedral, for performance before Henry VIII and evidently performed before the King some time between 1530 and his death in 1547. *Wit and Science* adopts the typical fall and redemption pattern that we have seen already in *Magnificence* and *King Johan*, except the fall in this instance is not so much religious or political as pedagogical. Wit is a dashing but baseborn young fellow about to be betrothed to a modest, wealthy damsel named Science; her father Reason has given Wit a mirror that allows him to behold "yourself to yourself" (line 3). Wit starts out bravely, helped by Study and Instruction, but soon allows Tediousness to bring him low. Honest Recreation revives him, along with other comforts, but Wit decides that Science is not for him: "Shall I tell you truth? / I never loved her" (lines 298–99). He throws off his academic gown, dances a galliard, and falls into the voluptuously soft lap of Idleness, who frightens off Honest Recreation. But things get worse: Ignorance enters and is subjected to a hilarious language lesson in which Idleness vainly tries to teach him to pronounce his own name. Ignorance and Wit trade clothing, and when Lady Science comes in to check up on Wit, she can see him only as Ignorance. And yet the love story continues. Looking in his mirror, Wit sees a face black as the devil's, recognizes how far he has fallen, is whipped by Shame, taken in hand once more by Instruction, and shown his goal of Mount Parnassus, where he will make Science his own. At play's end, though Science continues to express some doubts as to Wit's intentions, the planned love-match is reinstated and Wit is once again on the right path toward learning.

One could scarcely ask for a more seductive persuasion to learning than this romance between Wit and Science, promising the diligent student marital bliss, money, and security. The play's propaganda value for its performers, the choirboys of Paul's, is clear: hard work in the classroom will pay. But as Kent Cartwright points out, the play was performed at a time when Cardinal Wolsey and Henry VIII had made policy initiatives supporting the development of humanist education. At the point of his worst degradation, when Wit looks in Reason's mirror and sees himself as Ignorance, he tests the mirror by turning it on the audience:

> Other [either] this glass is shamefully spotted,
> Or else am I too shamefully blotted!
> Nay, by Gog's arms, I am so, no doubt!
> How look their faces here round about?
> All fair and clear they, everich [every] one,
> And I, by the mass, a fool alone,
> Decked, by Gog's bones, like a very ass!   (lines 806–12)

In all the company of noble auditors, he is the only ignorant fool. The audience is flattered by being numbered among the wise and witty, but also (at least by implication) encouraged to conserve their "fair and clear" aspect in Reason's mirror through continuing support for humanist education. *Wit and Science* combines the power of drama with many songs and dances in order to preach the value of what it also demonstrates – the skill and mastery of its schoolboy performers.

Not all early Tudor plays produced by educational institutions are so clearly self-referential. As critics have frequently marveled, did we not know that the rollicking farce *Gammer Gurton's Needle* originated as a university play in Christ's College, Cambridge, we would be hard put to connect it with the universities at all. *Gammer Gurton's Needle* was probably written and first performed during the early 1550s – before the death of King Edward VI in 1553, since it refers to the "king's name." The play's author is identified in a late printed edition (1575 and probably not the first) as "Mr. S.," probably William Stevenson, listed as Bachelor of Christ's College, Cambridge, in 1550, who went on to attain the MA degree and become a fellow of the college. The play itself is centered on the muck, mire, and dissension of village life in the north of England. Gammer Gurton has lost her prized, long needle, an implement whose phallic implications are exploited with much humor. Diccon, a "bedlam" and licensed beggar, has wandered into the village and, purely for the pleasure of entertaining himself and his audience, connives to set Gammer Gurton and her neighbors at odds over the needle and a supposedly stolen cock. The play's most unforgettable character is poor Hodge, Gammer Gurton's servant, whose breeches are torn in the most embarrassing possible place, a fact that enables numerous scatological jests on the part of himself and the other characters.

It would be a mistake to identify this play as singular in its carnivalesque preoccupation with the lower bodily strata. One of *Fulgens and Lucrece*'s low characters delivers a message to Lucrece from one of her suitors that is supposed to be about a kiss under a hollow ash, but he mistakenly asserts that she "fair kissed him on the nook of the arse" or the "hole," with predictably comic results. And in the *Four PP*, the Pothecary's cure depends on an elaborate contrivance by which a projectile is shot ten miles out of a woman's "tewel." Undoubtedly, the fecal humor common in these plays is one feature that made them repellant to neoclassical tastes later on. But the scatology of *Gammer Gurton's Needle* would have appealed to the play's first audience of young boys, aged ten or twelve to seventeen, at university.

Moreover, as Cartwright has suggested, since many in Christ's College were poor students who hailed from northern parts themselves, the northerners of Gammer Gurton's village would pointedly have reminded them of the foulness they had left behind them. For such an audience, the mock-heroic search for the needle would have been both an hilarious holiday escape from more serious endeavors and a reminder of how far they had progressed beyond their origins as a result of their devotion to learning. Diccon's escalating series of deceptions brings the rural society to confusion and, finally, gridlock, which is suddenly broken when he delivers Hodge a great "blow in the buttock." Hodge feels the blow as a bite – the long-lost needle, unwittingly left by Gammer in his breeches, is now impaled in his rump. All ends happily and Diccon gets off with only light punishment. What was his motive in producing this elaborate farce, beyond the odd rasher of bacon that he managed to procure on the side? To bring "good sport," as he avers several times during his stage-direction of the action, urging the musicians to pipe up during the intervals so that their "friends" in the audience will not lack "mirth," and, at the play's close, almost hating to abandon the audience. The madman-director abhors the vacuum that will be left when the interaction between players and the audience has ended.

Although these early Tudor plays have their antifeminist moments, in general they accord women considerable agency. This characteristic is visible already in *Fulgens and Lucrece*, where a Roman patrician gives his daughter the right to choose her own husband; it is yet more visible in the anonymous *Godly Queen Hester* (c. 1529), in which Queen Hester, obviously a highly educated woman, pleads successfully for the lives and welfare of her subjects. Indeed, throughout the early Tudor period, powerful, well-educated, and well-connected women had strong impact upon the subjects and ideology of the drama, and the resulting power of women within the plays may be one of the things that made them vaguely uncomfortable for readers of later periods. Walker has suggested that the queen in *Godly Queen Hester* is to be identified with Henry's first wife Katherine of Aragon, who was lobbying strongly and bitterly against the King's plans to divorce her and thereby weaken his ties with the Catholic church. In the play, Hester argues that a queen must have the same ability to rule as a king does, and indeed Katherine of Aragon had served as Regent during Henry's 1513 campaign in France. In real life, Katherine was unsuccessful, but in the play, which was almost certainly intended for performance before the divorce was finalized, she succeeds in winning her husband from his tyrannous ways and thereby saves her subjects.

The pattern of woman heroines continues in Mary Tudor's reign with *Respublica*, probably written by Nicholas Udall, a humanist schoolmaster who was closely connected with Mary's court and the children of the

Chapel Royal; the boys probably performed the play before the Queen herself. According to its manuscript title page, the play was "made in the year of our Lord 1553, and the first year of the most prosperous reign of our most gracious sovereign Queen Mary the first." In this interesting play, the reading of allegorical persons becomes genuinely perplexed. According to its carefully worded prologue, the play will demonstrate the abuses that beset "all commonweals" and Nemesis, the *deus ex machina* at the end who comes down to restore order, represents "Mary our sovereign and queen," sent down by God to reform "th'abuses which hitherto hath been" (lines 49–50). Such an allegorical scheme makes the play a Catholic answer to Bale's *King Johan*: Respublica, a lamenting female figure reminiscent of Bale's Widow England, has been ruined by her credulous acceptance of false counselors, whose abuses recollect the Edwardian religious reforms. One of them, whose actual identity is Oppression, is renamed Reformation and proceeds to enact abuses that strongly resemble Protestant inroads of the previous decades on the rituals and religious foundations of the English Catholic church. Read on this allegorical level, the play lauds the beginning of Mary's rule as a time for ecclesiastical recovery and reconsolidation. Lady Nemesis at the end deploys Justice tempered with Mercy to carry off Oppression/Reformation and his fellow Vices; she leaves Respublica under the protection of the Virtues, and announces "I must go hence to another country now, / That hath of redress the like case that was in you" (lines 1926–27). Presumably this "other country" is another Protestant nation in need of restoration to Catholicism, which Mary is proposing to restore to truth as she has Respublica. The play ends with Pax (Peace) and other Virtues lauding Queen Mary and her counselors and wishing them a long and peaceful reign.

But there are other cogent ways of reading the play which the Prologue, by insisting so strongly on the necessity of reading Mary as Nemesis, may actually provoke. Could it be that the author of the play had Mary's own vulnerabilities more centrally in mind? On another level of political allegory, it is almost impossible not to identify Mary with Respublica, and indeed, according to the theory of the "King's Two Bodies," the ruler, as a composite entity, was held to partake both of human weaknesses and need (like Respublica) and of divine perfection and power (like Lady Nemesis). If Mary in her "mortal body" is identified with Respublica, the play becomes in many ways a female version of *Magnificence*; and like *Magnificence*, which celebrated reforms initiated by Mary's father Henry VIII, *Respublica* shows a monarch beset by vices of her own making that threaten to bring down her government. Respublica's chief flaw, however, is not youth and folly but credulity: she mistakes devouring Avarice for

Policy, Adulation for Honesty, Oppression for Reformation, and Insolence for Authority. Throughout the play, her motives are good, as was indeed true of the historical Mary Tudor, known largely to later history as "Bloody Mary" because of her persecution of obdurate Protestants.

Unlike Magnificence in his play, however, Mary as Respublica is deeply concerned with the sufferings of People, who is harried and beaten as a result of Respublica's poor administrative choices. In her empathy for her suffering subjects, she closely resembles Queen Hester, and therefore Mary Tudor's mother Katherine of Aragon, whom, as argued earlier, Hester was designed on one level to represent. Interpreted on this level, *Respublica* artfully integrates patterns from earlier plays celebrating reforms either introduced or contemplated by both of Mary's parents. If Respublica is identified with Mary, Udall's play does not so much look backward at Protestant abuses as forward toward Mary's own potential for failure. The play is both cautionary and predictive: it movingly portrays Mary's dilemma as a champion of religious truth who manages to produce great suffering; when she seeks divine guidance, her prayers are answered. Truth shows her the mistakes she has made and redeems her; Nemesis appears as a *deus ex machina*, or as Mary herself in her "immortal body" as monarch, to set Respublica and her People to rights. This Marian play is far more complex than either interpretation taken alone would suggest, and demonstrates the flexibility and continuing vitality of allegory as revelation and political intervention during the 1550s.

After the accession of Queen Elizabeth in 1559, woman-centered drama took a seemingly odd turn. Plays like *The Tribulations of Mary Magdalene* and *The Play of Patient Grissell* began to emphasize women's victimization rather than their achievement. There are many possible explanations for this development, but one surely is that Queen Elizabeth herself was an important national symbol of martyrdom and resistance to tyranny. As a "second person" under Mary Tudor, she had come close to execution on more than one occasion for alleged treasonous activities designed to take over Mary's throne and restore the kingdom to Protestantism. Indeed, she herself admitted in her speeches later on that she could easily have become involved in such machinations. But she chose instead a path of heroic endurance.[5] The story of Elizabeth's noble sufferings is movingly told in Foxe's *Book of Martyrs*, even though, unlike most other martyrs in that volume, she managed to avoid execution. Elizabeth's motto was *semper eadem* – always the same – but with an oxymoronic feminine twist, in that her use of *eadem* instead of the usual masculine *idem* associates the feminine gender with steadfastness rather than the more stereotyped flightiness and changeability.

Beginning with its memorable treatment in the writings of Petrarch, the story of patient Griselda had become an exemplum for resistance against political tyranny.[6] We now see Griselda only as a masochistic sop who allows her husband to dominate her and haul her children off to be murdered; but in Petrarch's Latin version of the story, Chaucer's "Clerk's Tale," and the early Elizabethan *Play of Patient Grissell* (c. 1558–61), written by John Phillip, Griselda is rather a pattern of heroic steadfastness in the face of adversity, a pattern held up for emulation by women and men alike. The preface to the undated quarto edition of the play from the mid-1560s seems likely to have been part of the play in performance, and counsels its readers or viewers:

> Let Grissell's Patience sway in you, we do you all require,
> Whose history we unto you in humble wise present,
> Beseeching God we always may in trouble be content
> And learn with her in weal and woe the Lord our God to praise.
> My time is past, my charge is done, I needs must go my ways.
>
> (Preface, lines 17–21)

This early Elizabethan play parallels Chaucer's more familiar version in terms of plot, but lays rather more emphasis on the idea of tyranny. The low-born Grissell's loutish noble husband Gautier is persuaded by Politic Persuasion to deprive her of her children and finally even her marriage, as he sends her back to the humble cottage from which she came and makes plans for a new wedding. Every time they push her further, Gautier and Politic Persuasion watch closely for any sign of revolt, but to the long series of atrocities Grissell utters not one word of protest, although she movingly laments her sorrow and refers more than once to the "tyranny" of their proceedings. To my knowledge, no one during the period seriously advocated passivity and duty in a wife so profound that she would fail to protect the lives of her children, but many contemporaries did argue for heroic passivity as the only just response against tyranny. As Kent Cartwright has pointed out, the outraged reaction of women in Grissell's household points toward a normative response to Gautier's tyranny, and makes her own steady silence appear all the more uncanny.

During the tumultuous years before Elizabeth's accession England had in fact required very similar sacrifices on the part of her dutiful subjects. Cranmer and other Protestant notables were burned at the stake; many others were hounded into exile; families were divided and children lost. Without portraying Elizabeth's precise experiences under Catholic persecution, *Patient Grissell* gestures toward both her own and her nation's required fortitude under Mary's attempted reimposition of Catholicism. It is not uncommon for the drama, a sensitive barometer of public opinion, to help its audiences "work through" a major national calamity. Plays of the early 1590s obsessively replayed motifs relating to England's victory over the Spanish Armada in 1588 and her continuing vulnerability to Spanish invasion. Similarly, after 1660 the English stage convulsively reenacted elements of the traumatic civil war and execution of Charles I. In *Patient Grissell* and other similar plays of heroic endurance from the late 1550s and early 1560s, we can identify the same phenomenon, centered on the charismatic, iconic figure of Queen Elizabeth and heroines who resembled her, but celebrating the survival and steadfastness of a persecuted people who had suffered under the many cataclysmic alterations in the national destiny since the reign of Henry VIII, particularly Mary Tudor's forced reinstitution of Catholicism, which had abruptly been reversed upon the accession of Elizabeth. *The Play of Patient Grissell* closes by naming Elizabeth and the "lords of the Council" in a way that both links England's Queen with Grissell in the play and warns her and her government to "govern aright" so that they will avoid the tyranny illustrated in Gautier.

One effect of Gautier's cruelty in *Patient Grissell* is that he appears destined to die without heirs, as Mary Tudor did, until he reveals to Grissell that her children were not murdered, but secreted away. Contemporaries may have seen a parallel with Elizabeth's imprisonments at the Tower and Woodstock – a seeming extinction from which she yet emerged to carry on the Tudor line. A key concern of Elizabeth's subjects during the early years of her reign was the securing of heirs through her marriage (a fate that she managed to resist), or, failing that, through her designation of a list of successors to take over the throne in the event of her sudden death (a list that she steadfastly refused to make). The final play to be considered in this brief survey is also the most famous: *Gorboduc* or *Ferrex and Porrex*, written by Thomas Sackville and Thomas Norton for Twelfth Night during the 1561–62 Christmas revels of the Inner Temple and performed at court on 18 January 1562.

The Inns of Court were famous for their Christmas revels: during the 1561–62 holiday season, according to the diary of a London citizen, a lord of misrule rode through London, gorgeously dressed and accompanied by a hundred horsemen with chains of gold, into the Inner Temple, "for there was great cheer all Christmas . . . and great revels as ever for the gentlemen of the Temple every day, for many of the [Privy] Council were there" (*Gorboduc*, Cauthen, ed., p. xi). Usually, misrule meant jollity and comic topsy-turvydom. It is difficult for us to imagine the stark, powerful tragedy of *Gorboduc* as part of such revelry. But *Gorboduc* demonstrates the dangers of misrule on a national level by enacting the annihilation that resulted from the bad choices of an ancient British king. Part of the shock of *Gorboduc* for its contemporaries must have come from its startling innovations: it was, so far as we know, the first English play to use blank verse instead of rhyme, and the first to use dumbshows. Each of the play's five acts begins with a mute visualization of the essential meaning of the act that follows it. The technique is reminiscent of early English plays, in that, like the earlier Vices and prologues, the dumb shows of *Gorboduc* serve to create a space for performance, focus the audience's attention upon it, and suggest directions for interpretation. But *Gorboduc*'s dumbshows do not so much seduce the audience into participation as stun them into silent horror. The first depicts six wild men dressed in leaves who try to break a "fagot of small sticks," but do not succeed. Then they draw out one stick at a time, and easily dismantle it. In the main action of the first act, Gorboduc resolves to divide his kingdom between his two sons, Ferrex and Porrex, during his own lifetime, so that their strength can be occupied and he can guide them while going into semi-retirement. His counselors disagree among themselves about the wisdom of his action, but the dumbshow has already shown a truth Gorboduc himself does not see. Act Two is preceded by a dumb show of a king offered wine in a glass, which he refuses, and wine in a golden goblet, which he drinks. The wine in the goblet contained poison, and the king falls dead. So, during the second act, Gorboduc's two sons Ferrex and Porrex, both invested with their halves of the kingdom, "drink" bad counsel and plot each other's deaths. Act Three begins with a dumbshow of mourners; in that act Gorboduc learns that his younger son Porrex has murdered Ferrex. And so things continue from bad to worse: Gorboduc's Queen, outraged at Porrex's killing of her favorite son, murders Porrex; the angry people rise up and kill Gorboduc and his Queen, and by act Five there is war of all against all; the land is desolate, famine-ridden, and consumed by fire. The moral of all this? According to the final speech of the play, the fate of Gorboduc shows the vital importance of Parliament's declaring an order of succession so that modern England will not share the fate of Gorboduc's ancient Britain. But we can get more specific than that, because *Gorboduc* adds elements that are not in the play's chronicle sources. In *Gorboduc*, Porrex, the younger brother who kills his sibling, is the brother who held a kingdom from the Humber northward – he is therefore associated with the territory of sixteenth-century Scotland. Similarly, in the last act of the play, Fergus, Duke of Albany, looks down upon the waste of England and resolves to seize the throne. Albany was traditionally a Scottish title. *Gorboduc* warned Queen, Council, and Parliament of the importance of creating an order of succession in the event of Elizabeth's death. A few months before *Gorboduc*, she had told the Scots ambassador that such a move would be folly of the highest order: "Think you that I could love my winding-sheet?"[7] But further, with its portrayal of menacing Scots, *Gorboduc* was advising Elizabeth herself to remove the name of Mary Queen of Scots from the line of the English succession and thereby cancel out the horrific vision of Catholic Scottish engulfment of a vulnerable Protestant England. This vitally interesting play deserves more attention than can be afforded it here. Suffice it to say that *Gorboduc* offered Elizabeth advice that was probably most unwelcome. As our brief survey of early Tudor drama has suggested, it was the frequent plight of Tudor monarchs to be entertained with dramatic performances that showed the consequences of their mistakes and offered advice for good rule. But *Gorboduc* also does something that earlier plays discussed here did not – through the sheer terror of its visual images of dissolution, it awed its audiences into a submissive silence that made them spectators rather than co-creators of the action. If, as suggested earlier, the development of fixed stages eventually taught audiences to sit mutely and watch, ignored by the play itself, then *Gorboduc* was a step along the way.

NOTES

1 See John Orrell's essay on "The Theaters" in *A New History of Early English Drama*, ed. John D. Cox and David Kastan, (New York: Columbia University Press, 1997), pp. 102–12. For subsequent references to texts referred to by author's name in my chapter, readers are referred to the "Further reading" section at the end.

2 See John M. Wasson, "The English Church as Theatrical Space," in *New History*, eds. Cox and Kastan, pp. 25–37; and Richard Dutton, "Censorship," in *New History*, eds. Cox and Kastan, pp. 287–304.

3 See Dutton, "Censorship."

4 See Theresa M. Kelley, *Reinventing Allegory* (Cambridge and New York: Cambridge University Press, 1997), pp. 1–42.

5 I am indebted to Mary Beth Rose's chapter in progress on Elizabeth I in a forthcoming book tentatively entitled *Versions of the Heroic*.

6 See David Wallace, "'Whan She Translated Was': A Chaucerian Critique of the Petrarchan Academy," in *Literary Practice and Social Change in Britain, 1380–1530*, ed. Lee Patterson (Berkeley: University of California Press, 1990), pp. 156–215.

7 "Queen Elizabeth's Conversations with the Scottish Ambassador. William Maitland, Laird of Lethington, September and October, 1561," cited from *Speeches, Letters, Verses, and Prayers of Queen Elizabeth I*, ed. Leah S. Marcus, Janel Mueller, and Mary Beth Rose (Chicago: University of Chicago Press, 2000), Speech 4.

FURTHER READING

Anglo, Sydney, *Spectacle, Pageantry, and Early Tudor Policy* (Oxford: Oxford University Press, 1969).

Bale, John, *The Complete Plays of John Bale*, 2 vols., ed. Peter Happé (Cambridge, England, and Dover, NH: D. S. Brewer, 1985–86).

Bevington, David, *From "Mankind" to Marlowe: Growth of Structure in the Popular Drama of Tudor England* (Cambridge: Harvard University Press, 1962).

Boas, Frederick S., ed., *Five Pre-Shakespearean Comedies* (London: Oxford University Press, 1934).

Cartwright, Kent, *Theatre and Humanism: English Drama in the Sixteenth Century* (Cambridge: Cambridge University Press, 1999).

Cox, John D., and David Scott Kastan, eds., *A New History of Early English Drama* (New York: Columbia University Press, 1997).

Medwall, Henry, *The Plays of Henry Medwall*, ed. Alan H. Nelson (Cambridge: D. S. Brewer, 1980).

Phillip, John, *The Play of Patient Grissell*, ed. R. B. McKerrow and W. W. Greg, Malone Society Reprints (n.p.: The Malone Society, 1909).

Rastell, John, *Three Rastell Plays*, ed. Richard Axton (Cambridge: D.S. Brewer, 1979).

Records of Early English Drama, University of Toronto; published volumes to date include Chester (1979), Coventry (1981), Newcastle upon Tyne (1982), Norwich (1982), Cambridge (1989), and others.

Redford, John, *Wit and Science*, in *Medieval Drama*, ed. David Bevington (Boston: Houghton Mifflin, 1975).

S., Mr., *Gammer Gurton's Needle*, in *Five Pre-Shakespearean Comedies*, ed. Frederick S. Boas (London: Oxford University Press, 1934), also includes texts of *Fulgens and Lucrece* and *The Four PP*.

Sackville, Thomas, and Thomas Norton, *Gorboduc or Ferrex and Porrex*, ed. Irby B. Cauthen, Jr. (Lincoln: University of Nebraska Press, 1970).

Skelton, John, *Magnificence*, ed. Paula Neuss (Baltimore and Manchester: Johns Hopkins University Press and Manchester University Presses, 1980).

Udall, Nicholas, *Respublica*, ed. W. W. Greg, Early English Text Society, original series no. 226 (London: Oxford University Press, 1952).

Walker, Greg, *Plays of Persuasion: Drama and Politics at the Court of Henry VIII* (Cambridge: Cambridge University Press, 1991).

Westfall, Suzanne R., *Patrons and Performance: Early Tudor Household Revels* (Oxford: Clarendon Press, 1990).

White, Paul Whitfield, *Theater and Reformation: Protestantism, Patronage, and Playing in Tudor England* (Cambridge: Cambridge University Press, 1992).

Wickham, Glynne, *Early English Stages, 1300–1660*, 3 vols. in 4 (London: Routledge and Kegan Paul, 1959– 81).

8

SUZANNE GOSSETT

Dramatic achievements

THE CULTURAL NICHE

In 1575, when Christopher Marlowe and William Shakespeare were eleven years old, Ben Jonson three, and John Lyly and George Peele Oxford students, they could hardly have envisaged their eventual careers as actors, playwrights, theatrical administrators and investors. There were no permanent theatres in London. Playing in the area was irregular, produced by traveling companies performing occasionally in inn yards. Yet the next year saw the construction of a playhouse at Newington Butts, the opening of the Theatre in Shoreditch to the north, and the movement of the Chapel Children into a hall theatre in the Blackfriars, thus establishing both the types of theatres – outdoor, multistory "public" amphitheatres and smaller, enclosed "private" theatres – and the types of company personnel – adult men, with a few boys to act the women's parts, or entirely boy choristers – that would obtain until the closing of the theatres in 1642. In 1583 a playing company bearing the Queen's name was established. In 1594 a reorganization officially restricted playing to two companies at two playhouses, the Lord Chamberlain's Men at the Theatre and the Lord Admiral's Men at the Rose. Nevertheless, by June 1600 the proliferation of houses and companies was so great that the Privy Council issued an order "to restrain the excessive number of playhouses and the immoderate use of stage plays in and about the city."[1]

English drama in the last quarter of the sixteenth century was created to fill what Gary Taylor has called a new cultural niche. As Taylor argues, the new theatres generated a voracious demand for fresh wit and plays. This milieu, characterized by innovation, competition, and complex forms of collaboration, exemplifies Taylor's paradigm that "strong stimuli cluster."[2] Opportunities in the playhouses drew writers from other literary genres. Plots were borrowed from successes like Sidney's *Arcadia*, Spenser's *The Fairie Queene*, or Greene's *Pandosto*. The humanist revival of the classics helped shape tragic and comic form and attitude. More than half of the plays were written by more than one author, and almost all playwrights participated in such work. Other plays reveal the hand of that asynchronous collaborator, the revisor. Such circumstances made for rapid advances, so that plays of the 1580s look old-fashioned from the perspective of 1600; it is not only bardolatry that argues for a teleological development in which *Hamlet*, *Twelfth Night*, and *Henry V*, all 1599–1601, could not have existed without Thomas Kyd's *The Spanish Tragedy* (1587), Lyly's *Gallathea* (c. 1585), and Marlowe's *Tamburlaine* (1587).

Many elements of the culture indirectly supported the explosive growth of commercial drama. By the mid-1570s, when James Burbage opened the Theatre, Sebastian Westcott opened a playhouse for Paul's Boys and Richard Farrant did the same for the Blackfriars boys, Elizabeth had survived excommunication and the Northern Rising, had established long-lasting policies of "defensive neutrality" and financial stability, and was beginning the period of exploration that would lead to economic and geographic expansion. By the more difficult 1590s, when the country was troubled by disease, bad harvests, and war, the industry was entrenched, able to survive plague closings, religious objections, and such direct threats as a 1597 Privy Council order to destroy the theatres. London was the center of intellectual, social, and cultural life for those elements of the society – courtiers, students at the Inns of Court, wealthy merchants, visiting country gentry – who had leisure and means to attend the theatre frequently; apprentices, city wives, soldiers, artisans, and prostitutes elbowed their betters in the penny-entrance standing room and occasionally in the more expensive gallery seats. Although the theatres were physically on the margins of the city, their cultural significance was widely recognized. Complaints (to these "schools of licentious liberty ... more people resort than to sermons or prayers"), compliments (our plays are "a rare exercise of virtue" beating down "pride, lust, whoredom, prodigality ... drunkenness"),[3] calls for companies to furnish plays for the entertainment of the Queen, even attempts at regulation, all demonstrate the centrality of drama to the Tudor world that constructed it and was depicted and reconstructed by it daily.

The repertory system was intended to bring audiences back day after day, and the constant need for material once companies played in London six afternoons a week encouraged experimentation in style and subject. After 1594 the Admiral's and Chamberlain's staged new plays approximately once every two weeks. The remainder of the performances were continuations and revivals. Closely monitoring their rivals, the companies imitated each other's successes, revised or added sequels to their own, and spun off noteworthy characters or topics to new productions.

Competition in this theatrical milieu was personal as well as commercial and intellectual. Robert Greene objected to Shakespeare, the upstart-crow player, moving into the sphere of educated writers entitled to call themselves "university wits"; Jonson killed an actor and bragged that he had beaten John Marston; Kyd informed the authorities that Marlowe was responsible for the blasphemous opinions in writings found in their room. Francis Meres' *Palladis Tamia: Wit's Treasury* (1598), ostensibly "a comparative discourse of our English poets with the Greek, Latin and Italian poets," devolves into a purely English struggle, evaluating "our best for tragedy" and "the best for comedy" (Chambers, *The Elizabethan Stage*, vol. IV, p. 246). Yet rivalry between writers and companies was often fruitful, unlike the perpetual hostility of those who would have banned all theatrical activity. Following the 1572 Act for the Punishment of Vagabonds, which classified actors "not belonging to any baron of this realm or ... other honorable personage of greater degree" with other rogues and sturdy vagabonds (Chambers, *The Elizabethan Stage*, vol. I, p. 279), the companies found it essential to carry the name of one of the great aristocrats who used their services and did not share Puritan objections to playing. These Privy Councillors proved crucial in protecting the actors from their enemies, especially the powerful London authorities. The players thus benefited from two types of patrons: their nominal lords, and the theatrical entrepreneurs, primarily Philip Henslowe at the Rose and James Burbage and his sons at the Theatre, who furnished capital for scripts, costumes, and playhouses. All shared an interest in keeping the theatres open.

Hardest to distinguish are the contributions of the individual men – writers, actors, and producers were all men in the period, though by 1592 Mary Sidney had published her translation of Garnier's *Tragedie of Antonie* – and those of the theatrical environment in which they found themselves. The material conditions of production had an immediate formal impact. The "two hours' traffic of our stage" (*Romeo and Juliet*, Prologue, line 12) could only be a bit more in an outdoor, afternoon performance. Stage "mansions" or houses were used at court, but there was no scenery in the amphitheatres. Creation of the Queen's Men, which had twelve men where previous companies were no more than eight, permitted "large cast" plays (Gurr, *The Shakespearian Playing Companies*, p. 59), many of which were English histories. Was the explosive interest in this subject the effect of more plentiful personnel to "fight over York, and Lancaster's long jars" (Jonson, *Every Man In His Humour*, 1616, Prologue), of the rising nationalism embodied in such works as Holinshed's *Chronicles* or Camden's *Britannia*, or of the patriotism and taste of individual playwrights?

The ultimate shaping of a script was done by the companies' direct supervisor, the Master of the Revels – from 1578 to 1610 Edmund Tilney – as part of an ongoing negotiation between the state and the drama. The Master licensed plays for performance from 1574 and for the press from 1606. A 1559 proclamation had already prohibited staging discussion of religion or the government of "the commonweal." If, as some modern scholars and many Elizabethan opponents of theatre argue, the drama was significantly dissident, even radical, the authorities had reason to seek control. Occasional failures only parallel their failure to control other socially marginal voices. If the drama instead served as a safety valve, staging subversion as a means of containing it, excessive censorship would have been counterproductive. Jean Howard's proposal, that the stage functioned in a "complex and contradictory fashion within the interstices of a social formation which was not static,"[4] is borne out by the notable paradox of dramatic censorship: throughout the period control was extended over playhouses, companies, scripts, and published texts, but recurrent crises, in which texts were censored, playwrights jailed, theatres closed, and the boys' companies suppressed, demonstrate that control was erratic or intentionally inadequate. Although threatened with punitive measures and encouraged to self-censorship, playwrights still ventilated contentious topical issues. The licensing practices of the Master of the Revels suggest that he, too, collaborated, his allowance serving simultaneously as restriction and permission.

STYLE, FORM, SUBJECT

The power of Elizabethan drama comes from a number of related factors: characters who give an impression of interiority, a rich variety of styles, functional dramatic conventions, meaningful and coherent structure, generic innovation, and a sometimes dangerous willingness to engage major social and political issues. Twentieth-century critics have used different theoretical languages to insist that a dramatic character is no more than the lines he or she speaks, a text-effect or impression of subjectivity discursively produced and without past, future, or depth psychology. The consistent response of audiences from the sixteenth through the twentieth centuries has instead been to treat characters as unified selves with identities like real people. According to legend, royalty shared this reaction: Queen Elizabeth asked for more Falstaff; Charles I retitled his copy of *Much Ado About Nothing* "Benedick and Beatrice." Rather than denying the force of these characters, therefore, some recent analyses attempt to describe how the illusion of reality is created. Katharine

Maus relates the impression to Renaissance epistemological beliefs. In a "culture in which truth is imagined to be inward and invisible," individuals on stage, as in life, demand that the viewer search for "selves" not displayed but assumed to be present.[5] Among methods creating the "subjectivity effect" Alan Sinfield includes "self-reference and self-questioning (including soliloquy), indecision, lying" and "the appearance of entertaining more than one discourse at a time."[6] Even so, gender and rank limit the style and degree of subjectivity permitted.

The illusion of individuality is created largely through language. Meres' criteria include "fine wit" and "glorified phrase," and as dramatic blank verse makes a radical jump from its beginnings in the end-stopped lines and formal verse paragraphs of *Gorboduc* (1562) to the "high astounding terms" of *Tamburlaine* (1587) and then develops more gradually, it gains flexibility, richness of imagery, and specificity to the speaker. Falstaff, parodying the alliteration and balance of Lyly's euphuistic style, assumes his audience recognizes the growing naturalism of prose. By the end of the century, in plays like *The Shoemaker's Holiday* or *Henry V*, prose and verse intertwine as indications of class, style, and subject. Yet language visibly decorative, self-delighting, and intended for enjoyment in itself, persists. Especially favored was the highly patterned rhetoric of trial scenes.

The range of convention was broad; along with surprisingly realistic details this drama derives strength from its use of "gests" or bold dramatic images combining visual elements with dialogue.[7] Hieronimo rising from his "naked bed" to discover his son's body was one of the most frequently remembered. The mutilated Lavinia of *Titus Andronicus* or Barabas the Jew of Malta falling into his own cauldron are resonant symbols in environments of political intrigue. Sidney objected to "two armies ... represented with four swords and bucklers,"[8] but history plays required that movement through time and space be handled with maximum efficiency: "Barkloughly Castle call they this at hand?"; "O, call back yesterday, bid time return, / And thou shalt have twelve thousand fighting men!"(*Richard II*, III.ii.1, 69–70).

Structural development was from variety and multifariousness to meaningful multiple plotting. In Thomas Preston's *Cambises* (c.1565), which combines gods, allegorical figures, and ordinary folk, a sword wounds the king "by sudden chance." In later plays plots and characters are parallel or contrasted, action causal. Robert Greene's *Friar Bacon and Friar Bungay* explores the power of magic in interrelated actions; couples in John Lyly's *Endymion* represent stages on the platonic ladder of love. Movement between locations takes on thematic significance, and entertainments illuminate and often advance the main action.

The playwrights desired a self-conscious audience, aware of the con-structed nature of performances before them. Frames were a favorite device: *The Spanish Tragedy* (1587) opens with Revenge inviting Andrea, "Here sit we down to see the mystery, / And serve for Chorus in this tragedy" (lines 90–91); as Madge in Peele's *Old Wives Tale* (c.1593) begins to talk, Frolic observes, "Soft Gammer, here some come to tell your tale for you" (lines 129–30). The majority of frames intrude into the developing fiction. Sly in *The Taming of the Shrew* (c.1590–93) disappears after the first act, possibly to strengthen the misogynistic taming plot, but in the anonymous *The Taming of A Shrew* he comments throughout. These interruptions break the audience's suspension of disbelief, reminding them of such theatrical conventions as doubling and cross-dressing, methods of exposition, and the "abridgement" that reduces "th' accomplishment of many years / Into an hourglass" (*Henry V*, Prologue, Chorus to Act 5). Similar "alienation" effects are created by the staging of interior plays or, in *Friar Bacon and Friar Bungay*, by Bacon's magic mirror (scene 6, line 128).

Metatheatrical references demonstrate that Elizabethans, like Polonius, thought of drama by styles, types, and genres (*Hamlet*, II.ii.397–99). In Ben Jonson's *Poetaster* (1601–02) Tucca's pages audition by demonstrating "King Darius' doleful strain," an "amorous vein," a "horrible fierce soldier," "the ghost" of revenge tragedy, "the Moor" (from *The Battle of Alcazar*), and a Machiavellian intriguer. Unclassical mixtures, characteristic of the period, were often charming and successful. The extant works of George Peele, "a working Elizabethan writer whose literary product owes less to the artist's individual nature than it does to the corporate natures of the audiences he sought to entertain,"[9] constitute a cross-section of these unsynthesized genres. *The Arraignment of Paris*, a court play, was an "experiment in versification"[10] as well as flattery, assigning the golden apple to "the Nymph Eliza a figure of the Queen" (1137. s.d.). *The Old Wives Tale* is a romance coupling literary satire and a diatribe against parish burial fees with a fairytale magician and man-turned-bear. *David and Bathsebe*, based on biblical "discourses," incorporates contemporary dramatic subjects – sexual license, political succession, a Faustian desire for knowledge. *The Battle of Alcazar* merges the grand historical theme, "three bold kings ... contending for a crown," (Induction) with topical concern for racial "others" encountered through exploration or trade.

Edward I is even more heterogeneous. Lluellen, the Welsh prince, disguises as Robin Hood, and the popularity of this part may have encouraged Henslowe to commission two Robin Hood plays (Chambers, *The Elizabethan Stage*, vol. III, pp. 446–7). Lluellen's double-agent brother is an intriguing Machiavel. The Queen's deathbed confession to the King, which Webster borrowed for *The White Devil*, and her illegitimate daughter's "groveling" death are as lurid as Jacobean tragedy. For "gests" there are the Friar playing dice against an invisible St. Francis, or the Queen sinking into and rising from the earth. This wicked Queen is Spanish. Her murder of the Mayoress displaces class tensions onto female reproductive jealousy, and her adultery renders illegitimate the genealogy justifying the Spanish Infanta's claim to the throne of England (Braunmuller, *George Peele*, pp. 96–97). The play promotes a vision of national greatness with a strong central monarchy, while participating in the "people's history of England" that the Henslowe companies staged.[11] Problems in transmission of the text, and conflicting sources, make for occasional incoherence, but Shakespeare remembered the death of the Mayoress, nursing an asp at her breast, for *Antony and Cleopatra*.

Ultimately these plays looked as much outward as inward. Cultural discourses on rightful authority in home and state, on marriage, on class relations, on the exclusive or inclusive limits of the nation, circulated through these plays, which were both "historically determined and determining modes of cultural work."[12] Even *Romeo and Juliet*, that timeless tragedy of love and death, participates in Elizabethan debates on matchmaking, private revenge, illiteracy, criminalization of the poor, divided loyalties to blood and milk parents, homosocial bonding, and effeminization through heterosexual love.

COURT DRAMA

Plays were written and produced specifically for the court as well as being brought to court by the public troupes, whose productions were sustained by the defensive fiction that all performances were rehearsals of potential court entertainments. Both kinds of plays might contain flattery, criticism, and advice, although the latter elements were concealed under allegory of varying impenetrability. We can never know how topical a performance was, since there might be unscripted insertions or silent parody. But many plays were political actions in a culture of barely-suppressed contestation. The Queen was quick to find analogies, for example between herself and Richard II, and equally capable of ignoring them. Her reputed desire to see Falstaff in love suggests that she preferred a different focus from the recurrent concern of Shakespeare's Henry IV plays with legitimate succession – she had herself been declared illegitimate – and their validation of "performative masculinity" as the sign of kingship.[13]

In the 1580s the playwright most successful in finding a mode of court address was John Lyly. His plays repeatedly verge on specific allegory, but just as Diana or Cynthia seems about to "be" Elizabeth he retreats to a safe, vague relevance, suiting the goals of comedy announced in the Prologue to *Sappho and Phao*, "to move inward delight, not outward lightness," and to give pleasure through "counsel mixed with wit." Lyly's plays never actually incorporate the Queen, although *Campaspe* and *Sappho and Phao* (1584) have separate prologues for court performance. Both depict a ruler over-coming personal desire; both resist attempts to make the details match the candidates among Elizabeth's suitors. This indefiniteness is intentional: Lyly writes transparent satire of Philip II of Spain in the gold-seeking, ass-eared Midas who admits to enticing "the subjects of my neighbor princes to destroy their natural kings" (*Midas*, III.i. 38–39). Allegory intended for the Queen was safer than that about her.

The complexity of Lyly's method is best seen in *Endymion*, produced by Paul's Boys at Greenwich on Candlemas, 2 February 1588, during rumors of impending invasion. The unchanging moon/queen Cynthia obviously suggests Elizabeth, and Endymion may represent Lyly's employer the Earl of Oxford, one of a group of courtiers suspected of open or assumed Catholicism. In this allegorical framework, Tellus becomes the outwardly beautiful, inwardly corrupt Catholic church rather than a specific woman, and the play "asks for royal tolerance of English Catholics provided they take the crucial step of proclaiming their loyalty."[14] At the same time, Endymion, sleeping forty years and rewarded for adoration only with indefinite promises, carries overtones of the frustration that male courtiers felt toward the ageing Queen, as well as Lyly's own chagrin at failing to receive court advancement. Beneath the engagingly decorative surface of euphuistic prose is a surprising amount of social resonance. Problems of adequate employment, misogyny – Tellus and the witch Dipsas are oblique aspects of Cynthia, who is "contaminated by her apparent opposites" (Montrose, *The Purpose of Playing*, p. 164) – resistance to authority, witchcraft, and social mobility all emerge. It is not so surprising that Lyly and his boys were drawn into the religious and political Marprelate controversy, although it is unclear whether indiscretion or competition from the "new large-scale adult company plays like *Tamburlaine*" led to the closing of Paul's Boys, effectively ending Lyly's career (Gurr, *The Shakespearian Playing Companies*, p. 226).

Ultimately, performance at court, while valuable for prestige and com-pensation, could be treacherous, like every interaction between theatre and authority. Allegorical representations of the monarch could encounter objections. *Cynthia's Revels* (1600), which resolves with the appearance of the "Queen and huntress, chaste and fair," was nevertheless, according to Dekker, "misliked at court" (*Satiromastix*, Act 5, scene 2). Contemporary understanding of such reactions is found within the plays. A court audience might, like Claudius in *Hamlet*, choose not to hear, or like Theseus in *A Midsummer Night's Dream*, treat the occasion as more important than the entertainment. Yet the actors recognized their own responsibility. In *The Spanish Tragedy* Hieronimo's presentation of his court entertainment in "sundry languages" (IV.iv.74) symbolizes the actors' desire to speak and yet not to speak, to be understood and yet – as in Hieronimo's finally biting out his tongue – to be silent "rather than to reveal" under compulsion.

TRAGEDY: HEROIC AND DOMESTIC TRANSGRESSION

As Henslowe's surviving diary demonstrates, most of the repertory of the leading Elizabethan companies consisted of histories and comedies: trage-dies were "rare and valuable commodities."[15] In the Induction to the anonymous *A Warning for Fair Women* (>1599), Tragedy claims to "reign as queen / In great *Apollo's* name and all the *Muses'*." Such triumphant classicism is ironic in a domestic tragedy, but the important tragic plays of the period share a grandeur that recalls the Senecan tragedy studied by Elizabethan schoolboys and transcends other differences, like the morality framework of *Dr. Faustus* or the blurring into history that led Meres to praise among Shakespeare's tragedies "his *Richard the 2, Richard the 3*" (Chambers, *The Elizabethan Stage*, vol. IV, p. 246).

The first key period for Elizabethan tragedy roughly coincides with Marlowe's short and productive life in the theatre, beginning in 1587 when he introduced "the Scythian Tamburlaine / Threatening the world with high astounding terms" (Prologue, 4–5) and ending with his murder in May, 1593. *The Spanish Tragedy* appeared either just before or just after the 1588 Armada; *Dr. Faustus* is now thought to have followed *Tamburlaine*; *Titus Andronicus* was new for Sussex's Men in January 1594, but may have been performed by other companies earlier. These plays have in common a larger-than-life, transgressive hero, a detailed historical or political frame-work, and an interrogation of major cultural issues such as the limits of patriarchy, the conflict between individual aspiration and established authority, or the state's ability to provide adequate justice. Ethics are never entirely separate from politics: religious attitudes in the A-text of *Dr. Faustus* reflect the radical Protestantism of the English war party in the 1580s and 90s.[16]

Tamburlaine has been convincingly dubbed a "Herculean hero," like his mythical forebear operating outside the moral norms of ordinary men. Declaring that "Nature that framed us of four elements ... Doth teach us all to have aspiring minds" (II.vii.18–20), he claims to "hold the fates bound fast in iron chains" (I.ii.174). In Part I his success and magnificence come, significantly, as much from "working words" (II.iii.25) as conquering arms. He captures the Soldan's daughter in an ambiguously "offensive rape," yet Zenocrate soon desires only to "live and die with Tamburlaine!" (III.ii.6, 24). His pride brings down no divine retribution. As an eastern alien, Tamburlaine is both barbarous and awe-inspiring; but this alluring and terrifying fantasy represents unchecked forces in early modern England: ambitious men rising with "giantly presumption" (II.vi.2); sturdy rogues and decommissioned soldiers whom travelers might encounter in the countryside; half-piratical merchant explorers.

In the second part Marlowe seems less assured as he confronts immutable limitation: even "Tamburlaine, the scourge of God, must die" (Part II, v.iii.249). Not the chariot but Zenocrate's traveling hearse is the major property. Tamburlaine slays an effete son, reversing his earlier displacement of father-kings, and becomes ever more a "desiring machine" producing violence and death.[17] Marlowe teases his audience's religious sensibilities: it is after burning the "Turkish Alcoran" and challenging Mahomet that the hero falls ill, and Tamburlaine's apparently orthodox conclusion that "The God that sits in heaven ... is God alone" is astonishingly qualified by the agnostic challenge, "if any God " (Part II, v.i.199–200). Dramatists like Lodge, Peele, and Greene, capitalizing on Marlowe's smash hit, imitated his rhetoric and glamorous stage effects but avoided similar violations of conventional attitudes.

The Spanish Tragedy is the other seminal tragedy of the period, consolidating the dominance of the revenge play. It is a compendium of imitable and endlessly imitated models: contrasting male and female madness, a letter written in blood, Machiavellian conniving, grotesquely comic death, a fatal entertainment, rhetorical excess like "O eyes, no eyes, but fountains fraught with tears!" (III.ii.1). Its brief moment of romantic love, the erotic hand combat of Bel-Imperia and Horatio, is recycled for *Romeo and Juliet*. Dramatically the play is a "parade of great theatrical emblems," and Hattaway suggests that Kyd "created the 'scene' as the elemental dramatic unit" (*Elizabethan Popular Theatre*, pp. 105–06). Kyd maintains control through consistent irony. Hieronimo, Knight Marshall of Spain, is expected to dispense justice but can find none. Andrea's revenge receives approval from the classical gods, yet apparently he died fairly on the battlefield. Bel-Imperia resists being the conduit of a royal alliance, yet rather than romanticizing her choice, Kyd depicts her violating "status, kinship, and gender norms" by illicit sexual activity.[18] Most shockingly, dutiful, socially-circumscribed Hieronimo destroys two royal houses.

The popularity of *The Spanish Tragedy* is evident in the ubiquitous parody of its lines and in the commissioning of two sets of additions. *Dr. Faustus* was even more elaborately revised and enlarged. The A-version, now deemed closer to the original of Marlowe and an unidentified collaborator, focuses intensely on the pressing paradox of post-Reformation Calvinism, the significance of human action in a universe of predestination. Where violation of social and political norms in *Tamburlaine* exalts the spirit, Faustus' rebellion against God leads only to the terrifying hour – summarized in a magnificent soliloquy – in which Faustus, unable to reach Christ's blood though it "streams in the firmament!" waits for the clock to strike and the devils to carry him off. Almost all of Faustus' actions are attempts to escape from the spiritual isolation of the individual soul. In this way he is as much the progenitor of Hamlet as is the revenger Hieronimo.

Dr. *Faustus* has been a particular template for interpretations. Earlier readers saw it as an embodiment of "Renaissance" humanist intellectual aspiration, but many postmodern readers stress indications that for Faustus freedom is an illusion. In the A-text the Good Angel offers only the dubious promise that it is "never too late, if Faustus can repent" (II.iii.79). The tragedy is deepened by parodic moments that remind audiences of the emptiness for which Faustus rejects salvation: Faustus asks Helen to "make me immortal with a kiss" (v.i.93); his servant aspires to "make all the maidens in our parish dance at my pleasure stark naked before me" (II.ii. 3–5). The magician's grandeur is thus deflated even before he is dragged away mouthing a last, futile offer to renounce intellect and magic: "I'll burn my books. Ah, Mephistopheles!" (v.ii.123).

Senecan influence is especially clear in *Titus Andronicus*, which combines a "serious critique of Roman ideology"[19] with ghoulish horrors, resonant emblems, and stoic suffering. The scene in which Titus recognizes Tamora through her disguise as Revenge fittingly represents the play's generic self-consciousness and complexity. As in Kyd, political ambitions are played out on women's bodies. Yet the play disorients audience sympathies by obliterating distinctions between the innocent and the corrupt. "That ravenous tiger, Tamora" (v.iii.194) gains compassion when she sheds "A mother's tears in passion for her son!" (I.i.109), but later she becomes a murderous mother, determined to kill her inconveniently black baby. Mutilated Lavinia terrifies her nephew, and her mouth becomes a disturbing upper body displacement for her abused womb. Most important, Titus is a mistreated patriot, but he kills his own son and causes the invasion of Rome. In Shakespeare's later works these jarring elements would be separated, the political scenes nourishing English and Roman histories, the major characters – Titus, Tamora, Aaron – helping to generate Lear and Goneril, Othello and Iago.

Although *Titus* and *The Spanish Tragedy* are heroic tragedies, they link political revolution to sexual violation. The idea that a culture speaks through private as well as public action was familiar to Elizabethans from conduct manuals and homilies which stressed the parallels between the domestic and political spheres. Recently it has helped breach the critical firewall dividing heroic from domestic tragedy. Plays like *Arden of Faversham* (>1592), *A Warning for Fair Women* (1598–99), and Thomas Heywood's *A Woman Killed With Kindness* (1603), once slighted because of the reduced scale of their action and because the central transgressor is female, still engage tragic conflicts. While maintaining a homiletic pattern of sin, discovery, repentance, and punishment, they depict what Catherine Belsey has called "the breakdown of order – the rape of women and property – which follows when the exchange of contracts in a market economy supplants old loyalties, old obligations, old hierarchies."[20]

Arden of Faversham is based on a real crime sufficiently heinous to be recounted in Holinshed's *Chronicles:* husband murder was petty treason, as were attacks on a master by servants.[21] Yet Alice's act of rebellion against the marital authority of her husband is embedded in a framework of social and economic disruption centered on him. Thomas Arden is a "new" man, beneficiary of the land distribution that followed the breakup of the monasteries and indifferent to the sufferings of former tenants. His pride is punished by both men and gods: his eventual murderer resents his social contempt – "There's for the pressing iron you told me of" (scene 14, line 235) – and he is fittingly found on ground he held "by force and violence" (Epilogue, line 11).

Arden and Frankford in *A Woman Killed* are inadequate domestic statesmen who leave their homes rather than purifying and fortifying them. Because he has not properly ruled his realm, Arden is safer anywhere else: repeated attempts to kill him outside fail, and he is murdered at his own table, while Mosby usurps the master's chair. Frankford actually introduces his betrayer – a male "companion" (scene 4, line 72) – into his household, instructing his wife to use him as "a present Frankford in his absence" (scene 6, line 80). After Anne does "use" Wendoll, Frankford avoids murder by cleaning house. He will keep neither Anne nor her belongings. Her penitent self-starvation constitutes her refusal to consume any more of his property once she has allowed his most valuable possession to be violated.

The social significance of these plays emerges from their lack of romanticism. None of the adulterous relationships is satisfactory: sexual sin is not merely condemned, it is not pleasurable. The women have agency only to do ill and possess little subjectivity. All three women are at last contained and under observation, and all speak the voice of the restored patriarchy as they publicly express repentance. The plot of *A Woman Killed with Kindness* (1603) has many parallels with *Othello* (1603–04), Shakespeare's most domestic tragedy, yet there is no similar sense of mysterious evil. As Anne dies, the major male characters readjust their alliances; the betrayer Wendoll contemplates new employment. The power of domestic tragedy comes instead from its imbrication in the social fabric. No individual loss interferes with its continuity.

THE HISTORIES: SELF AND NATION

The English history play is largely the creation of Shakespeare, whose *Henry VI* plays seem to have been preceded only by the anonymous *The Famous Victories of Henry V*. The vogue was short-lived, almost entirely confined to the 1590s. Though recognized in its own time, the genre was amorphous, identified primarily by the national subject matter and the frequent presence of "drum and ensign" (Induction, *A Warning for Fair Women*). Yet the history plays do have a consistent purpose: in them late-Elizabethan culture recounts the fifteenth century to explain the sixteenth. Jean Howard and Phyllis Rackin claim the plays are an "ideological apparatus for the construction of an emergent national consciousness" (*Engendering a Nation*, p. 47), but this consciousness was not unitary. Instead the histories resist closure, asking questions on which national consensus had to be built: who and what constitutes the nation geographically and demographically? What do populace and leader owe each other? Is there a mystical basis legitimizing the political structures, or are they pragmatic arrangements imposed by force and maintained for the benefit of those in power?

In *Henry VI* and *Edward II* Shakespeare and Marlowe examine the same phenomenon, the weak king caught between obligation and desire. The ideological stance of the three *Henry VI* plays is open to conflicting interpretations. Whether the scenes of Jack Cade's rebellion seem sympathetic or satirical depends partly on whether one sees Shakespeare's histories echoing their source, Holinshed's *Chronicles*, in working out "something like political liberalism,"[22] or instead as concerned "above all with the consolidation and maintenance of royal power" (Helgerson, *Forms of Nationhood*, p. 234). Stylistically these histories fluctuate between morality structures and the realism of a campaign headquarters: Edward II's anal penetration by a hot spit emblematizes all he has lost through sodomitical obsession, yet his relation to Gaveston is pragmatically acknowledged by the Mortimers: "The mightiest kings have had their minions" (1.iv.390). Their real objections are to the favorite's class mobility and the waste of military pay. Not until *Richard III* does Shakespeare's first tetralogy fully integrate political and psychological motivation. In *Henry VI Part III* Richard is a self-proclaimed theatrical icon, the "murderous Machiavel," but in *Richard III* the strategizing tyrant's dreams, memories, and compensatory fantasies create the illusion of "interior being."[23]

In *Richard II* all classes, from analogizing gardeners to "neuter" York, participate in a five-act meditation on the foundations of rule and the dilemma of conflicting loyalties. The confrontation between incompetent legitimacy and politically-savvy usurpation is won but never resolved. In broad terms Richard and Henry, rightful king and able administrator, represent residual and emergent forms of political power. As Howard and Rackin suggest, the victory of the claimant who leans on performance rather than heredity, like the domestic confinement of women and the identification of the nation with geographical space rather than monarch's body, marks the second tetralogy as incipiently modern, but the personal and political losses are evident (137–215).

By *Henry IV, Parts I and II*, metaphor, emblem, and historical reality merge. Multiplying fathers, Shakespeare explores simultaneously the psychological and political transmission of heritage. Falstaff is the carnivalesque representation of bodily life, a "reverend Vice," the surrogate parent who warms "the cold blood [Prince Harry] did naturally inherit of his father" (*Part II*, iv.iii.116–117), but he is also a man who claims battlefield victory unjustly and who separates the prince from a worn and needy father. Here, unlike *Tamburlaine*, it is not the effete son who is killed by the warrior father; instead the martial Hotspur, anachronistic in his inability to play even family politics, is abandoned on the battlefield. Meanwhile the consummate actor/son saves his father's life before taking the crown and, with an absolutism even he cannot believe and that three plays have called into doubt, claiming that "plain and right must my possession be" (*Part II*, 4.5.222).

Throughout the second tetralogy, Shakespeare complicates the ideal national ethos embodied in Gaunt's vision of "this sceptered isle." Hotspur, Mortimer, and Glendower are as ready to divide "this fortress ... this little world" (*Richard II*, ii.i.40–45) as the inhabitants of the Eastcheap tavern are to misappropriate the king's press, the "laws of England" (*Part II*, 5.3), the sacred body of the heir apparent – even the language which unites those institutions. The oscillation of the *Henry IV* plays across the countryside becomes a symbolic representation of the difficulty of controlling both geographic and social marginality. Henry banishes his detractors but the English audience, facing the end of a dynasty, a Scottish claimant, and an Irish revolt, could not so easily resolve the complexities of national identity.

COMEDY: ROMANTIC, NATIONALISTIC, SATIRIC

Elizabethan comedy is primarily romantic, joining magic, music, clowning and pastoralism to tales of love and imaginative adventure. It is much enriched by the incorporation of patriotic, realistic, and satiric strands. The stylistic progression is toward satire and the domestic realism that in the Jacobean period would become city comedy. By 1599, Mitis in Jonson's *Every Man Out of His Humour* looks back nostalgically – though, in light of *Twelfth Night* (1600–01), a little prematurely – to plays "of some other nature, as of a duke to be in love with a countess, and that countess to be in love with the duke's son, and the son to love the lady's waiting maid: some such cross-wooing, with a clown to their servingman, better than to be thus near, and familiarly allied to the time" (Grex, III.vi.195–201). Nevertheless, even romantic comedies incorporate "familiar" social and historical issues, particularly gender transgression, family conflict, and class and ethnic tensions.

Lengthy female rule, a theatre that notoriously "took boys for women," and a continuing controversy about woman's nature all encouraged a dramatic focus on permutations of gender. The production realities of all-male casts infuriated preachers and moralists, who inveighed against cross-dressing as a violation of biblical prohibition, and who may have been right that for some of the male audience effeminate boy actors provided homo-erotic titillation. Female audience members, Stephen Orgel suggests, took equally disruptive pleasure in seeing a "youth in skirts" not as "possessor or master, but as companionable and pliable."[24] The performative nature of the actor's staged gender, with its subversive implication that all gender is socially constructed, was especially thematized within comedies, notably by cross-dressed characters. Such figures threaten the "normative social order based upon strict principles of hierarchy and subordination" (Howard, *Stage and Social Struggle*, p. 94). Yet because the dramatic energy of disguise always risks focusing on the work of the actor rather than the literary representation, the interaction between play and cross-dressed player created an obsessive meditation on theatrical fiction to which gender was assimilated as a major instance.

The arbitrary construction of gender identity is clearly suggested in Lyly's *Gallathea* (1584–85), where the problem posed by two young girls who fall in love with each other while disguised as boys is resolved by letting Venus "turn one of them to be a man"; which one is neither revealed nor obvious from distinctions between them. Furthermore, each girl suspects the other's true sex. The virgin sacrifice which the girls escape represents heterosexual union as rape, and Lyly suggests homoerotic sexuality by Phyllida's invitation, "let us into the grove and make much one of another" (III.ii.55). Even in *Twelfth Night*, Shakespeare's play where homoerotic desire circulates most openly, all the characters but Antonio are repositioned by the "bias" of nature. In *Gallathea* the final image is of single-sex marriage.

Plays of cross-dressing vary in their challenge to traditional stereotypes. Dorothea in Greene's *James IV* and Viola in *Twelfth Night* demonstrate "female" weakness despite male disguise: forced to fight Sir Andrew, Viola offers the Lacanian aside, "A little thing would make me tell them how much I lack of a man" (III.iv.302–03). Female disguise, as in Haughton's *Englishmen for My Money* (1598), may facilitate "breeding ... a jolly boy" (line 2662). But Portia in *The Merchant of Venice*, though she has announced herself as "an unlessoned girl, unschooled, unpracticèd" (III.ii.159), once disguised violates the real and symbolic boundaries of the married woman, the closed house and the closed mouth. She leaves by the "common ferry" for Venice, where she manipulates fundamental instruments of the patriarchy: oratory, law, money, and inheritance. She is no longer cross-dressed when she threatens ultimate openness – "I'll not deny him anything I have, / No, not my body nor my husband's bed" (V.i.227–28) – but through male disguise she has regained control of her resources and herself.

Arranged marriage is the most common issue of family contention in comedy, though legal manipulations over inheritance and property are also pervasive. There was inherent tension between the comic form inherited from Terence and Plautus, which insistently sided with independent young lovers, and contemporary homilies and domestic conduct manuals, which assured parents of their right to determine their children's future, though counseling them to allow a veto. In practice there was wide variation in the freedom experienced at this liminal moment. One dramatic solution, exemplified in *Friar Bacon and Friar Bungay* and *The Taming of the Shrew*, was to finesse the issue by including two marriages – one arranged, one stolen – and by collapsing the apparent opposition between love and arrangement. Those of high station were most constrained: in *Friar Bacon* Prince Edward renounces his beloved, "I must go see and view my wife; / I pray God I like her as I lovèd thee" (scene 8, lines 148–49), while Lacy achieves his choice. In *Taming* Bianca and Lucentio evade her father's daughter-auction, but his father still assures Baptista "we will content you" (V.i.127). Most radically, Petruchio asserts that the marriage arranged for Kate bodes peace and love as well as "awful rule, and right supremacy" (V.ii.112–13), a statement characterized by masculinist authoritarianism but apparently supported by Kate's final speech, whether read as a sign of co-optation or of a learned ability to play games.

Comic conflict over marriage frequently reveals real class tensions. A steward like Malvolio might dream of his mistress because "there is example for 't. The lady of the Strachy married the yeoman of the wardrobe" (*Twelfth Night*, II.v.38–39), while Master Page wants his daughter to avoid a husband "too great of birth" (*Merry Wives of Windsor*, III.iv.4). In *Friar Bacon* Margaret's unwanted suitors include her father's landlord, who insinuates he will raise his "due" unless she accedes. Only rarely is class conflict more general, for instance in the Robin Hood plays; the physical abuse of servants and the hunger of pages are usually treated as amusing.

Yet in a London fearful of invasion and tense about sharing resources with foreign merchants and artisans – against whom there were riots in the 1590s – even romantic comedies may participate in delicate cultural negotiations over inclusion and exclusion. *Englishmen for My Money* and *The Merchant of Venice* (1596–97), like Marlowe's tragedy *The Jew of Malta* (*c*.1590), center on the foreign merchant in a commercial city with penetrable borders. In all three plays, an alien father's fear of sexual invasion of his daughter symbolizes and inverts the city's fear of invasion by him; in all three the daughter's lover belongs to the dominant local caste, so ethnic and cultural hegemony is transmogrified into social and religious union, meant to exclude the foreign father while absorbing his assets. These purposes are especially clear in *Englishmen*, which foregrounds the economic while eliminating the doctrinal (the Portuguese usurer is probably a Marrano, but the text never identifies him as such). The play is roaringly chauvinistic: English laws, language, and husbands win out, as in *Merchant* "the laws of Venice" (IV.i.309) are Portia's defense against Shylock the Jew, and she gives "gentle riddance" not only to all of Morocco's "complexion" (II.vii.78–79) but to all "strangers" (I.ii.121).

Occasionally Elizabethan comedies move beyond domestic concerns into historical romance. *Friar Bacon* concludes with a "mystical" prophecy of the royal bud who will "overshadow Albion with her leaves." More audaciously, Greene's James IV is a Scottish king married to the King of England's daughter, and the play, a decade or more before James I's accession, insists on the power of "those lands / Which, if they join in one, command the world" (v.vi.102–03) – a tantalizing possibility at least since the 1586 Treaty of Berwick.

Thomas Dekker's *The Shoemaker's Holiday* (1599) shows how a London setting facilitated both romance and realism. The concluding fantasy of social harmony is characterized by love, food, economic privilege, and patriotic cohesion, as embodied in Simon Eyre's tag line, "Prince am I none, yet am I princely born" (scene 21, lines 17, 35–36).

Here the Dutch shoemaker is really an English aristocrat. Yet the Lord Mayor and the Earl of Lincoln are mutually suspicious representatives of new money and old nobility. Not only does aristocratic Lacy evade the war while journeyman Rafe is conscripted, but Rafe returns wounded and unrecognizable. His absence reduces his wife Jane's status: having found Jane "more stately than became her," the shoemaker's wife "checked her, and so forth. Away she flung, never returned ... we heard not of her." Margery's unwitting double entendre, "If she had wanted, she might have opened her case to me or my husband or to any of my men" (scene 10, lines 93–102), reveals how such a woman could support herself. Even Jacobean dramatic confrontations between citizen wives and gallants are adumbrated when Jane is harassed in her shop. Such confrontations would become more overt in two new forms, city comedy and "comical satire."

Satire, a rapid-response weapon in a small and self-obsessed theatrical world, fed into Elizabethan comedy from multiple sources. Chapman inaugurated the "humours" style in *A Humorous Day's Mirth* (1597, Admiral's); the Chamberlain's Men immediately competed with Jonson's *Every Man In His Humour*. Then in 1599 the bishops' ban on verse satire drove ambitious poets like John Marston to seek a new outlet in the theatre, which may have stimulated Jonson to the increased harshness of his *Every Man Out of His Humour* (1599). These stylistic developments intermingled with the "poetomachia" or "war of the theatres," differing titles indicating the dual focus of a quarrel that involved simultaneously hostilities between individual playwrights and competition between the men's public companies and the newly revived boys' companies in the private theatres.

The general generic movement is from magic to "deeds, and language, such as men do use" (*Every Man In*, 1616 Prologue), from romance to sexual intrigue. Along with traditional social satire Chapman stages age-mismatched couples and risqué jokes. Intense artistic self-consciousness is pervasive in Jonson. He carefully defines humours: physiologically the "choler, melancholy, phlegm, and blood" flowing in the human body, determining personal temperament, "by *Metaphor*" the term may apply "when some one peculiar quality / Doth so possess a man, that it doth draw / All his affects, his spirits, and his powers / In their confluctions, all to run one way" (*Every Man Out*, Opening Grex, lines 99–108). (In modern terms humours approximate obsessive-compulsive behavior.) Jonson uses frames and appoints commentators to "strip the ragged follies of the time" and to sit as "censors. ... upon every *Scene*" to direct audience response (*Every Man Out*, Grex, lines 17,153–55). Eventually, in *Poetaster* (1601), Jonson will claim the classical high ground, identify with the Roman poet

Horace, and announce his intention to "spare men's persons and but tax their crimes" (Folio, III.v.134). But by forcing Crispinus/Marston to vomit words from *Histriomastix* (1599) and parodying *Twelfth Night* (1600–01), Jonson still participates in conflict between personalities, companies, and literary styles which dominated comedy at the century's end. The importance of the new satires thus lay not in their brief vogue but in their contribution to a new tone.

1599

By 1599 the cultural niche, modified significantly since 1576, was changing again. In the fall the Globe opened. The repertory included *As You Like It*, Shakespeare's first play for the new theatre, *Julius Caesar*, seen by the visiting Thomas Platter in September (Gurr, *The Shakespearian Playing Companies*, pp. 291, 294); and *Every Man Out*, premiering after *Julius Caesar*, which it quotes. *Henry V*, staged during Essex's mission to Ireland, as the Globe was being built, was moved there. In the fall the boy players began again at Paul's, either with Marston's *Antonio and Mellida*, possibly designed for their opening night, or with his *Histriomastix*. To keep abreast, Henslowe was staging *The Shoemaker's Holiday*, planning the new Fortune theatre, for which he would sign a contract in January of 1600, and commissioning the first part of *Sir John Oldcastle*, a response to the "plaudites" of Falstaff. This was a moment of expectation and fear of change: the famine was over but conflict in Ireland and on the Continent continued. Elizabeth was sixty-six. With the two-company monopoly breaking down – Worcester's Men were in London by the end of the decade (Gurr, *The Shakespearian Playing Companies*, p. 319) – there were expanded opportunities, but the competition was stronger and more diverse.

The plays register their self-awareness through metatheatrical references: *Henry V* asks for "imaginary forces" to supplement what can be shown "within this wooden O"; Caesar is barely dead before Cassius anticipates "How many ages hence / Shall this our lofty scene be acted over" (III.i.112–13). Humours and satirical drama use formal means to articulate insider judgments. The Induction to *Antonio and Mellida* brings on the boy players "with parts in their hands, having cloaks cast over their apparel," discussing how to "personate" their parts and joking about cross-dressing and old-fashioned language, "Rampum, scrampum, mount tufty Tamburlaine!" (line 91). The banishment of Sir Owlet's men in *Histriomastix* indicates the improved status of the "sturdy rogues and vagabonds." These players are expelled not for poor acting, but for failure to pay taxes and relieve the poor. In 1599 the grant of heraldic honors was confirmed to Shakespeare's family.

The condition of tragedy in 1599 may be exemplified by *Julius Caesar*, which explores the fatal intersection of personal psychology, public persona, and large historical forces. The rhetoric of debate is never more powerful than in the orations of Brutus and Antony, two politicians arguing a fundamental ideological question, the meaning of revolution. But both men simultaneously expose "selves." Similarly, when Portia wounds herself, she is both a daughter of the republic and a neglected wife implicitly challenging the values of Roman history. The wound anticipates the forcibly feminized body of Caesar, bleeding uncontrollably from "poor poor dumb mouths" (III.ii.226), and the final rash of suicidal stabbings, all logical consequences of the ideology of Roman masculine *virtus*. Brutus' inability to discuss Portia's death in IV.iii. suggests private, inward grief, yet when he – if the text is correct – pretends ignorance of her death to Messala, he publicly models how "great men great losses should endure" (IV.iii.192). The appearance of Caesar's ghost adds a metaphysical dimension to a profoundly political play: "Art thou any thing?" Brutus asks (IV.iii. 280), anticipating Hamlet's philosophical queries.

Henry V, despite the King's obsessive attribution of victory to God, concludes Shakespeare's major history sequence focused on the pragmatic political questions that had preoccupied the entire series: sovereignty and the constitution of the nation. The Welsh, Irish, and Scots, symbolized by their captains, are included, and the French princess may be, provided that she yield "maiden cities," language, and body to the man who opened the gates of Harfleur with threats of rape and destruction (V.ii.326). But territorial breadth is more easily obtained than social union. The hero of Agincourt asserts that he that "sheds his blood with me / Shall be my brother" (IV.iii.61–62), but not only Falstaff and Bardolph are excluded. The philosophizing gardeners of *Richard II* have become cynical soldiers, distrusting the King's promises. Henry's lengthy meditation, "what infinite heartsease / Must kings neglect that private men enjoy!" (IV.i.228–82), is subverted by Williams' description of potential casualties (IV.i.129–41), by Henry's own contempt for wretched slaves, and by its astonishing similarity to his father's insomniac soliloquy in *Henry IV, Part II*, III.i.4–31, which concludes, "Uneasy lies the head that wears a crown." This "conquering Caesar" (Chorus to Act V, line 28) is another cool Lancastrian politician, publicly providing "cheerful semblance" (Chorus to Act IV, line 40), privately tormented by "the fault / My father made in compassing the crown!" (IV.i.291–92).

Competing forms of comedy at the turn of the century are exemplified in the Admiral's *Shoemaker's Holiday*, the Chamberlain's *As You Like It* , and Paul's Boys' *Antonio and Mellida*. The jolly nationalism of Dekker would turn darker in *The Honest Whore* (1604), where Bedlam joins the citizen shop as a London location, but *Shoemaker's Holiday* is neatly poised between the romances that had dominated and the cynicism to come. *As You Like It* is the culmination of the "festive comedy" of the 1590s, moving from the court to the woods, embodying "holiday humor" in songs, foolery, and game playing, and concluding with marriages and restoration of title and property. Shakespeare does put pressure on these conventions. The boy actor/Rosalind/ Ganymede/"Rosalind" is his most sedimented case of cross-dressing, "a particularly volatile symbol of liminality."[25] Touchstone dismisses the pastoral ideal (III.ii.17–18). The folk-tale of the winning younger brother is balanced by the hostilities bred by primogeniture; the loving relation of the Duke and his lords is balanced by Oliver's abuse of Adam. Rosalind as bride apparently confirms female subordination to husband and father, yet she arranges the appearance of Hymen – a hired woodman? a god? – and reappears as the ambiguously gendered epilogue for one final defiance of "the fashion." Still, the conclusion to *As You Like It* is magic, a "theatrical *source* of social conciliation."[26]

Marston, cognizant of the competition as he started carving out his theatrical niche, may have seen *As You Like It* as he was completing *Antonio and Mellida*. In the final act his Rosaline's suitor weeps "to the senseless trees" (v.i.64) in Orlando-like lines, and there are a banished duke, the cross-dressed daughter of another, songs, a satirist, and a fool. But Marston exaggerates each element. For example, he cross-dresses both hero and heroine, creating a spectrum of hetero- and homoerotic wooing scenes, and Felice, his "rare firking satirist" (III.ii.13), is more pungent than Jaques in his scenes of "rare sport" (III.ii.161). Marston is deeply uncertain of his tone: the happy ending in which Antonio rises from his coffin would reappear in Jacobean comedy, but the angry satire, stoicism, and Timon-like scene of Andrugio eating roots all make it less astonishing that *Antonio's Revenge* begins in blood and reveals that the reconciliation at the end of *Antonio and Mellida* was feigned.

The achievements of Elizabethan drama cannot be summarized briefly. For those who lived the busy rhythm of commission, composition, collaboration, opening and revival, the pattern of development was perhaps just occasionally glimpsed. As the century ended Shakespeare, for the first and only time, nostalgically quoted the dead shepherd, Marlowe, and according to legend persuaded the Chamberlain's Men to risk producing Jonson's *Every Man In His Humour*. This career-building rival more contentiously tried to purge objectionable new styles, but even he could fantasize a poet seated at the right hand of an emperor. The new century would see royal patronage of the companies and increasing acknowledgement of authorship. The theatres closed in 1642; the plays, miraculously, remain.

NOTES

1 Andrew Gurr, *The Shakespearian Playing Companies* (Oxford: Clarendon Press, 1996), p. 110.
2 Gary Taylor, *Cultural Selection* (New York: Basic Books, 1996), pp. 44–54.
3 E. K. Chambers, *The Elizabethan Stage*, 4 vols. (Oxford: Clarendon Press, 1923), vol. IV, pp. 237–39.
4 Jean E. Howard, *The Stage and Social Struggle in Early Modern England* (London: Routledge, 1994), p. 82.
5 Katherine Maus, *Inwardness and Theatre in the English Renaissance* (Chicago: University of Chicago Press, 1995), p. 32.
6 Alan Sinfield, *Faultlines: Cultural Materialism and the Politics of Dissident Reading* (Berkeley: University of California Press, 1992), pp. 59–67.
7 Michael Hattaway, *Elizabethan Popular Theatre* (London: Routledge & Kegan Paul, 1982).
8 Philip Sidney, *An Apologie for Poetrie*, in G. Gregory Smith, ed., *Elizabethan Critical Essays*, 2 vols., (Oxford: Oxford University Press, 1904), vol. I, p. 197.
9 A. R. Braunmuller, *George Peele* (Boston: Twayne, 1983), p. 6.
10 G. R. Hibbard, "'From iygging vaines of riming mother wits' to 'the spacious volubilitie of a drumming decasillabon,'" in *The Elizabethan Theatre XI* (Port Credit: P. D. Meany, 1990), p. 70.
11 Richard Helgerson, *Forms of Nationhood: The Elizabethan Writing of England* (Chicago: University of Chicago Press, 1992), p. 237.
12 Louis Montrose, *The Purpose of Playing* (Chicago: University of Chicago Press, 1996), p. 1.
13 Jean E. Howard and Phyllis Rackin, *Engendering a Nation: A Feminist Account of Shakespeare's English Histories* (London: Routledge, 1997), pp. 187ff.
14 David Bevington, ed., *Endymion* (Manchester: Manchester University Press, 1996), p. 33.
15 Roslyn L. Knutson, "Influence of the Repertory System on the Revival and Revision of *The Spanish Tragedy* and *Dr. Faustus*," *English Literary Renaissance* 18 (1988): 260.
16 Leah S. Marcus, *Unediting the Renaissance* (London: Routledge, 1996), pp. 38–67.
17 Stephen Greenblatt, *Renaissance Self-Fashioning: From More to Shakespeare* (Chicago: University of Chicago Press, 1980), p. 195. See also C. L. Barber and Richard P. Wheeler, *Creating Elizabethan Tragedy* (Chicago: University of Chicago Press, 1988).
18 Frank Whigham, *Seizures of the Will in Early Modern English Drama* (Cambridge: Cambridge University Press, 1996), p. 26.
19 Coppélia Kahn, *Roman Shakespeare* (London: Routledge, 1997), p. 47.
20 Catherine Belsey, *The Subject of Tragedy: Identity and Difference in Renaissance Drama* (London: Methuen, 1985), p. 133.

21 Frances E. Dolan, *Dangerous Familiars: Representations of Domestic Crime in England, 1550–1700* (Ithaca, NY: Cornell University Press, 1994).
22 Annabel Patterson, *Reading Holinshed's* Chronicles (Chicago: University of Chicago Press, 1994), pp. 198, xii.
23 Janet Adelman, *Suffocating Mothers* (London: Routledge, 1992), pp. 1–2.
24 Stephen Orgel, *Impersonations* (Cambridge: Cambridge University Press, 1996), pp. 70, 81.
25 Bruce R. Smith, *Homosexual Desire in Shakespeare's England: A Cultural Poetics* (Chicago: University of Chicago Press, 1991), p. 153.
26 Louis Adrian Montrose, "'The Place of a Brother' in *As You Like It*: Social Process and Comic Form," *Shakespeare Quarterly* 32 (1981): 54.

FURTHER READING

Much valuable criticism is contained in the introductions and notes to modern editions, including major anthologies of Shakespeare and *Drama of the English Renaissance 1: The Tudor Period*, ed. Russell A. Fraser and Norman Rabkin (New York: MacMillan, 1976) and Arthur F. Kinney, ed. *Renaissance Drama: An Anthology of Plays and Entertainments* (Oxford: Blackwell, 1999), as well as in such series as The Revels Plays, the New Mermaids, the Arden editions of Shakespeare and the Oxford World's Classics. Editions of individual plays are not listed here. Fuller bibliography is available in Braunmuller and Hattaway, *Cambridge Companion*, and Cox and Kastan, *New History*, below.

Adelman, Janet, *Suffocating Mothers* (London: Routledge, 1992).
Altman, Joel B., *The Tudor Play of Mind* (Berkeley: University of California Press, 1988).
Barber, C. L. and Richard P. Wheeler, *Creating Elizabethan Tragedy* (Chicago: University of Chicago Press, 1988).
Barber, C. L., *Shakespeare's Festive Comedy* (Cleveland, OH: Meridian, 1963).
Bartels, Emily C., *Spectacles of Strangeness* (Philadelphia: University of Pennsylvania Press, 1993).
Bednarz, James, "Marston's Subversion of Shakespeare and Jonson: *Histriomastix* and the War of the Theaters," *Medieval and Renaissance Drama in England* 6 (1993): 103–28.
Belsey, Catherine, *The Subject of Tragedy: Identity and Difference in Renaissance Drama* (London: Methuen, 1985).
Berek, Peter, "*Tamburlaine*'s Weak Sons: Imitation as Interpretation before 1593," *Renaissance Drama* 13 (1982): 55–82.
Braunmuller, A. R., *George Peele* (Boston: Twayne, 1983).
Braunmuller, A. R. and Michael Hattaway, eds., *The Cambridge Companion to English Renaissance Drama* (Cambridge: Cambridge University Press, 1990).
Burnett, Mark Thornton, "Tamburlaine: An Elizabethan Vagabond," *Studies in Philology* 84 (1987): 308–23.
Cerasano, S. P. and Marion Wynne-Davies, *Renaissance Drama by Women* (London: Routledge, 1996).
Chambers, E. K., *The Elizabethan Stage* (Oxford: Clarendon Press, 1923).

Cox, John D. and David Scott Kastan, eds., *A New History of Early English Drama* (New York: Columbia University Press, 1997).

Dolan, Frances E., *Dangerous Familiars: Representations of Domestic Crime in England, 1550–1700* (Ithaca, NY: Cornell University Press, 1994).

Dollimore, Jonathan, *Radical Tragedy* (Chicago: University of Chicago Press, 1984).

Dutton, Richard, *Mastering the Revels* (Iowa City: University of Iowa Press, 1991).

Greenblatt, Stephen, *Shakespearian Negotiations* (Berkeley: University of California Press, 1988).

Renaissance Self-Fashioning: From More to Shakespeare (Chicago: University of Chicago Press, 1980).

Gurr, Andrew, *The Shakespearian Playing Companies* (Oxford: Clarendon Press, 1996).

Guy, John, *Tudor England* (Oxford: Oxford University Press, 1988).

Hattaway, Michael, *Elizabethan Popular Theatre* (London: Routledge and Kegan Paul, 1982).

Helgerson, Richard, *Forms of Nationhood: The Elizabethan Writing of England* (Chicago: University of Chicago Press, 1992).

Howard, Jean E., *The Stage and Social Struggle in Early Modern England* (London: Routledge, 1994).

Howard, Jean E. and Phyllis Rackin, *Engendering a Nation: A Feminist Account of Shakespeare's English Histories* (London: Routledge, 1997).

Hunt, Maurice. "Slavery, English Servitude, and *The Comedy of Errors*," *English Literary Renaissance* 27 (1997): 31–56.

Ingram, William, *The Business of Playing* (Ithaca, NY: Cornell University Press, 1992).

Jardine, Lisa, *Still Harping on Daughters* (Brighton: Harvester, 1983).

Kahn, Coppélia, *Roman Shakespeare* (London: Routledge, 1997).

Kamps, Ivo and Deborah E. Barker, eds., *Shakespeare and Gender* (London: Verso, 1995).

Kastan, David Scott and Peter Stallybrass, eds., *Staging the Renaissance: Reinterpretations of Elizabethan and Jacobean Drama* (New York and London: Routledge, 1991).

Kernan, Alvin, *The Cankered Muse* (New Haven: Yale University Press, 1959).

Knutson, Roslyn Lander, *The Repertory of Shakespeare's Company* (Fayetteville: University of Arkansas Press, 1991).

Levin, Richard, *The Multiple Plot in English Renaissance Drama* (Chicago: University of Chicago Press, 1971).

Magnusson, A. L. and C. E. McGee, eds. *The Elizabethan Theatre* xi (Port Credit, Ontario: P. D. Meany, 1985).

Marcus, Leah, S. *Unediting the Renaissance* (London: Routledge, 1996).

Maus, Katharine Eisaman, *Inwardness and Theatre in the English Renaissance* (Chicago: University of Chicago Press, 1995).

Montrose, Louis Adrian, "'The Place of a Brother' in *As You Like It*: Social Process and Comic Form," *Shakespeare Quarterly* 32 (1981): 28–54.

The Purpose of Playing (Chicago: University of Chicago Press, 1996).

Mullaney, Steven, *The Place of the Stage* (Chicago: University of Chicago Press, 1988).

Orgel, Stephen, *Impersonations* (Cambridge: Cambridge University Press, 1996).

Orlin, Lena Cowen, *Private Matters and Public Culture in Post-Reformation England* (Ithaca, NY: Cornell University Press, 1994).

Palliser, D. M., *The Age of Elizabeth* (London: Longman, 1983).

Paster, Gail Kern, *The Body Embarrassed* (Ithaca, NY: Cornell University Press, 1993).

Patterson, Annabel, *Reading Holinshed's* Chronicles (Chicago: University of Chicago Press, 1994).

Riggs, David, *Ben Jonson: A Life* (Cambridge: Harvard University Press, 1989).

Shapiro, James, *Shakespeare and the Jews* (New York: Columbia University Press, 1996).

Sidney, Philip, *An Apologie for Poetrie*, in G. Gregory Smith, ed., *Elizabethan Critical Essays*, 2 vols. (Oxford: Oxford University Press, 1904).

Sinfield, Alan, *Faultlines: Cultural Materialism and the Politics of Dissident Reading* (Berkeley: University of California Press, 1992).

Smith, Bruce R., *Homosexual Desire in Shakespeare's England: A Cultural Poetics* (Chicago: University of Chicago Press, 1991).

Taylor, Gary, *Cultural Selection* (New York: Basic Books, 1996).

Waith, Eugene M., *The Herculean Hero* (New York: Columbia University Press, 1962).

Whigham, Frank, *Seizures of the Will in Early Modern English Drama* (Cambridge: Cambridge University Press, 1996).

Wrightson, Keith, *English Society 1580–1680* (New Brunswick: Rutgers University Press, 1982).

9

HEATHER DUBROW

Lyric forms

DEFINITIONS AND DISTINCTIONS

Students with a keen sense of curiosity – or possibly merely a keen sense of mischief – could fruitfully exercise either predilection by asking their teachers for a brief definition of lyric. The complexities of responding to that demand, like the problems a similar query about tragedy would generate, demonstrate the complexities of the literary types in question. But despite the difficulty of defining lyric, exploring the forms it took during the English Renaissance can illuminate this mode as a whole, some of its most challenging and exciting texts, and the workings of the early modern era.

Aristotle posits an apparently clear-cut division of all literature into lyric, epic, and drama, basing the distinctions on the mode of presentation: lyric is sung, epic recited, and drama staged. This division remains influential, lying behind the work of Northrop Frye and many other modern theorists. Yet certain successors to Aristotle devise more elaborate subdivisions of poetry, adducing criteria that narrow the concept of lyric and lead to withholding that label from some forms of poetry. Thus, for example, in Book 1, Chapter 11 of his *Arte of English Poesie* (1589), George Puttenham distinguishes heroic, lyric, elegaic, and epigrammatic verse and nods toward the presence of other types as well; this list shows the influence of classical writers like Horace.

When they attempt to define and describe lyric, twentieth-century critics replicate the problems earlier writers confronted. Some try to categorize it through formal qualities; lyrics are generally considered to be short, though of course that criterion is frustratingly relative and imprecise. Some argue that stanzaic form is typical of lyric though not necessarily present in all poems deserving that title. Other definitions emphasize the connection between lyric and song, variously citing direct allusions to songs, such as *Carmina* (a title of Horace's poems), the presence of such characteristics as the refrain, and references to musicality like Keats' famous address to a nightingale.

Another approach is defining lyric in terms of its relationship to time. The claim that it rejects or ignores temporality, though common, is less persuasive than more subtle attempts to anatomize the complex and varied ways the lyric engages with time. Thus, for example, Sharon Cameron's trenchant study *Lyric Time: Dickinson and the Limits of Genre* suggests that the mode in question fears time, associating it with death, and works out ways of redefining that potential antagonist. But how does this imputed fear relate to the indubitable presence of history in many lyrics?

Yet another avenue toward a definition is characterizing the lyric speaker. Some argue that this form allows the poet to express his real feelings, but recently most critics have instead asserted that this, like virtually all types of writing, is mediated in so many ways that the concept of actual emotions risks naivete. It is common to claim that the lyric speaker is isolated; yet, as we will see, early modern pastorals, like many other lyrics of the period, not only celebrate community as a value but also are typically situated in a community of shepherds. One group of critics maintains that lyric speakers express universal feelings and represent all of us rather than individualized, historically situated people; another group, however, retorts that such speakers are often, or even necessarily, historicized.

Certain commentators in turn focus on the relationship between the speaker and his audience, with John Stuart Mill delivering the highly influential observation that the lyric speaker is overheard. Similarly, in opposition to the suggestion that lyric is fundamentally a social mode, Helen Vendler defends the isolation and universality of its speaker. The reader is present, she insists, as a kind of mirror: "a lyric is *a role offered to a reader;* the reader is to be the voice speaking the poem."[1]

Northrop Frye offers another seminal approach when he discusses lyric in terms of what he playfully terms "babble" and "doodle." Associated with sound or *melos*, the former, he suggests, signals its connections with the charm and is manifest in rhythm, alliteration, and puns. "Doodle," in contrast, is the realm of verbal pattern or *opsis*, and Frye connects it to another blood relative of lyric, the riddle.[2]

Influenced by the importation of influential Continental theorists such as Derrida, Foucault, and Lacan and by the emphasis on the instability of language that characterizes and arguably defines poststructuralism, in the final three decades of the twentieth century critics have challenged many preconceptions lying behind earlier descriptions of the lyric.[3] One of the most common moves of poststructuralist criticism, the dismissal of older conceptions of the autonomous individual as tainted products of humanist ideology, is manifest in focusing on the rhetoric and performativity of lyric in lieu of the experience of the speaker or author.

Feminism has also informed reconsiderations of the mode in question, with critics variously endorsing and questioning the frequently cited gendering of the lyric as female and of narrative as male. In addition, love lyrics pivot on gender more immediately in the relationship between speaker and object, the first generally male and the second female. Hence many critics have read the lyric as both source and symptom of its culture's suppression of women, pointing to the ways its addresses to the woman may silence her and its descriptions dismember and disempower her; in particular, the blazon, a part-by-part celebration of the female body based on the French *blason*, is seen as an assertion of control under the guise of praise. And the concern for the historical and political that characterizes many critical movements at the end of the twentieth century has variously produced both distaste for the lyric's imputed tendency to suppress historical imperatives and issues rather than merely ignoring them, and demonstrations of its putative participation in historical discourses despite assumptions to the contrary.

Finally, however, the controversies surrounding these and other attempts to define lyric mandate distinctions based on both historical periods and genres. David Lindley, the author of an excellent short overview entitled *Lyric*, brackets his attempts at definition by insisting on historical specificity.[4] As he and others have pointed out, many discussions of the mode are shaped – and misshaped – by their positing the Romantic lyric as the normative model. How and why, then, do sixteenth-century poets approach that protean form, the lyric?

PRINCIPAL POETS AND STYLES OF THE SIXTEENTH CENTURY

Even a brief and preliminary chronological survey of major developments and authors of the period provides some answers to that question – but in so doing generates yet more questions. Though born in the fifteenth century, John Skelton composed most of his important poetry in the sixteenth. His output is varied, encompassing spiritual meditations on death and salvation, a portrait of an alehouse, and a dream vision; one of his best-known poems is *Philip Sparrow*, a thought-provoking example of lyric lament. Equally thought-provoking is Skelton's approach to metrics; his short lines, so idiosyncratic that they are aptly termed "Skeltonics," may well be based on church music, especially plainsong.[5]

Sir Thomas Wyatt, who lived between 1503 and 1542, is not only one of the earliest poets of the period but also one of the most intriguing. His canon includes several forms that were to be popular throughout the period, such as satires and metrical translations of the Psalms; his love poetry is especially impressive for its often colloquial diction and its intensity. Adapting sonnets by his Italian predecessor Francis Petrarch, he variously fashions poems that are virtually translations and others that reformat Petrarch's lines in a darker, more bitter font. Henry Howard, Earl of Surrey, who was born fourteen years after Wyatt, also contributed to the development of the sonnet, working out the rhyme scheme discussed below that came to be called "Shakespearean." In contrast to the irregular metrics and tangled emotions of Wyatt's sonnets, those of Surrey are typically limpid and graceful.

George Gascoigne, indubitably among the most significant writers in the early years of Elizabeth's reign though he is often neglected, includes among his varied canon, *A Hundred Sundry Flowers* (1573) and *The Posies* (1575). These volumes contain skillfully crafted love poetry, some of which is reminiscent of Wyatt's bitterness and wryness, as well as instances of such forms as the epitaph and satire. Among his most moving lyrics is "Lullaby of a Lover," which plays the soothing reasssurances associated with the lullaby against its own caustic reflections on aging and desire. Gascoigne's contemporaries in this period experimented with a number of forms that were to become very popular later in the century; George Turberville, for example, translates the pastorals of the Italian monk Battista Spagnoli, often known as Mantuan. These decades also saw the publication of several collections of lyrics, notably the popular book known as *Tottel's Miscellany* (1557); this volume includes love poetry, pastoral, and satire and represents a wide range of authors, including Wyatt and Surrey.

Edmund Spenser's collection of pastorals entitled *The Shepheardes Calender* (1579), a text to which I will return in more detail, is often seen as inaugurating the extraordinarily rich production of poetry that characterizes the final decades of the sixteenth century. Certainly it manifests many characteristics that were to recur in its author's later poetry, such as his self-conscious and complex relationship to his literary predecessors, his engagement with the controversies surrounding English Protestantism, and his delight in stylistic experimentation, which in this instance is especially manifest in his range of verse forms and his use of archaic language. In his sonnet collection *Amoretti* (1595), Spenser laments the tension between working on *The Faerie Queene* (1590; 1596) and pursuing other types of writing; but he continued to produce lyric poetry throughout his career.

Often described as a seventeenth-century poet in order to substantiate a clear-cut break between the Elizabethan and Jacobean periods, John Donne in fact probably wrote many of his love lyrics and elegies during the 1590s. The rapid variations in tone and style from poem to poem, as well as within a single text, render his work as difficult to encapsulate as it is intriguing to read. The approaches commonly associated with him – the argumentative stance, the conversational voice, the witty playfulness, the intellectual knottiness – are famously present in such poems as "The Canonization" and "The Ecstasy," among many others. Such lyrics thus exemplify certain characteristics generally associated with metaphysical poetry: its philosophical speculations, its interest in abstract ratiocinations, and its so-called metaphysical conceits, startling images that typically link apparent opposites, such as sexuality and spirituality. Yet Donne's secular verse encompasses many other registers as well, including the lyric simplicity of songs like "Sweetest love, I do not go," a poem we would not be surprised to find in any Elizabethan miscellany. As such texts as "The Bait" and "The Funeral" demonstrate, Donne's canon also swerves from bitterly misogynistic poems, notably some graphically bawdy elegies, to ones that celebrate the beloved (or, as some readers claim, in appearing to do so primarily celebrate the speaker's power over her). (Some critics attempt to negotiate the infinite variety of Donne's lyrics by positing a chronological movement from the conventional language and eroticism of Petrarchism, a movement discussed in more detail below, to the refined spirituality of Neo-Platonism; but in fact these and other strains coexist in his work.)

The 1590s was a decade of not only extraordinary richness but also extraordinary variety in English poetry; remembering that John Donne may well have written many of his acerbic love poems during the period and that it also saw the development of formal verse satire provides a salutary qualification to generalizations about the lush, graceful verse conventionally associated with these ten years. Love poetry of many types flourished during the decade, drawing particularly on the erotic lyrics of Ovid and the sonnets of Petrarch. In particular, the sonnet tradition enjoyed a great vogue in the 1590s, inspired by the posthumous publication in 1591 of Sir Philip Sidney's collection *Astrophil and Stella*, which is discussed in more detail in the section on the sonnet below. Contributions to this genre during the 1590s range in tone and subject matter from the predictable but gracefully melodic verse in Samuel Daniel's *Delia* (1592) to the iconoclasm of Barnabe Barnes's *Parthenophil and Parthenophe* (1593), which ends in a startling fantasy of a rape.

In addition to love poetry, the 1590s saw the appearance of many other types of lyric. Witness, for example, the career of Michael Drayton, who during that decade alone published scriptural paraphrases, sonnets, pastorals, historical complaints, and historical epistles based on Ovid's *Heroides*. Indeed, some of the most intriguing lyric poems in the English language – variously intriguing in the ways they challenge their readers intellectually, impress them aesthetically, and woo them ideologically – date from the 1590s.

LITERARY AND CULTURAL CONDITIONS

Why, then, did the Renaissance lyric develop when and how it did? Literary, social, and cultural conditions in the early modern period inform it, and are in turn informed by it. To begin with, during that era the mode in question enjoyed, or more accurately endured, a lower status than certain other types of writing. Not only the problems of defining lyric but the imbricated challenges of evaluating and justifying it emerge with particular force in Sidney's *Defence of Poetrie* (1595), a treatise manifesting the defensiveness about the mode that recurs throughout the Tudor period. Sidney offers an impassioned justification of lyric: "who with his tuned lyre and well-accorded voice, giveth praise, the reward of virtue, to virtuous acts; who gives moral precepts, and natural problems; who sometimes raiseth up his voice to the height of the heavens, in singing the lauds of the immortal God."[6] Thus Sidney elevates and justifies the lyric by encompassing didactic poetry, the poetry of praise, and religious verse within the category in question. The text nervously proceeds, however, to answer the charge that lyric poetry includes amoral love poetry by suggesting such texts are an abuse of the potentials of the genre.

Other literary theories in the early modern period further complicated evaluations of lyric. A medieval formulation that remains popular during the Renaissance, the concept of the Vergilian wheel, states that Vergil moves chronologically from pastoral to georgic (literature about agricultural practice) to epic. This model encouraged later poets to define their careers in similar terms, thus spurring the writing of pastoral; yet the widely cited if historically inaccurate trajectory of the Vergilian wheel clearly privileges narrative forms over lyric. We encounter the same preference for narrativity when Aristotle posits a hierarchy of genres with tragedy at the pinnacle, a judgment adopted by many other writers as well; some Renaissance rhetoricians, including Sidney himself, offer an alternative ranking that privileges epic, reflecting the nationalistic aspirations of their era. But whichever of those systems one adopts, lyric does not win the lottery.

As I have already suggested, gender and gendering offer additional explanations for its dubious status. Love has been the subject of lyric poetry in many different eras, and in the early modern period in particular the connection between the two was intensified by the vogue the sonnet enjoyed in England in the 1590s, as well as by the popularity of love songs throughout the era. But the credo that love, including the activity of writing about it, is effeminate and effeminizing recurs throughout early modern texts. Or, to put it another way, one might say that in Renaissance aesthetics lyric adopts a female subject position to the male one of epic – not only inferior but also in some way threatening, much as female characters in both classical and Renaissance epics threaten the city that must be built, the nation that must be founded.

Yet sixteenth-century culture also offered many justifications for composing lyrics, even ones about love. Nationalism encouraged demonstrations that English poetry could rival the achievements of classical and Continental writers, including those of sonneteers. Attending to the commonplace that the Bible is a compendium of all genres, Renaissance lyricists could claim as their predecessor no less a figure than David, considered the author of the Psalms. Similarly, pastoral writers could dignify their work by adducing the revered Vergil as a forebear, as Spenser insistently does in his *Shepheardes Calender* (1579).

Prosodic developments and disagreements also shaped the aesthetics of the early modern lyric. Essentially English poets inherited two principal possibilities, accentual-syllabic and quantitative verse. The first, the main form of English poetry, grounds its metrical schemes both in where stresses fall and in the number of syllables. In contrast to these patterns, quantitative verse, practiced by Greek and Latin writers, ignores stress, relying instead on the length or quantity of its syllables. It is common – and broadly speaking accurate – to map the history of prosody in the sixteenth century as a movement from rough and unsuccessful experiments with iambic pentameter, the form of accentual-syllabic verse based on a pattern of five units that are typically iambic, to its triumphant execution in the mellifluous poetry of the 1590s. But this schema, while providing a sound overview, resembles the parallel assumption that the English sonnet was gradually moving from less successful rhyme schemes toward its natural form, the so-called Shakespearean sonnet; both trajectories have tempted critics to express a xenophobic nationalism, and both encompass as well the threat of underestimating the achievements of material that does not fit the pattern. Writers who do not achieve smooth iambic pentameter might be marching to, or rather composing for, a different drummer. Witness the debates about the decasyllabic (ten-syllable) lines of Sir Thomas Wyatt. Some read them as instances of crude early sorties into iambic pentameter; alternatively, critics have proposed a whole series of different systems that

Wyatt might be successfully shaping, such as the skillful combination of the versification of Lydgate and Italianate hendecasyllabic (eleven-syllable) patterns that George T. Wright identifies as the drummer in Wyatt's hauntingly irregular lines.[7]

A more extreme alternative to iambic pentameter was the possibility of importing a system of quantitative verse into English. Impelled by their respect for Latin and Greek verse, a number of poets in the period debated and experimented with this option. Edmund Spenser and an academic with whom he was friendly, Gabriel Harvey, exchanged a series of letters, published in 1580, about quantitative verse. Sir Philip Sidney, who delighted in experimenting with verse forms as well as with meter, also wrote some quantitative lyrics.

Debates about alternative metrical systems are closely related to controversies about whether rhyme is an appropriate ornament or a lamentable barbarism, since here too one central issue is whether English verse could and should imitate its classical predecessors. Despite his own success with rhyme, Thomas Campion, associating it with a lamentable neglect of classical principles of meter, mocks it in his *Observations in the Art of English Poesie* (1602): "the facilitie and popularitie of Rime creates as many Poets, as a hot sommer flies";[8] yet other sixteenth-century poets, notably Samuel Daniel, as vigorously defend rhyme.

Whatever their position on such debates, in practice sixteenth-century poets enthusiastically experimented with a range of stanzaic patterns. Courtly forms popular in the fifteenth century such as the rondeau, a French stanza in which the opening words recur, survive and flourish in the work of Sir Thomas Wyatt in particular – yet another warning of the dangers of stressing the modernity of the period at the expense of acknowledging its continuing affiliations with the past. Later in the century, poets, reveling in virtuoso performance, adopted a number of other difficult forms. For example, both Sidney and Spenser composed sestinas, a devilishly complex system of six six-line stanzas plus envoi that they inherited from Italian writers. The technical triumphs achieved in such challenging stanzaic patterns in turn pose challenges for us as critics: how can we most incisively reconcile – or perhaps most illuminatingly juxtapose – contemporary interpretations of the early modern writer as passive vehicle for cultural anxieties with the recognition that such poets were also agents effecting pyrotechnics of prosody?

The early modern lyric was, of course, shaped not only by rhythm in the literal sense but also by the rhythms of court life. Although the profound impact of the literary movement New Historicism and its English cousin cultural materialism have intensified critical interest in that environment, it was investigated from different perspectives by earlier students of the lyric. In particular, in *Music and Poetry in the Early Tudor Court*, a study published in 1961, John Stevens relates Renaissance poetry to conditions at the Tudor court, emphasizing in particular practices of setting poems to music and of passing lyrics among a circle of friends in what he terms "the game of love." Such connections between the Renaissance lyric and courtly music clarify debates about the workings of lyric in general, reminding us that in some important instances it is indeed linked with song – and, more significantly, linked as well with performance and courtly ritual, thus further calling into question generalizations about lyric as a spontaneous overflow of emotion.

The connections between lyric and song manifest the fascination with music that characterizes the English Renaissance, like its Continental counterparts. Philosophical treatises deploy music as a symbol for cosmic orders; the Renaissance schoolmaster Richard Mulcaster movingly advocates teaching it; poetic texts frequently fashion musical imagery. But this sibling art affected early modern poetry more immediately and directly as well. Songbooks were published throughout the sixteenth century, though they became especially popular and prevalent around the turn of the century. Songs ranged in form from the simple monophonic type called an "air," a form to which Thomas Campion and John Dowland contributed significantly, to the elaborately polyphonic madrigal, a form with Continental antecedents that was developed in England by William Byrd.

Musical settings survive for some well-known Renaissance lyrics, including the songs that were frequently incorporated into plays by Shakespeare and his contemporaries. A manuscript heading reminds us that no fewer than six of Donne's love poems were set to airs. Other poems allude to musical performance, as Wyatt famously does in "Blame not my lute" and "My lute, awake." Indeed, among the significant authors of Renaissance lyrics should be listed the composer Campion.

The second question Stevens had raised, the use of the lyric within social interactions, has been pursued from different perspectives by critics at the end of the twentieth century. Exemplifying the New Historicist privileging of politics in its many senses over the private spheres, Arthur F. Marotti's article "'Love is not love': Elizabethan Sonnet Sequences and the Social Order" (*ELH*, 49 [1982]: 396–428) impelled a revisionary redefinition of the functions of lyric. Sonnets that appear to be about love, Marotti argues, should really be read as statements about the author's struggle for patronage, a link encouraged by that supreme patroness Elizabeth's predilection for presenting herself as the mistress of sonnets. Marotti's assertion that struggles for place in the patronage system inform the more overt struggles for the affections of a disdainful mistress is persuasive. Yet, like many revisionist readings, this essay overstates its case: the insistence that poems that appear to be about love instead encode their primary concern with patronage is far less convincing than the alternative formulation that love lyrics, while centrally and often primarily concerned with romantic relationships, play love against courtly politics in ways that comment on both arenas.

Marotti and others have recently repositioned the Renaissance lyric in a different type of social context. Impelled by the materialist concern for the conditions of production, many critics have been tracing the consequences of the form in which Renaissance lyrics appeared. In particular, extensive and often exciting scholarship has illuminated the consequences of the movement from a manuscript to a print culture, with critics positing a radical change in conceptions of authorship.[9] As these studies indicate, numerous early modern lyrics were in fact circulated in manuscript, often in collections that included a range of poets and did not identify the authors; others appeared within popular collections such as *Tottel's Miscellany*; and yet others were published in single-author books, the format enjoyed by the posthumous volume of Sidney's *Astrophil and Stella*. All these patterns were complicated by the appearance of lyrics in commonplace books, collections compiled by an individual that might, for example, juxtapose poetry and recipes or scurrilous verse with more elevated poetry. Manuscript culture, according to the critics studying it, virtually erases the autonomy of the individual writer: a given poem might be significantly changed a number of times in transmission, and texts are seen as amorphous and permeable in ways that minimize the poet's identification with or control over his work. Print culture, in contrast, both impels and is impelled by a greater emphasis on the individual author, a perspective that such analyses see as tellingly parallel to the development of bourgeois conceptions of subjectivity.

Such arguments carry with them many intriguing implications about not only authorship but also content and style. For example, it is likely that the juxtaposition of disparate texts within a given manuscript both encouraged and was encouraged by the lyric's tendency to explore meaning relationally. That is, lyrics often comment explicitly or implicitly on alternative generic possibilities, which come to represent different perspectives and ideologies; for example, as Rosalie L. Colie demonstrates, the sonnet is on one level the opposite of epigram and on the other a host that welcomes epigrammatic couplets.[10] Moreover, the juxtapositions of texts in the practices of manuscript culture arguably encouraged as well an equally revealing phenomenon in the print culture of the period, the habit of publishing related but significantly different texts together in ways that invite comparison and contrast. Thus Spenser's *Amoretti* appears with his "Epithalamion" and some short lyrics in the form known as anacreontic.

Yet, despite these and many other important implications of the research that compares manuscript and print cultures, arguments about it need to be nuanced more than is sometimes the case. We have to recognize the coexistence of several models of authorship throughout the period, including very early versions of characteristics attributed to print culture. For example, the elaborate revisions visible on Wyatt's manuscripts suggest a pride in and concern for details of the text not usually associated with manuscript culture even though his poems were circulated in that form and, indeed, the kinds of laborious revision involved in crafting forms like the sonnet also suggest a model of authorship sometimes associated largely or even exclusively with a later period.

LYRIC GENRES

The significance of literary form in the period – a significance as paradoxical as it was profound – helps to explain why genre provides the best perspective on the sixteenth-century lyric. In England as on the Continent, generic classifications were at once studied sedulously and violated repeatedly. Forms not sanctioned by Aristotle, such as the romance, and so-called mixed genres or *genera mista* such as tragicomedy were variously condemned and pursued. Not coincidentally, in this combination of firmly established divisions and frequent violations of them the genre systems of the early modern period resemble its systems of social class and gender.

A wide range of literary types flourished during the sixteenth century. Given its intimate relationship to the sonnet, the epigram should also be read in relation to lyric. The epithalamium or wedding poem tradition, very popular in the seventeenth century, produced only a few sixteenth-century examples; but this select company includes Spenser's *Epithalamion* (1595) and his cognate poem the *Prothalamion* (1596), the latter celebrating nuptials of sisters rather than a marriage. The complaint, a type of poem whose speaker delivers a lament, often though not invariably about love, also proved popular in the period, encompassing such texts as Daniel's *Complaint of Rosamond* (1592). In 1591 Spenser published a group of poems, including "Prosopopoia," "Muiopotmos," and "Visions of the Worlds Vanitie" under the title *Complaints;* they demonstrate the variety in the genre, with the first a fable; the second a description, sometimes read allegorically, of a butterfly's capture; and the third visionary sonnets influenced by Du Bellay and Petrarch.

The elegy is another sixteenth-century form with complex valences. In classical literature, the term refers to a particular meter, the alternation of hexameter and pentameter lines. In sixteenth-century England, however, the label "elegy" was used loosely for a range of literary types, generally lyric – in particular, funeral poetry and solemn meditations on many different subjects, including love. Hence instances range from Spenser's funeral lament *Daphnaida* (1591) to a series of Ovidian poems by Donne. The popularity of the elegy in the early modern period and the recurrent, in fact obsessive, references to loss in many other genres signal the intimate relationship between lyric and loss. Although this relationship occurs in many periods, it is particularly marked in the English Renaissance because both the sonnet and pastoral are genres of loss. The versions of repetition – the recurrence of a refrain, a word, an action – that are so characteristic of lyric may be a way of negotiating loss and recovery: subsequent versions of the repeated element remind us of the absence of the original one and yet offer the hope of recovery via substitution.

Although the category of religious poetry is too loose clearly to constitute a genre, it represents another important type of sixteenth-century poetry. It is no accident that the sixteenth-century flowering of the English lyric coincided with the development of Protestantism, for the Reformation's emphasis on interior states and meditation is clearly very congenial to lyric poetry; tellingly, medieval religious poems often celebrate Mary or Christ rather than scrutinize the soul of the speaker. Protestantism also, of course, informed religious poetry more directly. Thus it generated an outpouring of hymns, the genre to which that deeply Protestant poet Sidney repeatedly alludes in his *Defence of Poetrie*; their influence is manifest, when, for example, Donne deploys the term in three of his divine poems, "A Hymne to Christ, at the Authors Last Going into Germany," "Hymne to God my God, in my Sicknesse," and "A Hymne to God the Father." This is not to deny, however, that the period also encompasses significant religious lyrics by Catholics, notably Robert Southwell.

Like the hymn, the sonnet form attracted many poets writing about religion and spirituality. Some critics have even suggested that a rejection of secular for spiritual love is central to the sonnet, although it is in fact present more intermittently and ambivalently. In any event it is clear that the struggles between the Augustinian concepts of *caritas* and *cupiditas*, which may roughly be rendered as the attraction of the soul toward God and its pull toward the corporeal, were sometimes enacted in the implicit or explicit juxtaposition of religious and spiritual poems; thus Barnabe Barnes published *Parthenophil and Parthenophe*, a highly eroticized collection of sonnets, in 1593, and two years later brought out what was virtually a palinode, *A Divine Centurie of Spirituall Sonnets*. Another type of religious poetry, metrical translations of the Psalms, was so common in the period that composing such texts has been described as a virtual initiation rite for fledgling poets. Sidney's sister Mary, Countess of Pembroke, participated in that vogue, while another woman writer, Anne Lok, wrote a collection of sonnets based on the fifty-first Psalm.

As such instances demonstrate, while women such as Louise Labé composed sonnets and other types of verse on the Continent, the principal mode of writing for sixteenth-century Englishwomen was religious verse, whether they translated it or, as in the case of Lok, composed it themselves. The argument that this was a less threatening arena for women's voices is persuasive; Lok not only writes spiritual poetry but also quite literally locates her voice within patriarchal strictures by appending her poetry to her translation of Calvin. But equally persuasive is the assertion that such poems demonstrate at least some measure of resistance to and even subversion of patriarchy; female poets were turning to a form whose value was unassailable and in so doing arguably implying as well that a higher audience would attend to their words even if their contemporaries did not.

THE SONNET

Love poetry was of course composed in a range of forms, including that broad category generally called "song." Even – or especially – collections of poems termed "sonnet sequences" frequently encompass a number of other stanzaic forms; *Astrophil and Stella*, for example, incorporates eleven songs. But arguably the sonnet and pastoral were the two most popular and characteristic lyric forms of the period. Hence exploring these two genres in greater depth than others can help us to address many questions about the workings of lyric in the sixteenth century.

One of the few instances in which a genre is defined in terms of a verse form, the sonnet can most safely be categorized as a fourteen-line poem that often, although not invariably, follows one of a handful of specified rhyme schemes and often, although not invariably, concerns love. One mark of the variety and experimentation that characterized the lyric during the early modern period, however, is the instability of even that loose a definition. In 1582 Thomas Watson published *Hecatompathia*, a collection of eighteen-line sonnets, and throughout the period other writers occasionally deviated from the fourteen-line pattern; moreover, the term "sonnet" was sometimes used loosely for love poetry, so that Donne's lyrics were termed *Songs and Sonets* even though few of them have anything like the length or rhyme scheme usually associated with the term.

But normative models were also available and frequently imitated. Thus the so-called Petrarchan sonnet may rhyme *abba abba cde edc*; the first eight lines, the octet or octave, are fixed in their rhyme scheme, while the final three, the sestet, can assume a range of other shapes, such as *cdecde* or *cdcdee*. The sonnet labeled Shakespearean consists of three four-line units known as quatrains and a couplet, so it assumes the form: *abab cdcd efef gg*. All these versions of the sonnet play subdivisions against each other, the octet versus the sestet in the Petrarchan form and the quatrains versus the couplet in its English cousins; in addition, patterns of rhyme and meaning create further subdivisions, so that English sonnets, like their Italian predecessors, often include a significant break after line eight as well as the secondary shifts between quatrains. In the English sonnet these relationships among prosodic and semantic units tend to be varied and unstable. For example, while the Shakespearean sonnet often effects closure on a reassuring note of epigrammatic finality, couplets may undercut what has come before, or they may undercut the apparent neatness of their own unit, as when Shakespeare's Sonnet 35, a poem engaged throughout with the loss of comfortingly predictable patterns, begins its final statement in the twelfth, not thirteenth, line. Thus the form itself may enact an imperiled and often unsuccessful attempt at resolution.

Sidney's *Astrophil and Stella*, which signals both the speaker's connection with and distance from the author by naming him "Astrophil" or "star-lover," demonstrates the dramatic immediacy and psychological complexity the form could achieve. The sequence also demonstrates its author's delight in experimenting with verse form, rhyme, and rhetorical devices such as complex patterns of repetition. These poems, whose author attained a virtually mythic status after his early death, enjoyed an extraordinary popularity, as did many of Sidney's other writings. Spenser's *Amoretti* (1595) is sometimes contrasted with Sidney's collection as more melodious and descriptive in its style and less troubled in its responses to love and desire, though Spenser does in fact include some extraordinarily bitter invective as well as soaring praise of his lady. Similarly, it is customary to contrast the graceful lyricism of Samuel Daniel's *Delia* with the Sidneyan drama of Michael Drayton's sonnets, but such generalizations also need qualifications. Many of the poems in the first edition of Drayton's *Ideas Mirrour* (1594) are indistinguishable from Daniel's work; some of the putative distinctions in question gradually emerged as Drayton saw the volume through eleven editions, including three significant revisions in the seventeenth century, but the collection remained varied in tone and style. Other poets of the period produced not only some impressive sonnet sequences but also enough indifferent or truly dreadful ones to inspire Sir

John Davies' witty parodies entitled "gullinge sonnets" (appearing only in a manuscript miscellany, not in printed form, during the early modern period and speculatively dated 1594). Although many of the other poems in the tradition were indeed as humdrum as Davies' mockery suggests, some distinguished themselves in significant ways. Richard Barnfield, for example, writes homoerotic sonnets. The sonnet became less popular around the turn of the century, though the first English sonnet sequence by a woman, Lady Mary Wroth's *Pamphilia to Amphilanthus*, appeared in 1621.

English sonnets have multiple and intertwined roots, including the poetry of the troubadours, the idealized visionary love poems in Dante's *Vita nuova*, and Neo-Platonic philosophy. The Italian poet Petrarch's collection, variously known by the revealing titles *Rime sparse* ("scattered rhymes") and *Canzoniere* ("songs"), is, however, the principal source of the English sonnet tradition. Although the *Rime sparse* encompasses a range of verse forms and subjects, most of its poems are sonnets concerning the speaker's relationship to Laura, a woman who may or may not have been fictive. These lyrics model several characteristics that English sonneteers were to imitate: a typically unhappy relationship with a woman who is often idealized but sometimes demonized (feminism has trenchantly glossed the reactive dynamic that structures that paradox), a preoccupation with representation itself, a struggle between a commitment to secular love and an attempt to disavow it, whether in the name of its spiritual counterpart or simply common sense and self-protection. Petrarch contributed as well a number of formal characteristics that recur in English sonnets. From him English poets borrowed the signature trope of the genre, the oxymoron, which combines opposites, generally in the form of an adjective–noun phrase such as "icy fire" or "sweet warrior." They adapted as well images for love that appeared in Petrarch and his predecessors, such as references to a hunt or a careening ship. Their interaction with the author of the *Rime sparse* was, however, mediated not only by his own commentators (his immense popularity generated ten major commentaries, so that his poems often appeared with elaborate and lengthy glosses) but also by the later Italian and French poets who themselves imitated him and thus implicitly commented on him. Four poems Daniel published in *Delia* derive from Du Bellay, for example, and Lodge bases several of his poems on sonnets by Ronsard, sometimes virtually plagiarizing them.

Indeed, nationalism, so central to the English early modern period in England in other ways, shapes its sonneteering as well, with an impulse to appropriate, nationalize, and surpass Continental models among its principal motivations. But, as I have already suggested, this is only one of several explanations for the extraordinary popularity of sonneteering. The sonnet attracted poets and readers in part because it enacted many of the central struggles of the age, often distancing them through transposition: its swings between power and powerlessness, for example, staged contemporary concerns about the uncertainties of social status.[11] Above all, though, Petrarchism served variously to intensify and resolve early modern negotiations about gender. As many critics have demonstrated, the genre provides reassuring scenarios for controlling the threats associated with the female body and female subjectivity; for example, the blazon, that part-by-part description of the female body, can provide an instance of divide and conquer. And yet such generalizations, though widely accepted, risk oversimplification: despite the conventional wisdom about the silencing of women in early modern culture, Petrarchan mistresses not only speak but are praised for their voices, and in fact the sequences most often manifest not the power of the male speaker but an unresolved struggle between power and powerlessness. Indeed, the Petrarchan sonnet models gender relations elsewhere in the culture above all in its complexities, contradictions, and ambivalences.

PASTORAL

Pastoral was also especially popular in and characteristic of early modern English literature. But whereas the sonnet enjoyed a relatively brief but extraordinarily intense vogue during the sixteenth century, pastoral poetry was written virtually throughout the period, being variously deployed for love poetry, funeral elegies, meditations on religious and ethical problems, and satire, especially of the church; Spenser's *Shepheardes Calender* includes all of these approaches to the mode. Important and highly influential precedents to the English tradition include the *Eclogues* of Vergil (which attracted interest in part because the fourth poem was interpreted as prophesying the birth of Christ) and the lyrics of the Greek poets Theocritus, Bion, and Moschus. English poets were also familiar with their Continental predecessors in the genre; for example, Mantuan provided a significant precedent for using pastoral to discuss religion.

Probably the most famous pastoral of the period is Spenser's *Shepheardes Calender*; his choice of this form for his virtual poetic debut (he had previously published some translations) reflects both the continuing power of the model of the Vergilian wheel and the significance of this genre for his culture. Twelve eclogues comprise this collection, each accompanied by a woodcut, a motto, and elaborate notes by one "E.K.," who may or may not be Spenser himself. Among the many pastorals included in Sidney's prose romance, the *Arcadia* (1590), is "Ye goteherd gods"; the poet here skillfully deploys the repeated rhymes of the sestina to stage the obsessiveness of mourning. Another influential and revealing version of the genre is Christopher Marlowe's "Passionate Shepherd to his Love," a poem whose speaker attempts to seduce a lady by promising her the delights of the countryside; this lyric inspired a number of retorts in its own day, notably Sir Walter Ralegh's "Nymph's Reply to the Shepherd" and Donne's "Bait." In our own century Marlowe's text was turned into a cabaret song in Ian McKellan's cinematic version of *Richard III*, thus figuring the destruction and deformation of the values the poem ostensibly celebrates.

Once one moves beyond the obvious generalization that pastoral concerns the countryside, engaging with the values it represents and playing them against those of court or city, it becomes more complicated to define and describe the form. Certain conventionalized situations and formats do recur in the pastorals of many periods: shepherds often participate in singing contests, and they lament the sorrows of love. Often, too, pastorals describe invasions into the pastoral world, though this characteristic of the genre has not received the attention it deserves; whether effected by the intruders on whose threatened arrival Vergil tellingly opens his collection or by death, such intrusions mime and comment on the presence of other genres within pastoral, such as references to epic and satiric rebukes. Dialogues are common within pastoral, as is the Chinese-box effect of a frame story within which other stories are told. And pastoral, a strikingly reflexive genre, characteristically incorporates commentaries on its own practices, such as the act of writing poetry. Indeed, it is not only metapastoral but also metalyric in that the questions it raises about temporality, loss, and the workings of poetry itself are at the core of the lyric mode.

But what values and ideologies characterize pastoral? Some assert that it focuses on the relationship between man and nature, while others instead draw attention to its eroticism. Some claim pastoral is simple and idyllic, while others stress the complexities and ambivalences exemplified by the statement attributed to death in pastoral, *Et in Arcadia ego* ("I am even in Arcadia"). Some associate it with detachment, while others trace the ways pastoral allegorizes political, social, and religious controversies, as Spenser famously does in his *Shepheardes Calender*. In a major study of the genre, *What Is Pastoral?*, Paul Alpers negotiates a number of these debates, incisively arguing, for example, that pastoral typically neither denies nor drowns in the threats it engages but rather suspends them. And pastoral is, he suggests, often concerned primarily with the interactions in human communities.[12]

To understand the workings of pastoral in the early modern period, one needs to look more closely at additional characteristics and predilections as well. Its emphasis on the contrast between the *here* of the country and the *there* of city or court is the spatial analogue to its recurrent temporal preoccupation with *then* and *now*; the former is generally represented as the idyllic time before the pastoral world is threatened, whether by the new inhabitants who displace the shepherds in Vergil's first eclogue, by love, or by that figure who is both enemy and sibling of love in pastoral, death. This contrast between *then* and *now* is sometimes figured in the combination of narrative and lyric elements in pastoral. Pastoral is also typically concerned with the unstable relationship between loss and recovery. Thus, for example, in a sense the pastoral landscape is a second Eden, and yet it too is under threat (a pattern that recurs in dramatic pastorals such as Shakespeare's *As You Like It* as well as their lyric counterparts); and when a shepherd sings a song associated with another shepherd, he both recuperates that lyric and signals the absence of its original author. Pastoral, the genre that on some level represents a lost home, is also deeply concerned with threats to an abode; witness Vergil's telling decision to open his eclogues on a story of a shepherd being dispossessed.

Although these characteristics recur throughout the history of pastoral, they would have been especially appealing in the early modern period. Its interest in time and change attracted an era that was fascinated with history and historicity. Its emphasis on both the loss and restoration of home interested a culture that mythologized itself as a second Troy – and that feared that that Troy, like the first one, was subject to invasions, notably from the Catholic powers in Europe. Seamus Heaney, whose own poems are so often written within, about, and in defiance of history, observes, "A poem floats adjacent to, parallel to, the historical moment."[13] Even when pastoral does not comment directly on history and politics, it may trope them, floating adjacent to and thus variously refracting, redefining, and reinterpreting them.

But pastoral is often more directly connected with its culture as well, and this too helps to explain its appeal. Two of the most significant rhetorical treatises of the sixteenth century emphasize its congeniality to allegorical treatments of political and social issues. Although pastoral was seen as a low form during the Renaissance, involving both language and speakers less elevated than their counterparts in, say, epic, Sidney stresses that it could perform an important social function. "Is the poor pipe disdained, which sometime out of Meliboeus' mouth can show the misery of people under hard lords or ravening soldiers? ... sometimes, under the pretty tales of wolves and sheep, can include the whole considerations of wrongdoing and patience" (*Defence of Poetrie*, p. 116). Sidney does precisely what he describes in his romance, the *Arcadia*. And in Book 1, Chapter 18 of his

Arte of English Poesie, Puttenham asserts that the impetus behind pastoral was not in fact the exploration of love "but under the veil of homely persons, and in rude speeches to insinuate and glance at greater matters."[14] Exploring and expanding the commentaries by Sidney and Puttenham, recent studies have trenchantly traced how pastoral glances at "greater matters" of English Renaisssance politics and culture. Thus Annabel Patterson traces references to patronage, while Louis Montrose demonstrates the ways this genre explores, often in safely allegorical form, questions about power, status, and patronage.[15]

CONCLUSION

But much as Shakespeare's sonnets end on ostensible summaries that often instead challenge what has come before, so a survey of the genres of lyric poetry should terminate on an acknowledgment of the instability of that category. Some genres regularly encompass both lyric and narrative modes: witness the range of poems in Spenser's *Complaints*. The so-called lyric epithalamium dovetails both modes, insistently temporal in its chronicle of the events of the wedding day and lyric in its meditations on them. Similarly, the nymphs' song in Spenser's "Prothalamion" signals a change of mode through a change of speakers. But one of the best examples of the interplay between lyric and narrative is the sonnet tradition. Individual sonnets often tell stories; witness the whole host of mythological tales so popular in the genre, such as the seventeenth poem in Sidney's *Astrophil and Stella*. The tension between the attempt to find a plot in a collection of sonnets published by a given poet and the insistence that the poems in question reject narrativity is manifest in the terms used for such collections: "sonnet sequence" versus "sonnet cycle." The soundest approach to these debates moderates (in both senses of that verb) the extreme arguments on both sides: we need to recognize that the balance between lyric and narrative elements differs significantly from one group of sonnets to the next, but often a single author's collection of sonnets will juxtapose poems that are discrete meditations and might as plausibly be arranged in a different order with groups of sonnets that appear to tell a story. In any event, however one resolves the disagreements about the presence of narrative plots, in the sonnet as in many other genres the interaction among lyric, narrative, and dramatic elements stages the tensions among differing visions of problems ranging from temporality to gender.

　We are now in a position briefly to return to my initial questions about the problems of defining lyric and relating it to sixteenth-century culture. Not only should definitions and descriptions be historically specific; the variety lyric manifests even within a single historical period, such as the early modern one, offers further caveats about generalizations. One can, however, say that in the Renaissance the connection between lyric and song is central. One can also assert with confidence that Renaissance lyrics variously qualify and challenge definitions that emphasize an isolated speaker overheard rather than participate in social interactions. To be sure, some poems, notably in the sonnet tradition, are indeed internalized meditations, and often their so-called plots are far more amorphous than critics more accustomed to reading narrative and drama like to acknowledge. But many other Renaissance lyrics evoke a social situation, whether it be that of the shepherd communicating with other shepherds or of the elegiac poet addressing the dead person or other mourners. And even the poems that involve internalized reflection often presume as well an audience who is not simply overhearing private thoughts but rather being indirectly addressed. The lament in a sonnet, for example, may present itself as a private outpouring of sorrow but also function as implicit pressure on the lady and an implicit complaint about her behavior to a male audience. Thus, though this predilection has not received the attention it deserves, Renaissance lyrics frequently address not just a single audience but rather multiple and different audiences.[16] In an age fascinated by rhetoric, the lyric poet is typically a consummate rhetorician, adorned with the literary skills and shadowed with the ethical dangers of that role.

The presence of multiple audiences aptly figures the ways contemporary critics can most fruitfully read the sixteenth-century lyric. We need to eschew generalizations that neglect its own multiplicity, and we need to approach it from many critical perspectives, alert to both technical virtuosity and ideological imperatives and thus to the complex interplay between formal potentialities and cultural history.

NOTES

1 Helen Vendler, "*Tintern Abbey:* Two Assaults," in *Wordsworth in Context*, ed. Pauline Fletcher and John Murphy, (Lewisburg and London: Bucknell University Press and Associated University Presses, 1992), p. 184.

2 Northrop Frye, *Anatomy of Criticism: Four Essays* (Princeton: Princeton University Press, 1957), pp. 275–80.

3 For a useful overview of these changes, see Chaviva Hošek and Patricia Parker, "Introduction," in *Lyric Poetry: Beyond New Criticism*, ed. Hošek and Parker (Ithaca, NY: Cornell University Press, 1985).

4 David Lindley, *Lyric* (London: Methuen, 1985), pp. 22–24.

5 For this explanation of Skelton's prosody, see Arthur F. Kinney, *John Skelton; Priest as Poet: Seasons of Discovery* (Chapel Hill: University of North Carolina Press, 1987), esp. pp. 46–51.

6 The reference is to Sidney, *An Apologie for Poetrie*, ed. Geoffrey Shepherd (London: Nelson, 1965), p. 118.
7 George T. Wright, *Shakespeare's Metrical Art* (Berkeley: University of California Press, 1988), pp. 27–37.
8 The citation is to Campion, *Observations in the Art of English Poesie* (London, 1602), p. 4.
9 See esp. Arthur F. Marotti, *Manuscript, Print, and the English Renaissance Lyric* (Ithaca, NY: Cornell University Press, 1995); Wendy Wall, *The Imprint of Gender: Authorship and Publication in the English Renaissance* (Ithaca, NY: Cornell University Press, 1993).
10 Rosalie L. Colie, *Shakespeare's Living Art* (Princeton: Princeton University Press, 1974), ch. 2.
11 For a more detailed discussion of this and cognate explanations for its popularity, see my study *Echoes of Desire: English Petrarchism and Its Counterdiscourses* (Ithaca, NY: Cornell University Press, 1995).
12 On suspension see Paul Alpers, *What Is Pastoral?* (Chicago: University of Chicago Press, 1996), pp. 68–69, 173; he discusses community in a number of places, but see esp. pp. 81–82.
13 Heaney, *The Government of the Tongue: Selected Prose 1978–1987* (New York: Farrar, Straus and Giroux, 1989), p. 121.
14 I cite Puttenham, *The Arte of English Poesie*, ed. Baxter Hathaway (Kent, OH: Kent State University Press, 1970), p. 53.
15 See two essays by Montrose: "'Eliza, Queene of shepheardes,' and the Pastoral of Power," *English Literary Renaissance* 10 (1980): 153–82; "Of Gentlemen and Shepherds: The Politics of Elizabethan Pastoral Form," *English Literary History* 50 (1983): 415–59; Patterson, *Pastoral and Ideology: Virgil to Valéry* (Berkeley: University of California Press, 1987).
16 Multiple audiences are also common in love poetry in particular, a point Christopher Martin demonstrates, though from perspectives different from mine, in *Policy in Love: Lyric and Public in Ovid, Petrarch and Shakespeare* (Pittsburgh, PA: Duquesne University Press, 1994).

FURTHER READING

Alpers, Paul, *What Is Pastoral?* (Chicago: University of Chicago Press, 1996).
Bahti, Timothy, *Ends of the Lyric: Direction and Consequence in Western Poetry* (Baltimore: Johns Hopkins Press, 1996).
Biester, James, *Lyric Wonder: Rhetoric and Wit in Renaissance English Poetry* (Ithaca, NY: Cornell University Press, 1997).
Bush, Douglas, *Mythology and the Renaissance Tradition in English Poetry*. rev. edn. (New York: Norton, 1963).
Cameron, Sharon, *Lyric Time: Dickinson and the Limits of Genre* (Baltimore: Johns Hopkins University Press, 1979).
Colie, Rosalie L., *The Resources of Kind: Genre-Theory in the Renaissance* (Berkeley: University of California Press, 1973).
Dubrow, Heather, *Echoes of Desire: English Petrarchism and Its Counterdiscourses* (Ithaca, NY: Cornell University Press, 1995).

Ferry, Anne, The "Inward" Language: Sonnets of Wyatt, Sidney, Shakespeare, Donne (Chicago: University of Chicago Press, 1983).

Frye, Northrop, Anatomy of Criticism: Four Essays (Princeton: Princeton University Press, 1957).

Greene, Roland, Post-Petrarchism: Origins and Innovations of the Western Lyric Sequence (Princeton: Princeton University Press, 1991).

Greene, Thomas M., The Light in Troy: Imitation and Discovery in Renaissance Poetry (New Haven: Yale University Press, 1982).

Haber, Judith, Pastoral and the Poetics of Self-Contradiction: Theocritus to Marvell (Cambridge: Cambridge University Press, 1994).

Hedley, Jane, Power in Verse: Metaphor and Metonymy in the Renaisssance Lyric (University Park: Pennsylvania State University Press, 1988).

Henderson, Diana E., Passion Made Public: Elizabethan Lyric, Gender, and Performance (Urbana: University of Illinois Press, 1995).

Hollander, John, Rhyme's Reason: A Guide to English Verse, 2nd edn. (New Haven: Yale University Press, 1989).

Melodious Guile: Fictive Pattern in Poetic Language (New Haven: Yale University Press, 1988).

The Untuning of the Sky: Ideas of Music in English Poetry, 1500–1700 (Princeton: Princeton University Press, 1961).

Hošek, Chaviva and Patricia Parker, Lyric Poetry: Beyond New Criticism (Ithaca, NY: Cornell University Press, 1985).

Lever, J. W., The Elizabethan Love Sonnet, rev. edn. (London: Methuen, 1966).

Lindley, David, Lyric (London: Methuen, 1985).

Low, Anthony, The Reinvention of Love; Poetry, Politics and Culture from Sidney to Milton (Cambridge: Cambridge University Press, 1993).

Marotti, Arthur F., Manuscript, Print, and the English Renaissance Lyric (Ithaca, NY: Cornell University Press, 1995).

Martin, Christopher, Policy in Love: Lyric and Public in Ovid, Petrarch and Shakespeare (Pittsburgh: Duquesne University Press, 1994).

Norbrook, David, Poetry and Politics in the English Renaissance (London: Routledge and Kegan Paul, 1984).

Patterson, Annabel, Pastoral and Ideology: Virgil to Valéry (Berkeley: University of California Press, 1987).

Sidney, Sir Philip, An Apologie for Poetrie, ed. Geoffrey Shepherd (London: Nelson, 1965).

Smith, Hallett, Elizabethan Poetry: A Study in Conventions, Meaning, and Expression (Cambridge: Harvard University Press, 1952).

Stevens, John, Music and Poetry in the Early Tudor Court (Lincoln: University of Nebraska Press, 1961).

Woods, Susanne, Natural Emphasis: English Versification from Chaucer to Dryden (San Marino, CA: The Huntington Library, 1984).

Wright, George T., Shakespeare's Metrical Art (Berkeley: University of California Press, 1988).

10

DONALD CHENEY

Narrative, romance, and epic

As early as 1484, William Caxton translated the fables of Aesop from the French version of Steinhöwel; over the course of the following century numerous editions of Aesop and Aesopian beast-fables were to appear, in verse and prose, and in Latin as well as in English. A version in Scots by Robert Henryson was published in 1570, and one in "tru ortŏgraphy" in 1585. As Annabel Patterson has shown,[1] these fables or "apologues" proved extraordinarily adaptable to a wide array of purposes: superficially attractive in themselves as entertaining little narratives making minimal demands on a humble listener's attention span, they could be used to advance or subvert the ruling class's agenda.

In the final quarter of the century, Edmund Spenser adopted the genre as a recognizable part of his repertory, and thereby signaled its place in the native literary tradition that he was advertising and "illustrating" (in the sense of Du Bellay's "Defense and Illustration" of the French language, both embodying and ennobling it, making it more lustrous). His fable of the Oak and the Briar in the "February" eclogue of *The Shepheardes Calender* (1579) is told by the aged shepherd Thenot to rebuke young Cuddie; readers today continue to wonder whether it shadows one or another contemporary dispute, despite (or perhaps because of) the editor E.K.'s bland emphasis on its simple pleasures: "This tale ... he telleth as learned of Chaucer, but it is clean in another kind, and rather like to Aesop's fables. It is very excellent for pleasant descriptions, being altogether a certain Icon or Hypotyposis of disdainful younkers."[2]

A comparable suggestion of topical allegory attaches to such other poems by Spenser as *Muiopotmos*, where the careless butterfly who awakens a spider's envy recalls the fate of many a courtier, or *Virgils Gnat*, itself a fable about a fable by which the earlier poet rebuked his patron's ingratitude. For a later Aesopian venture of Spenser's, *Mother Hubberds Tale*, included in the 1591 *Complaints* volume, though it was described by the poet in his dedicatory epistle as a "simple" product of "idle labors ...

long since composed in the raw conceit of my youth" (*Shorter Poems*, p. 334), its more inescapable topicality apparently led to its being "called in" by the censor, with unsold copies of the work impounded; the poem was omitted from the 1611 edition of Spenser's collected works. Allusions to this scandal by such contemporaries as Harvey, Nashe, Middleton, and others suggest that anxiety over censorship may have been accompanied by an eagerness to document those cases where the authorities were prepared to read and show some concern over the idle labors of poets. Patterson has called attention to the legendary life of Aesop which accompanied editions of his fables, by which the genre was said to have originated with an Aethiopian slave, physically grotesque, whose conspicuous "otherness" gave him a unique position from which to understand and criticize his masters, comparable to that of a court jester whose deformity and lack of social status rendered him unthreatening and therefore unpunishable for acts of *lèse majesté*. Later writers in the Aesopian mode similarly appealed (as "E.K." had done) to its rustic simplicity as licensing any satire to be found therein, real or imagined.

That such appeals were disingenuous should come as no surprise: authors, translators, and readers alike were far removed from the humble or rustic life, and their experience of Aesop's works was likely to have originated in school exercises where they rendered such texts into and out of the classical tongues. Like E.K., they would know and appreciate an Icon or Hypotyposis when they saw one. So, although these fables appear, chronologically, at the beginning of a survey of sixteenth-century story-telling, they are scarcely the primitive or naive beginnings of a tradition from which the English novel emerges, to "rise" to its full flowering of sophistication and moral resonance in the eighteenth century. Rather, the works to be discussed in this chapter seem at times startlingly "postmodern" in their rhetorical complexity and self-conscious infoldings of textuality; and small wonder, since writers and readers composed their thoughts and feelings with reference to rhetorical norms that seem esoterically erudite today. Furthermore, the new conditions of publication in a rapidly expanding book market created opportunities and anxieties that an author could never forget or ignore, as he sought to address a newly varied and shadowy audience.

It is suggestive of the dependence of all sixteenth-century fiction on these rhetorical bearings that the full title of Spenser's most scandalous fable should have read: *Prosopopoia; or Mother Hubberds Tale*. The name of the humble story-teller ("Base is the style, and matter mean withal," line 44) is literally secondary to the identification of the tale as an exercise in prosopopoeia or personification. Spenser need not have been familiar with

The Arte of English Poesie (1589), since the term was in common usage; but the Chaucerian examples given there are consistent with the tone of Spenser's opening. Puttenham (the presumed author of the work) speaks of three kinds of counterfeiting: *hypotyposis*, "or the counterfeit representation," a generalized feigning of "things" that never were; *prosopographia*, "or the counterfeit countenance," the description of actual or recognizable persons; and *prosopopoeia*, "or the counterfeit in personation," a description of imaginary persons or the giving of human attributes to non-human creatures.

Although the distinction between these two latter categories of writing seems at times to be our familiar distinction between non-fiction and fiction, expository writing and "creative" writing, Puttenham's examples of *prosopographia* are Homer's heroes or Chaucer's pilgrims, whereas examples of *prosopopoeia* are the allegorical figures in Chaucer's version of *The Romance of the Rose*; so it seems that in his usage, at least, the former term points to realistic or typical descriptions, not necessarily to matters of fact. *Prosopopoeia* is then *more* fictive because more patently unreal: *graphia*, the writing or describing, versus *poeia*, the making or inventing, of a human countenance (*prosōpos*, Latin *vultus*). As we shall see, this elastic pair of rhetorical terms corresponds to or engenders a frequently playful, sometimes anxious, polarity in the century's imaginative writings: elaborate epistolary frames may seek to identify or control the proper or original "audience" for a work, authenticate it or call into question its status; or else, references to contemporary persons or texts, bearing their own charge of questionable authenticity, may be imbedded in the text to ground it in fact or reorientate the reader.

UTOPIA

For all its popularity with readers in succeeding centuries, Thomas More's *Utopia* (1516; English translation by Ralphe Robynson, 1551) stands at the opposite pole from the ostensibly demotic Aesopian fables in view of its association with the learned international humanism of its day. The last surviving Neo-Latin text to remain (in translation, of course) on undergraduate and graduate reading lists as a monument of English literature, it had its origin as a reply to Desiderius Erasmus' *Encomium Moriae*, a wittily paradoxical Praise of Folly, *moria*, whose title punningly marked it as an affectionate tribute to his friend More. In his *Humanist Poetics*, Arthur F. Kinney[3] has traced in subtle detail the process by which More provides an answering Praise of Wisdom that similarly proposes a description of an ideal commonwealth, presented in a dialogue so lopsided that it is virtually a monologue by Utopia's witness, one Raphael Hythlodaeus, whose name identifies him as both angelic messenger and a speaker of nonsense – a nonsense comparable, presumably, to that which More's own name had suggested to Erasmus. But in this case, More has written himself into the dialogue as a largely mute Doubting Thomas who listens to Hythlodaye's long presentation but has to defer his qualms and queries to another day when dinnertime puts an end to Book II and to the work.

Clearly, the description of utopia is situated in a world of contubernial fraternity that extends from the pious fraternities of the Middle Ages, through the academic meeting places of the Republic of Letters and down to today's remnants of college fellowships and academic conventions. The turf bench in More's garden, a cloistered retreat from the world where Nature and Art weave temporary garlands of repose, is a locus where we find a *prosopographia* of the historical Thomas More, "Citizen and Sheriff of the Famous City of London" as he identifies himself on the title page, and a *prosopopoeia* of the definitely fictional and slightly fantastical Hythlodaeus, an "Icon or Hypotyposis" of those travelers who were bringing their tales of a new world back to London.

The prefatory and framing devices invite the reader to consider which side of this academic confrontation is the more soundly rooted in reality – the good citizen More, homeowner and family man, master of his household and diplomatic servant of his nation, or the world traveler and comparative sociologist Hythlodaeus. The question, like the conversation itself, is literally academic: Utopia is a hypothesis, "No Place" (Greek *ou-* + *topos*), though it is also presented as a "Good Place" (Greek *eu-*). Or rather, it is presented as a projection of the *desire* for a Good Place; and its praise in Hythlodaeus' long monologue could be characterized as an *Encomium Desiderii*, a double pun on the name of More's friend (since "Erasmus" is a Greek form of Latin "Desiderius," from *eros*). More is thus suggesting that he is both a Thomas and a More, a fool who needs convincing, while Desiderius Erasmus may be a double-barreled enthusiast, more fool he.

In his prefatory letter to Peter Giles, More (like Chaucer in the *Canterbury Tales*) presents himself as innocent reporter, to be judged on the accuracy of his recording what Hythlodaeus has said, not on the accuracy or plausibility of the description of Utopia itself. Thus he apologizes for his book's containing the statement that a bridge over the River Anyder is 500 paces long, when the river itself is only 300 paces wide; he is so vehement in affirming his determination to give a true report even if the facts are wrong, that he seems to overlook the fact that bridges are typically longer than the width of the rivers they cross. And beyond that, this carelessness obscures the greater comic disparity, that this is the River No-Water. Presumably this is More answering Erasmus in the voice of Moria, playing the role of folly in which his friend had cast him.

This pretense of anxiety on the part of a well-meaning but uncomprehending narrator prepares us for the ways in which the *Utopia* proper will both project and question our desires for a good, or a better, commonwealth. At heart this is very much a pragmatic Englishman's version of Utopia, in which a literalizing imagination tries to work out the details of an ideal state; repeatedly, Doubting Thomas can't keep his hands off a brilliant idea, and a communist paradise is always turning into what we recognize as a bureaucratic nightmare – unless, of course, our faith in the ideal is strong enough to make us ignore the absurdities in its working-out.

Although there are contradictions on every page, many of them hilarious, one example may serve. In cases of adultery, the Utopians punish the offender with slavery and permit the innocent spouse to remarry; since Erasmus was on record as believing that the church should allow remarriage (in addition to the permitted separation from bed and board) under such circumstances, this may seem to be one small but sensible step toward reason in a society based on rational principles. Yet we are invited to consider other scenarios as well. Ideally, if both adulterers are married, their spouses will marry one another – if they wish. Perhaps the wife loves her husband despite his offense: in such a case she can accompany him into slavery; and if their story is sufficiently touching the Senate may decide to pardon the couple; but if the husband should err again, the punishment will be death. If hard cases make bad laws, an enumeration of possible hardship cases, and of the exceptions they warrant, makes for a queer sort of utopia.

Like Plato's ideal republic from which it derives its ancestry, More's projection of an ideal commonwealth increasingly comes to appear dependent on a substratum of disenfranchised servants, some of them slaves in the literal sense and others who are slaves to their own baser natures; and as the long day's description of its organization wears on, amusing inconsistencies give way to more menacing shadows. The Utopians love peace, but annex neighboring territories as their own prosperity requires; they are diabolically skilled in playing on the frailties and corruption of others. Increasingly as the work unfolds, More's anatomy of Utopian society comes to seem prophetic of emergent British expansionism and colonialism, triggered in part by travelers' reports and in part by rumblings of reform and nationalism on the Continent. By the end of the sixteenth century, England would be heavily investing in such dreams, and Spenser would give the name of Fairyland to that heady world of secular self-actualization that More had named Utopia when it was still Nowhere. By then, of course, More would have long since become a martyr to his own unreadiness to see the laws of marriage made more elastic.

What seems uncannily prophetic in the *Utopia* is doubtless the product of More's profound involvement in the humanist culture of his time. A Renaissance that was late coming to the British Isles had long since made itself felt among the Continental members of the Neo-Latin republic of letters; and More's ability to move easily among his republican colleagues across the Channel enabled a rich irony that would soon become harder for British writers to achieve, after Henry's break with Rome. At the same time, the skeptical More who is represented in the *Utopia* as working out, with typically English pragmatism, the implications of Utopian desire, bears a striking resemblance to his contemporary, Sir Thomas Wyatt, who translated Petrarch's transcendent longings for Laura into earthy and impatient expressions of physical desire, and in doing so anticipated the projects of the major Elizabethan sonnet collections, in which Sidney, Spenser, and Shakespeare all created dramas in which – for all the lovers' desire to idealize their mistresses – "Desire still cries, 'Give me some food,'" (*Astrophil and Stella*, 71).

ADVENTURES OF MASTER F.J.

George Gascoigne's *Adventures of Master F.J.* (1573; revised version 1575) is an extraordinarily sophisticated and convoluted story of desire, and one of the century's finest narrative achievements; furthermore, it illustrates so many of the period's characteristic tropes and narrative motifs that it may serve as a principal illustration of early Elizabethan fiction. It anticipates Spenser's *Shepheardes Calender* of 1579 both in its claim to assimilate Continental and native literary materials and in its bristling apparatus of introductory notes and framing fictions, among which we catch fleeting glimpses of the anxious author, fearful of censure and envy. A preface by H.W. takes responsibility for having passed to the printer, A.B., a manuscript received from his friend, G.T., consisting of lyrics signed by F.J. to which G.T. has added increasingly verbose narrative descriptions of the occasions under which they were first written, copied, and more or less furtively conveyed to the lady who was their subject and their object.

In structure, *F.J.* resembles Dante's *Vita Nuova* or Sannazaro's *Arcadia* in its combining of poems with an explanatory background narrative in prose; but the generic similarity only underscores the suppression of spiritual or pastoral elements from this love story. G.T. tells of the young F.J.'s courtship of a married woman, Mistress Elinor, the daughter of his host, during a protracted visit to a country estate "in the north parts of this realm."[4] Although he is at first rebuffed, once her current lover, known only as her "secretary" (and described in F.J.'s biased terms as "in height the proportion of two pigmies" [*Anthology*, p. 15] – which seems to be a grudging way of characterizing a six-foot rival), is called off to London, F.J. observes a change in his lady's "style" and finds his way clear. Concealing his "naked sword" under his nightgown, he proceeds to the first of a series of rendezvous with her.

Meanwhile, F.J. has been befriended by an unmarried daughter of the house, Frances, in what promises to be a Platonic relationship contrasting with the physical affair he is beginning with Elinor. Whereas F.J. and Elinor refer to themselves as "HE" and "SHE" in their communications, F.J. and Frances choose the private names of "Trust" and "Hope." But although readers have tended to see Frances as the decent woman F.J. should have loved and married, her role in the story is more ambiguous. When she sees F.J. returning from Elinor, with "the point of his naked sword glistering under the skirt of his nightgown," she is "thoroughly tickled now in all her veins" (*Anthology*, p. 31), and with the aid of another gentlewoman steals the sword from his bedroom while he sleeps. It will be returned to him only after he has heard a teasing story from Frances of her dream of "a tall gentleman, apparelled in a nightgown of silk all embroidered about with a guard of naked swords" (*Anthology*, p. 35). As in the equally fictional dream told by Chaucer's Wife of Bath when she courted her fifth husband, a woman is affirming her authority over a male (or at least indulging a sensuous tickle) by appropriating a stereotypically male fantasy of phallic dominance.

Although F.J. might have taken warning from this episode, he continues to exult in his continuing triumphs with Elinor, without considering that his "sword" may be a two-edged one, capable of being turned against its owner, if it can be purloined so easily and circulated among the women of the house. His poems celebrate his erotic victories; and when Elinor's husband returns, he goes hunting with him as a pretext for writing about hunting horns and horned prey. But with the return of the "secretary" from London, F.J. falls into a fit of jealousy; and once Elinor finds him both violent and tedious she returns to her earlier diversions.

The narrative is distinguished by its evocation of two distinct points of view: the male G.T.'s, which seems to prefigure that of a more experienced and cynical F.J., and that of Frances, who shares some of Elinor's own amused, sympathetic, but unsentimental hedonism. F.J.'s increasing obtuseness as the story progresses is matched by an increased authority given to the women in the story; and when the unnamed gentlewoman of the earlier episodes is identified as (or perhaps replaced by) an older lady named Pergo

(Latin "proceed, as toward a conclusion"), there is a hint of the Three Sisters who have been unobtrusively spinning and weaving F.J.'s text to this point and are about to conclude it.

As William Nelson has shown,[5] Spenser drew on *Master F.J.*, and on the allegory of Sospetto from Ariosto's *Cinque Canti* that G.T. includes in his commentary, for his portrayal of Malbecco and Hellenore in *The Faerie Queene*, Book III; and he could have found in Gascoigne as well the sense of Hellenore (seduced by Paridell) as being a whorish Helen. Elinor is puzzled when one of F.J.'s poems refers to her as "my Helen," thinking that he is recycling a poem to an earlier lady by that name; and G.T.'s own uncertainties on the matter (like More's on the bridge over the Anyder) invite us to pause and consider the ways in which Elinor may indeed be, or not be, another Helen.

If there is one aspect of *Master F.J.* that sets it apart from, and above, other romances of the century, it is probably the skill with which the author gives the reader a detached perspective from which to view F.J.'s hapless journey from overweening lover to bewildered and disenchanted loser. We hear little from F.J. in his own voice, aside from the frankly derivative poems he has passed on to his friend. G.T.'s attitude of amused if sympathetic condescension toward the young lover prepares us for his fall; while the focus of interest on Frances and later Pergo as observers and participants – and as veteran residents of this bizarre household – keep us aware of how little F.J. understands of the rules of the game he thinks he is winning so brilliantly. When Elinor comes down to dinner the day after her "Moonshine Banquet" with her new lover, bearing the handwritten message "Contented" on her cap, this may seem a tribute to F.J., but we are merely told that "the lord of the castle of ignorance, and Dame Frances of great temperance, let it pass without offence" (*Anthology*, p. 34). For the men of the household, this seems to be a castle of ignorance indeed.

In his fecklessness, F.J. seems to mimic the public persona of George Gascoigne, whose most famous lyric, "Gascoigne's Woodmanship," features his failed marksmanship, and who chronicles his other near-misses as courtier with an almost perverse delight in self-effacement. Like other authors of his generation, he is one of the "Elizabethan Prodigals" memorably described by Richard Helgerson;[6] but instead of staging a narrative of repentance and self-improvement, he presents himself as continuing to blunder on amusingly and harmlessly – as perhaps befits any courtier whose virgin Queen permits no more purposeful activity for the men who surround and helplessly adore her.

In common with other works of the period, *Master F.J.* shows an awareness of Chaucer as the master story-teller to emulate. At the opening of the work, G.T. laments to H.W. "that amongst so many toward wits no one hath been hitherto encouraged to follow the trace of that worthy and famous knight Sir [sic] Geoffrey Chaucer" (Anthology, p. 5); and though his lament is itself Chaucerian in its digressiveness (he apologizes for having "wandered somewhat beside the path" [Anthology, p. 5]), F.J.'s confused pilgrimage leads him into a strange new world where women's desires are foregrounded (with teasing or tickling echoes, as we have seen, of Chaucer's Wife) and masculine teleologies frustrated – indeed, shrugged off as irrelevant.

Perhaps Gascoigne's own self-representation as humorously inept owes something to the figure of Pilgrim Geoffrey in The Canterbury Tales, whose attempt at a romance of chaste Sir Thopas is hooted off the stage that Poet Chaucer has constructed; but in any case it seems clear that for later ages Chaucer was a poet of unfinished tales; whether aborted or eroded by "cursèd eld" (as Spenser suggests) is unclear. It was not Chaucer's tale of Sir Thopas but his Squire's tale of "Cambuskan bold" that Milton's Penseroso dreamed of completing, a task already performed by Spenser in the titular legend of the fourth book of his Faerie Queene of 1596. Although the conspicuously abrupt endings of Elizabethan romances are not explicitly Chaucerian, they do seem to be associated with a Chaucerian sense of anxiety over their stories' drift, ratcheted to a new intensity by the conditions of print publication and attendant loss of control over one's audience. G.T. abruptly breaks off his story of F.J. with the remark that "It is time now to make an end of this thriftless history . . . I will cease, as one that had rather leave it unperfect than make it too plain." He apologizes for having used "sundry names for one person" (Anthology, p. 80), calling attention thereby to his failure to name his characters (or their location) in more than generic terms, "nothing doubting but you will easily understand my meaning" (Anthology, p. 80). He promises to stop his prose explanations of the poems, and to give henceforth (in the remainder of the 1573 volume of Hundreth Sundry Flowers) only the texts of various poems, "adding nothing of mine own but only a title to every poem" (Anthology, p. 80).

The anxieties implicit in these hasty concluding remarks by G.T. are realized and made explicit in Gascoigne's revised text two years later, where he apologizes profusely (and perhaps unnecessarily) for any indecencies or libels in the work, renaming the entire volume as Posies (divided into flowers, herbs, and weeds, in accordance with their alleged virtues or redeeming social merit) and presenting F.J. now as The Pleasant Fable of Ferdinando Jeronomi and Leonora da Valasco, translated out of the Italian riding tales of Bartello. G.T. disappears from the text, and the generic names of the protagonists are replaced by safely foreign proper names; the whole is now presented as a translation from a non-existent Italian original, whose "riding tales" relocate Chaucer's riding rhymes in a distant and famously vicious land. And a (slightly) moral ending is provided: "the worthy Lady Franceschina" dies of a miserable consumption, galled by the ingratitude of Ferdinando, who retires to "a dissolute kind of life" (*Anthology*, p. 80) in Venice, while Leonora continues to live a long and lustful life.

Richard C. McCoy[7] has suggested that Gascoigne's "castrated verses" may enact a drama of ostentatious apology and revision which calls attention to subversive elements in his writings that otherwise might escape notice. Here, too, Chaucer may be a source for a recurrent motif in sixteenth-century fictions, as regards both his apology in the General Prologue for any indecencies he may have to "report" in the *Tales* (echoed as we have seen by More in his letter to Giles), and his famous "Retraction" disavowing (by name) all his works which may not tend toward virtue. A similar "retractation" is found in Spenser's *Hymnes*, where allegedly earlier hymns to love and beauty are later "reformed" or reformulated in hymns to their heavenly counterparts. Protestant and nationalistic biases are brought into play as well, now, since Gascoigne's forbidden entertainments are assigned to Catholic Italy, whose abominations are beyond the reach of the English censor, at least during his waking moments.

ELIZABETHAN NARRATIVES

Other narratives partake in varying degrees of the formal and thematic elements seen in Gascoigne's. Lyly's *Euphues: The Anatomy of Wit* (1578) is chiefly known today for having given a name to an elaborately balanced style (already evident in works like William Painter's *Palace of Pleasure* of 1566 or George Pettie's *A petite pallace of Pettie his pleasure* of 1576) that was widely imitated in its day and as widely ridiculed immediately thereafter. Euphuism is perhaps best regarded as a necessary phase in the taming and "illustration" of English prose; it must have seemed almost magically effective when it was first encountered by English readers accustomed to the waywardness of their language when it was untethered by considerations of meter. A strenuously parallel sentence structure can suggest (while it is still a novelty) a disciplined mind and a language adapted to expressing the products of that mind. Hence the opening sentence of the work: "There dwelt in Athens a young gentleman of great patrimony, and of so comely a personage, that it was doubted whether he were more bound to nature for the lineaments of his person, or to fortune for the increase of his possessions" (*Anthology*, p. 89).

It is easy today to see that there are many facts of everyday experience that resist expression in so relentlessly parallel a form; and in fact the story of Euphues' prodigal friendship for Philautus and his equally prodigal love for Lucilla contains these in abundance. Madelon Gohlke[8] suggests that it is the very failure of this kind of language to cope with these kinds of situations that is central to the interest of Lyly's work; that the abandonment of the narrative (as abrupt as G.T.'s abandonment of F.J.'s story) and the subsequent turn to a series of didactic essays figure the protagonists' self-containment, their inability to communicate to any dramatic effect. Whether or not a contemporary reader would or could have thought of Lyly's work in just those terms, it seems plausible that he or she would have been amused (or bemused) by the ironic disparity between the joys of articulate self-expression and the frustrations of mutual self-contradiction. Lyly's protagonists keep their dignity and self-esteem at a terribly high price; and for a moment it seems that English prose narration achieves a newly lustrous prose while becoming measurably less effective as narrative.

Other writers of prose fiction during the final two decades of the century respond variously to the expanded reading public of the later Elizabethan period. Where Lyly had essentially defined himself as a courtier like Gascoigne, for better and (eventually) worse, albeit with a considerable popular success as the author of *Euphues*, both Greene and Nashe were university men who were widely prolific as professional writers addressing themselves directly to the new public. Greene's *Pandosto: The Triumph of Time* (first surviving edition, 1588) is of particular interest today as the source of Shakespeare's *Winter's Tale*. Its double plot, which combines a tragedy of jealousy in the first half of the narrative with a comic romance between the protagonists' offspring in the second, was thus to give birth – as a result of Shakespeare's adoption and adaptation of it – to what we have come to define as the very plotline of romantic tragicomedy. At the very least, the popularity of Greene's work (*Pandosto* had appeared in at least four editions when Shakespeare turned to it) marked it as expressing a popular taste that the playwright chose to respect and exploit. Furthermore, Greene's familiarity with Greek romances and his reliance on them and their many intervening imitations for his plots and secondary motifs – specifically here, the *History* of Apollonius of Tyre, translated from the Latin by Laurence Twine as *The Patterne of Painefull Adventures* (?1594; entered 1576) – provides a line of continuity in the English tradition for what Margaret Anne Doody has recently called "the true story" of the novel.[9]

In the 1580s, a work affirming the triumph of time in its title may well have echoed, or seemed to echo, Elizabeth's own triumphant accession to the throne a generation earlier, as famously reflected in her embracing of the image of Truth the Daughter of Time; and Henry's disparagement of her mother's chastity must then have been recalled in the story of Pandosto's fatal doubts of Bellaria. (By the time of *The Winter's Tale*, with James on the throne, it was doubtless the finally united kingdom of Sicily and Bohemia that would have caught the audience's attention.) The sententiously euphuistic style that is visible especially in Greene's dedicatory letters to the work would have further underscored its mixing of pleasure and profit, as would the two mottos on the title page: *Temporis filia veritas* (Truth the daughter of Time) and Horace's affirmation of the moral function of literature: *Omne tulit punctum qui miscuit utile dulci* (He wins full credit who mixes the useful with the delightful).[10]

Like Gascoigne, however, Greene shares with his contemporaries a taste for abrupt and perhaps intentionally puzzling endings. Once the two lovers have been revealed and formally united, Pandosto (whose wife, unlike Hermione in Shakespeare's version, has not survived the earlier tragic events) "fell in a melancholy fit, and to close up the comedy with a tragical strategem, he slew himself; whose death being many days bewailed ... Dorastus, taking leave of his father, went with his wife and the dead corpse into Bohemia where, after they were sumptuously entombed, Dorastus ended his days in contented quiet" (*Anthology*, p. 204). The "tragical strategem" seems to have been the author's as much as Pandosto's; and although Greene may not have meant to imply the death of Dorastus' young wife, an authorial taste for "contented quiet" and the hasty closing up of the comedy seems an oddly conspicuous part of this conclusion.

Thomas Nashe's brief but highly varied career sheds a somewhat different light on the movement from the patronage culture of the court to an urban readership developed and nourished by the popular stage and the publishing world. The work for which he is best known, *The Unfortunate Traveller* (1594), comes with dedicatory letters to both Henry Wriothesley, Earl of Southampton (who like Nashe had attended St. John's College, Cambridge), and to the "dapper Monsieur Pages of the Court" (to whom he offers this story of "a proper fellow page of yours, called Jack Wilton; [*Anthology*, p. 208] – the "pages" of which story can both entertain them and subsequently serve other needs such as drying and kindling tobacco). The episodes which ensue, as Jack follows his fortunes from court to battlefield and across Europe, range from the sentimental to the bloodthirsty, private liaisons and public executions, narrated by a voice that revels in its cynical virtuosity. Like Ben Jonson, with whom he collaborated on the notorious *Isle of Dogs*, Nashe shows a voracious appetite for the energies reflected and released by urban slang, and his protagonist here is always on the move, traveling from one lurid event to the next as if to avoid being overly marked or "impressed" by any.

Nashe's frequent puns on "pages" and impressions suggest that the rapidly changing landscape of this picaresque court- and camp-follower may be expressive of a necessary impermanence in the new world's literary output. His book is, in fact, what a publisher today would call a "page-turner": one spectacular piece of gossip after another calls out for our attention in the manner of supermarket tabloids, and in so doing the work seems to identify its reader as a curious outsider, a member of the great new, unwashed reading public reveling in the loves and terrors of the rich and famous. Although Jack occasionally claims to feel horror at the events he describes, his attitude is more often seemingly without affect, giving rein to the manic verbal energy in his self-appointed role as "outlandish chronicler" (*Anthology*, p. 308).

Like the other narratives of this period, Nashe's tale ends abruptly and with a gesture of reform after this life of a prodigal. "Mortifiedly abjected and daunted" by the horrific torture and execution of Cutwolf, Jack "married [his] courtesan, performed many almsdeeds, and hasted so fast out of the Sodom of Italy that within forty days I arrived at the King of England's camp" (*Anthology*, p. 308) – returning to the security of his own people and putting an end for now to his travels but promising "more pains in this kind" if his readers are pleased with what they have read. This final appeal to market demand identifies the reader's own desire as the reason for Jack's travels: it is not the mob in Bologna that cries out for Cutwolf's spectacular torments, but the reading public at home.

Thomas Deloney's *Jack of Newbury* (c. 1597) appeals to the fantasies of the new reading public in a less oblique or ironic sense, telling (as the title page promises) of the well-deserved rise to wealth and power of a Berkshire cloth-maker, "declaring his life and love together with his charitable deeds and great hospitality. And how he set continually five hundred poor people at work to the great benefit of the commonwealth. Worthy to be read and regarded" (*Anthology*, p. 313). Where Nashe's story painted an apocalyptic scene of the ravenous world beyond the Channel in the era of Henry VIII, Deloney's (similarly located under Henry) offers a far more benign view of English prosperity where desires are channeled into fruitful and profitable directions. In Deloney's world, middle-class diligence and native good humor invariably serve the interests of the entire community; this is a world of merry England in which the sanguine generosity and the dream of social mobility, "gentilesse," of Chaucer's Franklin are enabled by the expanding textile economy associated (at least nominally) with the Wife of Bath. By the end of the narrative, Jack has devised a trick whereby Sir

George has been obliged to marry Jack's maid, whom he had seduced, "and our King ... laughing heartily thereat, gave him a living forever, the better to maintain my Lady his wife" (*Anthology*, p. 392). It is both an ironic commentary on the dreams of the new class, and a reflection of the nation's changing centers of economic power, that Jack's final triumph should be the royal pension that marks him as a beneficiary of a system that was already obsolete. Deloney's fictions were selling these dreams to so large a public that he presumably had no more need for such a pension than did the prosperous clothier.

SIDNEY AND SPENSER

By century's end, two massive works, Sidney's *Arcadia* and Spenser's *Faerie Queene*, give the fullest expression to the narratives of desire that we have been examining in this chapter. Both survive in fragmentary and problematic torsos, evidence of their authors' ambition if not of a desire to emulate Chaucer in projecting an interminable work. Both are located in an ideal or notional setting which is both no-place and a projection of English dreams and memories. And both, in different ways, imitate Italian models in attempting a mixed genre in which romance narratives aspire to epic goals.

Of all the works we have considered, Sidney's romance is – or was, at the time of his premature death – the furthest removed from those anxieties over publication that haunted the Renaissance author. It was in a very strict sense *The Countess of Pembroke's Arcadia* (to give its full title); for as the dedicatory letter describes it, the work was "done in loose sheets of paper, most of it in your presence, the rest by sheets sent unto you as fast as they were done"[11] – that is, "delivered" to the Countess in bits and pieces and in haste, without a period of gestation such as might precede another book's delivery as finished product ready to see the light of day. And Sidney characterizes "this idle work of mine" as "done only for you, only to you ... or to such friends who will weigh errors in the balance of goodwill" (*Old Arcadia*, p. 3). As a series of personal, privileged communications from brother to sister, the work presents itself to our eyes as the kind of shared fantasy of an ideal space (Arcadia, a pastoral world where almost everyone writes poetry) that we can believe in as the province of loving siblings. And since the "hypocrite lecteur" (in Baudelaire's term) is both "mon semblable" and yet "ma soeur," there is a special irony to the story's emphasis on Pyrocles' disguise as an Amazon (in the "old" or earlier version, naming himself Cleophila, "turning Philoclea to myself" by reversal of syllables) while courting the princess Philoclea; and Sidney's use of the feminine pronoun in describing "Cleophila's" acts and feelings becomes as it were a playful means of meeting his reader's sensibilities half way.

The farcical confusions of desire that are especially conspicuous in the more purely comical *Old Arcadia* (Philoclea's father and mother separately fall in love with Cleophila, the mother being more shrewd in her intuition of the Amazon's true sex) make this a story that plays very sweepingly with the implications and ramifications of the Family Romance. Basilius' decision to flee the court and his responsibilities as King because of a mysterious prophecy can be seen as a father's (and mother's) attempt to keep their daughters from marriage and to present themselves as erotic alternatives. In the end, the parents learn to act their age (after "committing adultery" with each other) and the daughters gain husbands who have proven their desire through comic stratagems without knowing that they were pursuing marriages that had already been arranged by their families.

Sidney borrows his combination of pastoral narrative with interspersed pastoral "eclogues" from Sannazaro's *Arcadia*, and his interlace of multiple erotic plots from Ariosto's *Orlando Furioso*. Although the resulting text is far too complex to permit any simple statement of its thesis, it seems plausible that for the author and reader it was originally a work that ventilated private and public awarenesses of the peculiar state of contemporary dynastic ambitions, in a world where the Virgin Queen sought the indefinite deferral of her courtiers' marital desires. Sidney's revisions of the first three books of the *Arcadia*, left unfinished at his death, add a plethora of grim secondary narratives which make the central story seem less simply comical. That Basilius' pastoral truancy is now taking place in a far more threatening world probably reflects Sidney's own darkening view of contemporary events and/or his own political prospects. In Sidneian terms, the *motto* for the *Old Arcadia* might be: *Arcades ambo* (Both of us have been resident in Arcadia); and for the revised version: *Et in Arcadia ego* (Even in Arcadia, I – Death – am present).

With the death of Sidney in 1586, the Countess of Pembroke became a significant player in the attempts to define and exploit her brother's cultural and political capital. In publishing "authorized" versions of the *Arcadia*, first the revised fragment and subsequently the revision with a bridging passage linking it to the unrevised portion of the original story, she made it into *The Countess of Pembroke's Arcadia* by an act of appropriation, however innocent or calculated. The current of affectionate banter, or privileged communication, between brother and sister, which was already apparent in the work, takes on new significance when the Countess became her brother's literary executor and a patroness of the arts in her own right. It was perhaps in response to a new sense of a Sidney family romance that a rumor of incest became current, according to John Aubrey: "there was so great love between him and his fair sister that I have heard old Gentlemen say that they lay together ... "[12] The rumor is itself a trope for female usurpation of a male privilege; and as such it may reflect an accurate reading of the cultural significance of the *Arcadia* as an Elizabethan epic of the 1590s.[13] Sidney's legacy was to remain hotly contested, and Mary Sidney played an important and conspicuous role in the canonization and elaboration of the *Arcadia*'s text. We are only beginning today to appreciate the achievement of this remarkable woman.

In the letter to Ralegh that Spenser attached to the 1590 edition of Books I–III of *The Faerie Queene*, the chivalric romances of Ariosto and Tasso are seen as successors to the epics of Homer and Vergil, and all four authors are the "antique Poets historical" being followed in this present work whose general end is "to fashion a gentleman or noble person in vertuous and gentle discipline."[14] Something like the distinction between *prosopographia* and *prosopopoeia* is seen in the two kinds of settings and personages of the poem. As is most clearly shown in the parallel histories of Britain and Fairyland perused by Arthur and Guyon at the Castle of Alma (II.x), Britons inhabit a recognizable geography, and live and die with all their mortal frailties and historically documented failures and betrayals; at the same time, they inhabit a redeemed Christian universe of hope. Arthur is the clearest example of such a Briton, bearing a name that places him in history even though he does not yet know much about that place; he is described rather than invented like most of the other personages in the poem. The Red Cross Knight discovers at the House of Holiness that he too is a Briton, and will someday be known as Saint George and as such be a "signe of victoree" (I.x.61); we have all along "recognized" his prosopography, rather prematurely since he has been acting like an elfin knight.

Although the distinction between fairies and Britons is elusive and frequently ignored, most of Spenser's questing knights bear riddlingly allegorical names and obsessively focused if heroic motivation. They are all in the service of Gloriana, "That greatest Glorious Queene of *Faerie* long" (I.i.3), and like Chaucer's Squire they live "In hope to stonden in [their] lady grace" rather than in hope of seeing the New Jerusalem, since they are the unfallen creatures of a fallen and bound Prometheus (II.x.70). They may remind us of specific Britons (Arthur's squire, named as Timias at III.i.18, will come increasingly to resemble Ralegh), but they are daemonic, driven versions of such real people. "In that Faery Queene I mean glory in my general intention," Spenser tells Ralegh, "but in my particular I conceive the most excellent and glorious person of our sovereign the Queen, and her kingdom in Faery land."

Spenser's fairies and elves, then, are examples of *prosopopoeia* as fabulous inventions, counterfeits "in personation" as Puttenham puts it,[15] figures of the mask or persona worn by queen or courtier in the pursuit of glory, or temperance; or holiness for that matter, since the Red Cross Knight is bound to fail, desperately, in his elfin quest for a glorious victory over his dragon. Spenser has taken the romance world of Ariosto and his Italian predecessors, a locus for amused and frequently bemused analysis of the chaotic potential of erotic desire, and invested it with the political and economic dreams of his contemporary nation. His friend Gabriel Harvey was understandably puzzled or worried by the comic, even satirical potential of this mingling of epic and romance, and regarded this attempt to "overgo" Ariosto by invoking the low-mimetic realm of fairyland as a case of "*Hobgoblin* run away with the Garland from *Apollo*."[16]

Although the emulation of Ariosto will be most evident when Spenser's Britomart arrives on the scene in Book III, an obvious descendant of Ariosto's Bradamante with her mixture of martial and marital ambitions, the first book provides a more fundamental and general narrative of desire. Here at the outset, epic and romance are initially seen as opposed impulses. The Knight of the Red Cross is accompanied by a veiled lady (later to be named as Una, the One true object of his faith) whom he will have as his bride once he has conquered the dragon that imprisons her parents; but the principal interest of this "elfin" knight is the pursuit of glory, the "great adventure" of dragon-killing which will "wine him worship" and the good graces of Gloriana. Although the reader easily identifies him as the young St. George, his earthy origins (he was named George, "earth-tilling," by his adoptive father, a plowman) will remain repressed or denied to his self-consciousness until he is enlightened by Heavenly Contemplation later in the Book. His human capacity to love, and indeed to sin, is what he must know before enacting the legend that will truly win him worship as "Saint *George* of merry England, the sign of victory" (I.x.61). For now, however, like Basilius at the beginning of the *Arcadia*, he is in flight from an ominous eroticism that threatens his self-possession. The Red Cross Knight looks on Fairyland as an arena where a series of heroic achievements will construct a glorious commonwealth (much as the elfin histories in Book II describe the edification of Cleopolis); but it quickly becomes apparent in the first canto that this land's trees, each praiseworthy in itself, combine to form a Dantesque dark wood of error. The monster at the center of this wood is a fitting embodiment of the knight's fears, a monstrously fecund female, "Most loathsome, filthy, foul, and full of vile disdain" (I.i.14).

That it is the light of the Knight's virtue that enables him to see this "ugly monster plain" suggests that the disdain originates in the young man's mind.

Earlier we were told that "Right faithful true he was in deed and word, / But of his cheer did seem too solemn sad" (1.i.2.) – and this resistance to Charity, love, triggers the process that leads to his sexual fall in canto seven and his subsequent redemption. Book 1 is characterized by powerfully misogynistic imagery, with recognizable allusions to Protestant identification of Rome with the Whore of Babylon; but it should be noted that it is the young Knight himself who generates these images. He interrupts an erotic dream of Una and goes on (with Archimago's help) to project the sexual guilt on her, seeing her in another squire's arms; thereafter he is possessed by a sensuous Duessa who embodies his own divided self.

It seems fitting, therefore, that the Knight will only be in full possession of the "whole armor" of a Christian knight, possessing not only Faith and Hope but also Charity, after he has been purged at the House of Holiness and is ready to visit Charissa, a final, sanctified version of that image of a fertile woman, surrounded by her offspring, that had seemed so monstrous in the initial encounter with Error. Spenser, like Sidney, borrows the trappings of medieval romance to mingle the heroic with the erotic: for both writers, the hero must learn how to combine fierce wars and faithful loves. Yet the translation of Ariosto's epic romance to Protestant English soil raises problems that neither the authors nor their readers can easily resolve. Blair Worden has recently shown the degree to which Sidney's *Arcadia* resonates with the language of contemporary debate over Elizabeth's marriage. Both of these Elizabethan romance epics derive their complexity of tone and feeling from a sense of how unsatisfactory any single resolution of that debate must be. Even as Red Cross, good Protestant that he is, rejects Duessa once he has seen her sensuous corruption, he moves toward a Despair that can only be averted by a sense of redemptive Love – a love that England's Queen must reject.

If the letter to Ralegh is to be trusted, Spenser seems to have intended each book of the poem to show Arthur's "magnificence," the possession and perfection of all the poem's separate virtues, and to have given the prince something of the role of rescuer that he has most clearly in Book 1. By the same token, such a poem would apparently have developed Arthur's quest for Gloriana as leading to a marriage with her that could have represented a grand historical achievement of British glory. Yet there are reasons to doubt that this was ever his intention. Arthur exists in a time and with a separate body of received stories that would make any union with Gloriana almost inconceivable; and the fact that his dream of Gloriana is modeled on Chaucer's ludicrous Sir Thopas may well have given Harvey reason to fear that his friend's endorsement of Elizabethan glory was less than wholehearted.

The mixed genres of heroic poem and romance that were emerging with such vitality and critical controversy in sixteenth-century Italy gave Spenser as well as Sidney a model for exploring the contradictions in the nationalistic dreams of his own time and place. The Fairyland that had traditionally existed in native folklore as a pre-Christian, uncivilized locus of natural forces and genial lusts outside the city walls of Britain becomes in Spenser's hands the source of – or a figure for – the raging, expansionist desires of Elizabethan England. Fairyland in 1590 and 1596 (the date of the six-book version of the poem) was another Utopian vision of England – an England dreaming of going places, or an England going no-where. If the poem proposed a union of Arthur and Gloriana-Elizabeth, a new Camelot, readers who knew more of Arthur's story would recall that Arthur's dreamy union with another fairy, his half-sister Morgana (or Anna), would lead to the birth of Mordred. Although Una and Red Cross rejoice at Arthur's story (I.ix.16–17), the seed of Camelot's destruction may already have been sown by the time Arthur wakes to find "nought but pressed grass," and there may be a painful irony to Una's remark that "True Loves are often sown, but seldom grow on ground" (I.ix.16–17). The Aesopian fables of power that constituted the earliest British published tales evolved quickly and relentlessly into narratives of desire and its discontents, or at least its ominous possible sequels; and the heroic romances that emerged by the end of the century are conspicuous for the darkening shadows that threaten to overwhelm the dreams of dynasty.

NOTES

1 Annabel Patterson, *Fables of Power: Aesopian Writing and Political History* (Durham and London: Duke University Press, 1991).

2 Edmund Spenser, *The Yale Edition of the Shorter Poems of Edmund Spenser*, ed. William A. Oram et al. (New Haven: Yale University Press, 1989), p. 50.

3 Arthur F. Kinney, *Humanist Poetics: Thought, Rhetoric, and Fiction in Sixteenth-Century England* (Amherst: University of Massachusetts Press, 1986), chapter 2.

4 *An Anthology of Elizabethan Prose Fiction*, ed. Paul Salzman (Oxford: Oxford University Press, 1987), p. 6.

5 William Nelson, "A Source for Spenser's Malbecco," *Modern Language Notes* 68 (1953): 226–29.

6 Richard Helgerson, *The Elizabethan Prodigals* (Berkeley, Los Angeles, London: University of California Press, 1976).

7 Richard C. McCoy, "Gascoigne's 'Poëmata castrate': The Wages of Courtly Success," *Criticism* 27 (1985): 29–55.

8 Madelon Gohlke, "Reading *Euphues*," *Criticism* 19 (1977): 103–17.

9 Margaret Anne Doody, *The True Story of the Novel* (London: HarperCollins 1977).

10 Kinney focuses on this Horatian motto in his discussion of Greene, *Humanist Poetics*, pp. 181–229.
11 Sir Philip Sidney, *The Old Arcadia*, ed. K. Duncan-Jones (Oxford: Oxford University Press, 1985), p. 3.
12 John Aubrey, *Brief Lives*, cited by Jonathan Crewe, *Hidden Designs: The Critical Profession and Renaissance Literature* (New York and London: Methuen, 1986), p. 82.
13 A similar accusation was made against Isotta Nogarola in an anonymous pamphlet of 1438; see Anthony Grafton and Lisa Jardine, *From Humanism to the Humanities: Education and the Liberal Arts in Fifteenth- and Sixteenth-Century Europe* (Cambridge: Harvard University Press, 1986), ch. 2, "Woman Humanists: Education for What?" pp. 29–57.
14 Edmund Spenser, *The Faerie Queene*, ed. A.C. Hamilton (London: Longman, 1977), p. 737.
15 George Puttenham, *The Arte of English Poesie* ed. Baxter Hathaway (Kent, OH: Kent University Press, 1970), p. 246.
16 Edmund Spenser, *The Prose Works*, ed. R. Gottfried (Baltimore: Johns Hopkins University Press, 1949), p. 472.

FURTHER READING

Greenblatt, Stephen, *Renaissance Self-Fashioning: From More to Shakespeare* (Chicago: University of Chicago Press, 1980).
Helgerson, Richard, *The Elizabethan Prodigals* (Berkeley, Los Angeles, London: University of California Press, 1976).
 Self-Crowned Laureates: Spenser, Jonson, Milton and the Literary System (Berkeley and London: University of California Press, 1983).
Knapp, Jeffrey, *An Empire Nowhere: England, America, and Literature from Utopia to* The Tempest (Berkeley, Los Angeles, Oxford: University of California Press, 1992).
Lewalski, Barbara Kiefer, ed., *Renaissance Genres: Essays on Theory, History, and Interpretation* (Cambridge and London: Harvard University Press, 1986).
Lewis, C. S., *English Literature in the Sixteenth Century Excluding Drama* (Oxford: Clarendon Press, 1954).
Oram, William A., *Edmund Spenser* (New York: Twayne and London: Prentice Hall International, 1997). (Twayne's English Authors Series, No. 535.)
Salzman, Paul, *English Prose Fiction 1558–1700: A Critical History* (Oxford: Clarendon Press, 1985).
Van Dorsten, Jan, Dominic Baker-Smith, Arthur F. Kinney, eds., *Sir Philip Sidney: 1586 and the Creation of a Legend* (Leiden: E.J. Brill, 1986).
Worden, Blair, *The Sound of Virtue: Philip Sidney's Arcadia and Elizabethan Politics* (New Haven and London: Yale University Press, 1996).

11

ANNE LAKE PRESCOTT

The evolution of Tudor satire

It is hard, said the poet Juvenal as he looked around Nero's Rome, not to write satire (Satires 1.i). But what is "satire"? Sometimes a form, often a mode, it can double as diatribe, sermon, parody, joke, utopia, dystopia, epistle, or novel; its tone ranges from fury to faint irony, anguish to amusement. Is it, then, discourse with attitude? Any sendup or putdown? It must be more than irritability or grief, and that "more" is often some fantasy, conceit, myth, invention, or persona. Like allegory, it thrives in a fallen world of ambiguous signs, Augustine's "land of unlikeness." Not all Tudor writers explore a deconstructionist's "différance," but some adopt a distance or difference – fiction – that distinguishes their work from lament, polemic, or sermon.[1] When such work holds something up to amused or scornful scrutiny, and at some length, the result is satire.

Sharing a widespread ambivalence toward verbal hostility, satirists can be defensive, claiming to bark only at the rabid or apply caustics only to cure.[2] Tudor laws on slander were severe, moreover, and in any case Christians are told to forgive their enemies, not smite them hip and thigh with ridicule. Witness the dialogue between "Author" and "Treatise" that opens Jerome Barlowe and William Roye's satirical *Read Me and Be Not Wroth* (Strasbourg, 1528): "Author" wants to expose Cardinal Wolsey's "abominable" pride, but "Treatise" fears that sharp language "becometh not Christian charity." Not to worry, says "Author": Truth will be Treatise's "conservation." Whatever their relation to Truth, satirists often needed "conservation." From John Skelton calling Wolsey a "fat hog" in *Speak, Parrot* to Thomas Wyatt scorning a king's cruelty, from Edmund Spenser hinting at William Cecil's faults to young Londoners railing in the 1590s, satirists exposed themselves to potential disapproval.

Such satirists often saw themselves as part of a coherent tradition going back to ancient Rome: "As Horace, Lucilius, Juvenal, Persius, and Lucullus," says Francis Meres in his *Palladis Tamia* (1598), "are the best for Satire among the Latins: so with us, in the same faculty, these are the chief: Piers Plowman, [Thomas] Lodge, [Joseph] Hall of Emanuel College in Cambridge, the Author of Pygmalion's Image and Certain Satires [John Marston], the Author of Skialetheia [Everard Guilpin]." Renaissance writers sometimes distinguished the three chief Roman models: "Juvenal burns, Persius taunts, and Horace smiles," ran a famous formula in J. C. Scaliger's *Poetices libri septem* (1561, IV.98: "Juvenalis ardet, instat apertè, jugulat. Persius insultat. Horatius irridet"). Critics and poets, though, also held the mistaken belief that "satyre" comes from archaic Greek "satyr" plays. Chapter 13 of George Puttenham's *Arte of English Poesie* tells of early poets dressed as "gods of the woods, whom they called Satyrs or Sylvans," reciting "verses of rebuke"; William Webbe's *Discourse of English Poetrie* (1586) and John Harington's preface to his translation of Ariosto (1591) say the same – hence satire's potential tie to pastoral. Since satyrs are disreputable, "satyres" may legitimately taunt and prance: their very indecency keeps decorum. In 1605, Isaac Casaubon's *De satyrica graecorum poesi et romanorum satira* (II, ch. 4) traced "satire" to *satura* – "full, stuffed"; satire is a *lanx satura*, a platter heaped with varied foods – but satirists continued to prefer unkempt hairiness and heat.[3]

The first significant Tudor satire was by John Skelton. His 1499 *Bowge of Court* recounts Dread's dream of a shipload of vices (compare Sebastian Brant's German *Ship of Fools*, translated by Alexander Barclay in 1509, and the anonymous *Cock Lorrel's Boat, c.* 1518, in which a ship with such folk as dung farmers and priests sails through England). Skelton can be queasy about satire: a Latin coda to *Ware the Hawk* (between 1503 and 1512) claims the freedom to bite the morally obtuse, and "Against Garnesche" (1514?) insists that if "poets satirical, / As Persius and Juvenal, / Horace and noble Martial" were alive they too would attack this "Witless, wayward, Sir Wrig-wrag." Is it wrong to "bark" at Cardinal Wolsey in *Why Come Ye Not to Court?* (1522)? No: like Juvenal, Skelton is "constrained," for "Quia difficile est / Satiram non scribere."[4] Skelton can name Roman satirists, but he does not imitate them. The polyglot juxtapositions of *Speak, Parrot* (1521?) and the pounding rhythms ("Skeltonics") of *Colin Clout* (*c.* 1522), "Elinor Rumming" (*c.* 1517), and *Why Come Ye Not to Court?*; the mockery of heresy's willfulness, statesmen's pride, the folly and corruption of all three social classes – not least the clerical failings allegorized in *Ware the Hawk* – are largely *sui generis*. Skelton also had a talent for sarcasm ("He whistleth so sweetly he maketh me to sweat," says "Against a Comely Coystrown [kitchen boy]") and complexly ironic appropriations like the liturgical fragments in *Philip Sparrow* (1502–05).

It was Wyatt who introduced a Roman manner, like a good humanist adapting Juvenal and Horace or their Italian imitators to his own circumstance as a Christian and English courtier and diplomat. By 1536, when he began his satires, he had been in prison and seen friends executed. His first satire, on court life, does more than follow tradition, even if in words translated from Luigi Alamanni, who in turn owed much to Juvenal. Wyatt can burn indignantly (although less apt than some to confuse Roman satire with sermon or diatribe), but his tone is Horatian: reasonable, urbane, amused. Under house arrest, he writes to a friend that he is glad to leave court, being so inept at using "wiles for wit" or calling drunkenness "good fellowship" and cruelty "zeal of justice."[5] The claim to be at liberty "in Kent and Christendom" redefines freedom, while the gentleman-to-gentleman tone and mock humility invite us to find the satirist more engaging than the court's toadies, informers, and cheats. He has courage, too, for his inability to approve "high Caesar and damn Cato to die" may allude to Thomas More's execution, while a refusal to "call the lion of coward beasts the most" could not have pleased Henry. His next satire (1537?) tells of a country mouse who visits her city sister (cf. Horace, 11.6). Advocating stoic moderation that keeps the heart from being "knotted" by hope or dread, Wyatt's temperate voice makes the corruption he ridicules seem worse. And he changes the fable: unlike Horace's, his mouse is caught by a "traitor cat." The third satire is as bleak. Written by 1539, it adapts a dialogue by Horace (11.5) in which a cynical Tiresias tells Ulysses how to prosper: flee truth and "make thy language sweet."

While Wyatt was naturalizing the Romans, others perpetuated a native style. Such work can be sophisticated, of course; its puns and alliteration alone imply a world made opaque and perilous by ingenuity, illusion, and deceit. One such satirist was Robert Copland, a printer with a taste for piety, romance, and misogyny. It is unlikely that this last was fed by personal animus: impelled by several cultural energies, laughter at female sexuality, craft, or ambition was also a social game and, on one level, lightly meant. In penning it, Copland developed an ingratiatingly self-referential treatment of authorship and printing, chatting with "Quidam" ("Someone") in the preface to *The seven sorrows that women have when their husbands be dead* (c. 1526) about bad printers, prices ("A penny I trow is enough on books") and the risk of offending women with this "scoff."[6] *Sorrows* smirks with double entendres, as when the widow hopes to find someone to lay new "stones" on her path. Widows were common targets of such humor, perhaps because they had an independence denied wives; compare Walter Smith's *Twelve merry Jests* [i.e., Jests and Deeds] *of the Widow Edith* (1525), which mixes estates satire, Chaucerian irony, and a trickster criminality that Smith rather relishes.

Copland also tried scatology and the mock will. In *Jill of Braintford's Testament* (written *c.* 1535) a widow who possesses only farts bequeaths twenty-six and a half of them (the curate gets one plus the half, which he declines). Among the deserving are anyone who fails to repay loans, lets a neighbor drink first, allows a wife to boss him around, or "hath a faire wench in bed all night / And kisseth her not once e're it be daylight." *The Highway to the Spital House* (1529–36, printed 1536?) adapts Robert de Balsac's *Chemin de l'ospital* (1502; cf. Tomasso Garzoni's *Hospital of Incurable Fools*, trans. 1600). After assuring us that he spares the truly unfortunate and the poor in spirit, Copland gives a dialogue between himself and the hospital "porter" who welcomes gentleman wastrels, fake foreigners speaking bad French, drunks speaking worse Dutch, counterfeit doctors, pseudo-scholars, and con artists who pray in public and when alone swear by God's "arms, nails, wounds, heart soul and blood." This hospital evokes Purgatory or worse, and its shadow stretches over what Langland had called the field full of folk and Bunyan was to call Vanity Fair.

After the death of Henry VIII in 1547, as England turned for a time toward a more radical Protestantism, there was a surge of verse mocking the Mass, priests, Purgatory, and the Pope.[7] Social satire in the Colin Clout manner continued, as witness Thomas Churchyard's *Davy Diker's Dream* (1552?). More striking, though, is the way a satirical tone had already sharpened the polemics and drama of Protestants like Robert Turner, author of *The Hunting and Finding Out of the Romish Fox* (Bonn, 1543), or John Bale. Others tried more formal sorts of satire, sometimes with an apocalyptic edge. Despite the Reformation's mistrust of fantasy, a number of poets hoped to serve gospel truth with fiction, even fiction so minimal as the personification of the Catholic Mass as a whore, "Missa" (or, in William Punt's 1548 prose *New Dialogue*, as "mother Mass"). Pagan smiles or rage seemed less useful than native tones, especially those of Skelton's Catholic but downright Colin, tones that go with congregational singing, white walls, and vernacular scripture – not legends, idols, and priestcraft.

Luke Shepherd's *John Bon and Mast[er] Parson* (1547 or 1548) imagines talk between a skeptical plowman and a priest; the latter laments that the Mass, our means to grace, "is hated in every border / And railed on and reviled, with words most blasphemous," but John says mockingly that "ye have a great grace / To eat God and man in so short a space," so "mass me no more massings."[8] Similarly, the Skeltonics of Shepherd's *Upcheering of the Mass* (1548?) impersonate a Mass-lover who warns gospel-lovers that the papist day may come again and bursts into gloating semi-Latin: "Wherefore now totus mundus / That round is and rotundus / Be merry and jocundus" (sig. A5v). The poem ends with a farewell to Mistress Missa, who must "trudge" to the sea and then live "In regno Plutonico." Like many Catholics, the Protestant Shepherd mocks clerical ignorance. The Skeltonics of *Doctor Double Ale* (*c.* 1548) describe a priest who preaches drunk, enriches alewives with his boozing, calls the Pope God's equal, and murders Latin ("Ego volo quare / Cum tu drinkare," sig. a8). Similarly, William Kethe's *Ballad Declaring the Fall of the Whore of Babylon, entitled "Tie Thy Mare, Tom Boy* (1548) tells the "purple and scarlet" Roman church that "Your beads and your bead rolls / It was but abusion" and exults at her exile beyond Dover. More politically radical, Robert Crowley's *Philargyry of Great Britain* (1551) represents old papal tithes and new English greed as a silver-gobbling giant. The satirical fictions include Crowley's claim to have "feigned" a lie about the truth, Philargyry's oration on his metallic dietary needs ("Bring, bring, bring, bring / Always something"), a political speech by Hypocrisy, and the disguising of London as "Nodnol," a city "all one / With Babylon."[9]

The defiant papist of Shepherd's *Upcheering* was right – in 1553 Mary Tudor restored Mistress Missa. The Protestant Hugh Hilarie's *Resurrection of the Mass* (Strasbourg, 1554) imagines a long speech by Missa that extols her power to do everything from curing piles to inspiring adultery. She recounts her English career from the time she was "in my ruff" to when she felt her "buttocks for fear to quake." Now that she is back, she says, only "Gospellers" grieve at the restoration of pilgrimages and purgatory, images and saints. True, she admits, because her foundation is not set on God she will eventually "come unto confusion." The satire ends with a parodic rite invoking altars, oils, priapi, and sodomites. "Ite" [Go], says the last line (from the real Mass), "Missa est." Catholics, of course, saw things differently. John Heywood's handsomely illustrated dialogue, *The Spider and the Fly* (1556), tells of a kindly but firm housekeeper (Mary Tudor) who reluctantly squashes a talkative spider (heresy) on behalf of an aggrieved fly. Like Shepherd and Crowley, Heywood hopes to advance a royal agenda: the veil of fiction is thin enough for a monarch to see through and learn what to do.

Toward the end of Mary's reign, even as her government was indeed stepping on heresy, a few less pointed satires saw print in Richard Tottel's miscellany, *Songs and Sonets* (1557). "Of the Subtlety of crafty lovers" and "Description of an ungodly world" may be better called complaints, but they are ones with ironically observed detail ("they can halt and lay a salve whereas they feel no sore"), sarcasms ("then rumble they with instruments"), and anaphoric lists that nudge the verse into satire.[10] It was in the following reign, however, especially toward its end, that poets followed Wyatt's example in adapting Roman satirists, and there were translations of Horace by Lewis Evans (1565?) and Thomas Drant (1566, 1567), the latter adding a satire of his own to the volume. Elizabethan satire did not begin this move at once: in 1560 Thomas Churchyard, for example, reprinted his 1552 flyting with Thomas Camel, abusive scoffs in the Crowley and Shepherd manner. Much Renaissance satire, moreover, works as a mode affecting other genres: one of the age's best walking parodies, for example, is Philip Sidney's Latin-mangling pedant in *The Lady of May*, a pastoral entertainment for Elizabeth, and the vogue for Petrarch aroused sendups like John Davies' manuscript "Gulling Sonnets."

George Gascoigne's *Steel Glass* (1576) edges into classical territory, if not very far. Allegorizing the satirist's ancient nervousness, Gascoigne opens with a revision of Philomela's rape and metamorphosis into a nightingale: Slander accuses Plain Dealing's child Satyra (a "dame, / Or at the least a right hermaphrodite"), Misery cages her, and her sister Poesy's husband, Vain Delight, ravishes her. Although her rapist has cut out her tongue "with Razor of Restraint," she still can stammer reproofs "with harmless true intent" and make the reproved "see themselves."[11] She uses a mirror given her, she says, by Lucilius, inventor of Latin verse satire, but she speaks vernacular estates satire, criticizing king, nobles, clergy, and commons in turn and imagining a reversed world of well-behaved people. Despite Satyra's Roman mirror, then, earlier Tudor styles continued to seem comfortable.

They persist, too, in Spenser's *Shepheardes Calender* (1579). This set of twelve pastorals, says the prefatory "argument" by "E.K.," comprises "moral" eclogues (i.e., commenting on *mores*) that "for the most part be mixed with some satyrical bitterness." These are "February" (on the reverence due age), "May" (on "colored deceit," in this case Catholic efforts to seduce the young with "bells, and babes, and glasses"), "July" and "September" (on "dissolute shepherds and pastors"), and "October" (on "contempt of poetry and pleasant wits," not very "satyrical" but viewing spineless poets with some irony). To E.K., satire includes Aesopian fable expressed with a rusticity that looks to Vergil's pastorals and Reformation polemics. Like them, moreover, these eclogues imply political commentary: "July"'s "Algrin" is clearly Bishop Grindal, recently in trouble with a Queen allegorized here as an eagle who drops a shell on Algrin's bald head. As always, Spenser is elusive: brained Algrin looks as silly as the eagle looks careless.

Spenser continued to find the animal fable useful. His "Mother Hubberd's Tale," published in *Complaints* of 1591 but begun earlier, concerns an ape and a fox who try various scams and then, in disguise, take over a kingdom left vulnerable while its ruling lion snores until, aroused and roaring, the royal beast restores justice. Spenser had probably at first meant to criticize a projected marriage between Elizabeth and the unpopular duc d'Alençon. By 1591 the poem would have seemed more like estates satire with an anti-court emphasis, but the doings of its protagonists so evidently glance at the government and its complacent Queen that the authorities called in the volume. Like Wyatt, Spenser did not lack courage, although England's lion spared him arrest. Passages in the 1596 *Faerie Queene*, moreover, hint that had Spenser lived longer, fashion and his own evolving interests might have invited his return to satire. The "Legend of Courtesy," which treats its topic with some skepticism, ends by urging the author's verses henceforth merely to please, which "now is counted wisemens threasure." Such satirical bitterness, as E.K. might have called it, was now in the air. Nor did political animal fables cease; even the Earl of Essex wrote one, if indeed it is his.[12]

Written earlier (or so says the author, a lawyer) but published the same year as Spenser's *Calender*, Edward Hake's *News out of Paul's Churchyard* (1579) comprises eight "English Satyrs." The title page quotes Horace; a Latin tag assures us that he who admonishes does not bite and does not wound but cures; and a preface tells the Earl of Leicester that Hake means only to "rescind" sin and "erect" virtue. The satires hardly strain for Horace's urbanity or Juvenal's fire. Jouncing through alliterative four-teeners, they attack the greed, "wanton maids," and temptations lying in wait for "Sir Nummus" – wealth. Like Gascoigne's more adroit *Glass*, these poems gesture only vaguely toward Rome, preferring to exclaim ("O ardent force of flaming sin, / O rage, O riot, O") at those whom Hake or his speaker, Paul's Cathedral, calls backbiters, Minotaurs, Cyclops, sirens, papists, blockish badgers, snakes, and curs.

In the mid-1590s verse satire's tone changes, a shift demonstrated by the verse of Thomas Lodge. In "Truth's Complaint over England," from his *Alarum Against Usurers* (1584), the speaker walks out along the river – like many before him – and hears the "mournful Muse Melpomene" lamenting England's decline. Later, in stanzas published with *Scylla's Metamorphosis* (1589), Lodge imagines a "satyr" with stern looks and bushy locks who adores the god Discontent in terms that make the satyr a "malcontent" of the sort soon popular in drama and make the poem itself a paradoxical encomium to frowning dissatisfaction. By 1595, Lodge's *Fig for Momus* has dropped stanzas for couplets that borrow from Juvenal and approach an Augustan compression:

> If thou then see a troop of guarded knaves
> Wait at Argastos' heels like servile slaves,
> Be not aghast, admire not at his state;

For now the world is bent to serve and hate.
'Tis true: that slave whom Pompey did promote
Was he that first assayed to cut his throat.[13]

Lodge is also edgy, adopting in his preface a cynic/doggish defense: sheep "are soonest worried by curdogs because they are mild: but he that nips him soundly... purchaseth his own peace, and escapes much peril."

Lodge was the first of a group of young men, many with ties to the Inns of Court, who had read Horace and could adopt his moves but preferred the ragged zeal or obscurity of Juvenal and Persius. Their taste for whips, growls, filth, teeth, venom, vomit, quills, caustics, scalpels, and the sour yet heady wine of Diogenes' barrel, is largely bravado. Yet the sputtering sadism and incoherence that energize such satire must be related to social tensions in the London world of young males on the loose. Indeed, the satirists' youth seems an aspect of their enterprise, although there had been a moment when a different pattern had begun to emerge: a poem to Gascoigne, for instance, notes that "From lays of love, to satyres sad and sage, / Our Poet turns, the travail of his time, / And as he pleased the vein of youthful age, / With pleasant pen employed in loving rhyme, / So now he seeks the gravest to delight / With works of worth much better than they show" (*Works*, vol. II, p. 139). In the 1590s it was not the "gravest" whom satirists hoped to delight.

There were other tensions, equally important, as too many bright graduates sought too few jobs in a world shaken by an expanding capitalism, a still powerful Spain, religious divisions, and the political anxiety of watching a childless Queen come closer to the grave. Satirists (and epigrammatists like John Weever) ostentatiously turn from Petrarchan sighs and courtly myths. Even Ovidian stunts like Marston's semi-pornographic *Pygmalion's Image* (or, with less leering Ovid and more outright sex, Thomas Nashe's *Choice of Valentines*) stress desire itself more than the sensual poignancy of change. Yet these satires, for all their occasional courage and their pose of cynical contempt and choleric moralism, may be less radical than the diatribes or fables of Shepherd and Heywood. Whatever its dramatic gnashing and growling, late Elizabethan satire demands that the world live up to its own stated values. Shepherd and Heywood, with specific agendas (further Reformation, Catholic restoration) show more interest in strengthening royal policy than in expressing alienation, but what they want is a clean sweep and drastic action.

In 1597 and 1598, Joseph Hall, future bishop and author of a mock Utopia, *Mundus alter et idem* (1605), published his Juvenalian *Virgidemiae* (rods), three books of "toothless satyrs" and three of "biting" ones. Affecting fury at his day's corruption, whoredoms, pride, and folly, Hall responds with "hot blood's rage" in deliberately rough lines that scorn to write a "sonnet of my Mistress' face" or a fawning "tayle" (tale/tail?) to some great patron.[14] Lawyers, doctors, bad poets, clergy, professors, astrologers, burghers ("If Mammon's self should ever live with men, / Mammon himself shall be a Citizen," says IV.v.129–30), drunks, Petrarchans, travelers, Catholics ("Caesar's throne is turned to Peter's chair," IV.vii.12): all receive blows of the satirist's "ferrule" (IV.ii.174). Nor is Hall reluctant to lay about him with his pen, praising the boldness of "Antique Satyres" who knew that satire is a "Porcupine, / That shoots sharp quills out in each angry line" (V.iii.1–5). Hall thought himself England's first porcupine:

> I first adventure, with foolhardy might
> To tread the steps of perilous despite:
> I first adventure: follow me who list,
> And be the second English Satyrist ...   (Prologue)

Either Hall forgets his predecessors or thinks that only Juvenalian fire makes a "satyre." Real porcupines do not bother with complaints, Horatian smiles, or animal allegory.

Guilpin's *Skialetheia, or A Shadow of Truth, in Certain Epigrams and Satyres* (1598) followed soon, likewise burning with indignation.[15] Those sensibilities are hypermasculine, urban, witty, educated, and disabused. Yet Guilpin has no wish to redefine England's values, only to scold England for violating them. Late Elizabethan satire may prance rhetorically on cloven hoofs, but it does so on behalf of traditional morals; in this, of course, it resembles Juvenal, disgusted by Nero's Rome because he longs for a Rome he thinks lost. Guilpin's tone as he fans his own Juvenalian flames (in "words compact of fire and rage: / Terms of quick camphor and saltpeter phrases," says Satire 1) can be nasty, with its references to purgatives and emetics, its indecent wordplay and showy admiration of Aretino as the scourge of vice. On the other hand Guilpin claims in his "Satyre Preludium" to be dismayed by English poets who write obscenely, "filthing chaste ears with their pens' Gonorrhey." Such contradictions give the verse texture. And, like those makers of "whimp'ring sonnets" and "puling elegies" whom Guilpin mocks in the same satire, his speaker is fascinated by his self, claiming for it a stability belied by the verse's rattle and tumble: "My lines are still themselves," he tells his critics as he gives them a "fico" – a fig – "and so am I" (VI.190).

The same year John Marston published *Pygmalion's Image and Certain Satyres* and *The Scourge of Villainy*. A boasting prefatory poem asks "Is not my pen complete? are not my lines / Right in the swaggering humor of these times?"[16] The Juvenalian pen's targets include "lewd Priapians," Catholics, flatterers, cuckolds, whores, doctors, hypocrites, belching critics who piss like curs, ambitious courtiers, the envious, pederasts, women, and bad poets – the London scene. Marston imitates the Romans but he can also play Diogenes with his lamp: "A Cynic Satyre" mischievously begins "A Man, a man, a kingdom for a man." Yet if Marston's satirist is agitated by depravity, he is himself liable to something like madness, an odd mixture of violent egomania and death-wish. Although *Scourge* is dedicated "To his most esteemed, and best beloved Self" and its speaker claims – with some justice – "I am myself, so is my poesy," the last satire begs "hungry Oblivion" to "Devour me quick," hoping for a silence in which he may "sleep securely free from love or hate." Marston himself stopped writing verse satire, but Oblivion spared him and he turned to entertainments and the drama.

William Rankins' *Seven Satyres Applied to the Week* (1598) combines fashionable asperity with nonclassical methods: the verse is in stanzas, the organization would please medieval poets, and the assumption is that planetary influence explains social and individual enormity. Atheists and Machiavellian politicians, for example, show Saturn's impact. In 1599 came *Micro-cynicon: Six Snarling Satyres* by one T.M., attacking sodomy, pride, prodigality, cross-dressing, and so forth. By June the authorities had had enough. Perhaps they found personal allusions behind the "satyrical" obscurity offensive, but then any autocratic government would find such malcontent exuberance, even if a pose, the rhetorical equivalent of a riot. Governments prefer tidiness to the sound of snarls and tumult in Diogenes' barrel. An entry in the Stationers' Register records an order by the Archbishop of Canterbury and Bishop of London forbidding further printing of satires. To be called in and burned are satires by Hall, Guilpin, "T.M.," Marston, several misogynist works, Thomas Cutwode's obscurely allegorical *Caltha Poetarum*, Marlowe's translation of Ovid's elegies, and pamphlets by Nashe and Harvey. And henceforth let "no satires or epigrams be printed."[17]

Unnamed, probably because not yet in print, is John Donne, whose five "Satyrs" appeared posthumously, with prudent excisions, in 1633. Begun in 1593 when Donne was studying at Lincoln's Inn, the lines have a satyr's roughness recalling the Romans as they were then read. Similarly, the classicized names typical of such satire signal a revival of classical methods. But the poetry's jounce and obscurity also derive from the condensation and mental rapidity typical of Donne's wit, while the satirical personae, themselves not wholly in good moral health, are subtly imagined and not exempt from Donne's irony. The first satire adopts for London, so as to mock the city scene, the unwanted Roman who follows an exasperated Horace through the city (satire 1.ix). Donne's monstrous "motley humorist" has all the vices a bustling London affords, from his taste for a "muddy whore, or prostitute boy" to his care to launch "amorous smiles" at passing "silken" courtiers.[18] The second satire (1594?) mocks a corrupt and plagiarizing lawyer who is "sick with poetry." The third, on the difficult necessity of eventually deciding which is Christ's true bride among the several aspirants to that role, is harder to date. With remarkable courage Donne insists, perhaps recalling his upbringing in a Catholic family subject to prosecution, that mere power, whether in Rome, Geneva, Germany, or England, cannot offer sufficient guidance to the individual soul toiling up the steep craggy hill on which stands Truth. The anti-court fourth satire (1597?) also adopts Horace's tiresome companion, but with darker urgency as the stroll through London becomes in effect a descent to Hell. The hanger-on, a seedy and curious wanderer, has a diabolical look, his interest in the satirist's opinions perhaps due to a role as government informer out to send the imprudent into the jaws of "our giant statutes." The fifth satire (1598?), a more perfunctory performance, laments this "age of rusty iron" with its injustice and corruption and asks "greatest and fairest Empress, know you this?" No: "Alas, no more than Thames' calm head doth know / Whose meads her arms drown, or whose corn o'rflow." Hardly prudent words.

Despite the ban of 1599, poets continued to bark and cavort in print. In 1600 Samuel Rowlands published *The Letting of Humors' Blood in the Headvein, with a New Morissco Danced by Seven Satyrs upon the Bottom of Diogenes' Tub* and the following year saw the start of a series of "Whipper" satires by Weever, Guilpin, and Nicholas Breton (who also wrote "Pasquil" verse), criticizing yet perpetuating the recent manner (snarling, bitter satire). In the next reign, poets like Richard Brathwait, George Wither, and Henry Parrot (whose *Mastiff*'s title page shows a well-educated dog barking "Mordeo Mordentem" [I bite the biter]) continued to play the angry porcupine. Their quills seem duller, though, and by the time Dryden revived classical satire, Casaubon's scholarship had taken effect and the satyrs had departed, taking their porcupines with them. Pope and Swift could burn like Juvenal but with a more controlled fire and in tighter couplets.

PROSE SATIRE

Tudor prose satire can be even harder to define than its verse relatives. Impatient with borders and prescriptions, it can often be called "Menippean," after the Cynic philosopher, Menippus, although Renaissance and modern authorities disagree on who should count as Menippean.[19] Sometimes Lucian is included, sometimes not; so too with Apuleius, whose *Golden Ass* was translated in 1566 by William Adlington, while the Menippean aspect of Thomas More's *Utopia* tends to get lost in critical discussions. By 1595 English readers could read about this genre or mode, also called "Varronian" after the Roman Varro, and with ties to the "anatomy," in an essay probably by Pierre Pithou, editor of what he could find of Petronius' still fragmentary *Satyricon*. Pithou's explanation was attached to *La Satyre menippée*, written in the early 1590s by a group of moderate Catholic supporters of Henri de Navarre. The word "Menippized," explains Pithou, is not new, for the ancient Roman critic Varro had written prose satires called "Menippized" after Menippus, who had also written "salted jestings" and "merry conceits of good words, to make men to laugh, and to discover the vicious men of his time." Since then, says Pithou, we have had Petronius, Lucian, Apuleius, "and in our age that good fellow Rabelais" (trans. 1595, sigs. Bb1–Bb1v).

Pithou is unusual among humanist critics in omitting Seneca, whose *Apocolocyntosis*, on the postmortem "Gourdification" of the Emperor Claudius, was printed in 1513 and imitated by Erasmus in his savage *Julius Exclusus*. Menippus' own satires are, like Varro's, lost, but he often stars in the skeptical, even nihilistic, Greek dialogues by the second-century Syrian, Lucian. Lucian was hugely popular in the Renaissance despite his reputation as a currish atheist chewed to death by dogs. More and Erasmus translated some of his dialogues in 1506, unperturbed by his irreligion. "What difference does it make to me," asks More's preface, "what a pagan thinks about those articles contained in the principal mysteries of the Christian faith?" Lucian teaches us to "live a life less distracted by anxiety; less fearful, that is, of any gloomy and superstitious untruths."

Unlike Petronius, though, disgusted by Nero's Rome but unwilling to preach, and unlike the skeptical Lucian, Tudor satirists lived in a Christian world that defended literature on didactic grounds. Menippean satire offers a dangerous and ambiguous escape into gratuitous verbal play, paradoxes, fantasy, excess, the upending of solemnity, the leaky grotesque body, loose narrative structures like the journey, multiple voices, heaps of edible or fecal matter, and words. Especially words. Under its influence even serious satire is apt to evaporate into nonsense, break into festivity, and "anatomize" folly in ways revealing less its inner workings than its emptiness. Such perplexities make some satire more compelling, of course, and explain why many cannot decide how seriously More "meant" *Utopia*.

Menippean satire is baggy and shapeless, a sausage or stew of a genre –

and hence associated with Saturnalia or Carnival – into which the author has stuffed a variety of materials: parodies, tales, recipes, digressions, asides, lists, dialogues, imaginary languages, documents, mixtures of tongues, marginalia, feigned book titles, pictures, multiple voices, fantasy, diagrams, anything and everything. Indeed, the term "Menippean" is all too useful to literary taxonomists tempted to affix the adjective to any prose that shows generic confusion, narrative or structural bulges, a refusal to get to the point, a tendency to multiply words, a taste for paradox and disorienting perspective, or a spinning moral compass. Nevertheless one can locate a body of Renaissance texts that are either Menippean, like Rabelais' *Gargantua et Pantagruel*, or allied to it, like Robert Greene's translation of Louise Labé's *Débat de Folie et d'Amour* (1555, appended to Greene's *Gwydonius*, 1584), paradoxes such as *The Praise of Nothing* by E.D. (1585), underworld visions in the manner of Lucian's *Menippus* (such as an anonymous 1588 "News from Heaven and Hell," in which the Earl of Leicester performs sexual acrobatics that turn "his prick of desire" to "a pillar of fire"[20]), parodic or carnival inversions, and – especially in Stuart England – mock journeys and imaginary libraries.

The dialogue was especially popular. The most complex is doubtless More's *Utopia*, a thought-experiment about what might follow from changing a society's assumptions so as to eliminate pride and greed without help from revealed truth. Utopia is also a reversed world in which many details (the lack of lawyers, the use of gold chamberpots) parody or invert European practices and values. Even more Lucianic are the self-reference and paradox, the play on words for "nothing" or "nowhere" (the very title means "Noplace"), and the irony with which the main text's idealistic project is countered by suspect marginalia, self-mockery, and the name of the chief speaker, "Raphael Hythloday" – whose Christian name recalls an angel and whose surname means "speaker of nonsense." The first more strictly Lucianic dialogue in English, though, is *Pasquil the Plain* (1533), a "merry treatise" on political flattery by Thomas Elyot, fresh from translating *A Dialogue between Lucian and Diogenes*. The preface reminds us that Pasquil is the statue in Rome "on whom once in the year, it is lawful to every man to set in verse or prose any taunt that he will, against whom he list, how great [a statesman] so ever he be." The witty Italian statue, though, has acquired the sturdy plainness of Langland's Piers and Skelton's Colin. How? By sitting so long in the Roman street and "hearing market men chat, he is become rude and homely." He "noteth not any particular person or Country," however, so we should interpret "according to the best meaning" and when he speaks truth "defend him against venomous tongues and overthwart wits." The brisk talk that follows offers such ironies as the remark that if Pasquil would learn discretion he would win gilt and a new paint job. But unlike Lucian, Elyot has a religious commitment: a trim fellow who carries the New Testament in his hand and *Troilus and Cressida* near his heart offends the author's serious beliefs. Similarly, although Pasquil's vow that when all politicians are good counselors he will be as still as stone is very witty coming from a statue, in 1533, as Henry VIII was getting a divorce and a new title, jokes about political counsel had real bite.

Biting even harder after Edward VI's accession, many prose satirists joined in the volley of sarcastic anti-Catholic insults meant to help establish God's kingdom in England. Although it can be playful, such satire tends to be more plainly sarcastic than that of Lucian and more committed than the evasive *Utopia*. In the anonymous *Will of the Devil* (c. 1548), Beelzebub announces his bequests "In mine own name, Amen," hopes for burial in the "hearts of my darlings the Mass-mongers," and bequeaths such treasures as saints' days and chalices.[21] *Will* has a revolutionary's contempt for ancient practice, and its populism shows in the devil's gift of geldings to summoners so they can more easily serve subpoenas on the poor. But it remains securely patriarchal (the devil leaves "sovereignty, which they most desire" to women) and it scorns gaming, adultery, and sodomy: "Item, I give to all priests lemans [sweethearts], that will not marry, but persevere in their sodomitical, and abominable chastity, that they shall piss holy water all the days of their life" (sig. A7v).

William Baldwin's *Beware the Cat* (1553, printed 1570) is a subtler performance. Baldwin had just translated *Wonderful News of the Death of Paul the III*, by Matthias Flacius Illyricus, in which "P. Esquilles" (Pasquil) describes a cannibal Mass, clerical fornication, and a transformed pope bleeding menstrual blood into a chalice. *Cat* takes particular aim at the Mass, a rite that Protestants could find frightening as well as illusory and hence satisfying to exorcise by mockery. Imagining watchful and articulate cats in a realistic London setting, it serves up parody, impudent marginalia, a "hymn," a festive Christmas context, advice on eating hedgehogs, debate on animals' reason, rhymes, repetitions, lists, a magic stew, jests, anecdotes, fables, scatology, reversals ("The spring and neaping of the sea," we are informed, "causeth the moon to wax and wane"), imaginary books, and fancy prose: "And as soon as restless Phoebus was come up out of the smoking sea and, with shaking of his golden-colored beams which were all the night long in Thetis' moist bosom, had dropped off his silver sweat into Hera's dry lap, and kissing fair Aurora with glowing mouth had driven from her the adulterer Lucifer, and was mounted so high to look upon Europa that, for all the height of Mile-end steeple, he spied me through the glass window lying upon my bed, up I arose." And a magic spell parodies the Mass: "Shavol swashmesh, gorgona Iiscud ... Javol sheleg hutotheca Iiscud."[22] *Cat*'s agenda is serious, but its shifty perspectives and wordplay make for an unstable world.

Similar ambiguities complicate William Bullein's *Dialogue Against the Fever Pestilence* (1564). Bullein, a Protestant doctor and priest, imagines dialogues with a dozen speakers fleeing plague-stricken London. The concern for corruption and the commitment to Protestant reform seem serious, but Bullein's humor invites a reading that undermines the satire's moralism. The 1573 edition adds a reversed world, "Taerg Natrib" – "Antipody" of "Great Britain" – inhabited by the pious, loving, honest, peaceable, orderly, loyal. But it is described by Mendax, "Liar," in a paradox like More's invention of "Health-angel Nonsense-speaker" or Lucian's bland assurance in *A True History* that he tells nothing but lies, while in an inversion of carnival, Great Brita[i]n is wrong way round and Taerg Natirb, relentlessly good, has things right (even if its reversed names mock the notion that reform simply means flipping over present reality).[23] Bullein took his Protestantism seriously, yet his paradoxes also imply that the best way out of our dilemmas is laughter.

Toward the end of the century even more English writers adopted a Menippean manner, perhaps in part inspired by an increase in such Continental models as the 1581 *Satura Menippaea* by the Dutch humanist Justus Lipsius. Lucianic dialogues remained popular, as witness Nicholas Breton's charming *Wits Trenchmour* (1597) with its philosophical angler and a worried scholar. More generically complex are satires that jumble styles or tones, wander into digressions, enjoy self-reflexive ironies, mock learned solemnity, and praise what is marginal, low, even dirty. Their works also typify what happens when the tradition of Petronius and Lucian combines with outlooks that are in some degree Christian, with timely concerns and "popular" tastes. As always, such satire can be found in texts presented as something else. John Eliot's *Ortho-epia Gallica* (1593) is a guide to French made Menippean by "merry" dialogues, stories as "authentic" as Lucian's, and "fantastical pleasantries." Eliot both enjoys and mocks London's voluble stir and its proto-imperial taste for imported novelties: a milliner stocks hats made in "Babylonian fashion," for instance, and an art seller has pictures of Plato's Ideas, "the Atoms of Epicurus," and Echo.

Another example of generic seepage is *The Cobbler of Canterbury* (1590), a small volume of tales in which Menippean foolery undoes much of the realism of the setting (a barge journey from Billingsgate to Grave-send) and social types (gentleman, scholar, cobbler, and "old wife").[24] In his preface, the anonymous author calls himself a friar's son made hairless by the pox, compares himself to a dog, puts in a good word for taverns, addresses us as though physically present, and calls this volume a "gallimaufry" in which gentlemen may "savor their ears with jests" and rustics may "laugh, while their leather buttons fly off." After an epistle by "Robin Goodfellow," we meet passengers so merry that Cato himself would have laughed at their "knavish jests" and "prattles which seemed like a very chaos of sundry conceits." The text that follows includes a pseudo-scholarly analysis of different sorts of cuckolds and parody (a young lover invokes the muses: "Approach in place Pierides, / My vein in verses to bend: / Dame Chryseis which gav'st Homer suck, / Thy tender teats me lend"). *Cobbler*, says the author, is a riposte to *Tarletons News out of Purgatory* (1590), fictions framed by reports by the dead clown, Richard Tarlton, on what he saw in Purgatory. For example, the poet Ronsard, having loved too much, recites purgatorically bad poetry ("Down I sat / I sat down, /where Flora had bestowed her graces: / Green it was, / It was green / Far surpassing other places").

More purely satirical, perhaps, Thomas Nashe heaps his *lanx satura*, his pamphlets, with varied styles: lacerating jeremiads that spin into comic grotesquerie, show-off jigs of abuse, parody, typographical joking, digressions, puns, lists, asides, and piles of words, words, words. His aggressive energy makes some readers wonder if Nashe was more in love with words than committed to anything in particular beyond, perhaps, a contempt for religious radicals and poetry's enemies. His methods remained notorious: in 1630 William Vaughan, no mean Menippean himself, was to say in his *Newlanders' Cure* that this "scurrilous pamphleteer" would "drink *Aqua vitae* with gunpowder to inspire his malicious spirit with railing matter to shame Doctor Harvey and other adversaries of his, which inflaming potion wrought so eagerly upon his brain that he would often beat himself about the noodle, and scratch the walls round about him, until he met with some extravagant furious terms" (sig. B2v).

Nashe did not "meet" such terms at once, yet his 1589 *Anatomy of Absurdity* pushes hyperbole and metaphor into drama and caricature. How people are deluded, laments Nashe: hence our "new found songs and sonnets, which every rednose fiddler hath at his fingers end, and every ignorant ale knight will breathe forth over the pot, as soon as his brain waxeth hot."[25] Similarly, *A Countercuff Given to Martin Junior ... by the Pasquil of England* (1589) and its sequels, together with the antiepiscopal pamphlets by "Martin Marprelate," to whom Nashe is replying, show polemics' affinity for satire (cf. Thomas Norton's 1570 *Disclosing of the Great Bull*, which mocks the papal bull against Elizabeth with comic lists and cattle jokes). Nashe even has a satirist's defense: "Contention is a coal, the more it is blown by disputation, the more it kindleth: I must spit in their faces to put it out" (*Works*, vol. I, p. 110). Soon he found a more fully Menippean voice, if one still inflected by the discourse of moral outrage: *Pierce Penniless his Supplication to the Devil* (1592) promises "variable delights" and delivers verses, fables, anecdotes, scatology, Latin tags, a ghost story, praise of Aretino, an epistle to Lucifer politely addressing him as "your Hellhood" (vol. I, p. 165), a preface (mis)placed at the book's end calling the work a "senseless discourse," and – in keeping with a taste for supplement that satire shares with its *frère enemie*, romance – a poem that Nashe says Spenser forgot to include with *The Faerie Queene*. Nashe has also noticed the comic uses of marginalia, reaching out to grab the reader from the page's edge: "Mark these two letter-leaping Metaphors, good people" (vol. I, p. 181). From now on Nashe will more fully exploit the satirical resources of print, although *Countercuff* had already cocked a snoot at propriety by claiming to be "Printed between the sky and the ground, within a mile of an oak, and not many fields off from the unprivileged press of the ass-ignes of Martin Junior."

There are satirical aspects to Nashe's *Unfortunate Traveller* (1594), narrated by a seedy "page, or appendix" of the court and relishing parody, tricks, melodrama, and grotesques. It is in *Lenten Stuff* (1599), however, that Nashe takes off into the Menippean stratosphere. This paradoxical encomium celebrates red herring and Yarmouth, where Nashe stayed after offending the authorities by participating in writing the controversial *Isle of Dogs*. An exercise in digression, *Stuff* is Carnival rhetoric about Lenten food, its praise of salt herring implicitly praising *sal*, wit. The *sal* seasons a verbal rush that inscribes some fear of malicious interpretation, while Yarmouth's emergence from the salty mud at the kingdom's edges and its generous royal charters suggest a lost harmonious world free of censorious surveillance. And, of course, any paradoxical encomium plays at exalting the humble herring, Tom Nashe – and tumbling the mighty from their seats. Meantime, *Stuff* piles up stuff: puns, descriptions, stories, parodies (of genealogy, myth, neologisms, Marlowe), any "light friskin" of wit (*Works*, vol. III, p. 151) that Nashe could dream up.

Nashe aimed much of his mockery at Gabriel Harvey in a battle that perhaps began as performance but degenerated, on Harvey's part, into hurt and rage. Understandably so. In *Four Letters Confuted* (1592) and *Have With You to Saffron-Walden* (1596), for example, Nashe puts matter relevant to Harvey's astrologer brother into the blackletter familiar from almanacs and captions a woodcut so as to turn it into an image of Harvey untrussing in the privy. Verse fragments and parodies, lists, dialogues, nicknames like "Gorboduck Huddleduddle," a mock trial, imaginary scenes like that of Harvey taking a walk while "whole armies of boys" call out *"kulleloo, kulleloo, with whup hoo*, there goes the Ape of *Tully* [Cicero]: tee hee hee, steal *Tully*, steal *Tully*" (*Works*, vol. 1, p. 290) – make this the decade's most cruelly funny satirical show. Protesting that Nashe would "mowgh with his mouth, gnash with his teeth, quaver with his ten bones, and brandish his goose-quill" (*Pierces Supererogation*, 1593, sig. S4v), Harvey answered in kind. Nashe is a "Gargantua of prose" and "Babel of Rhyme" (sig. Z2). He is tricky, as witness his college pet, a fox cub whose "Acts and Monuments are notorious" (a joking allusion to John Foxe's martyrology). Given to "fantasticality" (*Supererogation*, sig. D2v), when "the sweet youth haunted Aretino, and Rabelais ... who so shaken with the furious fevers of the one: or so attainted with the French pox of the other?" (*A New Letter*, 1593, sig. B3). Not bad, but without Nashe's lethal lightness of touch. As Nashe put it in *Strange News* (1592), Harvey was less able to "writhe" words and "toss them to and fro nimbly" (*Works*, vol. 1, p. 282).

Sir John Harington was if anything more consciously Menippean than Nashe. The Queen's godson, Ariosto's translator, and a clever epigramma-tist, he identifies his *New Discourse of a Stale Subject, Called the Metamorphosis of Ajax* (1596) as a paradoxical encomium: with digres-sions, parodic hymns, illustrations, music, puns, anecdotes, imaginary conversations, addresses to the reader, and a courtroom trial of this very text, he sets out to praise the flush toilet or "jakes."[26] With mock gestures of apology, Harington imagines inventing the watercloset as a scatological episode in the epic of Rabelais' *Gargantua*, the giant who finds that a goose makes the best "arse-wipe." Like Rabelais, Harington jests at solemnity, pedantry, squeamishness, novel "projects," and famous books ("Of vaults, of sinks, privies and draughts to write" [*New Discourses*, p. 57] parodies the start of *Orlando Furioso*). His jests have point: we are flesh and should not pretend otherwise, the trivial has value, and with effort we could clean up our souls and bodies.

Thomas Lodge, maker of such semi-Lucianic dialogues as *Diogenes in His Singularity* (1591), is less paradoxical, yet even as he complains of London's moral turmoil he adds his own whirl of jokes, examples, quota-tions, and snatches of verse. *Wit's Misery, or the World's Madness* (1596) reports how demons spread the seven deadly sins through London. (Compare the "anatomies" of people dominated by various planets in Greene's *Planetomachia* [1585]. It is this liking for pattern that gives Renaissance collections of satires or epigrams a cousinship with the lyric sequence.) Lodge makes sin almost agreeable: Pride "playeth Lucian in lying," which sounds like fun; Lust calls adultery a "fit of good fellowship";

and Gluttony, calling for "one pottle more of that next the door," defends his swilling in rhyme:

> Mad is the knave and his wits have the colic
> That drinks good wine and is not frolic.

Demons haunt the theatre, too, but it is Lodge himself who has heard a stage ghost cry, "Hamlet, revenge" and Brawling Contention swear, "Pota d'iddio, putana d'iddio" (God's cunt, God's whore).[27] Good satirists are implicated in the world they mock, judge, condemn, punish, reform.

Lodge's very ambiguity is typical of much good satire: together with their flashes of temper, wit, and insight, it helps give these Tudor writers their poignancy and interest. Had Tudor satire also evolved as Tudor monarchs came and went, as official doctrine shifted, as printing houses proliferated, as Spanish gold, economic projects, and new discoveries dislocated English life and presented fresh topics for mockery and denunciation? Times change and satirists change with them. It is less clear that Donne, Marston, Harington, Nashe, and other late Elizabethans, whatever their rhetorical dazzle, were more adroit at imitating the classics than Wyatt and Elyot, more seriously engaged with their times than Skelton and Shepherd, or more sophisticated in manipulating voice and exploiting paradox or the look of a page than More and Baldwin. Tudor satire expanded with the years, and for a time acquired a "satyrical" shagginess not known much before the 1590s, but that it changed fundamentally is less certain and that it got better is less certain still. After all, "progress" is not a concept welcome in satire's funny but often cruel and wintry landscape.

NOTES

1 Dustin Griffin, *Satire: A Critical Reintroduction* (Lexington: University Press of Kentucky, 1994), discusses definitions and provides a fine bibliography of scholarship on satire.

2 On this anxiety see Robert Elliott, *Power of Satire: Magic, Ritual, and Art* (Princeton: Princeton University Press, 1960).

3 On editions and translations of Roman satirists, see Angela Wheeler, *English Verse Satire from Donne to Dryden: Imitation of Classical Models* (Heidelberg: Carl Winter, 1992).

4 John Skelton, *The Complete English Poems*, ed. John Scattergood (New Haven: Yale University Press, 1983), pp. 71, 133, 309.

5 Sir Thomas Wyatt, *Collected Poems*, ed. Kenneth Muir (Cambridge: Harvard University Press, 1940); the satires are on pp. 185–93.

6 Robert Copland, *Poems*, ed. Mary Carpenter Erler (Toronto: University of Toronto Press, 1993); the first extant edition is 1565.

7 John N. King, *English Reformation Literature: The Tudor Origins of the*

Protestant Tradition (Princeton: Princeton University Press, 1982), describes many such satires.

8 Luke Shepherd, *John Bon and Mast[er] Parson*, ed. John King, *American Notes and Queries* 5 (1992): 87–91.

9 Robert Crowley. *Philargyrie of Greate Britayne*, ed. John King, *English Literary Renaissance* 10 (1980): 46–75.

10 *Tottel's Miscellany*, ed. Hyder Edward Rollins, 2 vols., (Cambridge: Harvard University Press, 1965) vol. I, pp. 188 and 196.

11 George Gascoigne, *Complete Works*, ed. John W. Cunliffe, 2 vols., (1907; New York: Greenwood, 1969) vol. II, pp. 144–46.

12 Essex's animal fable, ed. Steven May, *Studies in Philology* 77 (1980): 62–64.

13 K.W. Gransden, *Tudor Verse Satire* (London: Athlone Press, 1970), prints these satires and notes the shift in manner.

14 Joseph Hall, *Collected Poems*, ed. Arnold Davenport (Liverpool: Liverpool University Press, 1949), IV.ii.174 and I.i.5–12.

15 Everard Guilpin, *Skialetheia, or a Shadow of Truth, in Certain Epigrams and Satyres*, ed. D. Allen Carroll (Chapel Hill: University of North Carolina Press, 1974).

16 *The Poems of John Marston*, ed. Arnold Davenport (Liverpool: Liverpool University Press, 1961), p. 65. *Scourge*'s title page quotes Persius; the second satire is titled "Difficile est Satyram non scribere."

17 In Davenport's edition of Hall, *Collected Poems*, pp. 293–94; Hall was reprieved.

18 John Donne, *The Satires, Epigrams and Verse Letters*, ed. W. Milgate (Oxford: Clarendon Press, 1967).

19 On the genre and for bibliographies, see Eugene Kirk, *Menippean Satire: An Annotated Catalogue of Texts and Criticism* (New York: Garland Press, 1980); Scott Blanchard, *Scholars' Bedlam: Menippean Satire in the Renaissance* (Lewisburg, PA: Bucknell University Press, 1995); and Devon Hodges, *Renaissance Fictions of Anatomy* (Amherst: University of Massachusetts Press, 1985).

20 Ed. D.C. Peck, "'News from Heaven and Hell': A Defamatory Narrative of the Earl of Leicester," *English Literary Renaissance* 8 (1978): 141–58.

21 Compare "Colin Blowbowls Testament," *c.* 1508, beginning "In Bacchus Nomine, Amen!" in William Hazlitt ed., *Remains of Early Popular Poetry* (London, 1864–66) vol. I, pp. 91–109.

22 William Baldwin, *Beware the Cat*, ed. William Ringler and Michael Flachmann (San Marino, CA: Huntington Library, 1988).

23 Bullein had two imitators: T.N., in *A Pleasant Dialogue ... Concerning the Government and Commonweal of the Great Province of Crangalor* (1579) and Thomas Lupton, in *Siuqila* (1580; "Siuqila" reverses "Aliquis"). See Elizabeth McCutcheon, "William Bullein's *Dialogue Against the Fever Pestilence*: A Sixteenth-Century Anatomy," in *Miscellanea Moreana: Essays for Germain Marc'hadour*, ed. Clare M. Murphy, Henri Gibaud, and Mario A. Di Cesare, (Binghamton, NY: Medieval & Renaissance Texts & Studies, 1989).

24 *The Cobbler of Caunterburie* and *Tarltons Newes out of Purgatorie*, ed. Geoffrey Creigh and Jane Belfield (Leiden: Brill, 1987).

25 Thomas Nashe, *Works*, ed. Ronald B. McKerrow, 5 vols., (Oxford: Blackwell, 1958 edn.) vol. I, pp. 23–24.

26 Sir John Harington, *New Discourse*, ed. Elizabeth S. Donno (New York: Columbia University Press, 1962).
27 Thomas Lodge, *Works*, ed. Edmund Gosse (London, 1883; New York, 1963), vol. IV, pp. 13, 52–53, 85, 62, 69.

FURTHER READING

Anselment, Raymond A., *"Betwixt Jest and Earnest": Martin Marprelate, Milton, Marvell, Swift and the Decorum of Religious Ridicule* (Toronto: University of Toronto Press, 1979).

Baumlin, James, "Generic Contexts of Elizabethan Satire," in *Renaissance Genres*, ed. Barbara Lewalski (Cambridge: Harvard University Press, 1986), pp. 444–67.

Blanchard, Scott, *Scholars' Bedlam: Menippean Satire in the Renaissance* (Lewisburg, PA: Bucknell University Press, 1995).

Gill, R. B., "A Purchase of Glory: The Persona of Late Elizabethan Satire," *Studies in Philosophy* 72 (1975): 408–18.

Griffin, Dustin, *Satire: A Critical Reintroduction* (Lexington: University Press of Kentucky, 1994).

Knight, Charles, "Imagination's Cerberus: Satire and the Metaphor of Genre," *Philological Quarterly* 69 (1990): 131–51.

Rawson, Claude, ed., *English Satire and the Satiric Tradition* (Oxford: Basil Blackwell, 1984).

Rhodes, Neil, *The Power of Eloquence and English Renaissance Literature* (New York: St. Martin's Press, 1992).

Selden, Raman, *English Verse Satire 1590–1765* (London: George Allen and Unwin, 1978).

Test, George A., *Satire: Spirit and Art* (Tampa: University of South Florida Press, 1991).

Wheeler, Angela, *English Verse Satire from Donne to Dryden: Imitation of Classical Models* (Heidelberg: Carl Winter, 1992).

12

LENA COWEN ORLIN

Chronicles of private life

The defining event of the sixteenth century was the Reformation. The break with Rome left its mark not only on the ecclesiastical, political, and economic spheres, but also on the private. Politically, the doctrine of the royal supremacy was advanced by the creation of an Anglican church headed by the English King. A principal way in which the monarchy justified its new power was through analogy to the "natural" structure of the private family: as the father was in his household, so the King was in his country, the uncontested center of authority. It was in the interest of the monarchy to produce an ideology which authorized the private household as the primary unit of social order and which reinforced the notion that the householder was absolute ruler within his household. Economically, repudiation of the Roman religion permitted the seizure of English lands and goods formerly held by churches, monasteries, and abbeys. The church had owned as much as a third of the country, and when the Crown not only appropriated these properties but also began to give them away and then sell them off, a relatively static land market exploded into activity. Meanwhile, an expanding market economy and an enlarging government bureaucracy generated sufficient wealth for a generation of "new," formerly unpropertied men to take advantage of the commodification of land and to establish their own great households. Standards of living rose for houses, goods, and furnishings across all ranks of society.

Whatever the political and economic advantages to the monarchy, however, the Reformation was *publicly* defined as an act of the King's conscience. Just as the political and economic upheavals had their enabling consequences for the lives of lesser men, so, too, did this formulation of a public role for private conscience. Along with the empowerment and enrichment of the householder came moral responsibility for the members of his household, a responsibility that was pursued through private access to scripture and through a culture of inwardness and self-examination. Against this epochal backdrop a literature of private life formed.

The scholarly revolution of the past two decades – the advent of postmodern theory and of such political criticisms as feminism, New Historicism, cultural materialism, postcolonialism, and queer studies – has undone the canon and made possible the rediscovery and reevaluation of this literature of private life. Of course the canonical literature has always included the private themes of family, friends, and household: *Hamlet* is as much about a son's loss of his father as it is about the royal succession in a kingdom. But canonical literature is not the first concern of this chapter. Rather, we will work to call attention to the genres which originated in private life, for which publication was often not the intended end, but through which personal concerns and histories have nonetheless survived: commonplace books, diaries, family correspondence, autobiographies, memoirs. This literature of private life is still expanding, as archives are plumbed, manuscripts are edited, and private voices are rediscovered both in these genres and in travel journals, account books, recipe books, and testamentary documents. For this reason, the present account can be only suggestive.

We will begin with the *public* literature of private life: that is, the texts that conveyed the ruling ideology. These texts addressed the purposes of matrimony, the selection of mates, the rearing of children, and the super-vision of servants. That their real concern was what was understood to be social stability can be seen from their strict focus on male enfranchise-ment, heterosexual alliances, hierarchical relationships, household struc-tures, and the dissemination of doctrine across the lines of age, gender, and rank. Even despite the fact that this political and religious doctrine made a faulty template for the social and economic life of early modern England, it nonetheless produced the conceptual underpinnings and the common language for the literature to which we will next turn, the private chronicles of Sir Thomas More, Lady Grace Mildmay, Lady Margaret Hoby, Nehemiah Wallington, and others. Their records reveal their struggle to shape their lives in accord with the tenor of their times. The struggle was not always successful; we occasionally find personal eco-nomic concerns outweighing public political ones, humor displacing seriousness of purpose, and emotion unsubdued by duty. Private life preserved some mysteries which no public ideology could adequately factor in or filter out.

THE IDEOLOGY OF PRIVATE LIFE

When in 1526 Henricus Cornelius Agrippa set out in "commendation of matrimony," he observed that matrimony giveth a great exercise to moral philosophy. For it hath a certain household commonwealth annexed, in ruling the which a man may soon learn and have experience of wisdom, temperance, love to God and his kin, and all other virtues, by which in loving his wife, in bringing up his children, in governing his family, in saving his goods, in ruling his little house, in procreating and enlarging his stock, he may lead a life most happy.[1]

To unpack this terse passage is to explode the ideological systems of early modern England into their many meanings for social organization, domestic politics, gender construction, economic activities, personal relations, and private life.

Agrippa's *Commendation* was dedicated to a powerful female patron, Marguerite de Navarre. It may be for this reason that his topic is given as the commendation of matrimony and that his point of departure is praise of the wife. This diversion cannot disguise how remote is his argument from that of romantic comedy, which was premised on the notion that world order was restored when eros had reached its end in a union forged in affect. Here, the household with all its social, political, and economic meanings is the object of desire. The wife is but the means to the household. When Agrippa asserts that the household ruler will love his wife, this is less a statement about the human heart than it is an echo of the proverbial doctrine that "love goeth downward, duty goeth upward" – that is, the wife and other subordinates in the ideal household offer their obedience to the household lord, and he in turn proffers love in its political sense, governance marked by care and benevolence.

"Loving," "bringing up," "governing," "saving," and "ruling" were grave responsibilities, not to be undertaken lightly. Only those who could not resist "procreating" and "enlarging" were encouraged to wed by such writers as William Whately, who approved marriage for the man who, "after diligent labor, convenient watching, due abstinence, earnest prayers, and a careful shunning of all times, places, companies, exercises, that may provoke ill affections, doth yet still find his heart so restlessly possessed with these desires, that he cannot withhold his will."[2] In fact, the writings of humanists Vives and Erasmus, the Office of Holy Matrimony established in 1559, the Homily of the State of Matrimony circulated from 1563 onward, the Roman Counter-Reformation catechism of 1566, and Puritan theology all agreed that the aims of marriage were, first, to provide a man with a companion or helper; second, to insure the lawful propagation of his children; and, third, to legitimate his sexual practice.

That which went unspoken – but was at least as much at issue – was that marriage established a man as a mature member of the social order. As Agrippa and many before and after him asked rhetorically, "how shall he rule a city that hath not learned to rule a house? how shall he govern a commonwealth that never knew his private and familiar business?" (sig. C7v). Marriage and householding were not separable institutions. They were so thoroughly intertwined that most men would not marry until they had the means and the opportunity to set up housekeeping. Economic and material constraints largely account for the late age at marriage in England – except for those at the highest social registers, where marriages were arranged early in the interest of property settlements. Elsewhere, however, men married at twenty-five or twenty-seven and women at twenty-three or twenty-four. They spent the years from early adolescence to matrimony in service of some sort, whether in apprenticeship to a trade or craft or as attendants in a great house. The preacher Henry Smith referred to this period as an apprenticeship to marriage as well as to profession: individuals had to "*learn* to be good husbands and wives, as though it were a trade of nothing but mysteries."[3]

These customs had a broad range of consequences for the normalized household as a social institution. First, it was not multigenerational, in the sense that newly married couples did not live with one or another of their parents. Again, the practices of those of the higher ranks varied, because the son and heir traditionally remained with his parents on the family estate. And at all levels houseroom was often found for the older widow who did not remarry. But the general rule was for one (male) head in each house; as political theorist Jean Bodin stated flatly, it was "the law of nature, which willeth, that every man should be master of his own house."[4] Second, the household was also not nuclear, because of its incorporation of servants. Only the poorest laborers would not have a servant or two. In fact, Bodin argued that a "family" could not be constituted with fewer than five people, which at its inception would have included householder, house-wife, and, in advance of children, three servants (sig. B5r). The universal custom of service relieved the usual pressures for youths to marry young and begin their own families early, because servants in England supplied the needs of child laborers in other countries. Third, the household was not socially stratified into the "upstairs" group of the principal family and the "downstairs" group of the servants. Instead, servants were often, roughly speaking, of a class with those who employed them, putting in the years of their "apprenticeship" to housekeeping. Upon marriage many would estab-lish themselves as the social equals of their former employers. Without clear social distinctions, what held servants in place during their tenure in service was the political structure of the household, what Agrippa called "governing" and "ruling."

According to Bodin, a family was "the right government of many subjects or persons under the obedience of one and the same head of the family" (*Six Bookes*, sig. B4v). For him, the family was a political organism, pure and simple. As he continued, "it is neither the walls, neither the persons, that maketh the city" or, by analogy, the family, "but the union of the people under the same sovereignty of government" (sig. B5v). Sovereignty resided in the householder, and wives, children, and servants were required to relinquish authority to him. Widely acknowledged to be the most troublesome in this regard was the wife, who was enjoined by Puritan William Gouge to acknowledge her husband's superiority; to obey him; to be subject to him; to use reverent speech to him; to bear his reproofs; to yield to him in dwelling where he would, coming when he called, and doing what he required; and never to think herself his equal, to stand on her own will, or to undertake to do anything without his consent.[5] According to Bodin, families, like other institutions, were "kept together and preserved by the mutual duties of commanding and obeying" (*Six Bookes*, sig. C1v).

Aristotle, whom Bodin knew and cited, allowed that there were different kinds of government, with monarchic and aristocratic (shared) rule being principal among them. But Bodin and other early modern political theorists were fully committed to the monarchic model. To justify the power and perquisites of royal sovereignty they sought to naturalize it, by outlining its analogy to a "natural" structure, the family. In order for the analogy to serve their purpose, however, the family had to be conceptualized along suitable (monarchic) lines. It could not be admitted that any government, even the domestic government, could function through shared rule – that is, with parallel roles for husband and wife. Bodin described the "domestical power" as of four sorts – husband over wife, father over child, lord over slave, head over servant – but these sorts were undivided in his ideal household, where the rule of the householder was absolute. The most obvious instance of the distorting effect of the analogy came in Bodin's defense of the father's power of life and death over his children (sig. C4v). Early modern culture did not condone infanticide; Bodin was really making a thinly veiled defense of the King's right of life and death over his subjects.

In practice, Agrippa's easy elision of the husband "saving his goods" and "ruling his little family" was difficult to achieve. The economic and political roles of the householder could not be made to cohere. Aristotle's aristocratic model was closer to practicable than was Bodin's monarchy, and even orthodox literature found itself admitting this conflict. The wife had too important an economic role to play in the household, as so official an organ of doctrine as the Homily on Matrimony testified: "Ye wives, be ye in subjection to obey your own husbands. To obey, is another thing than to control or command, which yet they may do, to their children, and to their family: But as for their husbands, them must they obey, and cease from commanding, and perform subjection."[6] The syntactic confusion, as the homily switches from an address phrased in the second person to explanation put in the third person, is indicative of the anxiety occasioned by the dual and sometimes incompatible roles of the household, political and economic. Whately tried to reconcile the two spheres by making a political philosophy out of economic necessity:

> in commanding, it must be regarded that authority descend not unto low, mean, and trivial things, which are not of any moment or importance in the family ... In such things he should let his wife rule under him, and give her leave to know more than himself ... He that will be drawing out his commandments for every light thing, shall find it at length regarded in nothing.[7]

In fact, the importance of the economic role of the household only grew over the course of the sixteenth century, as individuals accumulated more wealth and as standards of living rose. Chronicler William Harrison is the most frequently cited authority on the material transformations of the period. He celebrated widespread building activity as one of the glories of the Tudor age. He was particularly concerned to detail how goods and furnishings that "in time past" had "stayed" among gentlemen and wealthy citizens had come to "[descend] yet lower, even unto the inferior artificers and many farmers." They, too, he said, "learned also to garnish their cupboards with plate, their [joined] beds with tapestry and silk hangings, and their tables with carpets and fine napery." According to Harrison, the greatest changes involved the construction of chimneys, which replaced central hearths and made possible more heated spaces on more than one floor; the "amendment of lodging," which substituted mattresses, pillows, and sheets for rough pallets, logs, and coarse coverlets; and the "exchange of vessel," which replaced wooden table implements with platters and spoons of silver, pewter, and tin.[8] These improvements had gendered consequences. A standard dualism of the period, as voiced by John Dod and Robert Cleaver, was that "the duty of the husband is to get goods, and of the wife, to gather them together and save them."[9] As goods proliferated, clearly, the wife's sphere was enlarged.

When he collected and published his sermons, William Gouge had to defend himself against the charge of being "an hater of women"; the flash point for women in his congregation was his argument "restraining" the wife from "disposing the common goods of the family without or against her husband's consent" (*Of Domestical Duties*, sigs. ¶3v–¶4r). Gouge protested in his own defense that his draconian injunctions regarding wifely obedience taught "what a wife, in the uttermost extent of that subjection under which God hath put her, is bound unto, *in case* her husband will stand upon the uttermost of his authority" (emphasis added). When he discussed the duties of the husband, he objected further, he had stated "that he ought to make her a joint governor of the family with himself, and refer the ordering of many things to her discretion, and with all honorable and kind respect to carry himself towards her." If love, in Agrippa's political sense, is extended, then, as Gouge would say, "his wife can have no just cause to complain of her subjection" (*Of Domestical Duties*, sigs. ¶3v-¶4r). But the bad fit between political philosophy and economic necessity was undoubtedly one reason that Agrippa's sunny conclusion regarding house-holding as leading to "a life most happy" was not universally endorsed. Whately counselled men "to go unto Matrimony with fear of the worst," because "diverse houses are none other but even very fencing-schools, wherein the two sexes seem to have met together for nothing but to play their prizes and to try masteries" (*Care-Cloth*, sigs. A4r, A2v).

Most moralists in the sixteenth century wrote of aspirations not to "a life most happy" but of domestic "peace." The homilies read repeatedly in parish churches may have invoked public order as a stick to motivate householders, but preachers like Dod and Cleaver offered a carrot: "where the husband and wife performeth these duties in their house, we may call it a college of quietness" (*Godly Form*, sig. L6r). Shakespeare's Petruchio was not alone in describing his marital ambition as "peace" and "love" and "quiet life," nor was he unusual in believing that domestic harmony proceeded from the householder's "awful rule and right supremacy." But, once again, ideology did not keep pace with social reality. As the early modern economy required men to pursue their businesses outside the house, the house became more and more a place of refuge or sanctuary for the householder, with its tranquility increasingly important to him. The more absent he was from the house in pursuit of his business, however, the more the house became the woman's sphere. In the long term, the feminiza-tion of the household would lead inevitably to its devaluation as a social and political institution. In the short term, for the length of the sixteenth century, this meant that contests for the rule of the domestic space were not engaged only by the personalities of the husband and wife. They were structural, inherent.

REMEMBERING MORE, ATTAINING GRACE

In their different ways, Sir Thomas More and Lady Grace Mildmay were paradigmatic figures of the century. More, of course, has been the better known. Even though his story went against the grain of the Reformation, he was the man of the private sphere who matched Henry VIII for a notorious act of conscience. But while More's enduring celebrity unarguably derived from his martyrdom, this was not the sole defining element of his resonance in sixteenth-century popular culture. The man who merits mention in this chapter is not the Thomas More of the spectacular political career: barrister, aide to Cardinal Wolsey, favorite of Henry VIII, Speaker of Parliament, and Lord Chancellor of England. Nor is he the Thomas More of humanist scholarship and lasting literary fame: friend of Erasmus and Colet, author of the *Utopia*. Instead he is the More who in every contemporary incarnation is positioned in his "beautiful and commodious" home in Chelsea,[10] a man who consciously constructed a private life that accorded in point after point with the ruling tenets of the day. Whether More lived this life or whether he was only reported to have done so cannot be disentangled here, where in any case he has more to tell us as a cultural icon than a historical figure.

A principal source for More's life is the memoir of his son-in-law William Roper, who emphasizes his qualifications to write More's story by observing that "I was continually resident in his house by the space of sixteen years and more."[11] Roper nonetheless details life events in which he himself did not share, including More's youthful apprenticeships. More first joined the household of Archbishop Morton and then, in a variation on the custom of learning a trade, went to Oxford and to the Inns of Court to study law. Next came an early example of the religious practices which would set this man apart from others of his day: More spent four years in a Carthusian monastery, the London Charterhouse. He did not take holy orders, however, and in the end he may as well have followed the procedure that William Whately was to recommend a century later, of "due abstinence" and "earnest prayers" before embarking upon matrimony. When More emerged from Charterhouse, having accepted the invitation of a gentleman named Colt to enter his household, it was obviously to join the world on its terms. He soon wed Colt's elder daughter, Jane.

Roper allows us no romantic illusions about this union. More was evidently taking the necessary step toward social entitlement, not making a love match. In Master Colt's household, More's "mind most served him to the second daughter, for that he thought her [the] fairest and best favored." But, says Roper, "when he considered that it would be both great grief and some shame also to the eldest to see her younger sister in marriage preferred before her," More redirected "his fancy" (*Life*, p. 6). When this first wife later died, More took as his second wife a woman dismissed by Roper as "simple," "ignorant," and "somewhat worldly, too" (p. 82). More's sixteenth-century biographer, Nicholas Harpsfield, makes the meaning of such characterizations clear: More "rather married [her] for the ruling and governing of his children, house and family, than for any bodily pleasure."[12]

Harpsfield explains that despite Alice's putative limitations, More "entirely loved and most lovingly used" her, and Roper gives many instances of how love in its political sense descended in More's household. In the *Utopia*'s prefatory letter to Peter Giles, More himself describes how most of his days were devoted "in public to other men's affairs" and how, "When I have returned home, I must talk with my wife, chat with my children, and confer with my servants. All this activity I count as business when it must be done – and it must be unless you want to be a stranger in your own home."[13] Among other things, More took responsibility for the spiritual life of those under his authority. He prayed with his children and "nightly, before he went to bed, with his wife, children, and household [went] to his chapel, and there upon his knees ordinarily [said] certain psalms and collects with them" (Roper, *Life*, p. 25). In Roper's account, More anticipates the later advice of Anglican preachers that householders must be not only kings but also ministers to their households.

More's house was an appropriate extension of his status, learning, and aspiration. Alice described it as a domestic paradise: "a right fair house, your library, your books, your gallery, your garden, your orchard, and all other necessaries so handsome about you, where you might in the company of me your wife, [your] children, and household, be merry" (quoted by Roper, *Life*, pp. 82–83). More established residence at some remove from London, and, early on, he was so much the favorite of the King and Queen "that he could not once in a month get leave to go home to his wife and children (whose company he most desired)." Eventually, he began to "dissemble his nature" and disguise his wit (pp. 11–12), so that he became less the object of royal favor and more the master of his own leisure and liberty. For all the responsibilities it entailed, in other words, the Thameside estate at Chelsea also offered More sanctuary from the cares of the outer world and a brilliant career.

Not even Roper could argue, however, that in loving his wife, bringing up his children, and ruling his little house, More achieved what Agrippa called "a life most happy." Stephen Greenblatt has persuasively deconstructed the domestic idyll: More never entirely put aside the life of the Charterhouse.[14] As Roper reports, More "was desirous for godly purposes sometime to be solitary, and sequester himself from worldly company." Thus, "a good distance from his mansion house builded he a place called the New Building, wherein there was a chapel, a library, and a gallery," to which he retreated on Fridays for private devotions and spiritual exercises

(*Life*, pp. 25–26). He also "secretly" wore a hair shirt and "used also sometimes to punish his body with whips, the cords knotted" (pp. 48–49). In the course of his memoir, Roper shows us More's utter cynicism about the King's self-centeredness, his dismissive indulgence of his wife's simplicity. Only with respect to his children are we allowed a glimpse of a fully felt emotional life.[15] In the Tower, he told his daughter Margaret that if it were not for her and the rest of his family, "I would not have failed long ere this to have closed my self in as strait a room, and straiter, too" (p. 76).

Neither Roper's memoir nor Harpsfield's biography achieved publication in the sixteenth century. More's life story was suppressed during the reformist reigns of Henry VIII and Edward VI and in the authorized histories of Edward Hall and John Foxe. The flurry of Moreana that accompanied Mary I's succession to the throne, including not only works by Roper and Harpsfield but also a planned biography by William Rastell, was aborted with her early death, so that the Roper and Harpsfield texts thereafter circulated only in manuscript.[16] This does not alter the fact that they were written with an eye to a public audience, at least twenty years after More's death, and, in the case of Roper's memoir, in service to the family's reputation (it was believed that the story of Bishop John Fisher, who, like More, had been executed for refusing to take the Oath of Supremacy, had been given more public play). While these are filters through which we assuredly must read the accounts of More's exemplary private life, we cannot simply dismiss the chronicles as acts of flagrant misrepresentation. With varying degrees of personal struggle in doing so, many sixteenth-century individuals did accommodate themselves to the domestic doctrines of their day. More may well have been one of them; Lady Grace Mildmay almost certainly was.

Mildmay wrote an autobiography, compiled books of devotional meditations, and recorded notes and recipes which reveal her to have been a skilled practitioner of the early modern medical sciences.[17] (According to her daughter Lady Mary Fane, these last writings were "scatteringly and confusedly left to me in divers books and more than 2,000 loose papers" which Fane subsequently organized into four volumes; see *With Faith and Physic*, p. 110.) The autobiography and a collection of "advice" for Mildmay's grandson were certainly compiled, like Roper's memoir, with an awareness of others' perusing eyes, but her intended audience, unlike Roper's, was at least ostensibly the "private" one of her descendants. In these documents, Mildmay gave witness to the way in which a life could shape itself to fit the prevailing ideology.

Her "advice" digests sentences familiar from the public literature of sermons, conduct books, and official homilies, all framed by the political understanding that "A private household of family (which may resemble a whole commonwealth)" consists in instruction and governance.[18] She quotes: "Let wives be subject to their husbands"; "let the wife see that she fear her husband"; and "likewise the husbands dwell with them as men of knowledge, giving honour unto the wife, as unto the weaker vessel." Here, in a female-authored document, the early modern gender hierarchy is so thoroughly internalized that Mildmay reserves her sternest words of caution not for the troublesomeness of women but instead for that of servants and children. She warns that servants are "presumptuous" and "arrogant," that they "will seek to know all that their master knoweth and observe and watch all that he doth" and then will use that knowledge "for their own advantage." Children, meanwhile, must never be given their own will nor must they be spared correction, and they must be taught "to please their parents better than themselves" (*With Faith and Physic*, pp. 44–47).

In her more personalized autobiography, Mildmay gives evidence that as a child she herself practiced this last piece of advice. She was consigned to the tutelage of a young kinswoman, who would set her improving tasks: "to cast up and prove great sums," "to write a supposed letter to this or that body concerning such and such things," to read in books of herbs and surgery, to sing psalms, to practice fine embroidery. "Such," says Mildmay, "was her honest and faithful care to perform the trust which my mother reposed in her" (p. 26). Meanwhile, Mildmay's mother made herself responsible for her daughter's religious education. The sources of indoctrination into the prevailing ideologies were omnipresent: her caretaker advised her "that I should ever carry with me a modest eye and a chaste ear, a silent tongue and a considerate heart"; her mother warned her that "I should carry myself silent and humble in mine own conceit, esteeming others better than myself"; her eventual mother-in-law "instructed me likewise to become a faithful wife unto her son" (*With Faith and Physic*, pp. 27, 28, 34).

In consequence of this upbringing, Mildmay became a habitual reader. She recommends Foxe's *Acts and Monuments*, chronicle histories, laws and statutes, collections of philosopher's sentences, and, especially, the Bible. She counsels her own readers to begin with Genesis, read through to Revelation, and then start all over again. "I found," she observes, "that as the water pierceth the hard stone by often dropping thereupon, so the continual exercise in the word of God made a deep impression in my stony heart." Her program of Bible reading was, she says, "the only stability of my mind and my stay and comfort in all the troubles and calamities of my whole life" (p. 35).

As these last words suggest, Mildmay does not shrink from

acknowledging her adversities. These, like More's desire for the cloister, give texture to a life otherwise reported as having been lived according to pattern. With three daughters, Mildmay's father had originally divided his estate in thirds. When the eldest of the three died without heirs, her share was to have been split equally between the two survivors. Instead, on his deathbed, Mildmay's father "gave my sister two third parts of his best land and gave me but one third part of his worst land." Her mother had evidently conspired with the sister against Mildmay. This Mildmay calls an "unjust alteration" to his original intent, an "unnatural wrong." She reports that she told her sister that if God alone had moved her father to take this course, "then the will of God be done," but if, as she suspected, "you have labored my father by all means," then she would ask for God's aid "to right and defend my cause" (pp. 36–37). Only lawsuits assiduously pursued by her father-in-law successfully advanced Mildmay's claims.[19]

Mildmay reports her partial disinheritance in her autobiography, as also differences with her parents-in-law. But she concludes: "There was never any thing more blessed unto me in this life than mine afflictions and trials which were never greater than God enabled me to bear. I ever received them as the messengers and tokens of the love of God unto me, even as I have no less found and proved them" (*With Faith and Physic*, p. 39). Her editor, Linda Pollock, attributes Mildmay's forbearance from criticizing parents, husband, and in-laws to "a conditioned attitude of mind in which all of life's incidents were subordinated to illustrating the goodness of God to the faithful" (p. 17). Despite her private experience, Mildmay fit herself to the political and religious ideologies in circulation and evidently found in them her own state of grace.

MATTERS OF SUBSTANCE

If the ruling discourse of formal writings on private life – biographies, memoirs, and autobiographies – was political, that of personal records was economic. The most common and unselfconscious genres – household account books, wills, inventories, and, especially as the century wore on, diaries – all testify to the driving concern of early moderns with getting, keeping, and controlling their goods and property. In these records, the house was a center of production and consumption as much as a political unit.

Such was the testimony of clergyman and diarist Richard Rogers. On 12 January 1588 he observed the unexpected death of a neighbor woman and, as he undoubtedly urged his parishioners to do, searched this event from his daily life for its object lessons. With his own wife near childbirth, he was moved to contemplate his possible widowerhood and what it would entail:

First, the fear of marrying again, dangerous as 2^2 [sic] marriages are.
Want of it in the mean while.
Forgoing so fit a companion for religion, housewifery, and other comforts.
Loss and decay in substance.
Care of household matters cast on me.
Neglect of study.
Care and looking after children.
Forgoing our boarders.
Fear of losing friendship among her kindred.[20]

Rogers was concerned with the loss of a sexual partner ("want of it in the mean while"), and he regretted in advance the inevitable estrangement from his wife's extended family. But most of his list was given over to his wife's contributions to the household. She provided real economic value, preserving Rogers' "substance" and making it possible for the family to realize income from lodgers. Rogers understood further that the household and his children made their own demands, and that, without her, those duties would fall to him, leaving him less time for his religious studies. He justified his meditation on the grounds that he should "more thankfully use the benefit if it should be continued" (which, sadly, was not to be).

The range of responsibilities that made good huswifery "a trade of nothing but mysteries" is perhaps best suggested in the diary kept by Lady Margaret Hoby between 1599 and 1605.[21] Even as a gentlewoman, she either directly engaged in or oversaw the endless manual labors of a household. Her diary has her preserving quinces and pears, cooking meat, concocting sweetmeats and gingerbread and aqua vitae, making wax candles, mending and washing fine linen, dyeing wool, spinning and winding yarn, and packing for her occasional trips to York and to London. Nearly every day she "walked about the house" to supervise her servants, see to the meals, and give necessary orders and directions. Hoby also attended to the provisioning of the household, ordering honey, receiving goods bought in London, making her own purchases at a local fair, and dealing, too, with a goldsmith. She concerned herself with routine building maintenance and with the garden and farming, frequently visiting her workmen in the fields as wheat and corn were planted and apples were gathered. In various ways she made herself responsible for the well-being of people who came within her sphere, taking young women into service in her household, seeing to the religious instruction of her servants, entertaining guests and kinsmen, feeding the poor who arrived at her door, and acting not only as midwife but also as druggist and surgeon to members of the house and the occasional villager.

Many and varied as these tasks were, they seem to fall within the bounds of what Bodin and Gouge might have acknowledged to be the routine duties of a housewife. But there were also charges of such influence and gravity that the failure of political ideology to accommodate economic reality is exposed even in the records of this careful Puritan. Hoby paid household bills and servants' wages – and not only when her husband was away from home. On at least some occasions she kept the household account books and received rents. Herself a landed heiress, she collected the tithe corn and apples that conveyed with her property. Her husband consulted her on where to build cottages in the village, how to assign pews in the church, whether to sell a portion of her inheritance, whether to buy another house in the area, and how to pursue a suit that they pressed in Star Chamber. Hoby also represented her own material interests, both in conversation and in writing, when her husband urged her to settle some of her estate on him.

Margaret, née Dakins, was just twenty-five when she wed Thomas Posthumous Hoby, but, in the manner of people of property, she had first married much younger. At seventeen or eighteen she wed Walter Devereux; at twenty-one or so, Thomas Sidney. She was thus twice widowed when Hoby pressed his unwelcome suit. She wrote her longtime protector, the Earl of Huntingdon, to refuse Hoby, but Huntingdon died before the matter was resolved. When Huntingdon's brother succeeded to the earldom and immediately laid claim to Margaret's estate, she was advised that an association with Hoby's powerful friends would sway the judgment of the court of Chancery in her favor. Essentially, she was blackmailed into marrying Hoby in order to protect lands to which her husband almost immediately after the wedding himself laid siege. As is suggested by her story and that of Grace Mildmay, as well as by the later, notorious case of Anne Clifford, property disputes were rife in the period. We might imagine that the contests that distressed these women of status were played out at all social levels, although sometimes the object at issue was a cupboard or a featherbed rather than a landed estate.

Hoby, who faithfully reported her attempts to live a godly life – beginning and ending each day in private prayer, joining in public prayer, attending church, consulting with the household chaplain, and examining herself daily – also, despite the circumstances of her marriage, resolutely took on the further task that was enjoined her, that of being a companion to her husband. In entry after entry, she consults with him on household business, accompanies him to church services, breakfasts with him, dines with him, walks with him, goes to the fields and the village with him, attends him in illness, travels with him, writes to him in his absence as an "assured and loving wife" (*Diary*, ed. Meads, p. 268), and, simply, repeatedly, "keeps him company." Meanwhile, whatever his motivation for marrying her, Thomas Hoby may have made his own attempts at accommodation. One day, for example, the diarist describes being so ill with a toothache that she was confined to her room, and "Mr. Hoby read in the morning to me and prayed with me" (*Private Life*, ed. Moody, p. 113).

The marriage was to last for thirty-seven years (and one month, Thomas Hoby added at the end). When she died, his funerary monument to her declared that they had lived "in mutual entire affection to both their extraordinary comforts" (p. 222). It may be to the point that he had not long before prevailed in the property disputes. Childless herself, Margaret Hoby had made over her estate to her husband's heirs, requiring only that some lands be sold to the benefit of her kin and for charitable bequests. This concord was reached in 1632, thirty-two years to the month after she had first responded formally to her husband's property demands – and twenty-seven years after her final entry in the diary that has survived to us. With her diary either long abandoned or with subsequent entries lost, Thomas Hoby owned the last word.

The silence of Hoby's later life is particularly frustrating because she had lived into a different age from that into which she had been born. The less decorous diarists of the seventeenth century were willing to portray their disputes over substance more directly and vividly than she or other sixteenth-century authors seemed to feel licensed to do. For example, Adam Eyre recorded in 1647 that, "This morn I told my wife that if she would furnish me with £200 I would secure her all Hazlehead [his estate] for her life, and she should have the half of it for the present, if Edward Mitchell [his tenant] would part with it; and she refused, unless I would release her land in Scholes, which I refused." He threatened "never to come in bed with her"; she would not allow him "to go to bowls"; one night, she locked him out of the house. He began to wonder whether he could continue to live with her, even though he knew these were "wicked worldly thoughts." When the couple attempted a reconciliation, they vowed to put the past behind them, "and she promised me likewise she would do what I wished her in anything, save in setting her hands to papers" (*English Family Life*, ed. Houlbrooke, pp. 65–69). Political subordination she was able to accept, but when it came to her property she admitted no negotiation.

MYSTERIES OF PRIVATE LIFE

The national identity of early modern England was formed in history writing: Polydore Vergil, John Foxe, Raphael Holinshed, John Stow. Of all the genres of history writing, it was the chronicle on which the popular imagination seized, and we can assess its impact on the cultural consciousness by its elevation to the status of common reference, as notorious murders, marked virtues, brave achievements, and natural wonders were described as "worthy to be put in Holinshed's chronicle" or as "worthy Stow's Chronicle."[22] In the early modern imagination public history seemed finite, not infinitely expansive, as if only the most remarkable events put sufficient pressure on the historical record to effect their inclusion in the national narrative. This accounts for the anecdotal, even sensational, quality that surprises modern readers. In a culture in which the lines between public and private were not so clearly drawn as in our own time, diaries and letters often followed the forms and shared the concerns of public chronicles. One mark of the slippage between the two is the fact that when in her diary Anne Clifford mentions "looking at the Chronicles," it is unclear whether she has turned to the improving stories of public history that Grace Mildmay recommended or to the account Clifford was assembling about her own family.[23]

Margaret Hoby's private chronicle may have been an instrument of self-examination required by (and reviewed by) her household chaplain, Richard Rhodes. So speculates Hoby's first editor, Dorothy M. Meads, who notes further that Hoby's entries grow less regular after Rhodes moved away. Later entries are also less exclusively concerned with the day's litany of duties fulfilled – in fact, the diary becomes more like the public chronicles. There appears a hint of the fascination with rumor and report that was to characterize John Chamberlain's lively letters from London. Hoby writes: "William Heslerton was quit for coining of money, and his fellow that taught him hanged" (*Private Life*, ed. Moody, p. 184); "our late gracious Queen buried at Westminster" (p. 189); "This day was Waddie accused to have gotten a child, but he denied the fact" (p. 214). On 26 August 1601 Hoby records at more length that "I [had] a child brought to [me] that was born at Silpho, one Taylor's son, who had no fundament [anus], and had no passage for excrements but at the mouth: I was earnestly entreated to cut the place to see if any passage could be made, but, although I cut deep and searched, there was none to be found" (p. 161). This is the sort of story that could have found its way into the public pamphlet literature of monstrous births and natural wonders. But there it would not have carried the poignancy of Hoby's intimate contact with personal tragedy.

Such events surely marked every life, but too few left historical traces. And there are other gaps. For one thing, the sixteenth-century literature of private life is ineluctably skewed to persons of status like Sir Thomas More, Lady Grace Mildmay, and Lady Margaret Hoby. In part, this is a function of leisure; in part, of a certain level of education. But equally important is the fact that records were more likely to survive in the chests, evidence rooms, and garrets of houses that remained in family hands for generations. With the remarkable set of diaries left by a seventeenth-century London craftsman, Nehemiah Wallington, we have little idea which was more the freak of history: the man himself or the survival of his writings. In his diaries, he left extraordinarily vivid portrayals not only of spiritual struggles and patriarchal resolve but also of parental emotion and marital feeling.

He writes, for example, of his young daughter Elizabeth's merry mood one night. As her mother washed dishes in the kitchen, Elizabeth joked, "What do you here, my wife?" Later, in bed, she announced that she intended to buy her father a plum pie. But, says Wallington, "These were the last words that I did hear my sweet child speak." After two days of undiagnosed suffering, Elizabeth died, and "The grief for this child was so great that I forgot myself so much that I did offend God in it; for I broke all my purposes, promises and covenants with my God, for I was much distracted in my mind, and could not be comforted." Finally, Wallington's wife intervened. She described the cares they were rid of with this child's death, the troubles the girl would be spared, the joy she went to as the bride of Christ. Wallington asked, "Do you not grieve for this child?" And his wife answered resolutely that "I do as freely give it again unto God as I did receive it of him." When Wallington's son died three years later, his wife was again his comforter:

> Husband, say we should put our child forth to nurse; and when we see time fit we send for our child, and if Nurse should deny us our child and should think much at us that we fetch it home again, we should then be very angry with her. Even so stands the case with us, for God gave us this child to nurse for him for a while, and now he requires it of us again; therefore let us give it to him willingly.
>
> *English Family Life*, ed. Houlbrooke, pp. 142–44[24]

Wallington's chronicle is a revealing account of human emotion at war with religious dogma and orthodox political philosophy. Individual patterns of affection put more or less pressure on the accepted structures of private life, to varying degrees with differing life stories. But there is ample evidence of strong feeling between husbands and wives, masters and servants, brothers and sisters, parents and children. We have Sir John Harington's confiding letters to his wife, written with every evidence of spontaneous affection. "Dear Mall, how shall I speak what I have seen, or what I have felt?" he asks as he reports Elizabeth I's failing health. The letter closes: "Next month I will see thy sweet face, and kiss my boys and maids."[25] There are also Philip Gawdy's letters home from London, including his 1587 reply to his mother's anxious request that he "take heed how to live in this dangerous world." He wrote back: "I do every morning use the brick and wormwood as a remedy against all pestilence and infection that may happen to the body, and I have long since laid up your motherly good council, that I do every day meditate upon as a medicine against all bad company [and] other bad actions whatsoever" (*Letters of Philip Gawdy*, p. 9). This is an evocative hint at the power of a mother's imprint on her children – if not, until the critical turn of recent decades, on history.

In Wallington, Mildmay, and Hoby we see another imbalance in the early modern literature of private life, which is its overrepresentation of the godly, its suppression of the contradictions of political thought and social reality, its representation of compliance rather than resistance and violation. In this literature, recorded instances of serious transgression are rare. We learn of a household in which love did not descend as advised, in which a husband had beaten his wife "grievously," only because the wife's brother, Adam Winthrop, noted in his diary the reason he had taken his sister into his own house on 27 April 1597 (*English Family Life*, ed. Houlbrooke, p. 222). But, for the most part, we need to look to other records, such as cases pursued in the church courts, for evidence of how messy and disorderly private life could be.[26]

If human emotion was one radical in the ideological equation, so, too, was pleasure. While admonitory writings on family and household were serious and full of consequence, Sir Thomas More in his legendary afterlife became the receptacle for a countercultural insistance on the power of diversion and misrule in the personal realm. More's biographies may have gone unpublished in the sixteenth century, but his celebrity nonetheless flourished *outside* authorized media. Here, he was less a tragic martyr on the world stage than a man of many jokes in an explicitly domestic setting.

The comic note was struck early, with *Twelve Merry Jests of the Widow Edith*, supposedly compiled by one of More's men, Walter Smith, in 1525 (but republished as late as 1573).[27] In Jest 10, the Rabelaisian widow arrives at More's house in Chelsea and, with tales of her great "substance," large household, and profitable enterprises, soon attracts the attention of three young men. When she is revealed to be worth not so much as the "sleeve lace of a gown," her comic discipline is undertaken. Her potage and ale are laced with a powder causing rapid pulse, alternating chills and fever, and massive intestinal distress, and she is kept at table despite all pleas to be excused. The "Lady" of the house finally takes pity on her, and Edith races messily for the coalhouse, where the "stinking smoke" that marks her easement causes others to suspect a fire (sigs. F3r–v). Although More does not appear, presumably because it would not have suited the legend for him to have been taken in by the widow's tall tales in the first place, his home is associated with the comic license necessary to the narrative.

John Manningham, a London law student in 1602 and 1603, gave further witness to the nature of More's popular appeal. In a commonplace book, one of the principal Elizabethan genres of private life, Manningham recorded sermons he heard, poems he admired, gossip he entertained, and jokes he enjoyed.[28] One jest positions More at "the height of his prosperity," in his long gallery at home. There, More draws the attention of an old friend to the picture of a death's head with the motto, *Memento morieris*. More terms the work "most excellent for the device and conceit," but his visitor finds the sentence too common to merit remark. More then explains: "Sir, you remember sometimes you borrowed some money of me, but I cannot remember you have remembered to repay it; it is not much, and though I be Chancellor I have use for as little, and now me thinks this picture speaks unto you *Memento Mori aeris*: Remember to pay More his money" (Manningham, *Diary*, pp. 73–74). According to John Harington, More's epigrams "[flew] over all Europe for their wit and conceit."

Perhaps it is not surprising that More's legend also trailed tales of miracles. His grandson, Cresacre, recorded that until the dead body of William Roper was buried, "there was heard once a day for the space of a quarter of an hour the sweetest music that could be imagined, not of any voices of men, but angelical harmony, as a token how gracious that soul was to Almighty God and to the choirs of Angels" (Roper, *Life*, p. xliv). For those of us who today believe in miracles and angels, the tale may be sufficient unto itself. For others of us, though, this mystery may be a symptom of resistance to the overly intellectualized formulas that otherwise dominated the discourse of private life.

In 1607, Sir William Wentworth recorded a domestic miracle, too, and it was the story of his own generation.

> My father, having lived with my mother about xi years and having then issue only four daughters, it pleased God to visit him with a burning fever whereof he languished so that both my mother and his mother were almost in despair of his recovery. He lying thus very weak ... he saw stand by his bedside a well-favored gentlewoman of a middle age in apparel and countenance decent

and very demure; and thinking the sight very strange, he said to her, "Gentle-woman, from whence come you?" She answered, "Wentworth, I come from God." He said, "What is your name?" She said her name was God's pity and that God had sent her to signify unto him that he had compassion of him and that he should have no more fits of that fever. She told him he should live many more years and have a son born and thereupon she took out of her pocket a box of ointment and dipped some of her fingers therein and offered to put her hand into the bed about the middest thereof. But he, bashfully holding the clothes down, seemed to restrain her hand, but she said, "I must touch thee." Whereupon he suffering her, she put her hand into the bed and touched his privities and presently took her hand away and then said, "When thou art well, go to the well at St. Anne of Buxtons and there wash thyself and thank God for thy delivery" ... According to that prediction, he recovered his health, went to the well at Buxtons, washed himself and most humbly thanked God, etc. Afterwards it pleased God that I was born, being the last child he had.[29]

We could read this story many ways: as a miracle, a dream, a religious epiphany, a jest between the only men in a family, a story of pleasure outside marriage, a fantasy of alternative parentage. Perhaps most of all the tale gives evidence that, despite all efforts to codify it, to demystify it, and to find convenient ruling formulas for it, the private life of the sixteenth century was the stuff of legend as surely as was any chronicle of state or myth of nationhood. Of course its literature was shaped by culture and mediated by ideology, but this literature nonetheless gives us glimpses of interpersonal relations, forbidden pleasures, shared jokes, small tragedies, personal triumphs, and private miracles that defied doctrine.

NOTES

1 Henricus Cornelius Agrippa von Nettesheim, *The Commendation of Matri-mony* (1526), trans. David Clapham (London: 1540; STC 201, sigs. C7v–C8r). *The Commendation*, translated from the Latin in 1540, either shared a common source with or was quoted by many native English authors. Much of the material in this section is treated at greater length in my *Private Matters and Public Culture in Post-Reformation England* (Ithaca, NY: Cornell University Press, 1994), which should also be consulted for further bibliography.
2 William Whately, *A Care-Cloth* (London: 1624; STC 25299), sig. A4v.
3 Henry Smith, *A Preparative to Marriage* (London: 1591; STC 22685), sigs. H7r–v (emphasis added).
4 Jean Bodin, *The Six Bookes of a Commonweale* (1576), trans. Richard Knolles (1606), ed. Kenneth Douglas McRae (Cambridge: Harvard University Press, 1962), sig. C2r. Like Agrippa, Bodin was translated into English. His reception and influence can be attributed to the fact that his writing resonated with an English audience.

5 William Gouge, *Of Domestical Duties* (London: 1622; STC 12119), sigs. A1v–A2r.

6 *Certain Sermons or Homilies*, ed. Mary Ellen Rickey and Thomas B. Stroup (Gainesville, FL: Scholars' Facsimiles and Reprints, 1968), p. 242.

7 William Whately, *A Bride-Bush, or a Wedding Sermon* (London: 1617; STC 25296), sigs. D2r–v.

8 William Harrison, *The Description of England* (2nd edn., 1587), ed. Georges Edelen, Folger Documents of Tudor and Stuart Civilization (Ithaca, NY: Cornell University Press, 1968), pp. 200–01.

9 John Dod and Robert Cleaver, *A Godly Form of Household Government* (London: 1598; STC 5382), sig. L5v.

10 From *Il Moro: Ellis Heywood's Dialogue in Memory of Thomas More* (1556), ed. and trans. Roger Lee Deakins (Cambridge: Harvard University Press, 1972), p. 3.

11 William Roper, *The Lyfe of Sir Thomas Moore, Knighte*, ed. Elsie Vaughan Hitchcock, Early English Text Society, No. 197 (London: Oxford University Press, 1935), p. 3.

12 Nicholas Harpsfield, *The life and death of Sr Thomas Moore, knight, sometymes Lord high Chancellor of England*, ed. Elsie Vaughan Hitchcock and R. W. Chambers, Early English Text Society, No. 186 (London: Oxford University Press, 1932), p. 93.

13 *The Complete Works of St. Thomas More*, vol. IV, *Utopia*, ed. Edward Surtz, SJ, and J. H. Hexter (New Haven: Yale University Press, 1965), pp. 39–41.

14 See chapter one of *Renaissance Self-Fashioning: From More to Shakespeare* (Chicago: University of Chicago Press, 1980). For different readings, see Jonathan V. Crewe, "The 'Encomium Moriae' of William Roper," *ELH* 55:2 (Summer 1988): 287–307; and F. W. Conrad, "Manipulating Reputations: Sir Thomas More, Sir Thomas Elyot, and the Conclusion of William Roper's *Lyfe of Sir Thomas Moore, Knighte*," in *The Rhetorics of Life-Writing in Early Modern Europe: Forms of Biography from Cassandra Fedele to Louis XIV*, ed. Thomas F. Mayer and D. R. Woolf (Ann Arbor: University of Michigan Press, 1995), pp. 133–61.

15 On one occasion, More's daughter Margaret seemed near death of the sweating sickness. In prayer in the New Building, More was inspired to try a "glister," or enema. His intervention saved his daughter's life. Had Margaret died, More is said to have attested, he "would never have meddled with worldly matters after" (Roper, *Life*, pp. 28–29). See Crewe, "The 'Encomium Moriae,'" on the "incestuousness" of More's relationship with Margaret.

16 Such was also the case with the life compiled by Ro. Ba. around 1598. Heywood's *Il Moro* was published in Italian in Florence in 1556; Thomas Stapleton's *Vita Thomae Mori* in Latin in Douai in 1588. The play known as the *Book of Sir Thomas More* (c. 1593), by Anthony Munday and others, never reached the stage. An English translation of *Il Moro* may have been attempted in 1601, but if it was achieved it has not survived. Around 1630 Cresacre More's *Life of Thomas More* was finally published in English, but in Douai.

17 Grace Mildmay's writings are excerpted in *With Faith and Physic: The Life of a Tudor Gentlewoman, Lady Grace Mildmay, 1552–1620*, ed. Linda Pollock (New York: St. Martin's Press, 1993). All references are to this edition, but see

also Randall Martin's annotated transcription of "The Autobiography of Grace, Lady Mildmay," *Renaissance and Reformation/Renaissance et Réforme*, 18:1 (Winter 1994): 33–81.

18 Books of advice compiled by men were also highly conventionalized, a point I owe to Richard Helgerson. See, for example, *Advice to a Son: Precepts of Lord Burghley, Sir Walter Raleigh, and Francis Osborne*, ed. Louis B. Wright, Folger Documents of Tudor and Stuart Civilization (Ithaca, NY: Cornell University Press, 1962).

19 For a full account of this case and other "adversities," see Pollock's introductory section, "Family Affairs," in *With Faith and Physic*, pp. 4–22.

20 Excerpted in *English Family Life, 1576–1716: An Anthology from Diaries*, ed. Ralph Houlbrooke (Oxford: Basil Blackwell, 1988), p. 55.

21 For the convenience of the reader, citations are to *The Private Life of an Elizabethan Lady: The Diary of Lady Margaret Hoby, 1599–1605*, ed. Joanna Moody (Phoenix Mill, UK: Alan Sutton, 1998). This edition does not entirely supersede *Diary of Lady Margaret Hoby, 1599–1605*, ed. Dorothy M. Meads (Boston: Houghton Mifflin, 1930), and I am indebted to Meads for the biographical information given below.

22 For reference to Holinshed, see *Letters of Philip Gawdy ... 1579–1616*, ed. Isaac Herbert Jeayes (London: J. B. Nichols, 1906), p. 99. For Stow, see the anonymous play *The Puritan*, ed. A. F. Hopkinson (London: M. E. Sims, 1894), p. 75. These references are unusual for naming Holinshed and Stow, but the idea of "deserving a chronicle" was commonplace; many instances could be cited. On the genre, see Annabel Patterson, *Reading Holinshed's Chronicles* (Chicago: University of Chicago Press, 1994).

23 See *The Diaries of Lady Anne Clifford*, ed. D. J. H. Clifford (Phoenix Mill, UK: Alan Sutton, 1990), p. 82 for 27 December 1619. On 1 April 1619 Clifford had recorded that she "wrote in the Chronicles" (p. 71).

24 See also Paul S. Seaver, *Wallington's World: A Puritan Artisan in Seventeenth-Century London* (Stanford, CA: Stanford University Press, 1985). This account is all the more interesting given Lawrence Stone's notorious argument that parent–child relations were not affective; see *The Family, Sex and Marriage in England, 1500–1800* (New York: Harper & Row, 1977).

25 *The Letters and Epigrams of Sir John Harington*, ed. Norman Egbert McClure (Philadelphia: University of Pennsylvania Press, 1930), pp. 96–98.

26 See, for example, Laura Gowing, *Domestic Dangers: Women, Words, and Sex in Early Modern London*, Oxford Studies in Social History (Oxford: Clarendon Press, 1996); Martin Ingram, *Church Courts, Sex and Marriage in England, 1570–1640*, Past and Present Publications (Cambridge: Cambridge University Press, 1987); and the forthcoming work of Loreen Giese.

27 Walter Smith, *Twelve Merry Jests of the Widow Edith* (London: 1573; STC 22870). I am indebted to Anne Lake Prescott, "Crime and Carnival at Chelsea: Widow Edith and Thomas More's Household," in *Miscellanea Moreana: Essays for Germain Marc'hadour*, ed. Claire E. Murphy, Henri Gibaud, and Mario A. Di Cesare (Binghamton, NY: MRTS, 1989), pp. 247–64.

28 *The Diary of John Manningham of the Middle Temple, 1602–1603*, ed. Robert Parker Sorlien (Hanover, NH: University Press of New England for the University of Rhode Island, 1976). Manningham's diary gives evidence that the

anecdote recounted below, which was repeated in Cresacre More's biography of Thomas More, was in oral circulation for at least two decades before reaching print.

29 William Wentworth, in *Wentworth Papers, 1597–1628*, ed. J. P. Cooper, Royal Historical Society, Camden Fourth Series, 12 (1973), pp. 28–29.

FURTHER READING

Belsey, Catherine, *The Subject of Tragedy: Identity and Difference in Renaissance Drama* (London: Methuen, 1985).

Collinson, Patrick, *The Religion of Protestants: The Church in English Society, 1559–1625* (Oxford: Oxford University Press, 1982).

Cressy, David, *Literacy and the Social Order: Reading and Writing in Tudor and Stuart England* (Cambridge: Cambridge University Press, 1980).

Dolan, Frances E., *Dangerous Familiars: Representations of Domestic Crime in England, 1550–1700* (Ithaca, NY: Cornell University Press, 1994).

Erickson, Amy Louise, *Women and Property in Early Modern England* (London: Routledge, 1993).

Ezell, Margaret J. M., *The Patriarch's Wife: Literary Evidence and the History of the Family* (Chapel Hill: University of North Carolina Press, 1987).

Henderson, Diana E., "The Theater and Domestic Culture," in *A New History of Early English Drama*, ed. John D. Cox and David Scott Kastan (New York: Columbia University Press, 1997), pp. 173–94.

Houlbrooke, Ralph A., *The English Family, 1450–1700*, Themes in British Social History (London: Longman, 1984).

Hutson, Lorna, *The Usurer's Daughter: Male Friendship and Fictions of Women in Sixteenth-Century England* (London: Routledge, 1994).

Laslett, Peter, *The World We Have Lost – Further Explored*, 3rd edn. (London: Methuen, 1983).

Lucas, R. Valerie, "Puritan Preaching and the Politics of the Family," in *The Renaissance Englishwoman in Print: Counterbalancing the Canon*, ed. Anne M. Haselkorn and Betty S. Travitsky (Amherst: University of Massachusetts Press, 1990), pp. 224–40.

Mendelson, Sara Heller, "Stuart Women's Diaries and Occasional Memoirs," in *Women in English Society, 1500–1800*, ed. Mary Prior (London: Methuen, 1985), pp. 181–210.

Orlin, Lena Cowen, *Private Matters and Public Culture in Post-Reformation England* (Ithaca, NY: Cornell University Press, 1994).

Powell, Chilton Latham, *English Domestic Relations, 1487–1653* (New York: Columbia University Press, 1917).

Schochet, Gordon J., *Patriarchalism in Political Thought: The Authoritarian Family and Political Speculation and Attitudes Especially in Seventeenth-Century England* (New York: Basic Books, 1975).

Smith, Bruce, *Homosexual Desire in Shakespeare's England: A Cultural Poetics* (Chicago: University of Chicago Press, 1991).

Warnicke, Retha M., "Private and Public: The Boundaries of Women's Lives in Early Stuart England," in *Privileging Gender in Early Modern England*, ed.

Jean R. Brink (Kirksville, MO: Sixteenth-Century Journal Publishers, 1993), pp. 123–40.

Wayne, Valerie, Introduction to *The Flower of Friendship, a Renaissance Dialogue Contesting Marriage, by Edmund Tilney* (Ithaca, NY: Cornell University Press, 1992), pp. 1–93.

Wrightson, Keith, *English Society, 1580–1680* (London: Hutchinson, 1982.)

13

GARRETT SULLIVAN AND LINDA WOODBRIDGE

Popular culture in print

In *A Discourse of English Poetry*, 1586, William Webbe claims that the need for such a text, designed to aid readers in identifying a native poetic tradition, emerges out of the explosive proliferation of printed works and the problems they pose for exercising judgment.

> Among the innumerable sorts of English books, and infinite fardels of printed pamphlets, wherewith this country is pestered, all shops stuffed, and every study furnished, the greatest part I think ... are such as ... tend in some respect ... to poetry ... If I write something concerning what I think of our English poets, or adventure to set down my simple judgement of English poetry, I trust the learned poets will give me leave, and vouchsafe my book passage ... to stir up some other of meet ability to bestow [travail] in this matter: whereby I think we may not only get the means, which we yet want, to discern between good writers and bad, but perhaps also challenge from the rude multitude of rustical rhymers, who will be called poets, the right practice and orderly course of true poetry.

According to Webbe, so many books and pamphlets are being produced that they are pestering the country, stuffing both shop and study. How, then, to distinguish among them all? Webbe's answer is to produce a book of his own that identifies important poetic works, and then to appeal to "learned poets" to "vouchsafe [his] book passage" through the text-infested waters of English print culture. If Webbe here assumes an alliance of poet and critic, the figures against whom they are allied are those we might associate with popular culture: "the rude multitude of rustical rhymers." Like the stacks of books and pamphlets that promise to bury works of value beneath them, the disorder implicit in the presence of the rude "multitude" stands in opposition to "the right practice and orderly course of true poetry." These "rustical rhymers" appear further on as "the uncountable rabble of rhyming ballad makers and compilers of senseless sonnets" who "can frame an alehouse song of five or six score verses ... and perhaps observe just number of syllables." On the other hand, Webbe defines English poetry as "any work ... learnedly compiled in measurable speech, and framed in words containing number or proportion of just syllables, delighting the readers or hearers ... by the apt and decent framing of words."

Much could be said about the oppositions that undergird Webbe's analysis – rudeness vs. decorum, rusticity vs. urbanity, folk vs. Continental humanist tradition, multitudinousness vs. selectivity, ignorance vs. learnedness, alehouse vs. gentleman's study. Such distinctions are commonplace at the end of the sixteenth century, and Webbe's text offers a glimpse of an imperative that motivates them: a "popular" culture is generated in opposition to a high one. While Webbe sees himself as identifying a native poetic tradition, we suggest that he is helping to construct it. For Webbe, the construction of the popular is bred of the problem of print's spectacular growth in the sixteenth century. While print would seem to fix ideas, to render them permanent and widely available, the printing press's effects often suggested the opposite; as Jan-Dirk Muller shows, the widespread dissemination and massive production of texts made the orderly transmission of ideas, once enshrined in the manuscript culture of the medieval scriptorium, an impossibility. New ways needed to be generated to produce order out of the chaos of print. One way was the production of learned and popular cultures, which satisfied a need to classify (and to dismiss), and brought order to the "innumerable sorts" and the "infinite fardels." But, despite the present-day familiarity of these oppositions, they are not inevitable; in fact, efforts like Webbe's to construct a high tradition, coincident with a broader cultural program to elevate the status of the English language, mark a rupture from earlier conceptions of the social location of the texts that we would today designate as popular. If the seams of Webbe's tradition are showing – as when he asserts in one clause that the means are still lacking to "discern between good writers and bad," while in the next he insists that the "rustical rhymers" are to be challenged as false poets – that should remind us that both the tradition and that which it opposes are in the late sixteenth century still being stitched together.

This discussion of Webbe hints at several topics, each important for understanding popular culture in print: the conceptual and logistical problems posed by the growth of print; the relationship between the production, distribution, and consumption of printed texts and the principles by which they are classified; and the historical construction of elite and popular. We will touch upon these topics while focusing on the sixteenth-century history of three kinds of printed texts: broadside or street ballads, jest books, and rogue literature. Before doing so, however, we must confront the central question of this endeavor: what is popular culture?

POPULAR CULTURE

Peter Burke's *Popular Culture in Early Modern Europe*, arguably the most influential and important account of early modern popular culture, asserts that the sixteenth century marked the beginning of a gradual reformation of manners and morals that required the separation of elite and popular cultures. (For other theorists of popular culture, see Pierre Bourdieu, Stephen Kaplan, Lori Humphrey Newcomb, Scott Cutler Shershow, and Margaret Spufford.) Both clergy and members of elite society increasingly distanced themselves from "popular" practices that were seen as irreligious (if not pagan) and licentious. "In the case of the clergy," Burke writes, "withdrawal was part of the Catholic and [in England] Protestant reformations." As for nobles and members of the merchant classes who imitated them, they

> were adopting more "polished" manners, a new and more self-conscious style of behaviour, modelled on the courtesy-books ... The nobleman learned to speak and write "correctly," according to formal rules, and to avoid the technical terms and the dialect words used by craftsmen and peasants ... As their military role declined, the nobility had to find other ways of justifying their privileges: they had to show they were different from other people.

Burke's argument about the nobility, drawn from the work of Norbert Elias, obviously mirrors the process of tradition construction that Webbe advocated, and the reformations of manners and of verse, each with an emphasis on decorum, are clearly interconnected. As Burke's nobles "had to show they were different from other people," Webbe puts distance between "learned poets" and "ragged rhymers."

But who are these people and what are the practices that the social and literary elite felt the need to separate from? And what is "popular" about them? The first question is easily answered, the second less so. Burke talks of the distinction between the "great" and "little" traditions: "the great tradition was transmitted formally at grammar schools and universities," and the "little tradition" includes folk dancing, ballad singing, popular drama such as mumming or nativity plays, and puppetry. Importantly, as Burke notes, this little tradition did not belong exclusively to non-elite social groups, but elite participation began to diminish in the second half of the sixteenth century. However, the mere fact of this participation, no matter the degree to which it took place, poses a problem. Given elite involvement in the little tradition, in what way was it "popular"? Or, more broadly, how do we define the popular? This second question was first posed and answered almost two centuries after Webbe. As Burke's first chapter, "The Discovery of the People," makes clear, it is only in the late eighteenth and early nineteenth centuries that the kinds of practices labeled above as popular became the subject of European intellectual inquiry. This "discovery" was actually a creation, the constitution of a primitive culture of "the folk" celebrated for its "purity" and "communalism," its simplicity and closeness to nature (see Burke, *Popular Culture*, pp. 21–22). This act of creation is the obverse of the process we have witnessed as beginning in the late sixteenth century; but while there is a change in emphasis from vulgarity to purity, from crudeness to primitivism, from excoriating the "rude multitude" to celebrating it, still at each cultural moment the high is set up in opposition to the low or the popular.

Burke repudiates the scholarly definition of the popular as the articulation of the spirit of the folk. However, despite his recognition of elite involvement in "popular" activities, he cannot seem to avoid the high/low opposition upon which eighteenth- and nineteenth-century discussions of the popular are based. In fact, Burke understands the popular as that which the elite is not, defining popular culture "in a negative way as unofficial culture, the culture of the non-elite." Burke's initial definition gives way to others, but they pose new problems, as they shift the focus from culture to cultural forms: "Popular culture may be described as a stock of genres, but also, in close-up, as a stock of forms (schemata, motifs, themes, formulae)." Burke's first definition depends upon a negativity: popular culture is what elite culture isn't (i.e., "unofficial," "non-elite"). Popular culture as "a stock of genres" is positive, producing a body of materials that can be analyzed and evaluated. What this suggests is that we know what is meant by "popular culture," and that this meaning inheres in a set group of texts. But Burke's first definition is both more unsettling and more accurate. What marks popular culture as popular is not a set of textual attributes, but its place in a high/low binarism in which the popular is that which the elite is not.

As Peter Stallybrass and Allon White have shown, the high/low opposition is basic to "mechanisms of ordering and sense-making in European cultures." It is important to note that the high-low binarism exists in a complex and uncertain relationship to the social world, which includes "the middling sort." It may be, as Stallybrass argues in "'Wee feaste in our Defense'," that some of the work done by the construction of elite and popular traditions was designed to efface the middle classes. Nevertheless, both Burke and sixteenth-century commentators write repeatedly in terms of elite and popular, high and low. In recording their emphases we do not intend to accept them as accurate in their social description.

Concerning Burke, we emphasize first that in conceptualizing the popular the distinction must be maintained between *those texts classified as popular* and *the classifying process that produces the popular,* and second, that the definition of popular culture that underwrites analyses like Burke's is an anachronistic one, dependent upon the very process of separation between elite and popular that his book chronicles the emergence of. While Webbe creates a high tradition out of its opposition to the low and Burke creates a low tradition out of its opposition to the high, both traditions make sense only as categories that emerge over the course of the sixteenth century out of attempts to classify, to make orderly. Burke himself reminds us repeatedly that the elite were, at least for most of the sixteenth century, actively involved in those practices demarcated as popular. "In 1500," we are told, "popular culture was everyone's culture; a second culture for the educated, and the only culture for everyone else. By 1800, however, in most parts of Europe, the clergy, the nobility, the merchants, the professional men – and their wives – had abandoned popular culture to the lower classes, from whom they were now separated ... by profound differences in world view." But these examples trouble our sense of the category of the popular. If these activities are performed for, produced by and/or include the elite, what happens to the definition of the popular, predicated as it is upon opposition to the elite? Doesn't the fact that "popular culture was everyone's culture" demolish the popular as an historically specific descriptive category? While the distinction between high and low is fundamental to Burke's argument, in the early sixteenth century it is not the primary axis along which, say, ballad singing or participation in May Day rituals are read. Nevertheless, it is appropriate to see this period's importance to the construction of, in the service of its "opposite," what has come to be called the popular. We will argue, following Roger Chartier, not that intrinsically "popular" practices or texts were appropriated as such, but that the appropriation of such practices and texts entailed their designation as "popular." Appropriation, then, properly refers not to the simple taking up of a preexisting object or practice, but to the reconstitution of that object or practice in terms of a new interpretive paradigm: to appropriate is to construct. Three kinds of texts will help us track the ways in which the sixteenth century constituted "popular culture."

STREET BALLADS

Probably the most maligned of all early modern texts is the broadside or street ballad, described by Joy Wiltenburg as "a single printed sheet, usually decorated with rough woodcuts. A huge variety of subjects – including knightly adventure, ill-fated love, grisly news of murder or war, religious and moral precepts, jests, prodigies, and portents – appeared in songs, to be sold by street singers and country peddlers. Tunes were indicated by name, with no musical notation; audiences either knew the tune beforehand or learned it from the ballad seller." The topicality of ballads is one of their most important features, and it is partly this topicality that insures that even as ballads are denigrated by elites, they are consumed not only by the "people" but by representatives of all social levels. In the years before newsbooks, emerging in the late 1500s but not widespread until the seventeenth century, the news ballad was an important way of disseminating information. An example from 1596 tells the story of the fall of Calais in that year. "Calais, [her] woeful Lamentation for her hapless spoil," sung to the tune of "Crimson velvet," describes in garish detail the result of Spain's attack: "[A]ll her streets with blood doth run. / Her babes here murdered lie; / In vain her virgins cry, / Helplessly they are undone" (in *Shirburn Ballads*, ed. Clark). However, the news of Calais' fall is soon framed in terms of English concerns and national identity, matters of intellectual (not merely sensational) interest. After excoriating the Spanish for their brutality, and comparing their occupation of Calais with the earlier benevolent and paternalistic rule of the English, the ballad praises Queen and Country: "*England*, kind and fair, / God preserve and bless thee! / For thy royal Queen, / Lord prolong her days! / *Flanders* she hath helped, / And poor *France* distresséd, / To her endless fame / And eternal praise." The final stanza has Calais praying for England and wishing Elizabeth "many years and happy days"; at the same time, the ballad tacitly urges English military preparedness, for "*Spain*'s oppression hath no end."

If "Calais, [her] woeful Lamentation" disseminates news and celebrates England's glory, a ballad from 1585 entitled "The poor people's complaint" (sung to the tune of "Light a Love") describes in detail the decline of hospitality in sixteenth-century England. The first stanza offers a proleptic echo of Jonson's "To Penshurst" and its characterization of the stately households to which Penshurst is in opposition:

> We go to brave buildings of fair brick and stone,
> Where men of great calling live lordly alone.
> We ask it for God's sake, but none will come near us.
> We crave it for Christ's sake, yet no man will hear us.
> *Lord help us, Lord help us, Lord help us with speed.*
> *Come now, lord, and help thy poor people that need.*

Lamenting the death of the Earl of Bedford, a benefactor of the poor, the ballad conventionally alludes to a lost golden age, a "merry England" distinguished by the benign paternalism of its aristocrats and gentry, kind landlords all. The ballad thus takes up one of the crucial issues of the age, most pressing in the wake of Henry VIII's expropriation of the monasteries: the reconceptualization of land-based social relations under an emergent capitalism. Intervening in the gradual ideological transformation of land from the locus of a moral economy to an aggregation of saleable plots, the ballad reveals connections with traditions of agrarian complaint and reform, and of satire; it demands that "rich [estate] stewards take heed how they live," emphasizing the moral imperatives that should underpin land management, and castigates "rich worldlings that live without shame." Far from a simple outpouring of "popular" sentiment, "The poor people's complaint" intersects not only with "high" literary forms but with issues that in the sixteenth century were being negotiated at all social levels.

That the street ballad takes up issues crucial to all does not mean that it was taken seriously by all. The examples above reveal not only the timeliness but also the "crudity" of the verse we have come to see as "popular." In fact, such crudity helped enable the ballad's construction as "popular" during the late sixteenth century. While the folk ballad was still in evidence at this time, Natascha Würzbach notes that in critical discourse "the term 'ballad' . . . applied exclusively to the street ballad."

> Literary criticism at the turn of the sixteenth century and during the seventeenth century already indicated very clearly an awareness of the distinction between accepted literature which was legitimized and hallowed by patronage and cultural institutions on the one hand, and an inferior level of popular literature on the other, even though critics lacked the appropriate terminology. This is particularly obvious in the case of the street ballad. [See also the work of Sharon Achinstein.]

We can extrapolate from Würzbach's account to see that the street ballad functioned in the way discussed above, to help define "accepted" and "legitimized" literature by being constructed as its "popular" opposite.

While printed ballads had initially been composed by a range of writers, by century's end they were deemed appropriate only to the world of alehouse poets and vagrant songsters. Leslie Shephard charts changes in authorship: while at the beginning of the sixteenth century street ballads were written by the likes of John Skelton and Leonard Stopes, there soon arose "a class of professional balladists" which included "writers like William Elderton and Thomas Deloney. Elderton, sixteenth-century actor, comedian and ballad writer was famous for his love of liquor, and his red nose." From Skelton and Stopes, a poet laureate and a priest, to professional writers like the famously bibulous Elderton. Shephard's account of shifts in authorship also nicely limns the change in the social location of the street ballad, a form that was once aligned with courtiers and clergymen but that gradually became linked with, in Thomas Nashe's terms, "every rednose fiddler" and "ignorant ale knight."

While by century's end literary texts associate the street ballad almost exclusively with alehouses and pot poets, these broadsides circulated more widely and across all social classes, as evidenced by Pepys' famous seventeenth-century collection of printed ballads, or by the commonplace book that Tessa Watt adduces as proof that "the broadside was familiar amongst the most 'elite' groups of sixteenth-century society." Though this familiarity does not suggest that in 1700 all classes were engaged in *producing* broadsides, it does document the pervasiveness of their distribution and consumption. Thus, while the broadside ballad was routinely yoked to taverns, alehouses, and "such other places of base resort," and its singing was read by Robert Greene in *The Third and Last Part of Cony-Catching* as a pickpocket's ruse outside of a London playhouse, the ballad was distributed throughout the nation and to people of all social ranks, a fact that undermines any attempt we might make to figure the ballad as belonging solely to the "little tradition," or its topics as being intrinsically "popular." Nevertheless, critics do attempt to construct it as such, sometimes betraying the "guilty pleasures" of their own engagement with the texts they denigrate, as in Sir William Cornwallis' account of listening to the ballad singer whose efforts he mocks, or in Sidney's famous simultaneous dismissal and begrudging appreciation of "some blind crowder['s]" rendering of *Chevy Chase*. These gentlemen both engaged with "popular culture" and constructed distinct aesthetic/social spheres and practices that are necessary to the eventual configuration of the popular as a category opposed to the elite.

Just as important as the ballad's subject matter are the circumstances surrounding its production, consumption, and distribution. Consider Henry Chettle's description of

> a company of idle youths, loathing honest labour and despising lawful trades, [who] betake them to a vagrant and vicious life, in every corner of cities and market towns of the realm singing and selling of ballads and pamphlets full of ribaldry, and all scurrilous vanity, to the profanation of God's name, and withdrawing people from Christian exercises, especially at fairs, markets, and such public meetings.

The reference to "a vagrant and vicious life" is a pointed one, since the itinerant ballad sellers, who functioned also as singers of the ballads they sold, were commonly linked with vagabondage. In fact, as Watt shows, ballad sellers often were "guildless, 'masterless' men, and our records of them come almost solely from their prosecutions as vagrants." Moreover, the sites of their selling were "common" ones, such as "fairs, markets, and ... public meetings"; their very commonness not only inspired dismissiveness in many, but it also raised the spectre of revolt. The formation of groups, sometimes around vagrant ballad singers, represented the possibility of social disorder, a possibility heightened for Chettle by the fact that the ballad (or, for that matter, the alehouse) lured people away from orderly "Christian exercises."

Fear of such a possibility was increased by the perception that ballads were often seditious. While the Stationers' Company was incorporated in 1557 to regulate the production and sale of printed texts, Chettle assumes that ballads flout such regulation. According to Watt he is wrong, for about two-thirds of printed ballads were licensed, a ratio that holds for books as well. Nevertheless, Chettle explicitly links ballads to unlicensed printers, who are "Devil's instruments, intruders into printing's mystery, by whom ... religion [has] in the least measure [i.e. not insignificantly been] hindered ... These basilisks ... have first infected London ... [with that which is] in every street abusively chanted. This error (overspreading the realm) has in no small measure increased in Essex and the shires thereto adjoining." Whether metaphorized as infection or the proliferation of "error," the distribution of ballads from London to the country beyond indirectly refers to the movement of vagrant pedlars and ballad singers hawking pirated texts. Chettle's emphasis on the illegal production, sites of consumption, and means of distribution of the ballad is telling, for it suggests that the scandal of the ballad emerges not solely from the profane subject matter of many ballads. Instead, its pernicious "popularity," manifested in the fact it is "in every street abusively chanted," lies in the ballad's vagrant distributors, its irreligious sites of consumption, and its unlicensed point of origin.

JEST BOOKS

An important test case for the validity of "popular" as a cultural category for sixteenth-century texts is the jest book, to our century a quintessentially "popular" genre. In early Tudor England, "merry jest" was almost a technical term for broadly comic tales in prose or verse that rejoiced in untimely farts, picturesque petty revenges, and buffetings about the pate. Verse and prose jests share trickster heroes, slapstick humor, a repertoire of vulgarities, and delight in revenge. If "high" and "low" make any sense at all as descriptors, these vulgar jesting tales would seem to be "low."

The term "popular" was first applied to Tudor jest books, tellingly, in the late eighteenth and early nineteenth century, when Romantics were valorizing "folk" culture. Joseph Ritson's *Pieces of Ancient Popular Poetry* contained *A Merry Jest of the Friar and the Boy*, which he identifies as one of the "favorites of the people" and locates within oral tradition, to be sung "at marriages, wakes and other festive meetings ... [to] the tinkling of a harp." Edward Vernon Utterson's *Select Pieces of Early Popular Poetry* includes the verse jest *The Wife Lapped in Morel's Skin*, which a few years later William Hazlitt called a "valuable record and illustration of the manners of the *lower classes* in England" (emphasis his). The title of Hazlitt's collection, like Ritson's and Utterson's, posited the category "popular poetry," and in his collection *Shakespeare Jest-Books* he called these pieces "light literature." Twentieth-century scholars have largely accepted the categories adduced by Hazlitt and company. P. M. Zall, who edited the jest books in 1963, is representative: "The jestbooks are not 'literary' ... [not] works of art, with preconceived design and concern for artistic integrity of style and content." They are, in short, "popular."

Whether jest books are dismissed as popular and trivial, or valued for the earthiness that made them authentic emanations of the folk mind, Tudor jest books and their readers have routinely been situated on the "low" end of the "high/low" spectrum. It may startle us, then, to learn that a letter penned in 1603 reports that Queen Elizabeth listened to readings from *A Hundred Merry Tales* on her deathbed (see *Calendar of State Papers*). And as it happens, jest books were promulgated by Renaissance humanists of impeccable intellectual credentials; in fact, they formed an important part of the humanist program from its beginnings. The father of Italian humanism, Petrarch, composed a jest book in Latin, 1343–45, which included an elephant joke. An extensive collection, *Facetiae*, was assembled in the late fifteenth century by Poggio Bracciolini, a crucial figure in European humanism who unearthed long-neglected classical texts, thus enabling a revolution in classical learning. Even Erasmus framed a jest collection as a dialogue, "Convivium Fabulosum," with jest-tellers named Polymythus ("teller of many tales"), Gelasinus ("laughter"), Eutrapelus ("witty"), Philythlus ("lover of nonsense"), Philogelos ("laughter-loving"), and Lerochares ("joker"). (On the centrality of jesting to the humanist project, see Linda Woodbridge's forthcoming *Placeless in the Renaissance*. For an important collection of jests, see Barbara Bowen, *One Hundred Renaissance Jokes*.)

It is also a form that was often directed toward the elite. The English jest collection *Tales and Quick Answers* imitates Continental humanist collections, drawing most of its jests from Poggio and Erasmus; *A Hundred Merry Tales* borrows fewer, but still aims at educated readers – many of its jokes require knowledge of Latin. Serious writers such as Sir Thomas More or Hugh Latimer drew on jest books in humanist and theological works. A member of More's household wrote the jest book *Widow Edith*, and More's brother-in-law John Rastell was the printer of *A Hundred Merry Tales*, which several scholars have suspected More of writing. More himself published a verse jest in 1516, contemporary with *Utopia*.

Humanists gave educational, social, or medical reasons for purveying jokes: jests were useful to orators, essential to a gentleman's conversation, necessary to health. One section of the medical treatise *Mensa Philosophica* allied jest books with humanist medicine: its 241 jests promoted health through relaxing the mind. Such rationalizations suggest qualms: the jests *are* frivolous, vulgar, and cruel. The personnel of humanist jests are socially a cut above those in jest books not represented explicitly in humanist terms (legates and ambassadors rather than shoemakers and millers). But in individual jests, readers would be hard put to distinguish between the humanist jesting of Poggio, Erasmus, or Castiglione and the jesting in collections we dub "popular" – *A Hundred Merry Tales* or *A Man Called Howlglas*. Poggio's collection rejoices in a full complement of fart jokes, and Erasmus' concluding fart joke, which identifies words issuing from the mouth with farts issuing from the anus, bears a troubled relation to the humanist celebration of language. Jests – even crude belly-laugh jests reveling in the lower bodily stratum – loomed large in the humanist project. Though jokes are an accepted folklore genre, even folklorists credit their invention to Renaissance humanists, not the Folk (see, for example, Lutz Röhrich, *Folktales and Reality*, p. 52).

Given their humanist provenance, how did jest books get associated with popular culture? As with ballads, the shift happened during the sixteenth century. In the late Middle Ages and early Renaissance – from Poggio to Castiglione – jesting's class valence was patrician. Like the major jest theorist Cicero, Renaissance humanists offered jesting as a tool to help the well-born and educated get the better of their peers in an argument (judicial or social), ornament their writings, or show off elegant social graces. Poggio, a papal secretary, jested to skirmish with other papal secretaries; Castiglione sets jesting in the polished court of Urbino. Running alongside this jesting *inter pares* was a didactic tradition of jesting in sermons preached by educated clergy to an unlettered laity; socially, these jests flowed downward. Tudor jest theorist Thomas Wilson imagines jests used mainly in this way. In 1553, he advised that merry stories delight the "rude and ignorant": "Talk altogether of most grave matters ... and you shall see the ignorant ... either fall asleep, or else bid you farewell. The multitude must needs be made merry." By the late sixteenth century, some writers spoke of a conflict between high culture products like the works of Cicero and low-culture items like *Scoggin's Jests*: Gabriel Harvey complained, in 1593, "The Ciceronian may sleep, 'til the Scogginist hath played his part; one sure cony-catcher, worth twenty philosophers . . . the less of Cambridge, or Oxford." Other writings attest to Harvey's having read not only *Scoggin's Jests* but also *Skelton's Jests* and *A Man Called Howlglas*; far from withdrawing entirely from "popular" culture, the educated, like Cornwallis and Sidney with their ballads, consumed jest books even while scoffing at them. But as with ballads, the elite were no longer *producing* jest books by the 1590s. In 1516, Thomas More himself had written a jogging verse jest, *How a Sergeant Would Learn to be a Friar*; by the 1590s, no one remotely of More's stature would have dreamed of attaching his name to such a thing. "Jesters" and "rhymers," Samuel Ward declared in a sermon in 1617, belonged to "the rabblement." In the later sixteenth century, jest books were hived off into a lower cultural category, now seen as emanating *from* the masses and serving as a temptation to the educated. What looks like an elite appropriation turns out to have been *imposed* on the masses by the elite, and the process of disowning by which humanists relegated jest books to popular culture can almost be called a depropriation.

But though Renaissance humanists borrowed a few jests from classical sources, many others were medieval – couldn't this have been a true appropriation, a high-brow adoption from medieval peasant sources? We should not rule the possibility out of court. The German intellectual Heinrich Bebel, for example, describes his jests as homespun German tales, and he hailed from a peasant background. But the sources of jests are murky, nearly untraceable, and we are anyway less interested in their origins, which can never be located and always recede before the investigator, than in the way they were categorized and positioned during different periods. Even in the Middle Ages jests – at least as they have reached us – were more likely to be aimed downwards from the educated than to spring up from the peasantry. As Stanley J. Kahrl and others have shown, a major medieval source for humanist jests was the *exempla* or lively little tales with which preachers sauced sermons. This was a top-down operation: *exemplum* theory, notes Joanna Lipking, stresses "the intractable nature of ignorant audiences," their likeliness to sleep during sermons if not entertained. Time and again, what look like "popular" affiliations for jest books' sexy, earthy tales vanish under scrutiny. (The formulaic nature of Tudor verse jests is perhaps the best evidence linking these pieces to oral tradition; see Woodbridge, "New Light." Oral tradition itself, however, is no guarantee of a work's "popular" status – epics belonging entirely to oral tradition were sung in royal courts by singers of professional standing.) All we can really see from this historical vantage point is that jest books were disseminated by the educated; if there ever was a "popular" jest tradition, we have no access to it except as mediated through the writings of the educated.

Whose interests were served by the pretense that jest books were "popular"? Again, we may adduce Norbert Elias' theory that during the sixteenth century, the aristocracy differentiated itself from the middling sort by increasing refinement. Erasmus and other humanists wrote books on manners, recommending codes of conduct that avoided bodily contact, shunned spitting, avoided food others had touched. Reflecting humanism's increasing suspicion of the body and emphasis on the intellect, such civility kept the upper classes distinctly upper in a confusing age of social mobility. Good manners were taught by stigmatizing habits identified as lower class: "It is boorish to wipe one's nose on one's cap or clothing," dictates Erasmus; "to do so on one's sleeve or forearm is for fishmongers." In manners, a category of "low" was carved out expressly to preserve the distinctness of "high," much as William Webbe tried to distinguish "good writers" from "rustical rhymers." And the same thing happened with jest books. Once the elite started raising its standards of civility, jest books, repositories of all that was uncivil, gradually became an embarrassment.

To follow several incarnations of a single jest may be instructive. In the mid-fifteenth century, the prominent humanist Poggio Bracciolini purveyed the following misogynistic jest designed to suggest the obstinacy of women:

> A woman from my country was always fighting with her husband, contradicting everything he said, making fun of him, and insisting on the last word to show that she was superior. One day during a grave battle with her husband, she called him "lousy." In order to make her retract her words the man beat her furiously, but the more he punished her, the more she called him lousy. Finally ... he put a rope around her and lowered her into a cesspool, threatening to drown her if she did not change her tune. But she persisted in her verbal barrage, even when she was immersed up to the chin. Then, in order to shut her up once and for all, the man plunged her completely under the excrementious muck, hoping that imminence of death would make her improve her language. She, however, suffocating and speechless, said with her fingers what she could not with her mouth. Raising her hands above her head, she pressed her thumbnails together, thus by gesture still calling her husband lousy. For women kill lice with just these fingernails.

Lest we ascribe the jest's nauseating scatology to its folk-tale roots – "popular" literature – we should note that when the same tale appears among medieval sermon *exempla* compiled by Jacques de Vitry, the man merely pushes his wife into the water – it seems to have been Poggio

Bracciolini, a founder of Italian Renaissance humanism, who added the cesspool and the excrement. As thresholds of refinement were raised and the elite began to distance themselves from bodily vulgarity, the jest underwent a cleansing. Over a century later, Castiglione's version is so tidied up and excrement-free as to be unintelligible: "where obstinacy is bent, ... ye shall find some women that will never change purpose, as she that could no longer call her husband pricklouse, with her hands made him a sign."

But bowdlerizing was only one strategy. To preserve their civility in the face of their love of vulgar jest, humanists also eventually attributed the jests' vulgarity – and finally the jests themselves – to the lower orders. Tudor jest books nearly always associate their plenteous flatulence, mooning, and excrement with lower social orders or comic clergy. The freely-farting Howlglas and Widow Edith are vagrants. The title figure of Robert Copland's Jill of Brainford, a bequeather of farts, keeps an alehouse. (We recall "alehouse song" as the fare of "rustical rhymers" in William Webbe's formulation.) Such jests dealt not in thin, suggestive indecency but in full-blooded vulgarity: after dictating her flatulent will, Jill "groan[s] as panged with pain / Gripping her belly with her hands twain / And lift[s] up her buttock somewhat awry / And like a handgun, she let[s] a fart fly." As elite conduct grew perhaps oppressively fastidious, a wish to indulge in occasional bawdy, bodily humor is unsurprising, but increasing civility created inhibitions. The next best thing to abjuring vulgar tales was to relish them as evidence of lower-class vulgarity.

In disowning jest books, their own creation, humanists participated in the project we have been observing – to preserve elite literature as civil and decorous, they created a category that would one day be called "popular literature," and poured into it the discarded effluvium of their own earlier merriments, which now appeared unseemly, indecorous, too bodily, fit for the lower orders. Once again, high was high by virtue of what the elite succeeded in designating as low.

ROGUE LITERATURE

Ballads and jest books played a similar but not identical role in the construction of high and low: for example, although both saw an earlier participation by educated authors, who gradually withdrew from producing such texts, jest books boast a humanist pedigree of considerably greater elegance than anything ballads can offer. This should remind us that "popular culture" is not a unified field; it might be more precisely described as a cluster of appropriations that are sometimes only tenuously related. "Rogue literature" tells a third story, both familiar (after ballads and jest books) and peculiar to itself. Here we can only sketch in some of the issues involved in calling rogue literature popular.

Authors of "rogue literature" routinely claimed direct access to a "popular" world of real beggars, thieves, prostitutes, con men, and other underworld denizens. Thomas Harman claimed in *A Caveat for Common Cursetors* (1565–66) that as justice of the peace, he interviewed vagrants about their lives, bribing them for this information with a little cash and a good meal. In the 1590s, Robert Greene in his "cony-catching pamphlets" claimed to have infiltrated rogue society and become *au fait* with all its cheating practices. But Harman's posture as worldly-wise investigator, his stance as a reporter with first-hand knowledge of the underworld, is a sham: most of his evidence comes from literary tradition, from earlier exposés of vagrancy such as Awdeley's *Fraternity of Vagabonds* and ultimately the German *Liber Vagatorum*; and the literary lineage continued far beyond Harman: his work was generously plagiarized by Thomas Dekker and Samuel Rid, and his vocabulary lists of thieves' cant formed the basis of later slang dictionaries. Greene's exposés on cheating at cards and dice, claiming first-hand experience, are in fact plagiarized from Gilbert Walker's *A Manifest Detection of Diceplay*, 1552. Representing itself as the fruit of tough investigative reporting by fearless crime-fighters infiltrating a dangerous underworld, rogue literature is really a tissue of texts spawned by other texts. And again, it offers only illusory access to the "people," whose voices are ventriloquized by the educated – Harman was a public official versed in English law; Cambridge-educated Greene had traveled on the Continent, and dedicated works to such worthies as the Earl of Leicester and Lord Strange.

This is not to say that the genre was insulated from real life: actual vagrants were subject to many punishments including death, and works such as Awdeley's or Harman's, damning the unemployed as idle, shiftless, and criminal, seem to have influenced legislation governing vagrancy: the term "rogue" made its first appearance as thieves' cant in Awdeley and Harman's works, and within a decade appeared in the Poor Laws them-selves. That a humble genre like rogue literature could influence govern-ment policy points to a startling intersection of legislative and "popular" discourse that unsettles conventional boundaries between official and popular culture.

Although many have accepted rogue literature's sketch of Tudor low life as "in most particulars correct" (to quote A.V. Judges), Harman's *Caveat* and Greene's cony-catching pieces actually resemble jest books. Harvey, quoted above, set off elite culture in the person of "the Ciceronian" against not only the *Scoggin's Jests* but also against cony-catching pamphlets:

people thought of jest books and rogue literature in similar ways. Harman's *Caveat* is a collection of trickster tales, where practical jokes cause victims to be "laughed to scorn." Marks of the comic story-telling tradition are all over the *Caveat*. An old man's neighbors laugh heartily when he is held up by highway robbers, since he has absent-mindedly forgotten how much money he has about him. Bumpkins are bemused when their bedclothes are hooked off at night through a window by rogues, without waking them. Two rogues pull a scam to rob a parson, and have the last laugh by forcing him to drink their health in a tavern the next day. A traveler obligingly asks a habitual horse thief to walk his horse while he transacts some business. Some shifty operators of a "hospital" are stung when, at a midnight revel they are hosting for great lubbers who are feigning disability, some neighbors steal a roast pig off the fire while the hosts are mediating between their disorderly guests and a constable; the constable laughs up his sleeve. A gaggle of local wives ambush a lecher with his pants down, thrashing him soundly. Although Harman's categories of vagrancy make the work at first appear sociologically organized, it really is an old-fashioned tale collection with a narrative frame, like Tudor jest collections, and so are Greene's cony-catching works, which frankly employ the term "merry tale." In fact, it seems that jest books and rogue tales were often part of the same commercial vogue. During a second jest-book craze in the 1560s, when early Tudor jest books were reissued, Harman's *Caveat* first appeared. A third jest-book craze in the 1590s reached such a pitch that Edmund Spenser lent to Gabriel Harvey his own copies of *A Merry Jest of a Man that was Called Howlglas*, *Scoggin's Jests*, and *Skelton's Jests* (see Furnivall, *Captain Cox*, p. xlviii), and this was when Greene's cony-catching works appeared. A fresh edition of *Widow Edith* came out in 1573, the same year as a new edition of Harman's *Caveat*; both look like jest books about vagrants. One cannot draw firm generic lines around the jest – jest books often pilfered tales from other genres and jest-book material migrated into other genres. But the collection of funny stories, often with a narrative frame, was familiar when Harman and Greene wrote, and readers may well have placed their works as jests. The similarities made it easy to locate both genres within a category of "low" literary creation.

To lump rogue literature in with May poles and morris dances as a manifestation of popular culture, as Burke and others do, is to ignore the fact that while peasants and proto-proletarians *did* dance around May poles, practice folk medicine, and go mumming at Christmas, rogues did not write rogue literature. Far from bubbling up out of oral tradition, rogue literature, like jest books, was a creation of print culture. Certain printers specialized in jest books; some printed both jests and rogue pieces; and these same printers at other times published works of humanism. The concentration of jests and rogue literature in a few printers' hands suggests a kind of sponsorship of these genres, presumably for commercial profit. *A Hundred Merry Tales* and *Widow Edith* were printed by John Rastell, More's brother-in-law; the fact that Tale 9 is borrowed from Rastell's *The Nature of the Four Elements* suggests to some scholars that Rastell actually wrote *A Hundred Merry Tales*. Thomas Berthelet, who published Sir Thomas Elyot's profoundly humanistic treatise *The Book of the Governor* in 1531, the next year published the jest book *Tales and Quick Answers*. If "the folk" were more involved in some cultural forms than others, they seem hardly to have been involved with rogue literature or jest books at all. Considered from the standpoint of production and distribution, rogue literature and jest books are at a remove even from ballads, which were printed on a single large sheet of paper and hawked around by street vendors. The title pages of rogue literature and jest books regularly specify mainstream printers and distribution at respectable bookshops: Harman's *Caveat for Common Cursetors* was "printed in Fleet Street at the sign of the Falcon, by William Griffith," to be sold "at his shop in Saint Dunston's Churchyard in the west"; *Pasquil's Jests* was "imprinted at London for John Browne," to be sold "at his shop in Saint Dunston's Churchyard in Fleet Street."

In real life, the Tudor age witnessed desperate poverty – repeated crop failures, displacement through enclosures, rising prices, falling wages. The funnification of the poor in jest books and cony-catching pieces had serious consequences: public sympathy got blocked, not only because official theories judged the poor shiftless, lazy, untrustworthy, and responsible for their own misery, but also because so-called "popular" genres like jest books and rogue literature pronounced them funny – either so stupidly harmless as to be contemptibly comic, or so roguishly self-sufficient as not to need sympathy. This literature neither emanated from the people nor was meant for them to read. Rogue literature served the interests not of rogues, but of propertied, settled classes that perceived vagrancy and poverty as a threat. It was members of these classes who wrote rogue literature.

Elite participation is also visible in other genres that have been called "popular," such as the period's lurid accounts of crime and witchcraft: Frances E. Dolan has demonstrated that "some 'popular' pamphlets were written by legal personnel" including lawyers and judges. Concerning accounts of witch trials, Dolan describes an initial situation in which "popular and elite cultures were not discrete and ... each influenced and was shaped by the other"; but this gradually resolved itself into an elite attitude of skepticism which ascribed witchcraft beliefs to the people – another example of that early modern carving out of a category of popular culture against which elite culture defined itself. Another pertinent kind of text is controversialist works about women – the scholar who isolated these as a genre, Louis B. Wright, dubbed it "The Popular Controversy over Woman." Among literature he thought intended for the middle class, he found these pieces about women rather *lower* class – fare for small-time shopkeepers; definitely "popular." Other scholars often call the controversy about women a "pamphlet war," with "pamphlet" connoting slapdash composition and a popular readership. But closer inspection reveals yet again humanists behind the arras. The Tudor controversy about women, whatever its connections with the popular misogyny of the man in the street, was also strongly influenced by two Continental humanist works, *De nobilitate et praecellentia Foeminei sexus* by Henricus Cornelius Agrippa and *The Courtier* by Castiglione. In England, this so-called "popular controversy" included works by such major humanists as Sir Thomas Elyot and minor humanists like Edward More, grandson of Sir Thomas. Again, where are those shopkeepers? Where are the Folk in this picture?

"Popular" culture keeps receding as we approach. Whether or not the Folk ever significantly contributed to what looks now like "popular" literature, mediation by the educated seems always already in place.

In 1994, contributors to the volume *The Nazification of an Academic Discipline: Folklore in the Third Reich* struggled to come to terms with the fact that many German folklorists had enthusiastically collaborated with the Nazis. "It was an anomalous condition," Helge Gerndt assured readers, a "perversion of scholarship," but others entertained radical doubts about folklore study itself: Hermann Bausinger feared that Nazism had but emphasized "the primary ideas within this scholarly discipline." The practice of glorifying "the customs and the lifestyle of the simple people," casting peasants as "the foundation of the entire nation" (in Bausinger's quotation of Hitler) informs folklore as a discipline, reflecting its birth during the Romantic period. With folklorists' help, Nazi authorities did not discover but *created* the Folk as a category, and when they ran short of ancient customs, they created those too, including brand-new ancient May Day celebrations; but folklorists had been putting words in the mouths of the Folk since the Brothers Grimm. The elite creation of the Folk, the popular, as a category, in fact predates the Grimms – the Renaissance laid the groundwork. Where Elizabeth had tried to suppress popular entertainments, King James (for reasons no less politically expedient) tried to foster them. Peter Stallybrass shows how James, in his *Book of Sports*, along with writers like Herrick in *Hesperides*, celebrated a Merrie Olde England of May poles and church ales, in a transparent attempt "to create an alliance between top and bottom against the growing power of the Puritans" – a startling prefiguration of Hitler's desired coalition between ruling class and peasantry against Jews and the alienating forces of industrialization. We have seen by what shifty and mendacious means cultural productions such as ballads, jest books, and rogue literature were disowned by the elite and fathered upon the lower orders. But however questionable the process, once popular culture – the culture of the People, the Folk – had been created as a category, it was ever after available for ideological uses. Whether for glorification or vilification, popular culture was during the sixteenth century constituted as a separate world. John Florio's translation of *Montaigne's Essays* shows a firmly class-oriented concept of popular culture, and even the word "popular," in place by 1603: "It is a custom of popular or base men to call for minstrels or singers at feasts." The Renaissance posited a popular culture against which to define – and usually to exalt – high culture. Having glimpsed hidden wires behind this conjuring trick, should we go on using these categories as our own?

FURTHER READING

Achinstein, Sharon, "Audience and Authors: Ballads and the Making of English Renaissance Literary Culture," *Journal of Medieval and Renaissance Studies* 22 (1992): 311–26.

Anonymous, *The Book of Vagabonds and Beggars with a Vocabulary of their Language and a Preface by Martin Luther* (The *Liber Vagatorum*), ed. D. B. Thomas, trans. J. C. Hotten (London: Penguin, 1932).

Anonymous, *Tales and Quick Answers, Very Merry, and Pleasant to Read*, in *Shakespeare Jest-Books*, ed. William Hazlitt (London: Willis and Sotheran, 1864), vol. I, pp. 15–162. First printed 1532.

Awdeley, John, *The Fraternity of Vagabonds, c. 1561*.

Bausinger, Hermann, "Nazi Folk Ideology and Folk Research," in *Down and Lixfeld*, pp. 11–33.

Bourdieu, Pierre, *Distinction: A Social Critique of the Judgement of Taste*, trans. Richard Nice (Cambridge: Harvard University Press, 1984).

Bowen, Barbara C., *One Hundred Renaissance Jokes: An Anthology* (Birmingham, AL: Summa Publications, 1988).

Burke, Peter, *Popular Culture in Early Modern Europe* (New York: New York University Press, 1978).

Calendar of State Papers, Domestic Series. 287:51.

Castiglione, Baldassare, *The Courtier*, ed. W. E. Henley (London: David Nutt, 1900). Thomas Hoby translation, first printed 1561.

Chartier, Roger, "Culture as Appropriation: Popular Cultural Uses in Early Modern France," in *Understanding Popular Culture: Europe from the Middle Ages to the Nineteenth Century*, ed. Stephen L. Kaplan, (Berlin: Mouton, 1984), pp. 229–53.

Clark, Andrew, ed., *The Shirburn Ballads, 1585–1616* (Oxford: Clarendon Press, 1907).

Chettle, Henry, *Kind-heart's Dream* (New York: Johnson Reprint Corporation, 1972). First printed 1593.

Copland, Robert, *Jill of Brentford's Testament* (London: W. Copland, 1563).

Cornwallis, Sir William, *Essays*, ed. Don Cameron Allen (Baltimore: Johns Hopkins University Press, 1946). First printed 1600.

Dolan, Frances E., *Dangerous Familiars: Representations of Domestic Crime in England 1550–1700* (Ithaca, NY: Cornell University Press, 1994).

Down, James R., and Hannjust Lixfeld, eds. and trans., *The Nazification of an Academic Discipline: Folklore in the Third Reich* (Bloomington: Indiana University Press, 1994).

Erasmus, Desiderius, "Convivium Fabulosum," *The Colloquies of Erasmus*, trans. Craig R. Thompson (Chicago and London: University of Chicago Press, 1965), pp. 254–66.

De Civilitate Morum Puerilium. Collected Works of Erasmus, ed. Peter G. Bietenholz et al. (Toronto: University of Toronto Press, 1974–93), vol. xxv. First printed in Latin, 1530; in English, 1532.

Florio, John, trans., *The Essays of Montaigne 1603* (London: M. Flesher, 1632).

Furnivall, Frederick J., ed., *Captain Cox, his Ballads and Books; Or, Robert Laneham's Letter* (London: Ballad Society, 1871).

Gerndt, Helge, "Folklore and National Socialism: Questions for Further Investigation," in Down and Lixfeld, pp. 1–10.

Greene, Robert, *A Notable Discovery of Cozenage* (London: J. Wolfe, 1591). *The Second Part of Cony-Catching* (London: J. Wolfe, 1591). *The Third Part of Cony-Catching* (London: T. Scarlet, 1592). *A Disputation Between a He-cony-catcher and a She cony-catcher* (London: A. Jeffes, 1592).

Harman, Thomas, *A Caveat for Common Cursetors, Vulgarly called Vagabonds* (London: W. Griffith, 1567); first printed 1565–66.

Harvey, Gabriel, *Pierce's Supererogation, or a New Praise of the Old Ass* (London: J. Wolfe, 1593).

Hazlitt, William, *Remains of the Early Popular Poetry of England* (London: John Russell Smith, 1864).

Shakespeare Jest-Books (London: Willis and Sotheran, 1864).

Judges, A. V., ed., *The Elizabethan Underworld*, 2nd edn. (New York: Octagon, 1964); 1st edn. 1930.

Kaplan, Stephen L., ed., *Understanding Popular Culture: Europe from the Middle Ages to the Nineteenth Century* (Berlin: Mouton, 1984).

Kahrl, Stanley J., "The Medieval Origins of the 16c English Jest-Books," *Studies in the Renaissance* 13 (1966): 166–85.

Kinney, Arthur F., ed., *Rogues, Vagabonds and Sturdy Beggars: A New Gallery of Tudor and Early Stuart Rogue Literature* (Amherst: University of Massachusetts Press, 1990); 1st edn. 1972.

Lipking, Joanna, *Traditions of the "Facetiae" and Their Influence in Tudor England*, unpublished dissertation, Columbia University, 1970.

Muller, Jan-Dirk, "The Body of the Book: the Media Transition from Manuscript to

Print," in *Materialities of Communication*, ed. Hans Ulrich Bumbrecht and K. Ludwig Pfeiffer, trans. William Whobrey (Stanford, CA: Stanford University Press, 1994), pp. 32–44.

Nashe, Thomas, *The Anatomy of Absurdity*, in *Elizabethan Critical Essays*, ed. G. Gregory Smith, 2 vols. (Oxford: Oxford University Press, 1904), vol. I. First printed 1589.

Newcomb, Lori Humphrey, "'Social Things': The Production of Popular Culture in the Reception of Robert Greene's *Pandosto*," *ELH* 61 (1994): 753–81.

Poggio Bracciolini, Giovanni Francesco, *The Facetiae*, trans. Bernhardt J. Hurwood (New York: Award Books, 1968). First published in Latin, 1470.

Ritson, Joseph, *Pieces of Ancient Popular Poetry* (London: C. Clark, 1791).

Röhrich, Lutz, *Folktales and Reality*, trans. Peter Tokofsky (Bloomington: Indiana University Press, 1991).

Shephard, Leslie, *The Broadside Ballad* (London: Herbert Jenkins, 1962).

Shershow, Scott Cutler, *Puppets and "Popular" Culture* (Ithaca, NY: Cornell University Press, 1995).

Sidney, Sir Philip, *An Apology for Poetry*, ed. Forrest G. Robinson (New York: Macmillan, 1970).

Smith, Walter, *The Twelve Merry Jests of the Widow Edith*, in *Shakespeare Jest-books*, ed. William Hazlitt (London: Willis and Sotheran, 1864), vol. III, pp. 27–108. First printed 1525.

Spufford, Margaret, *Small Books and Pleasant Histories: Popular Fiction and Its Readership in Seventeenth- Century England* (London: Methuen, 1981).

Stallybrass, Peter, "'Wee feaste in our Defense': Patrician Carnival in Early Modern England and Robert Herrick's 'Hesperides'." *English Literary Renaissance* 16 (1986): 234–52.

Stallybrass, Peter, and White, Allon, *The Politics and Poetics of Transgression* (Ithaca, NY: Cornell University Press, 1986).

Utterson, Edward Vernon, *Select Pieces of Early Popular Poetry* (London: T. Davison, 1817).

Vitry, Jacques de, *The Exempla or Illustrative Stories from the Sermones Vulgares of Jacques de Vitry*, ed. Thomas Frederick Crane (London: Folk-lore Society, 1890).

Walker, Gilbert, *A Manifest Detection of the Most Vile and Detestable Use of Diceplay* (London: Abraham Vele, 1555). Reprinted in Judges and Kinney anthologies.

Ward, Samuel, *Balm from Gilead to Recover Conscience* (London: T. Snodham, 1617).

Watt, Tessa, *Cheap Print and Popular Piety, 1550–1640* (Cambridge: Cambridge University Press, 1991).

Webbe, William, *A Discourse of English Poetry*, in *Elizabethan Critical Essays*, ed. G. Gregory Smith, 2 vols. (Oxford: Oxford University Press, 1904), vol. I. First printed 1586.

Wilson, Thomas, *The Art of Rhetoric*, ed. Peter E. Medine (University Park: Pennsylvania State University Press, 1994).

Wiltenburg, Joy, *Disorderly Women and Female Power in the Street Literature of Early Modern England and Germany* (Charlottesville: University Press of Virginia, 1992).

Woodbridge, Linda, "New Light on The Wife Lapped in Morel's Skin and The Proud Wife's Paternoster," *English Literary Renaissance* 13 (1983): 3–35.

Placeless in the Renaissance: Vagrancy and Identity in English Renaissance Literature. Forthcoming.

Wright, Louis B., *Middle-Class Culture in Elizabethan England* (Chapel Hill: University of North Carolina Press, 1935).

Würzbach, Natascha, *The Rise of the English Street Ballad, 1550–1650,* trans. Gayna Wells (Cambridge: Cambridge University Press, 1990).

Zall, P. M., ed., *A Hundred Merry Tales and Other Jestbooks of the Fifteenth and Sixteenth Centuries* (Lincoln: University of Nebraska Press, 1963). *A Hundred Merry Tales* first printed 1526.

14

RAYMOND WADDINGTON

Rewriting the world, rewriting the body

Possibly the most heated critical controversy in English Renaissance studies has concerned the question of personal identity, the existence of the self. New Historicists and cultural materialists have maintained that the self is always a social construct, branding their opponents as naive essentialists. From a less parochial viewpoint, the argument may seem reminiscent of the heredity-versus-environment debate that vexed sociologists earlier in the century or, indeed, the universal-versus-particular controversies during the Renaissance itself. If, with Shakespeare's Prospero, we take rational speech to be the distinguishing mark of humans, we may not be surprised that the "either/or" choice can be resolved into "both." Modern linguistics has found that structures of language are deeply embedded within the human mind. Human speech, then, is both innate and acquired, consisting of a "Universal Grammar" and a learned dialect, corresponding nicely to an essential identity that is complemented by the cultural construct.

By the end of the sixteenth century the number of dialects or, since we are considering written speech, varieties of discourse, had burgeoned in a manner both alarming and exhilarating to contemporaries. *Discourse* itself is a term we should pause over, since it meant different things then and now. In literary theory "discourse analysis" denotes the study of a text as the reflector of social organizations, institutions, and power relations, exhibiting all the tensions and conflicts those might imply. To Shakespeare "discourse" meant either power of rational speech or simply conversation; however, as the common phrase "art of discourse" suggests, spoken or written speech was always closely linked with rhetorical performance. It might be accurate to suggest that in sixteenth-century discourse, the habits of thought and composition ingrained by the rhetorical tradition – argument by polarity and by analogy, organization from particular to general and vice versa, the reliance on commonplaces and on copiousness – functioned as the performance equivalents to that Universal Grammar within the circuits of the mind itself.

If the rhetorical tradition provides the Universal Grammar, what fostered the proliferation of discourses? The shift in writing from Latin to vernacular languages and the parallel phenomena of urbanization and nationalization explain much of it. Over the course of a century and despite grievous plague losses, the population of London increased nearly fourfold to c. 200,000. City life begets economic specialization, which begets jargons. Ben Jonson, a Londoner with a remarkable ear, gives us, in *The Alchemist* and *Bartholomew Fair*, the language of small householders, clerks, tobacconists, gamblers, religious sects, occult sciences, and a host of more marginal occupations – street vendors, buskers, con-men, pickpockets, and prostitutes. Shakespeare, always more a countryman, never lost the rural facility for responding to the speech of "outsiders" as comic, populating his plays with ridiculous-sounding foreigners, although the threat of attack or invasion lent a menace to such figures. In *Henry V*, a play written during the threat of a new Armada, Shakespeare invented a plot device now overly-familiar from war movies. A regionally and dialectally diverse set of characters – English, Scots, Irish, Welsh – at first bicker among themselves, but, under fire, bond into a "band of brothers" against the common enemy, the French, who are stigmatized as effeminate.

A major force in the development of new discourses was the widespread sense that, through knowledge and technology, the relation between humans and the external world, nature itself, was changing; everywhere one looked, life was suffused with innovation, newness. Polydore Vergil, shortly to be Henry VII's humanist historian, wrote a history of inventions, *De inventoribus rerum* (1499; translation Langley, 1546), that became one of the most popular books in the sixteenth century. John Dee, the Elizabethan magus, exemplified such attitudes, providing in his preface to Euclid (1570) a blueprint for the control of nature through mathematics and technology, and writing treatises to prove that Tycho Brahe's 1572 discovery was, indeed, a new star, a *nova*.

A particularly resonant index to this wonderment of new knowledge and ideas can be found in a popular set of engravings, the *Nova Reperta* ("new discoveries"), designed by Giovanni della Strada. Many of the "discoveries" are far from new; but the engravings document the harnessing of animal and elemental power (e.g., stirrups, water and wind mills) and the technological innovations of the Renaissance that advance the arts and crafts (the printing press, engraving, oil painting, gunpowder, and armor-polishing). Improvements in personal comfort and health constitute a large category (spectacles, medicines, silk production, mechanical clocks, sugar, and olive oil). Finally, there is the technology (magnetic compass and astrolabe) enabling the discovery that Strada presents first, the New World.

Strada's image of America (figure 13) represents the continent as a woman awakened from sleep by the newly-arrived explorer, Amerigo Vespucci; the Latin caption tells us that he called her but once and thenceforth she was always awake. In the left background, improbably close to shore, is the ship, with no crew in sight. Vespucci, dignified and formally clad despite weeks at sea, represents all the Old World; he holds a banner with his discovery, the Southern Cross, and an astronomical ring, signaling his fame as a cosmographer. America – naked except for a woven cap, a band around her calf, and a loin-cloth of feathers – arises from a hammock suspended between trees. In the central background, at the apex of a triangle formed by the shore and tree lines, natives roast human limbs over open fires. The juxtaposition of hammock to cannibals gives us an instant conflation of the "soft" and "hard" modes of primitivism, effectively indicating the ambivalent response to the New World.

Exotic though the subject is, Strada's visual vocabulary relies on the lexicon of Renaissance Italian art. The composition is organized by the conventions of perspective; and the treatment of the central figure, America, draws on a sixteenth-century tradition of representation. The male discovery of a sleeping, nude woman is a subject charged with erotic potential; but Strada has chosen to depict awakening, rather than discovery. America's posture – knees spread, left leg bent at a forty-five degree angle; torso supported by the left arm with right arm outstretched, slightly bent as if in welcome or embrace – seems to derive from a familiar design of "Leda and the Swan." If so, Strada wittily plays, as does Shakespeare in *The Tempest*, on the topos of explorers presenting themselves as gods to credulous Amerindians. The caption, *Semel vocauit inde semper excitam*, easily lends itself to the sexual innuendo with *semper excitam* translatable as "always called" or "always aroused."

Except for her costume and hair, America looks no different from a European, in this, too, consistent with the conventions of discovery discourse. "[I]n all my life I have seldom seen a better favored woman," Sir Walter Ralegh wrote. "I have seen a lady in England so like to her, as but for the difference in color, I would have sworn might have been the same."[1] In the New World, perhaps surprisingly, the women are the "same"; the men are the "other." The sameness is punningly reinforced by the first part of the caption: *Americen Americus retexit* ("Americus discovers the American"). Vespucci reached the coast of South America and recognized it for a *mundus novus*, rather than a trade route to the Indies. Here, though, the discovery (not *reperio* but *retego*, "uncover" or "lay bare") is the nude body of a woman with his name.

Much scholarly ink has been expended on the "discourse of colonialism"

13 "America," engraving from Giovanni della Strada (Jan Van der Straet), *Nova Reperta* (Antwerp, 1600?).

and the "inscribing" of the New World as text. It is, therefore, irresistible to point out that, in Strada's visual discourse, the expected tropes of power, domination, and submission are nowhere to be found. Vespucci has voyaged to a place that is both strange and familiar; there he encounters an "other" disconcertingly like himself, even sharing his name. The encounter is represented as sexual discovery; and, if Vespucci began with the presumption of godlike power and prerogative, his slightly alarmed expression indicates he has thought better of it. America is the dominant figure here. Despite the protective bulk of Vespucci's costume, she has the larger and more muscular figure; like her European sisters, she is sexually voracious, always aroused; and this appetite is dangerous to males. The visual composition makes it possible to read the background cannibalism as an "after" to the foreground encounter: male bodies destroyed in the fires of lust. The set of topics – the attractiveness of the native women, their insatiable lust, its destructiveness to males, the cannibalism – recurs through Vespucci's published letters; and the engraving invents only in imaginatively linking the last two.

In Strada's interpretation, the discovery of America, fraught with tensions and paradoxes, is as much a voyage inward as outward, the New World providing a mirror in which the Old reads its image. For the remainder of this chapter, we shall take *Americen Americus retexit* as a metaphor, looking at some representative figures and exploring a variety of discourses that are partially old and partially new. In each instance, the "Universal Grammar," a structure of argument or ideas deriving from classical authority, is rewritten in a modern dialect, a new "discourse." To point the comparisons more sharply, we shall focus on one subject, well foreshadowed in the engraving, the sexuality of the human body, attitudes toward which genuinely do undergo a change.

DISCOVERING THE BODY

Two of the discoveries celebrated by Strada, mechanical printing and engraving, are reproductive means of disseminating information; and they are the instruments that made a celebrity of Pietro Aretino (1492–1556), the first vernacular writer to earn a living from the popular press. Like the *poligrafi* who followed his example, Aretino turned his hand to anything that would sell; but he was most famous for the volumes of his personal letters, a genre he invented, and for his pornography.

John Donne pays grudging tribute to both in *Ignatius his Conclave*, a prose satire that is a negative counterpart to the *Nova Reperta*. Always an intellectual conservative, Donne examines various innovators who have affronted antiquity by inducing "doubts, and anxieties, and scruples"[2] to determine who has the greatest claim to a place in Hell. Among other claimants such as Copernicus, Paracelsus, and Machiavelli, appears "Peter Aretine" who is known both for "his licentious pictures" (*Complete Poetry and Selected Prose*, p. 343) and for his letters, "a long custome of libellous and contumelious speaking against Princes" (p. 344). A cobbler's son, Aretino did, indeed, have the effrontery to publish his correspondence – a mixture of flattery, advice, and wheedling for reward – with Charles V, Francis I, and a host of lesser princes; but Donne is only partially accurate in ascribing the licentious pictures to him.

Giulio Romano made drawings of couples in sixteen different sexual positions; these were engraved by Marcantonio Raimondi; and, when the prints commenced to circulate in 1524, both artists were in trouble with the Pope. The prints were destroyed; Giulio fled from Rome; and Marcantonio was imprisoned. Aretino, who helped obtain the engraver's release, was moved to compose sonnets, turning the engravings into "speaking pictures." The engravings were then published with the sonnets and again destroyed, but too late, as they were copied and circulated in cheap editions with crude woodcuts. "Aretine's Postures" thereafter became a byword for pornography.

Aretino, typically, published a letter, explaining his motives with a paean to the human penis: "What harm is there is seeing a man mounting a woman? Should beasts, then, be freer than we are? We should wear *that thing* nature gave us for the preservation of the species on a chain around our necks or a medal on our hats."[3] Aretino's insistence on the naturalness of human sexuality reflects an atmosphere in which artists emphasized the sexuality of Jesus Christ as a sign of his full humanity; and Aretino was as good as his word, commissioning medals of himself, the reverses of which displayed a satyr's head composed of penises.

Pornography, as Donne points out, was not a new invention when Aretino wrote the *Sonetti lussuriosi* and later his *Ragionamenti*, dialogues about the lives of prostitutes. But the printing press democratized pornography, bringing it within the purview of ordinary people and not just those who could afford the luxury of special manuscripts; as the harbinger of printed sexual discourse, Aretino had a definitive impact on English imagination. Marcantonio Raimondi's engravings and the woodcut copies were a parallel advance in visual discourse, as nude sexual activity had only rarely been represented. "What coital positions did people use in the sixteenth century?" one historian has asked and answered, "We hardly know."[4] Thanks to "Aretine's Postures," however, we know what it was possible to *imagine* in the sixteenth century; and that must have been a revelation to many viewers, *nova reperta*.

If the bare human body was to be represented naturally and accurately, advances were required in both representational technique and anatomical knowledge. In competition with engraving, the older art of the woodcut was pushed to remarkable refinement, together raising book illustration to a level of achievement seldom matched. The resources of Venetian printing and illustration made possible the enduring fame of the precocious professor of surgery, Andreas Vesalius, for his *De humani corporis fabrica libri septem* (Basel, 1543). The woodblocks and accompanying text were prepared in Italy and transported to the publisher with Vesalius' anxious instructions for the actual printing. The spectacular title page of the anatomical theatre is deservedly famous; but perhaps more revealing is the portrait of Vesalius dissecting the hand of a cadaver (figure 14). This choice of action both insists on comparison with Galen, in whose exposition the anatomy of the hand is central, and challenges his model, since Galen was able to dissect only the hand of an ape. The graphic juxtaposition of hands – living, functioning to dead, dissected – and the instruments – scalpel for cutting and pen for recording – show the physician learning and teaching. Since the knife cuts wood as well as flesh, it also alludes to the role of the artists without whose collaboration the anatomical text would not have been possible.

That the workings of the body could be seen more clearly did not, of course, mean that there was agreement on what was seen, as the discourse of sexuality reveals. Aristotle, notoriously, described women as deformed, incompletely developed males, the consequence of insufficient heat in generation having caused their sexual organs to remain internal. From his authority comes the "one-sex model" (i.e., the lack of a separate concept of the female), reinforced by Galen's description of the homology in genitalia (female being an inverted form of male), two beliefs that, mistakenly, have been regarded as universal in the sixteenth century. Yet advances in anatomical description and theory eventually disproved the genital correspondence; and, while Aristotle and Galen predicated a humoral physiology, the latter's belief that both men and women contributed semen enabled a more balanced view of the sexes. By the century's end, medical theory, although confused, remained largely Galenic, with both Aristotle and some moderns viewed more skeptically. On this collective journey of mapping the human body, the discourse of discovery provided a vocabulary; and the ancient analogy of man as microcosm was revitalized and extended in all directions – anatomical-geographical analogies, the body politic, the king's two bodies, the world's body. Wittily, in *The Faerie*

14 Portrait of Andreas Vesalius, probably by Jan Stephan van Calcar, from *De humani corporis fabrica libri septem* (Basel, 1543).

Queene (I.vii.1–15) Spenser takes the correspondence between earthquake theory and male physiology (heat and air in both) to make the giant Orgoglio a macrocosmic symbol of the Red Cross Knight's sexual arousal.

TREATING THE BODY

A new self-consciousness of the body's sexuality was paralleled neatly by the threat of sexuality to the body's health. In 1494 Charles VIII of France invaded Italy, occupying Naples before withdrawing nine months later; Charles' mercenaries left behind and carried away a terrible new disease, *Morbus Gallicus* or "French Pox," later to be named syphilis. Most authorities quickly recognized that it was a venereal disease, genuinely new, and one popular myth attributed the pandemic to a New World origin, transported to Europe by Columbus' sailors. Readers of Vespucci's letters might be forgiven such an assumption: "Their women, being very lustful, make their husbands' members swell to such thickness that they look ugly and misshapen … many men lose their members which rot through neglect and they are left eunuchs."[5]

Faced with the appalling physical effects of syphilis and a mercury treatment that was nearly as debilitating as the disease, most practitioners took refuge behind an older, providental rhetoric. William Clowes thundered: "Lues Venerea, the pestilent infection of filthy lust: a sickness very loathsome, odious, troublesome, and dangerous. A notable testimony of the just wrath of God against that filthy sin." Philip Barrough agreed, while adding anti-Catholic prejudice, and advised avoidance, the Tudor equivalent of "Just say No" campaigns: "eschew the cause of this infirmity and filthy, rotten, burning of Harlots etc."[6] In such moralistic responses, the assumption that the lustfulness of women destroys men is often overt, Barrough making common cause with Vespucci in this. An odd correlative occurred with the superstition that a man could be cured of the infection by sexual intercourse with a virgin. In the early, most helpless, years of the disease, prayers for the intercession of the Virgin Mary were a frequent defense; and this might be seen as an extension of her protective powers. Acknowledgments that the selfless virgin herself will contract the pox as a consequence of the curative process, however, would suggest that this is another variation on the "virgin or whore" paradigm; as soon as women become sexually active, all virtue is gone.

The sixth of Strada's new discoveries is *Hyacvm, et lves venerea* ("Guaiacum and venereal infection"; figure 15). Guaiacum, wood of the gaiac tree, also known as *lignum Indicum* or "Indian wood," was imported from central America in 1517 and proved to be a more effective and less

15 "Hyacvm, et lves venerea," from Giovanni della Strada, *Nova Reperta* (c. 1600).

traumatic treatment than mercury. Strada's engraving is a double "before and after" testimonial. The scene depicts two rooms of a house, divided by the wall down the middle. The right side represents a kitchen with the preparation of the medicine in a simultaneous narrative: in the foreground, a workman chips the logs; middleground, a woman at a table with a scales reduces the chips to powder; in the background, another woman decocts the medicine over a fire. In the bedroom on the left, a penitent patient drinks the medicine. On the wall hangs a picture, an inset moralization of the kind later exploited by Hogarth, illustrating the first "before": in the foreground, a banqueting scene (aroused appetite) and, in the back, a man embracing a woman as he leads her to a canopied bed. QED. Lest the genre picture escape our attention, the artist has designed an ascending visual sequence: in the center foreground is a table with a lighted candle, the flame of which points to a close-stool with the lid open and, directly above it, the picture. The lighted candle is necessary illumination, but we also register its conventional symbolism, the flame of lust and the brevity of human life, whereas the close-stool associates sexual appetite with unclean-ness, "filthy lust." The moralistic interpretation of syphilis is obvious enough; but the Latin caption is further suggestive. On the right side, *Leuabit ista sorpta coctio arboris* ("That concoction of the tree when ingested will relieve"); on the left, *Grauata morbo ab hocce membra mollia* ("The weak limbs weighed down by this disease"). Literal enough at first glance; however, *membrum* can mean the penis and *mollis* not merely weak but sexually incapable or impotent. The caption reinforces the moralism of the inset picture with an implicit misogyny.

In such responses to syphilis, medicine crosses a line from bodily health to bodily control. Alternative medicine, however, gave women some means of controlling their own bodies. John Gerard's famous *Herbal* (1597), itself derived from the Belgian Rembert Dodoens' work, affords the careful reader information on plants useful as contraceptives and abortifacients. Such natural remedies doubtless were handed down in an oral tradition by midwives and village "wise women," a forbidden knowledge for which they could be stigmatized as witches.

HABEAS CORPUS

There was, of course, no lack of formal institutions concerned with controlling the body's sexuality. Under Henry VIII England became a Protestant state, which, among other changes, instituted a shift in attitudes toward marriage. Although Protestants might seem to devalue marriage by denying that it was a sacrament, the opposite was true. Roman

Catholicism, with the negative view of sex against which Aretino was reacting, always ranked the celibate life above marriage; conversely, Protestantism encouraged a married clergy and tended to regard conjugal sex as a natural and positive part of marriage, not merely a necessary means of procreation or a remedy against "burning."

The thrust of mid- and late-Tudor sexual prohibitions, therefore, was directed against extramarital sex. It is symptomatic that prostitution, in the brothels or "stews" of Southwark across the Thames from London, was regulated – officially tolerated – until banished by Henry VIII's decree of 1546. Banishment by no means implies elimination, as the *Homily Against Whoredome And Uncleanness*, issued under Henry's daughter, Elizabeth, makes vehemently clear: "the outrageous seas of adultery (or breaking of wedlock), whoredom, fornication and uncleanness have not only burst in but also overflowed almost the whole world."[7] Words from the pulpit evidently were backed by deeds, as there is evidence of an increasing crackdown on illicit sexual activity.

Just how much crime, including sex crimes, plagued Tudor London is a vexed issue. Some urban historians, over-relying on literary evidence, have projected a city on the verge of anarchy; but this is a bit like deriving rural homicide statistics from mystery novels. Revisionists have documented a more stable and orderly society. Whatever the exact proportions, however, if there is crime, it follows as the night the day, there will be punishment; and there was, to our eyes, a confusing welter of Tudor courts with overlapping jurisdictions. Shakespeare's line, "The first thing we do, let's kill all the lawyers" (2 *Henry VI*, iv.ii.76), though referring to Jack Cade's Rebellion in 1450, also plays upon the prejudice of a London audience in 1590, uneasy about the burgeoning legal profession, its political influence, and its power over the lives of ordinary citizens.

The vast majority of lawyers were trained in the common law at the Inns of Court and Chancery; they were complemented, and increasingly opposed, by a far smaller cohort of civil lawyers, who had earned a doctorate at university and were trained in the civil law of Rome, the Justinian Code. England had, and still has, a profound attachment to common law, a legal system based on custom, precedent, and interpretation, as in Sir John Davies' definition (1612): "For the *Common Law* of *England* is nothing else but the *Common Custom* of the Realm."[8] Davies asserts the superiority of common to statute law, made "by the Edicts of Princes" and "imposed upon the Subject," highlighting the conflict that had emerged.

James I, determined to extend the royal prerogative, found himself opposed by his Chief Justice, Sir Edward Coke, who viewed the King as subject to God and the Law. James, not inaccurately, saw common law rendering him subservient to his judges. In his view, the law was only the expression of the monarch's will, a position with which the Justinian Code was understood to be sympathetic. James' advocates were the successive Lord Chancellors, Thomas Egerton and Francis Bacon, which position gave them authority, as judge in the equity court of Chancery, to reverse some common law judgments. In Coke's struggle to resist the encroachment of Chancery, the threat of civil law, and the expansion of the royal prerogative, he was doomed to lose, suffering both loss of his position and, later, imprisonment. Although he lost the battle, he won the war. Coke's memorable declaration, "Magna Carta is such a fellow, that he will have no sovereign,"[9] became a rallying cry in Parliament's resistance to royal prerogative; and in 1649 Charles I would lose his head for placing himself above the common law.

Roman law, the *Corpus Juris Civilis*, was a written code, a body of doctrine, the interpretation of which Justinian explicitly attempted to limit and control; conversely, the genres of common law are those of *reportage* – year books, notebooks, reports – records of particular cases and decisions, the study and interpretation of which, in rather Platonic fashion, give insight to the unwritten code. Coke's monuments are his *Reports* (1600–15) and his *Institutes* (1628), which provide his idea of "the ancient law of England" with form and a local habitation. The title of the *Institutes* and the announced, four-book structure allude to the Justinian *Corpus*, but the systematic organization of that work is subverted by the seemingly random accumulation of cases, just as, implicitly, imperial prerogative is subverted by English populism. Coke disabuses us of the expectation that Roman law is the Universal Grammar and common law the dialect; the other way around, he insists.

Turning from the body politic to the body natural, we may find Coke's account of one sex crime, "Of Buggery or Sodomy," gives a sense of his method and language. He first defines the "detestable and abominable sin" in a paraphrase of Leviticus 18:22–23. The speech act of the following philological excursus is to identify the sin as foreign: "*Bugeria* is an Italian word ... *Paiderastes* is a Greek word ... the Lombards had brought unto the Realm ..." He then reviews "ancient authors," all of whom agree on death as the appropriate penalty; and the statute of Henry VIII earns approval for its agreement with the ancients. Coke next expounds the meaning of his definition, phrase by phrase. Here biblical taboo jostles with precise legalism (the act of penetration, evidence, consideration of minors, accessories), until he reaches "by womankind with brute beast," at which point the fabulous enters: "somewhat before the making of this Act [25

Henry VIII, cap. 6], a great Lady had committed Buggery with a Baboon, and conceived by it, etc."[10] The improbable anecdote reveals that, with Coke, the transition from marvelous to factual evidence is not yet complete, and custom is still shaped by fear of female sexuality.

In the battle over royal prerogative, the main antagonists, Coke and Bacon, both were losers, the Lord Chancellor deposed when he was convicted of bribery by Parliament. Bacon, however, continues to lose as his once-exaggerated position in the "Scientific Revolution" dwindles. Discriminating scholarship has shown the extent to which his thought was a mixture of neo-Aristotelianism, natural magic, and biblical prophecy; even the emphasis on observation and experimentation was something he shared with the Paracelsians and "empirics" such as herbalists. Bacon's real scientific contribution may have been popularizing the idea of an experimental method. The titles of Bacon's major works – *The Advancement of Learning* (1605), the skeletal *Instauratio Magna* and the *Novum Organum* (both 1620), the *New Atlantis* (1626) – all proclaim his commitment to innovation, but innovation of a particular kind. All of human knowledge will be advanced, renewed, rebuilt; and the ancient authorities, Aristotle (*Organum*) and Plato (*Timaeus* and *Critias*) rewritten. Bacon equally faulted theory without experimentation and experimentation without theory, seeing the need for a *via media*: "The men of experiment are like the ant; they only collect and use; the reasoners resemble spiders, who make cobwebs out of their own substance. But the bee takes a middle course" (*Novum Organum*, I, xcv).[11] In formulating his inductive method for this mediation – generalization from experiences by process of elimination – Bacon was significantly aided by his training in dialectic at Cambridge and by his professional experience at law. The reweaving, the combination of old and new, will be evident; but the scope and ambition of his "great instauration" also should be acknowledged. In parallel to Coke's project with the law, Bacon rewrites the body of scientific knowledge to center on nature and technology, and, not least, make it English.

The *New Atlantis* stands as an epitome of Bacon's scientific vision. It begins with the metaphor of discovery; the first page might be out of Hakluyt, although this voyage is to the Indies of the mind. Intertextually, Bacon positions his narrative as a corrective to Plato and to More's *Utopia* and, less overtly, a rewriting of Christian revelation to invest science with the mantle of religion. Arriving on the island of Bensalem, the seamen undergo a period of purification and initiation, during which they are instructed in its history, religion (Christian), contacts with the outside world, and secrecy. Having passed these tests, the men are given the freedom of the island, progressing from doctrine to observation, confirming their knowledge of the inhabitants. In the last stage of revelation, a Father of Salomon's House, the institutional center of Bensalem, relates its purpose: "the Knowledge of Causes, and secret motions of things; and the enlarging of the bounds of Human Empire, to the effecting of all things possible" (Bacon, *Essays*, p. 480). Descending to particulars, he describes the research facilities for the investigation of everything in nature. For the House's "ordinances and rites," there are galleries with statues honoring the principal "inventors" whose discoveries have advanced knowledge. Bacon conceived of his "fable" as "a model or description" of an experimental college, and it became an inspiration for founding the Royal Society (1662).

Bacon's writing is charged with procreative imagery, but always as a metaphor for intellectual productivity: "the noblest works and foundations have proceeded from childless men, which have sought to express the images of their minds, where those of their bodies have failed" (*Essays*, p. 19). Childless himself, at forty-five Bacon married an heiress thirty-one years his junior. Bacon was rumored to be homosexual, with "Ganymedes and Favourites"; but William Rawley's report that he drank a broth of saltpeter "every morning for thirty years" rings truer. Whatever his sexual orientation, repression is the right note.

In the *New Atlantis*, the state honors propagation with a "Feast of the Family," necessary, presumably, because the scientists' research in genetic engineering has not advanced to cloning. Bacon's description of sex and marriage on Bensalem is both distanced and displaced, narrated by an outsider, the Jewish merchant Joabin, thus evading embarrassment to a native while witnessing to truth. Joabin criticizes More's "Feigned Commonwealth" for permitting betrothed couples to view each other naked; Bensalem allows such viewing only obscured by bathing and vicariously, displaced to a friend. Excoriating European lasciviousness, Joabin praises Bensalem as the absolute "Spirit of Chastity": "As for masculine love, they have no touch of it" (*Essays*, p. 477). *Masculine love* was the common, period phrase for homosexuality; and *touch* carries a double sense – not even the slightest amount, and sexual contact. Among Bacon's unwritten projects is *Historia Veneris, ut species Tactus* ("history of Venus as a species of Touch"); and it is telling that the House of Salomon contains "perspective-houses," "sound-houses," and "perfume-houses; wherewith we join also practices of taste" (*Essays*, p. 487). Only the last of the five senses, touch, is omitted. Bacon's vision of a religio-scientific Utopia is as asexual as that of the recent Heaven's Gate cult.

BAWDY AND SOUL

Bacon's perspective houses for experimentation with light and optics boast of both telescopes and microscopes; and the gallery of inventors wisely includes a statue of the (unknown) inventor of glass, the enabling technology. Strada's engraving of *Conspicilla* ("spectacles"; figure 16) celebrates the invention that released humans from darkness. To the left, an early optician sells magnifiers and spectacles; the citizens on the right exhibit the benefits of these devices. Convex lenses were first used to assist ordinary vision with spectacles; the same craftsmen produced glass magnifiers, simple microscopes. Venice was producing spectacle-quality glass by the mid-fifteenth century. An Englishman, Thomas Digges, discovered the principle of the telescope about 1550; in 1608 Dutch spectacle-makers petitioned for monopolies in manufacturing such an instrument. The spectacular consequences of the technological innovation were quickly announced in Galileo's *Sidereus Nuncius* (1610). In Latin epigrams, a Scot, Thomas Seggett, lauds Galileo as greater than Columbus: the one gave us lands to be conquered by bloodshed, the other new worlds harming none.

But if glass allowed scientists to see both the pock-marked moon and the world in a grain of sand, a less famous application probably had more impact on ordinary people: mirrors allowed them to see themselves. In the Middle Ages mirrors were made by polishing metal; but in the sixteenth century high-quality glass mirrors, the backs painted with "silver," were a leading Venetian export. The fascination of self-discovery is registered in Parmigianino's *Self-Portrait in A Convex Mirror*, a painting once owned by Pietro Aretino.

What does one see in the mirrored image – the mystery of the ineffable spirit or the primacy of the body, tangible and appealing? Vision, once considered the most reliable of senses, became eroticized; "*Much Use* of *Venus* doth *Dim* the *Sight*," Bacon observed and attached a Shakespearean causation, "the *Expense* of *Spirits*."[12] Perspective glasses, distorting lenses or mirrors, were associated with both erotic pleasure and the unreliability of the senses. Jonson's Sir Epicure Mammon fantasizes about "my glasses / Cut in more subtle angles, to disperse / And multiply the figures, as I walk / Naked between my succubae" (*Alchemist* II.ii.45−48).[13]

Predictably, discourse of the soul mutated over the century as well. Like theology itself, writings on natural philosophy show a drift to simplify explanations and an increasing materialism. Francesco Suárez could cite both Aristotle and Vesalius for authorities. In the traditional faculty pyschology, humans are endowed with three souls – vegetative, sensitive, and intellectual; the sensitive soul motivates the entire body through

Ioan. Stradanus invent.   *Ioan. Collaert sculp.*   *Philip Galle excud.*

16 "Conspicilla," from Giovanni della Strada, *Nova Reperta* (c. 1600).

spiritus, a subtle vapor diffused from blood. Some writers simplified this scheme by eliminating the sensitive soul; others by retaining the triad and collapsing the distinction between *spiritus* and sensitive soul. Poets were willing to simplify and materialize even more radically, eliminating the sensitive and identifying the intellective soul with *spiritus*. The belief that the sensitive soul is diffused through the entire body was expressed in a Latin tag, *tota in toto, et tota in qualibet parte* ("all in all and all in every part"). Aretino, prophet of sexuality, used this motto on his medals with the phallic-headed satyr, proclaiming that his penis, his sexuality, is his soul; and a host of English poets spiritualized love-making through the "all in all" topos.

A number of currents come together in the inventor of the essay, Michel de Montaigne. As with those of his follower Bacon, Montaigne's *Essais* (1580, 1588; Florio's translation, 1603) display their origins from commonplace-book composition; in other respects, they could not differ more. Whereas Bacon is terse, aphoristic, and rigorously impersonal, Montaigne is expansive, anecdotal, remarkably personal, creating a self-portrait of a mind in motion and a living body. Deeply influenced by the newly available texts of ancient skepticism, Montaigne became persuaded that the reason and senses are unreliable, opinion contradictory, custom arbitrary; he used his humanist training of argument *in utramque partem* (both sides of a question) to subvert the certainties of commonplace thought. "Of Cannibals" comments on what is admirable and what deplorable in the behavior of Amerindians, reflecting on the often worse qualities of Europeans. Socratic self-knowledge is the desired end of Montaigne's self-portraiture; and, because he always perceives an intimate unity of mind and body, he must describe his body completely – its appearance, likes and dislikes, the effects of its aging, illnesses, its functions. Among the last, his sexuality: "Each of my pieces are equally mine, one as another ... My whole portraiture I universally owe unto the world."[14]

With rueful amusement, Montaigne concedes: "It vexeth me that my Essays serve Ladies in lieu of common ware and stuff for their hall: this Chapter will prefer me to their cabinet [boudoir]" (*Essays*, p. 508). The chapter "Upon Some Verses of Vergil" (III.5) is extraordinary, the most sustained and comprehensive meditation on human sexuality in the century. The two spindles upon which Montaigne weaves his essay are quotations, from Vergil and Lucretius, describing passionate love-making. About them he threads his reflections on prudery, the prohibitions on speaking of the act "so natural, so necessary, so just" (*Essays*, p. 508); the role of sex in a marriage; the sexual appetite of women; the cultural conditioning of young girls; phallic worship; unrealistic expectations of sexual prowess; jealousy, chastity, reputation, laws; his own sexuality; and, a sustained motif, the importance of imagination to sexual response. Montaigne denies that anything in life is either purely corporeal or purely spiritual, arguing that the role of the soul in bodily pleasures needs to be accepted. He ends, striking a blow for sexual equality: "I say, that both male and female, are cast in one same mould; instruction and custom excepted, there is no great difference between them" (*Essays*, p. 537).

Extracting the sexual discourse from Montaigne's essay would be an exercise in redundancy because the entire essay is that. Writing in his "old age" (*c.* fifty-three) with sexual drive declining, Montaigne elevates the familiar metaphor of creation as procreation through a sustained equivalence between rhetoric and sexuality. As literary creation, the essay demonstrates his sexual potency; it also is a manual on the arousal of sexual desire. In its commonplace dimension, the essay is a tissue of quotations on sex, by which Montaigne illustrates what excites the imagination. Urging complete candor in sexual discourse, he analyzes the Latin vocabulary of the two central quotations to show its natural, masculine vigor. Montaigne explains his efforts to achieve an affectively equivalent style in the vernacular, using, for example, Gasconisms and vocabulary from hunting and warfare. Finally, since he had described the *Essais* as "consubstantial" with himself, it follows that, in the self-portraiture of "Some Verses," he represents – in a renewed image from the *Timaeus* – the "disobedient, skittish and tyrannical member" (*Essays*, p. 516) of his own body, both picturing and viewing himself as a sexual being. *Americen Americus retexit.*

IMBECILLITAS CORPORIS

Montaigne's emphasis in "Some Verses" on the power of imagination over sexual performance twins it with an earlier essay, "Of the Force of Imagination" (I.21), the heart of which concerns the phenomenon of transitory impotence (*imbecillitas corporis* or "nouements d'aiguillettes"), a condition that, some scholars infer, he had experienced. Opposing the prevailing belief that such episodes are caused by witchcraft and sorcery, Montaigne asserts they are "but the impressions of apprehension, and the effects of fear" (*Essays*, p. 41), explaining how he cured a fearful bridegroom of the condition with the placebo of an astrological talisman. Eight years later, he is less sanguine. An express purpose of "Some Verses" is to compensate for his waning physical potency with imagination, writing about sex with sufficient virility to excite the reader. But he fears failure because, so intimately related are mind and body, that the mind turns traitor, forsaking him to follow the body; and, at the end, he depreciates his "notable commentary" as "a flux of babbling" (*Essays*, p. 537). Whether a litotes or a frank admission of the mind's physical dependency, we cannot be sure.

The preoccupation with impotence was not idiosyncratic to Montaigne, but "a virtual epidemic in the late sixteenth century."[15] As always, we need to resist assigning demographic weight to literary evidence; but Montaigne's plight echoed across the Channel in English poetry. George Gascoigne, similarly ageing, sings his "little Robin" to sleep ("The Lullaby of a Lover," 1573); but Gascoigne's serenity is lost by the 1590s. Donne, variously, can express revulsion at female bodies ("Love's Alchemy"); over-anxious incapacity, "I had loves pinnace overfraught" ("Air and Angels"); and post-coital depression at the self-destructiveness of the act ("Farewell to Love"). Thomas Nashe's *Choice of Valentines*, widely circulated in manuscript, narrates the misadventures of Tomalin, a bumpkin who seeks his sweetheart, Frances, and discovers her in a London brothel. At their sexual reunion, Tomalin too quickly is exhausted, leaving Frances to satisfy herself with what we would now call a "sexual aid," one of the more notorious examples of Murano glass-making that Nashe christened, in English, a "dildo."

To recapitulate the journey we have been mapping: during the sixteenth century medical science gradually came to accept that women were not malformed or imperfect males, but another sex – separate but equal, one might say. In tandem with this, the acknowledgment of human sexuality as, not a token of the Fall, but something "natural" had the effect of enfranchising female sexuality, as do the "Postures" of Aretino. These movements toward equality are subverted, however, perhaps more than anything by the still-pervasive hierarchical perception of reality. Lacking a horizontal vision of equality or mutuality, men appeared to feel that, if women were not inferior, they must be superior. Thus, women's sexual appetites, even when acknowledged as only natural, cannot be merely equal, but must exceed those of men.

At the very beginning of this era, a Venetian sailor, Nicolò, when charged with impotence by his wife, arranged for his parish priest and a scribe to observe him making love to a prostitute, at the climax of which he ejaculated into the hand of a witness. Not much sexual anxiety there. But Vespucci's grotesque New World report of men literally emasculated by rampant female sexuality is a more accurate predictor of the period's sensibility. Aretino's paradise of recreational sex merges with Montaigne's melancholy vision of rapacious female appetite and fading male capacity. The Tudor age ends with a chorus of male voices, some angry and

misogynistic and others wistfully insecure, complaining of women's insatia-
bility. Thus, the sometime libertine Donne can consign Aretino to Hell for
having "taken away all courage and spurres from youth" (*Ignatius his
Conclave*, p. 343).

Donne's marvellous Elegy XIX might serve as a case in point:

> Licence my roving hands, and let them go,
> Before, behind, above, between, below.
> O my America! my new-found-land,
> My kingdom, safeliest when with one man man'd.
> My Mine of precious stones: My Emperie,
> How blest am I in this, discovering thee!   (lines 25–30)

To a recent critic, Donne "deployed the language of discovery . . . to evoke a
sinister combination of sensuality and physical exploitation."[16] This
America, however, is not a kingdom. As with Elizabethan England, the
sovereign is a queen regnant; and, at the poem's end, he is still appealing,
his petition ungranted; she remains dressed, undis-covered. The woman
commands the power of her sexuality, whether she decides to use or
withhold it. The man's disconcerting discovery reprises *Americen Americus
retexit*.

CODA

"As liberally, as to a midwife, show / Thy self," Donne had implored'
(Elegy XIX, lines 44–45); and with Jane Sharp, a midwife "above Thirty
Years' we have a woman's body described in what has been missing, a
woman's voice. Conscious that she may offend modesty by the vernacular,
Sharp nonetheless describes "the parts of generation . . . purposely omitting
hard names."[17] *The Midwives Book* (1671) gives us a sense of what women
might have thought three generations earlier. Sharp can speak of excessive
desire: the clitoris "being nervous, and of pure feeling, when it is rubbed
and stirred it causeth lustful thoughts"; and Plato lives in her image of the
womb ("it hath a kind of animal motion to satisfy its desire"). She
understands the limitations of Galen, but firmly embraces the "two-seeds"
theory:

> Man in the act of procreation is the agent and tiller and sower of the ground,
> woman is the patient or ground to be tilled, who brings seed also as well as
> man to sow . . . this ground or field which is the woman's womb . . . we
> women have no more cause to be angry, or be ashamed of what Nature hath
> given us than men have; we cannot be without ours no more than they can
> want theirs.

The sown-ground metaphor insinuates that sex is natural and the partners have an equal role, as Aretino and Montaigne maintained. Her imagery for the process retains the traditional ones of fluid and temperature, but introduces a newer concept: "[the womb] hath also an attractive faculty to draw in a magnetic quality, as the lodestone draweth iron." Beyond her professional experience and concern for physiological precision, Sharp insists on pride and pleasure that women should take in their bodies, as in her description of the *mons veneris:* "a little bank called a mountain of pleasure near the wellspring and the place where the hair coming forth shows virgins to be ready for procreation." Sharp's discourse of the body, like the others, is a mixture of the old and new, Universal Grammar and local dialect; but, as with Montaigne's, we can recognize in it an authentic bridge to the modern.

NOTES

For advice and suggestions in writing this chapter, I am indebted to Peter Schaeffer, Winfried Schleiner, Michael T. Walton, Kathleen M. Ward, and Arthur H. Williamson.

1 Sir Walter Ralegh, "Discovery of Guiana," in Richard Hakluyt, *Voyages and Discoveries*, ed. Jack Beeching (Harmondsworth: Penguin, 1972), p. 397.

2 *Ignatius his Conclave*, in John Donne, *Complete Poetry and Selected Prose*, ed. C. M. Coffin (New York: Modern Library, 1952), p. 320.

3 Lynne Lawner, ed. and trans., *I modi. The Sixteen Pleasures* (Evanston: Northwestern University Press, 1988), p. 9. She presents the surviving copy in facsimile.

4 Roy Porter, "History of the Body," in *New Perspectives on Historical Writing*, ed. Peter Burke (Oxford: Polity Press, 1991), p. 210.

5 Luciano Formisano, ed. and David Jacobson, trans., *Letters From A New World* (New York: Marsilio, 1992), p. 49.

6 Quoted from Winfried Schleiner, *Medical Ethics in the Renaissance* (Washington, DC: Georgetown University Press, 1995), pp. 167 (Clowes) and 166 (Barrough).

7 Quoted from Lloyd Davis, ed., *Sexuality and Gender in the English Renaissance* (New York: Garland, 1998), p. 5.

8 Quoted from J. G. A. Pocock, *The Ancient Constitution and the Feudal Law* (Cambridge: Cambridge University Press, 1987), p. 32; see pp. 30–55 on "the common-law mind."

9 Cited in *Oxford Dictionary of Quotations*, 3rd edn. (1980), p. 154, no. 16.

10 Quoted from Russ McDonald, *The Bedford Companion to Shakespeare* (Boston: St. Martin's, 1996), pp. 291–93.

11 Quoted from Francis Bacon, *Essays, Advancement of Learning, New Atlantis, and Other Pieces*, ed. R. F. Jones (New York: Odyssey, 1937), p. 313.

12 Quoted from *Sylva Sylvarum, or, A Natural History in Ten Centuries* (London, 1639), p. 142.

13 Quoted from *Drama of the English Renaissance, II: The Stuart Period*, ed. R. A. Fraser and N. Rabkin (New York: Macmillan, 1976), p. 155.

14 Quoted from *The Essays*, trans. John Florio, London 1603 (facsimile edn., Menston: Scolar Press, 1969), p. 532.

15 See Lee R. Entin-Bates, "Montaigne's Remarks on Impotence," *Modern Language Notes*, 91 (1976): 640–54, quotation p. 642.

16 Jonathan Sawday, *The Body Emblazoned* (London: Routledge, 1995), p. 27.

17 Sharp is quoted from Charlotte F. Otten, ed., *English Women's Voices, 1540–1700* (Miami: Florida International University Press, 1992), pp. 197–205. Sawday, *The Body Emblazoned*, p. 214, notes that Sharp's anatomy is "far more complex than the 'one-sex model.'"

FURTHER READING

Archer, Ian W., *The Pursuit of Stability* (Cambridge: Cambridge University Press, 1991).

Brundage, James A., *Law, Sex, and Christian Society in Medieval Europe* (Chicago: University of Chicago Press, 1987).

Cave, Terence, *The Cornucopian Text* (Oxford: Oxford University Press, 1979).

Helgerson, Richard, *Forms of Nationhood: The Elizabethan Writing of England* (Chicago: University of Chicago Press, 1992).

Landau, David and Peter Parshall, *The Renaissance Print* (New Haven: Yale University Press, 1994).

Lloyd, G. E. R., *Polarity and Analogy* (Cambridge: Cambridge University Press, 1966).

Pinker, Steven, *The Language Instinct* (New York: William Morrow, 1994).

Rappaport, Steve, *Worlds Within Worlds: Structures of Life in Sixteenth-Century London* (Cambridge: Cambridge University Press, 1989).

Rattansi, P. M., "The Scientific Background," in *The Age of Milton*, ed. C. A. Patrides and R. B. Waddington (Manchester: Manchester University Press, 1980), pp. 197–240.

Regosin, Richard L., *Montaigne's Unruly Brood* (Berkeley: University of California Press, 1996).

Rosand, David and Michelangelo Muraro, eds., *Titian and the Venetian Woodcut* (Washington, DC: International Exhibitions Foundation, 1976).

Schmitt, Charles and Quentin Skinner, eds., *The Cambridge History of Renaissance Philosophy* (Cambridge: Cambridge University Press, 1988).

Shapiro, Barbara, "The Concept 'Fact': Legal Origins and Cultural Diffusion," *Albion* 26 (1994): 239–42.

Schiffman, Zachary, *On the Threshold of Modernity* (Baltimore: Johns Hopkins University Press, 1991).

Steinberg, Leo, *The Sexuality of Christ* (Chicago: University of Chicago Press, 1996).

Waddington, R. B., "Socrates in Montaigne's 'traicté de la phisionomie,'" *Modern Language Quarterly* 41 (1980): 328–45.

"What's Past Is Prologue." *English Literary Renaissance* 25 (1995): 461–64.

15

RICHARD HELGERSON

Writing empire and nation

"This realm of England is an empire, and so hath been accepted in the world."[1] With these words Parliament in 1533 declared England's independence from the Pope in Rome. Although our more familiar sense of *empire* as a political unit encompassing far-flung territories and heterogeneous peoples was current in the sixteenth century, the meaning here concerns absolute sovereignty. An empire is a polity that owes fealty to no one under God. Because England is an empire, England's king has, in Parliament's words, "plenary, whole, and entire power" in all matters within his kingdom. In place of the overlapping patchwork of regional, national, and international jurisdictions that had characterized medieval governance in Western Europe, monarchs in England and elsewhere were intent on seeing their rule penetrate more evenly into all aspects of life in the territories under their control. This "improvement of the sovereignty," as the Elizabethan poet and historian Samuel Daniel was to call it, had an inevitable cultural dimension.[2] If England was truly an empire, it needed to show the expected signs of imperial greatness. It needed a language and a literature comparable to those of the ancient Roman Empire, on which all early modern empires modeled themselves. And it needed to have its history written and its land described. In Spain and France, England's chief sixteenth-century rivals, similar projects of imperial self-making were well underway. Only at the cost of foregoing some measure of the sovereignty it was so intent on asserting could England fail to keep up. The English thus wrote their newly declared empire in a spirit of anxious emulation. But out of that anxious writing of empire something else emerged: the sense not just of a sovereign political order but also of a people, the sense of an English nation. Those efforts and that emergence, as they can be seen in language and prosodic reform, in history, drama, and poetry, and in topographically oriented antiquarian study, are the subject of this final chapter.

REFORMING LANGUAGE AND POETRY

In 1492, the year in which Spain conquered the last Moorish stronghold on the Iberian peninsula and Columbus took his famous voyage, Antonio de Nebrija published the first formal grammar of any European vernacular, his *Gramatica Castellana*, with the claim that "language has always been the companion of empire."[3] Some four decades later King Henry VIII took practical steps to see that English would be the companion of his empire. He commanded that henceforth laws be administered in Wales not in Welsh but in English, and that all Welsh officers or fee holders speak English, "the natural mother language used within this realm" (*Statutes* III.563). But in both Spain and England, there was serious doubt whether the mother tongue was up to the new tasks being imposed on it. Nebrija's grammar marks an early attempt to fit Castilian for imperial rule, an attempt that was seconded by generations of Spanish language reformers and poets. In England a similar constellation of humanists and poets worried about the inadequacy of their native language and went to work remedying its obvious defects.

To get a feel for the mixture of anxiety and ambition that drove this enterprise one could dip into any of the large number of books on grammar, spelling, poetics, and pedagogy that appeared in these years or, for that matter, into the prefatory matter of almost any sixteenth-century English book on any subject, so widespread was the concern and so common the ambition. But here is just one example, from William Webbe's *Discourse of English Poetry* (1586):

> It is to be wondered at of all and is lamented of many that whereas all kind of good learning have aspired to royal dignity and stately grace in our English tongue, being not only founded, defended, maintained, and enlarged, but also purged from faults, weeded of errors, and polished from barbarousness by men of great authority and judgment, only poetry hath found fewest friends to amend it.[4]

Wonder and lamentation are, for Webbe, the appropriate response to the continuing laggardness of English poetry in joining the general reform that had, in his view, already lifted English prose from "barbarousness" to "royal dignity and stately grace." Empire is much at issue here. Achieving royal dignity and stately grace would prove English and England's fitness for rule. Persisting in barbarousness leaves both vulnerable to base subjection. But as Webbe's busy line of verbs suggests, getting from one condition to the other would be no mean feat. To be raised to the level of Webbe's imperial aspiration, English had to be founded, defended, maintained, enlarged, purged, weeded, and polished.

So successful were these sweaty early modern efforts at language reform that only with difficulty can we recapture the sense of radical self-alienation they originally provoked. Look at a list of words like *describe*, *ticket*, *adapt*, *system*, *inflate*, *balcony*, *design*, and *fact* and it may be hard to believe that before the sixteenth century they and thousands of others that are today no less familiar were not part of the language and still harder to believe that the introduction of each produced at least a momentary shock of disorientation. The failures – and there were many – convey that sense of estrangement far more readily. Here, for example, are just a few of the many words that were tried but did not stick: *devulgate*, *obtestate*, *aspectable*, *ingent*, *temulant*, *accersited*, *expede*, *panion*, and *demit*. And here is a sentence written in an orthographical system that proved equally unsuccessful: *ei kan not blạm ani man tu fiink ðis maner ov niu ureiting stranʒ, for ei du konfés it iz stranʒ tu mei self.*[5] What that sentence says once we have deciphered it – "I cannot blame any man to think this manner of new writing strange, for I do confess it is strange to myself" – points to an experience that must have been widely shared. It is, in fact, just the reaction the editor, E.K., expected from the readers of Edmund Spenser's *Shepheardes Calender*. "Of the many things which in him be strange, [the framing of his words] I know will seem the strangest." But, strange or not, Spenser insisted on his peculiar framing because, as E.K. puts it, he hoped it would "bring great grace and … auctority to the verse" (*Elizabethan Critical Essays*, ed. Smith vol. 1, p. 128). Grace and authority were precisely what many thought the vernacular lacked, precisely what it would need if either England or Spenser were to attain the imperial status toward which both aspired. But such qualities could not be achieved without risking self-estrangement. To be made imperially graceful and authoritative English had first to be made strange.

The wholesale recovery of archaic words that gives strangeness to *The Shepheardes Calender* was not Spenser's only experiment in language reform, nor, for our purposes, is it the most revealing. At about the same time that he brought out *The Shepheardes Calender*, Spenser and a group of other young men, including Philip Sidney, Edward Dyer, and Gabriel Harvey, were trying to replace English riming verse with a verse form based on the quantitative meter that had governed classical Latin and Greek poetry. In so doing, they were following the lead of the influential mid-century humanist Roger Ascham. As Ascham had made clear, rime stood for Gothic barbarousness, quantitative verse for ancient civility. Choosing between them should thus not have been hard. But, unfortunately, the English language was proving resistant. Frustrated at his attempt to get the word *carpenter* to obey the classical rules, Spenser burst out in a letter to

Harvey, "Why a God's name may not we, as else the Greeks, have the kingdom of our own language?" (*Elizabethan Critical Essays*, ed. Smith, vol. I, p. 99). Having the kingdom of one's own language, making the language abide by the dictates of civility, goes to the very essence of the early modern project of imperial self-writing.

But here we have more than an uncomfortable feeling of estrangement. We have a response that suggests a quite different system of values. Objecting to Spenser's mangling of *carpenter*, Harvey exclaims, "Is there no other policy to pull down riming and set up versifying but you must ... against all order of law and in despite of custom forcibly usurp and tyrannize upon a quiet company of words that so far beyond the memory of man have so peaceably enjoyed their several privileges and liberties without any disturbance or the least controlment?" Unlike Spenser, Harvey would not make *carpenter* – or any other word – "an inch longer or bigger than God and his English people have made him" (*Elizbethan Critical Essays*, ed. Smith, vol. I, p. 117). And twenty-three years later in his *Defence of Rhyme* (1603), Samuel Daniel made the anti-imperialist ideology of Harvey's rebuke still more apparent. For both Harvey and Daniel, law and custom stand against the tyrannous usurpation of imperial fiat. Though they were as concerned as Spenser about the insufficiencies of English, they resisted any reform that would undo what "God and his English people have made."

Neither Spenser, nor Harvey, nor Daniel would consistently maintain the positions they adopt in these exchanges. Like most sixteenth-century Englishmen, they wavered between a resolute reforming zeal and a fear that they might be destroying the very fabric of the Englishness they sought to empower. But what the exchanges do give us is a freeze-frame view of the opposing positions and a suggestion of the ideological entailments of each. "Having the kingdom of our own language" means ruling English, as English would itself rule. Respecting law and custom means basing one's identity on what one already has. At some level, everyone must have known that the second was impossible. To fill the new demands that were being placed on it in religion, government, learning, and poetry, English would have to change. It could not do what Latin and Greek had done, what in their own century Italian, Spanish, and French were beginning to do, without becoming more like those other languages. It would have to enlarge its vocabulary, regularize its spelling and grammar, and establish its rules of prosody – all of which involved at least a measure of self-alienation. But, at the same time, if this new linguistic regime was not to feel like a new enslavement to foreign-inspired tyranny, it would have to disguise itself in the cloak of ancient tradition. That is what Parliament did when it claimed to find in "divers sundry old authentic histories and chronicles"

(*Statutes* III.427) evidence that England had always been an empire. And that is what Daniel did in defending the Gothic origins of rime. Although the mellifluous riming verse he and his contemporaries wrote was in fact no older than the quantitative movement itself, Daniel succeeded in making it feel natural and native. Thus the new empire Spenser, Daniel, and the others joined Parliament in writing could present itself as an old nation dating back "far beyond the memory of man." Generalizing on this phenomenon and adapting Antonio de Nebrija's sentence, we might say that nation has always been the companion of empire – that is, where the latter imposes itself, the former, replete with suitably ancient traditions, will be invented. But in this companionship of empire and nation, tensions, as we have already begun to see, inescapably arise.

CHRONICLING ENGLAND

In the sixteenth century, any book in English might be taken to be as much about the language – a demonstration of its powers and an enhancement of its range – as it was about the book's ostensible subject, whatever that happened to be. In this respect, all books in English contributed to the writing of England. But many contributed to that writing in a more direct way as well: by being about England. And of those, none had a greater impact than the many massive chronicle histories of England.

The sixteenth-century writing of English history began, however, not with a native chronicler but with an Italian humanist, who published in Latin for a largely Continental audience. Initially sent to England as a representative of the papacy, Polydore Vergil composed his *Anglia Historia* (1534) in an obvious (and successful) bid for royal patronage from the first Tudors, Henry VII and Henry VIII, whose claim to the throne needed bolstering. Bolstering that claim – but now for an English audience – was still more obviously the work of Edward Hall's *Union of the Two Noble and Illustre Families of Lancaster and York* (1547), which confined itself to the period from Richard II to Henry VII and discovered a providential design in the Tudor rise to power. In the primacy both books grant kings and matters of rule, Polydore's *Historia* and Hall's *Union* may be thought of as "imperial" histories. More "national" in their focus are the sprawling chronicles of the latter half of the century: Richard Grafton's *Chronicle at Large* (1569), Raphael Holinshed's *Chronicles* (1577), and John Stow's *Chronicle* (1580) and *Annals* (1592). These books do, of course, say much of kings and their doings, but they also give generous attention to material of quite other sorts: to urban government and civic pageantry, to robberies and murders, to price fluctuations, to guilds and mercantile activity, to freezes and droughts, and to such miscellaneous wonders as beached whales, monstrous births, and shooting stars. Though, like Polydore and Hall, they could all have joined Grafton in declaring that their histories were "merely and only of England, not mingling the same with foreign matters impertinent to our own state," they had an extraordinarily capacious notion of pertinency.[6] If it happened in England or involved an Englishman, it could get in.

The usual explanation for the hodge-podge quality of sixteenth-century chronicles is that their compilers did not know any better. Their preoccupation with England may have distinguished them from the urban, monastic, and universal chroniclers of preceding centuries, but little else did. Although they borrowed freely from Polydore, the Italian's humanist lesson of narrative coherence was lost on them. As F. J. Levy has remarked, "The criterion by which a historian was judged was the quantity of information he managed to cram between the covers of his book." The result, in Levy's phrase, was history "by agglomeration."[7] More recently, Annabel Patterson has argued that, at least in the case of Holinshed, chronicles are richly miscellaneous not by ignorance but by design. They were "conceived from the start as 'documentary history'"; they make diversity of opinion a virtue; they intentionally include "the voices and views of ... the common people"; and they are shaped by a principle Patterson defines as "the right to know."[8] In sum, chronicles work to empower readers of all sorts by giving them the information on which to decide for themselves.

Even if one supposes the form of sixteenth-century English chronicles, including Holinshed's, to be less deliberate than Patterson claims, their empowering effect would remain much the same. By including economic as well as political issues, women and commoners as well as aristocratic men, defendants as well as their official accusers, Parliament as well as the King, chronicles provided a national, more than an imperial, perspective on English history and England's communal identity. Not simply an expression of sovereign power, the chronicles' England is an uneven patchwork of competing rights, interests, and communities. Grafton, though he contributed to this undertaking, caught something of its menace when he attacked Stow's first *Summary of English Chronicles* (1565) for "the defacing of princes' doings" and claimed that in Stow's work "the gates are rather opened for crooked subjects to enter into the field of rebellion, than the hedges or gaps of the same stopped."[9] Although it is unlikely that Stow or any other chronicler harbored such subversive intent, the very shape of their commercial and antiquarian enterprise opened gates to multiple rethinkings of England and its constitutional order and, in the process, threatened to make active citizens of passively obedient subjects.

The form of the chronicle – a temporally ordered collection of more or less heterogeneous documents, facts, and narratives – was also adopted for two more specialized books that contributed greatly to the sixteenth-century writing of England: John Foxe's *Acts and Monuments* (1563) and Richard Hakluyt's *Principal Navigations of the English Nation* (1589). After the English Bible, which first made God speak English, and the *Book of Common Prayer* (1549), which allowed worshipers to answer back in the same national language, Foxe's *Acts and Monuments* did most to make England's national and religious consciousness one. The terms of this union were ideally imperial. Foxe makes much of the fact that the first Roman emperor to embrace Christianity was the British-born Constantine, and he depicts Elizabeth, who had once again joined imperial power to the true faith, as a second Constantine. But for most of the church's history, in England and elsewhere, power and faith have been at odds. That opposition, particularly since John Wycliffe's fourteenth-century renewal of the true faith, produced the persecutions that fill most of Foxe's pages and give *Acts and Monuments* its popular name: Foxe's *Book of Martyrs*. From the hundreds of documents Foxe prints, a sense clearly emerges that the true English nation, like the true church of Christ, is made up rather of those martyrs than of the kings and bishops who torment them. Foxe thus prepared the way for a dissenters' Englishness that even the Elizabethan establishment he so ardently supported would find it impossible to stamp out.

Hakluyt's navigational chronicling fed no comparably oppositional construction of English nationhood, but it too worked by unsettling agglomeration rather than tidy selection. Taking as his goal a description of the whole world through the accounts of English voyagers, Hakluyt betrays an imperial ambition of the most far-reaching sort, the ambition to expand England's newly sovereign power over the entire globe. But that ambition, which finds more or less explicit expression in at least a few of the documents he prints, is countered by the image that emerges from hundreds of others of England as a trading, rather than a warring, nation. Trade not conquest, merchants not gentlemen adventurers, are central to the England these voyages imagine. Hakluyt never favors one of these positions over the other, never so much as acknowledges that they might be at odds with one another. Instead, in familiar chronicle manner, he gives both full and unrestricted say. The daring-do of Sir Humphrey Gilbert, Sir Walter Ralegh, Sir John Hawkins, and Sir Francis Drake is there, but so are the mundane trading records of the Muscovy and Levant Companies. Both count as voyages of the English nation. Choosing between them or putting them together into some composite idea of Englishness is a job Hakluyt leaves to his readers.

With Foxe and Hakluyt added to Grafton, Holinshed, and Stow, it is clear that the chronicle was the dominant form of English self-writing for the greater part of the sixteenth century. But that form also attracted much scorn. "Voluminous Holinshed," the *Chronicles* were soon being called, "full of confusion and commixture of unworthy relations"; "trivial household trash"; "vast, vulgar tomes ... recovered from out of innumerable ruins" (Patterson, *Reading Holinshed's Chronicles*, p. 3). As these blasts suggest, the scorn arose precisely from the chronicles' lack of a clear imperial focus. Reviving the politic and humanist values of Polydore's *Anglia Historia*, a new generation of writers emerged from the conflicts of the 1590s to demand that history be stripped of the popular accretions with which the chroniclers, themselves stigmatized as "the dregs of the common people," had laden it.[10] There is, in the words of Sir Francis Bacon, the intellectual leader of this movement, a hierarchy "of books no less than of persons, for as nothing derogates from the dignity of a state more than confusion of ranks and degrees, so it not a little embases the authority of a history to intermingle matters of lighter moment ... with matters of state," and the others clearly agreed. "It standeth," wrote William Camden in the preface to his *Annals of Queen Elizabeth* (1615), "with the law and dignity of history to run through business of highest weight and not to inquire after small matters." Similarly, Sir George Buck, in his *History of King Richard the Third* (1646), bragged that he had "omitted nothing of great matter or moment, nor anything else but some slight matters, and such as are to be seen in the common and vulgar chronicles and stories and which are in the hands of every idiot or mere foolish reader and to no purpose and for the most part not worth the reading."[11] Books like Bacon's *Henry VII* (1622), Camden's *Annals*, and Buck's *Richard III* show what would be worth the reading: sharply focused and internally coherent accounts of royal power. Eschewing any broadly inclusive notion of national history, these writers concentrate on the strategies by which empire has been won and lost.

The humanist history of Bacon and his followers effectively discredited chronicling. Stow's *Annals* went on being updated and reprinted for another several decades, Hakluyt got a huge extension in Samuel Purchas' *Hakluytus Posthumus* (1625), and Foxe's *Book of Martyrs* had a still more vigorous afterlife, but the loose and baggy chronicle with all its generous inclusiveness was for all serious purposes a spent force by the end of the sixteenth century. Until the recent emergence of social history, the history of crime, women's history, local history, economic history, and anecdotal history, history as both intellectual discipline and mode of national self-representation remained firmly within the imperial boundaries the humanist historians of the 1590s had set for it. But if the popular concerns that had claimed such a large place in the mid-sixteenth-century chronicles were banished from the formal writing of history, they nevertheless found expression in a whole range of other genres: newsletters, chapbooks, ballads, other poems, and plays, many of which drew on the chronicles for their stories. These borrowings were, however, necessarily partial and resulted in a continuing split between those writings of England that emphasized the imperial center of power and those that looked rather at a nation of subjects and citizens.

STAGING EMPIRE AND NATION

Easily the best known of the borrowers – so well known that the chronicles are now most often studied only because they served as his source – is William Shakespeare. Fully thirteen of the thirty-seven plays usually accepted as Shakespeare's take plots and characters from Holinshed. These include nine English history plays from the 1590s – the three parts of *Henry VI, Richard III, King John, Richard II,* the two parts of *Henry IV,* and *Henry V* – and four plays from the early years of the seventeenth century: two tragedies, *Macbeth* and *King Lear,* a romance, *Cymbeline,* and a late history play, *Henry VIII.* But if Shakespeare took much from the chronicles, his emphasis on the politic order of particular reigns more nearly resembles that of the humanist historians. For him, as for them, the England that deserved writing was a "royal throne of kings," a "sceptered isle," an "earth of majesty," a "seat of Mars." These familiar phrases come from John of Gaunt's prophetic deathbed speech in *Richard II* and lead to Gaunt's lament, provoked by the prodigal behavior of King Richard, that "England, that was wont to conquer others, / Hath made a shameful conquest of itself."[12] Conquering others or, more often, being self-conquered by internal division are the imperial issues on which Shakespeare's chronicle-derived plays center.

We saw earlier the self-alienation endemic to early modern language reform. No one represents the self-alienating effect of sovereign power more insistently than Shakespeare. It is, after all, Shakespeare who has given us Henry VI, sitting on a molehill envying the lot of a homely swain; Richard III, bereft of pity, love, and fear, counting himself but bad till he is best; Richard II, mistaking the name of king for the substance of power; Henry IV, dreaming of a cleansing crusade his usurped office will never allow him to undertake; Macbeth, knowing he must forego honor, love, obedience, and troops of friends; Lear and Cymbeline, unable to tell love from flattery; and, most troubling of all, the future Henry V, studying his companions like a strange tongue to be known and hated – most troubling because, unlike the others, "this star of England" is so successful. Alienation is not only the punishment for evil, incompetence, or encrusted age. It is, Shakespeare lets us know, the very condition of even the most triumphant imperial power. "A little touch of Harry in the night," a phrase the chorus in *Henry V* uses to describe the King's disguised encounter with his troops on the eve of battle, is one of the chillier breezes to blow through English history.

Yet clear-sighted as Shakespeare is about the cost of empire, empire nevertheless remains the object of his theatrical gaze. Kings and aspirants to kingship provide most of the excitement and pathos in his English history plays, as well as in his tragedies and romances, whether based on chronicle sources or not. Even in comedy, a genre that is supposed to feature people of middle or lower rank, Shakespeare gives rulers a surprisingly large role. His comic repertory begins with the Duke of Ephesus in *The Comedy of Errors* and carries on with the King of Navarre, the Duke of Milan, the Duke of Athens, the Duke of Venice, the Prince of Aragon, Duke Frederick and Duke Senior, the Duke of Illyria, the King of France, and the Duke of Vienna. Even *The Taming of the Shrew* has its omnipotent "Lord" in the Induction, and *The Merry Wives of Windsor*, the only other comedy without an on-stage sovereign and the only comedy Shakespeare set in England, takes place in the shadow of Windsor Castle, concerns the humiliation of the carnival king Falstaff (imported from the *Henry IV* plays), and ends with a masque presided over by the Queen of Fairies, a familiar type of Queen Elizabeth. In comedy, as in history and tragedy, sovereignty is Shakespeare's most persistent subject. But where sovereignty is a background issue in comedy, in history and tragedy it is central, with the result, especially in the chronicle-based plays, that women and commoners are either marginalized or demonized. Mistress Ford and Mistress Page, the virtuous, articulate, and efficacious Windsor wives, have no counterpart in Shakespeare's representation of English history, and even in their own play they belong to a world of farce rather than to one of high seriousness.

Several other English history plays from the early 1590s, when the form was just getting started, share Shakespeare's fixation on monarchy and the person of the monarch: George Peele's *Edward I* (1591); Christopher Marlowe's *Edward II* (1592); *Edward III* (1590), which is sometimes claimed for Shakespeare; and *Edmund Ironside* (1593). But in these same years the chronicles also furnished the plot for a play of a very different kind, the anonymous *Arden of Faversham* (1591), which tells of the murder of a small-town merchant by his wife, her lover, and a host of accomplices. Holinshed himself worried that this "private matter" would be thought "impertinent" to his history, though he included it anyway, and it is just the sort of "unworthy relation" the humanist historians were most eager to banish. But *Arden* nevertheless became part of the theatrical writing of England and even led the way for a whole genre of domestic crime plays, none of which has ever counted as "history."

Almost as marginal to the usual definitions of history but no less dependent on chronicle sources is a group of plays that attend not to the getting and keeping of sovereign power but rather to the effect of that power on ordinary people. An early version of these concerns is the anonymous *Life and Death of Jack Straw* (1591), a play based on chronicle accounts of the 1381 Peasants' Revolt. But more characteristic of the vision of English history that rivaled Shakespeare's on the London stages of the 1590s and the first decade of the seventeenth century are the anonymous *Thomas of Woodstock* (1592); *Book of Sir Thomas More* (1595), written by Anthony Munday and a number of others; Munday and Henry Chettle's two-part *Robin Hood* (1598); Thomas Heywood's two-part *Edward IV* (1599); the multi-authored, two-part *Sir John Oldcastle* (1599); the anonymous *Thomas, Lord Cromwell* (1600); Thomas Dekker and John Webster's *Sir Thomas Wyatt* (1602); Samuel Rowley's *When You See Me, You Know Me* (1604); and Thomas Heywood's two-part *If You Know Not Me, You Know Nobody* (1604). One of these plays, *Sir John Oldcastle*, was written in specific response to Shakespeare's maligning of Oldcastle, a fifteenth-century proto-Protestant martyr celebrated in Holinshed and Foxe, in the character who got renamed Falstaff. But any of them, most of which were produced by the companies that competed with Shakespeare's, could be taken as rewritings of Shakespeare. Where he focused on kings, they focus on figures who, though intensely loyal to the reigning monarch, identify with the people's sufferings and, as a result, often end as victims of royal power. Oldcastle is just such a figure. Others are the title characters of *Woodstock*, *More*, *Robin Hood*, *Cromwell*, and *Wyatt*, Jane and Matthew Shore in *Edward IV*, Thomas Cranmer in *When You See Me*, and Princess Elizabeth in the first part of *If You Know Not Me*. In place of the heady, if sometimes disillusioning, excitement of empire and its pursuit that we get from Shakespeare's protagonists, these characters perform rites of mediatory suffering that bind subjects to a distinctly national past. Because of their dependence on the apocalyptic historiography of Foxe's *Book of Martyrs*, the last of these plays, beginning with *Oldcastle* in 1599, have been identified with the myth of the "elect nation," the idea that God chose England for a starring role in world history.[13] But all of them, including especially the powerfully moving Jane Shore episodes of Heywood's *Edward IV*, staged what were in effect the secular saints' legends of the

English nation, a nation that emerges in relation to the imperial power of monarchy but that makes its own claim to affective, if not actual, sovereignty.

ENGLAND IN VERSE

Shortly after her emotionally sensational appearance in the two parts of Heywood's *Edward IV*, Mistress Shore, to whom Heywood had given the familiar name of "Jane," began showing up regularly in broadside ballads. Movement between ballads and the non-Shakespearean history plays, both of which catered especially to a middle- and lower-class audience, was frequent around the turn of the century. But no figure marked that intersection more clearly than Jane Shore. The wife of a London tradesman, the favorite mistress of King Edward IV, and the victim of Richard III's campaign to demonstrate his own superior sexual morality, she was perfectly positioned to touch the emotions of a popular London audience. It is thus surprising to learn that the future "Jane" Shore made her written debut far from either ballad or play, in the first humanist history produced by an Englishman, Thomas More's *History of Richard III* (1513), a book that was included in every sizeable chronicle history of England from Grafton on, without having the slightest effect on the historical methodology of any of them. From More's *History*, all later versions of the Jane Shore story derive. But already in More there is a marked sense of generic transgression. Like Holinshed, when he put the Arden story in his chronicle, More feared a charge of impertinence, feared that readers might think Mistress Shore "too slight a thing to be written of and set among the remembrance of great matters."[14] As it happens, the most conspicuous of those disapproving readers turned out to be William Shakespeare. Though Shakespeare based his *Richard III* on More's *History*, he kept Shore's wife off-stage, mentioning her only in a few salacious asides – a marginalization Heywood massively rectified in *1* and *2 Edward IV*. But long before Heywood and the balladeers turned Shore's wife into Jane Shore and made her such a compelling figure that she easily outshone the kings who seduced and punished her – indeed, even before Shakespeare suppressed and degraded her – she had emerged from More's *History* to take a leading role in two closely related and highly significant verse writings of England: the mid-century *Mirror for Magistrates* and the 1590s female complaint.

If we classify, as I have been doing, writings of England along a spectrum from empire to nation, with the rough supposition that those nearest the imperial end will primarily focus on princes, great lords, and matters of rule and that those at the national end will give at least equal attention to women, commoners, and everyday life, *The Mirror for Magistrates* is notably imperial. Written to give a purely English expression to the tradition of poems concerned with the fall of princes and addressed to all those responsible for government, it confines its regard almost exclusively to kings, lords, and pretenders to kingship. One of the very few exceptions is Shore's wife. Added to the second edition of the *Mirror* in 1563, her lament, written by Thomas Churchyard, quickly became the most prized of all. Although to our ears the verse in which she tells her story plods no less tiresomely than that of the princes who surround her, Elizabethan readers found it irresistibly appealing. Here was a distinctly new tragic voice, the voice of a London wife and royal mistress who could claim only the rights of suffering subjecthood and the office of mercy her charitable acts had won her but whose fate seemed nevertheless to demand the full measure of pity and terror.

The best evidence of this appeal is that Mistress Shore's lament – and hers alone – opened the way to a new way of writing England. In 1592 and in obvious imitation of Churchyard's "Shore's Wife," Samuel Daniel found another tragic royal mistress and gave expression to her woes in *The Complaint of Rosamond*. The next year, Thomas Lodge found still another, Elstred, the abandoned mistress of the legendary British king Locrine, and Michael Drayton followed in 1594 with Piers Gaveston, the male lover of Edward II, and Matilda, the chaste victim of King John's frustrated lust, whose lament was quickly repeated by Richard Barnfield in his *Complaint of Chastity*. Nor was Shore's wife forgotten by the fashion her story had started. In 1593, Anthony Chute published *Beauty Dishonored, Written under the Title of Shore's Wife*; Thomas Deloney opened his *Garland of Good Will* with ballads on Rosamond and Shore's wife; old Churchyard issued a much augmented version of his poem from *The Mirror for Magistrates*; and in 1597, Drayton featured letters between Shore's wife and King Edward, along with others linking a dozen pairs of royal and noble lovers, including Rosamond and Henry II and Matilda and King John, in *England's Heroical Epistles*.

These "female complaints," as such poems are often called, are not all female, nor are they all complaints. But all do inhabit some part of the territory opened by More's *History of Richard III* and by Churchyard's "Shore's Wife," a territory invaded by imperial desires but alienated from them, a territory marked by passionate sensuality and abject suffering. Furnishing classical warrant for this radical rewriting of England was the example of Ovid and particularly of his *Heroides*, a set of verse letters from famously abandoned women to their departed lovers. Already in his own time, Ovid's rewriting of Greek and Roman history and legend had positioned itself in opposition to the imperial writing of Vergil – though it should be remembered that Vergil's own Dido is the prime exemplar of a tragically abandoned imperial mistress – and it is as an alternative to the imperial vision that Elizabethan poets wrote their female complaints. Ovid was always considered a dangerous example, and the female complaint was no less objectionable. "I smile," wrote the elder Giles Fletcher in a poem that tried to reclaim the complaint for the kind of men who had dominated it in *The Mirror for Magistrates*,

> to see the poets of this age,
> Like silly boats in shallow rivers tossed,
> Losing their pains and lacking still their wage,
> To write of women and of women's falls,
> Who are too light for to be Fortune's balls.[15]

And at least the two most ambitious of those poets who had written "of women and of women's falls" covered themselves by producing long poems of a more manly and imperial sort. Choosing the same field of fifteenth-century dynastic warfare that gave Shakespeare the subjects for eight of his nine English history plays of the 1590s, Samuel Daniel wrote his *Civil Wars* (1596) and Michael Drayton his *Mortimeriados* (1596), later revised as *The Barons' Wars* (1619). Together the two kinds of poem – female complaints and epic accounts of war – provided a stereoscopically bi-gendered image of England to match the similarly multiple image of ancient Rome Elizabethans found in Vergil and Ovid.

Gender works in a notably different way in the most ambitious of all sixteenth-century poetic writings of England, Edmund Spenser's *Faerie Queene* (1590). As the poem's title suggests, supreme rule is here – as, of course, it was in Spenser's England – in the hands of a woman. But, oddly, that sovereign woman never gets into the poem. Although the Faerie Queen is said to have commanded the quests of the knights who do appear – the Red Cross Knight, Guyon, Scudamore, Artegall, and Calidore – and is herself the object of Prince Arthur's quest, we never see her. Instead, we see the "private" virtues of her model, the Queen of England, allegorically represented in the long-suffering Una and the chastely heroic Belphoebe and Britomart, and we see images of a woman's "public" rule set forth virtuously, though weakly, in the Elizabeth look-alike Queen Mercilla and demonically in the tempting and tyrannical Duessa, Lucifera, Philotime, Acrasia, Malecasta, and Radigund. These last six were certainly not the "mirrors" in which Spenser invited his Queen to see herself reflected, but they do suggest the poem's profound ambivalence concerning the imperial power it pretends to celebrate. Although nominally devoted to the Faerie

Queen, Spenser's heroic knights are repeatedly threatened and weakened by the actual women rulers they meet in the poem.

The Faerie Queene is an allegorical and chivalric romance, a fantastic collection of loosely interwoven adventures. As such, it depends heavily on the example of Lodovico Ariosto's *Orlando Furioso* (1516) and falls necessarily on the Ariostan side of the great sixteenth-century debate over the respective merits of Gothic romance and classical epic. Just as Renaissance humanists worked to replace the sprawling medieval chronicle with a more focused and exclusionary form of political history, so they worked to replace the equally sprawling and unfocused romance with the more sharply unified epic – with, that is, the kind of poem that Vergil had written and that sixteenth-century poets like Torquato Tasso and Luís de Camões were imitating. This was in part an aesthetic choice between cultures. The humanists wanted to follow the civilized Greeks and Romans, not the barbarous Goths. But it was also a matter of political difference. Empire demanded imperial forms. Where the chronicle gave undue attention to urban institutions and to the concerns of people of middling rank, romance granted excessive autonomy to wandering knights. Both thus resisted the hegemony of the monarchic state. For all its adoration of "the most high, mighty, and magnificent empress" (from the dedication to *The Faerie Queene*), Queen Elizabeth, *The Faerie Queene* is guilty of just such resistence. Like many others, Spenser's is a writing of England caught between the rival claims of empire and nation. But the nation Spenser writes is significantly unlike the others we have encountered: not Harvey's "quiet company of words," nor the chronicles' citizen subjects, nor Foxe's martyrs, nor Hakluyt's merchants, nor the non-Shakespearean drama's suffering intercessors, nor the female complaint's abandoned women, but rather a nation of semi-feudal aristocrats, only restively submissive to the imperial power of their female sovereign.

THIS LAND OF ENGLAND

Close behind *The Faerie Queene* in size and ambition is another massive poem about England, Michael Drayton's *Poly-Olbion* (1613). Although not published until the early seventeenth century, *Poly-Olbion* was begun in the 1590s and belongs to a genre that got started a couple decades earlier with the publication of William Lambarde's *Perambulation of Kent* (1576), Christopher Saxton's *Atlas of England and Wales* (1579), and William Camden's *Britannia* (1586). What, one might ask, would justify putting this heterogeneous set of books – a long poem, a county guide, a collection of maps, and an antiquarian treatise – in the same genre? In our modern distribution of knowledge, they would seem to belong to quite separate disciplines: *Poly-Olbion* to literary history, Lambarde's *Perambulation* to local history, Saxton's *Atlas* to cartographic history, and Camden's *Britannia* to the history of learning. But in the sixteenth century the same words, *survey, description,* and *chorography,* name all four. Furthermore, all four adopt the same organizational scheme, a general description followed by particular descriptions that move in a perambulatory way from place to place. All four concern England and its geographical features. And all four, joined by such other works as John Norden's unfinished *Speculum Britanniae* (1596), John Speed's *Theater of the Empire of Great Britain* (1611), John Stow's *Survey of London* (1598), and dozens of county chorographies from Richard Carew's *Survey of Cornwall* (1602) to Sir William Dugdale's *Antiquities of Warwickshire* (1656), had a shared ideological effect. Together they contributed to a shift of primary loyalty from king to country, from the dynastic state to the land-based nation. Books like these made it possible to imagine England less as a system of rule than as a place.

Simply lining up in chronological order the frontispieces of Saxton's *Atlas*, Camden's *Britannia*, and Drayton's *Poly-Olbion* illustrates this shift. Where Saxton's book starts with an engraving of Elizabeth enthroned, Camden has a map of Britain as his frontispiece, and Drayton turns that map into an allegorical personification, a goddess-like woman with crown and sceptre, dressed in a map. The land has, in effect, displaced the sovereign and assumed for itself the signs of rule. The maps each book contains tell the same story. Where the royal arms prominently mark each map in Saxton, Camden strips the arms from forty-five out of fifty-six of his maps, and Drayton drops them altogether, filling his maps instead with personifications of the land and its natural features. In part, these changes result from changing material conditions. The Queen's government sponsored Saxton's *Atlas*. Clearly, that government felt entitled to put its stamp on the book. Camden's *Britannia* and Drayton's *Poly-Olbion* were, by contrast, private undertakings, supported, as were the great chronicles of the mid-sixteenth century, by a growing community of antiquaries and printers. But the changing material conditions are themselves signs of tension. The Privy Council pulled the plug on Norden's *Speculum Britanniae*, and when some members sought official recognition for the Society of Antiquaries Camden had founded, they were first ignored by Elizabeth and then suppressed by James. Although the antiquaries had promised to avoid matters of state and religion, even their private meetings were thought threatening.

Perhaps they were threatening. Although it is hard to find any antimonarchic sentiment in the chorographies that were the antiquaries' chief published products, simply by redirecting attention from king to country they were guilty of involuntary – and, in a few instances, perhaps not-so-involuntary – *lèse-majesté*. Not that empire was foreign to their concern. Camden began his great chorographic project as a way of uncovering the traces of the Roman imperial province of Britannia in present-day England, and Speed presented his book as a "theatre" in which one could view the Jacobean "Empire of Great Britain." But the very chorographic method, its focus on place and particularity, moved away from the singularity of empire and toward national multiplicity. In that regard, Drayton's title better captures the effect of chorography. Chorography always represents a poly-Olbion, a multiple England.

But there are other shifts in the early modern chorographical description of England than the one from king to country. Most obvious is the move from the large-scale national survey imagined by Lambarde and Norden and realized by Saxton, Camden, Drayton, and Speed to the more local focus of the seventeenth-century county chorographers. Linked to this is a shift, visible especially in the successive editions of Camden's *Britannia*, from an international audience of humanist scholars to a local audience of gentleman landowners. Abraham Ortelius, the Flemish humanist and map-maker, whose world atlas gave Saxton his model, prompted Camden to undertake his *Britannia* as part of a European-wide recovery of Roman antiquity. Like Polydore Vergil's *Anglia Historia*, Camden's *Britannia* was thus written in Latin. But by the time it made its way into English in Philemon Holland's 1610 translation, its character had changed as much as its language. The records of Roman Britain were still there, but they had been joined by a vast collection of more recent material, including numerous genealogical and property records. Camden had by then left his position at Westminster School to become an officer of the College of Arms, so his new interest in genealogy may be thought a professional deformation. But English chorography as a whole was moving in the same direction: from an antiquarian study that represented a common national heritage to a much more exclusive focus on individual ownership of the land. What emerges from these changes is no longer the imperial England of Shakespeare's history plays or the humanist histories, nor the more democratic England of the chronicles and the early chorographies, but rather an oligarchic England, an England that belongs to its great landholding families.

Drayton's chorographic poem participates in this parceling out of England, but only to a point. In *Poly-Olbion*, the land belongs not to gentleman landowners but rather to itself. This chorography's kings and queens are the land's natural features, Forest of Dean, the Malvern Hills, the Vale of Evesham, the Isle of Man, and the River Thames. They, along with dozens of others, are the poem's speakers. It is from them that we hear of the ancient settlement of Britain and of all the subsequent claims that have been made to it. The rivers of Wales recount the conquests of Arthur and the English rivers answer with the glorious deeds of the Saxons. But finally the history of these various human invaders matters less than do the immemorial loves and hates, rivalries and alliances, of the rivers, seas, hills, valleys, forests, and fields themselves. Although it would no doubt be wrong to think of Drayton as an ecological poet – the natural relations he describes have more to do with mythmaking than with science – his *Poly-Olbion* is certainly the "greenest" early modern writing of England, the one that gives the fullest say to the natural substratum of both empire and nation.

THE ONE AND THE MANY

In the preceding pages, I have emphasized differences between writings of England that lean more to the imperial or to the national side, differences between those that construct the nation in a way that privileges one set of interests and those that privilege another. Had I been able to conduct a still more comprehensive survey, one that included, to cite just a small part of what I had to leave out, John Leland's manuscript itineraries, Archbishop Matthew Parker's Anglo-Saxon studies, the legal writings of Edward Coke and Francis Bacon, William Harrison's description of England and its adoption by John Lyly in *Euphues and his England* (1580), and Thomas Deloney's middle-class fictions, the differences would have multiplied still further. But the remarkable and unprecedented agreement, already amply illustrated in the texts I have been able to invoke, that England demanded writing would only have been made more evident. As momentous as any of the great political and cultural events that marked England's history in the sixteenth century – the consolidation of rule after the civil wars of the fifteenth century, the separation from Rome, the rivalry with Spain, the development of exploration and trade on a global scale, the spread of humanist learning, the enormous increase in the market for printed books, the opening of permanent public theatres – and linked to all of them, was the emergence of England itself as the focal point for writing of all sorts. Whether we think of it as empire or nation, England defined the ambition of both individuals and communities, even as they defined England. Since they served different interests, theirs was a competitive enterprise. But it was also a concerted one. As they separately wrote many Englands, so they together wrote one multifaceted England. And, in doing so, they helped establish the uniquely central position the nation-state continues to hold in that configuration of obligations and attachments we have come to call modernity.

NOTES

This survey borrows and extends ideas from my *Forms of Nationhood: The Elizabethan Writing of England* (Chicago: University of Chicago Press, 1992). An article forthcoming in the *South Atlantic Quarterly*, "Weeping for Jane Shore," has also been pillaged for a few sentences on the female complaint.

1 24 Henry VIII. c. 12. See *The Statutes of the Realm* (1817; rep. London: Dawsons of Pall Mall, 1963), III.427. Spelling and punctuation in quotations and titles in the text of this chapter have been freely modernized. Titles in the notes appear in their original spelling.

2 Samuel Daniel, *The Complete Works in Verse and Prose*, ed. Alexander B. Grosart, 5 vols. (London: Spenser Society, 1885–96), vol. IV, p. 77.

3 Antonio de Nebrija, *Gramatica de la Lengua Castellana*, ed. Ig. González-Llubera (London: Oxford University Press, 1926), p. 3.

4 In *Elizabethan Critical Essays*, ed. G. Gregory Smith, 2 vols. (Oxford: Oxford University Press, 1904), I.227.

5 John Hart, *An Orthographie* (London: William Seres, 1569), sig. M4v.

6 Richard Grafton, *A Chronicle at Large and Meere History of the Affayres of Englande* (London: Henry Denham, 1569), fol. 2v.

7 F. J. Levy, *Tudor Historical Thought* (San Marino, CA: The Huntington Library, 1967), pp. 168 and 184.

8 Annabel Patterson, *Reading Holinshed's* Chronicles (Chicago: University of Chicago Press, 1994), p. 7.

9 Richard Grafton, *Abridgement of the Chronicles of Englande* (London: Richard Tottle, 1570), sig. ¶iiv.

10 Edmund Bolton, *Hypercritica* (1618), in *Critical Essays of the Seventeenth Century*, ed. J. E. Spingarn, 3 vols. (Oxford: Clarendon Press, 1908), vol. I, p. 96.

11 Francis Bacon, *Works*, ed. James Spedding, 14 vols. (London: Longman, 1857–74), IV, p. 310; William Camden, *Annales*, trans. R.N. (London: B. Fisher, 1635), sig. c3v; cf. Sir George Buck, *The History of King Richard the Third*, ed. A. N. Kincaid (Gloucester: Alan Sutton, 1979), pp. 7–8.

12 II.i.40–41 and 65–66. I quote from rev. *The Riverside Shakespeare*, ed. G. Blakemore Evans (Boston: Houghton Mifflin, 1997).

13 See Judith Doolin Spikes, "The Jacobean History Play and the Myth of the Elect Nation," *Renaissance Drama* 8 (1977): 117–49.

14 Thomas More, *The History of King Richard III*, ed. Richard S. Sylvester (New Haven: Yale University Press, 1963), p. 56.

15 *The English Works of Giles Fletcher, the Elder*, ed. Albert C. Baugh (Madison: University of Wisconsin Press, 1964), p. 124.

FURTHER READING

Blank, Paula, *Broken English: Dialects and the Politics of Language in Renaissance Writings* (London: Routledge, 1996).

Fussner, F. Smith, *The Historical Revolution: English Historical Writing and Thought, 1580– 1640* (New York: Columbia University Press, 1962).

Helgerson, Richard, *Forms of Nationhood: The Elizabethan Writing of England* (Chicago: University of Chicago Press, 1992).

Howard, Jean, and Phyllis Rackin, *Engendering a Nation: A Feminist Account of Shakespeare's English Histories* (London: Routledge, 1997).

Jones, Richard Foster, *The Triumph of the English Language: A Survey of Opinions Concerning the Vernacular from the Introduction of Printing to the Restoration* (Stanford, CA: Stanford University Press, 1953).

Knapp, Jeffrey, *An Empire Nowhere: England, America, and Literature from Utopia to* The Tempest (Berkeley: University of California Press, 1992).

Levy, F. J., *Tudor Historical Thought* (San Marino, CA: The Huntington Library, 1967).

McEachern, Claire, *The Poetics of English Nationhood, 1590–1610* (Cambridge: Cambridge University Press, 1996).

Patterson, Annabel, *Reading Holinshed's* Chronicles (Chicago: University of Chicago Press, 1994).